IS FOR

JUNK
ECONOMICS

A Guide to Reality
in an Age of Deception

MICHAEL HUDSON

ISLET

2017

© 2017 Michael Hudson / ISLET-Verlag
First Edition © January 2017
www.michael-hudson.com
www.islet-verlag.de

Books are available at quantity discounts for events by contacting the publisher at **michael-hudson.com**. Professor Hudson is available for consulting and speaking engagements.

Although the author and publisher have made every effort to ensure that the information in this book is correct, they do not assume, and hereby disclaim, any liability to any party for any loss, damage or disruption caused by errors or omissions, whether such result from negligence, accident or any other case.

Set in Times New Roman and Baskerville boldface
Design and typesetting by Edit/Design Productions
Charts and tables by Cornelia Wunsch and Lynn Yost
"The Miracle of Compound Interest" illustration courtesy Nigel Holmes
Rosetta Stone (British Museum) © AdobeStock

Companion to KILLING THE HOST by Michael Hudson

Hudson, Michael, 1939–
J is for Junk Economics: A Guide to Economic Survival in an Age of Deception
Michael Hudson
ISBN: 978-3-9814842-5-0

Table of Contents

ESSAYS AND ARTICLES

AUTHOR INTERVIEW: KILLING THE HOST (Companion book)

ABOUT THE AUTHOR

Foreword

Economies – and Economic Theory – at the Crossroads

*T*he 2008 banking and junk mortgage crisis saw the United States and Europe save banks and bondholders, not their economies. While governments spent trillions on bailouts and "quantitative easing" to save large creditors and speculators from losses on their bad loans and gambles, public and private infrastructure has been left to crumble and median wages are drifting down. Pension savings are being stripped, and pressure is rising to cut back Social Security.

Junk Economics is the cover story for all this. Claiming to be scientific, it is sponsored by financial interests to redistribute income and wealth upward, reversing the policies urged by the 19th-century classical economists and Progressive Era reformers. Instead of progressive taxation, this ideology advocates shifting taxes off the One Percent onto the 99 Percent.

The effect is to suck money out of economies, while driving the middle class into debt, mainly to the One Percent. The resulting austerity is used as an excuse to privatize the public assets and natural resources that classical economists hoped would provide the tax base for administering the proper functions of government. Debt-strapped local and national governments are forced to sell off public infrastructure to pay creditors.

The pretense is that this will lower the cost of these basic services. But public infrastructure is being turned into opportunities for new owners to charge monopoly fees for themselves, resulting in a loss of affordable basic services. In the United States, compulsory privatized Obamacare is squeezing family budgets, while in Britain privatized railroads and water are among the most blatant examples.

Instead of leading to the promised leisure economy of abundance by freeing society from the legacies of feudalism and the hereditary privileges of aristocracies, bankers and monopolists, today's financial elites promote Junk Economics to increase their time-honored "free lunch" at society's expense. The debt overhead they create for the economy at large was well identified a century ago as avoidable.

But today's financial class has idealized running into debt as the way for *economies to get rich by inflating asset prices. Wages, profits and rents are being turned into a flow of interest payments that are growing exponentially. Meanwhile, national statistics divert attention away from how debt service is siphoning household and business income up to the top of the economic pyramid.*

The suffering caused by the resulting financial austerity is unnecessary, not a result of any natural law. This reversal of the classical ideal of a "free market" – a market free <u>from</u> land rent, monopoly rent and predatory finance – has been promoted with a new vocabulary of Orwellian Doublespeak. For example, the term "reform," as used today, means reversing *the Progressive Era reforms that helped create a prosperous American and European middle class. It has been forgotten that what made the 20th century great was progressive taxation and public infrastructure spending to lower the cost of basic economic services – along with the New Deal and other legislation making money and finance a public utility instead of the predatory monopoly it has become.*

To revive a more reality-based analysis and policy-making, this book aims to reconstruct economics as a discipline, starting with its vocabulary and basic concepts.

• • •

Preface and Acknowledgements

I drafted this dictionary and its accompanying essays more than a decade ago, for a book to have been entitled *The Fictitious Economy*. It did not find a publisher. My warnings about how debt leveraging would lead to a crisis hardly qualified as a timely how-to-get-rich manual of the sort that publishers consider to be popular "economics books." Most readers were making easy money in the stock market and real estate. As stock prices recovered from their dot.com crash of 2000, home owners and investors were getting rich by debt leveraging, while pension funds remained solvent without having to increase employer or employee contributions.

Nobody wanted to hear that the gains couldn't be permanent while so much was there to be taken. Most of all, people did not want to hear that the financial sector that they thought was making them rich actually was undermining the economy and paving the road to the debt deflation that has made the economy poorer since the 2008 crash. Poorer, that is, for the 99 Percent whose incomes are now being paid to the One Percent as debt service and economic rent.

Flooding the stock market with debt-leveraged liquidity provided a propitious opportunity for President Bush and the Republicans to privatize Social Security. Their dream was to steer the monthly flow of wage withholding into the stock market, inflating a stock market boom along the same lines that Pension Fund Capitalism had been fueling since the 1950s. The aim was to generate soaring prices for speculators and a tidal wave of fees for Wall Street's money managers.

I met the editor of *Harper's*, Lewis Lapham, at a meeting of the Thorstein Veblen Society in 2004, and we discussed the need to warn against the idea that money could be made purely by financial engineering without building up the "real" economy. My cover story in 2005[1] on the proposed Social Security swindle reminded readers that stocks could fall as well as rise. The market's downturn that year dampened enthusiasm for privatization of Social Security, and a rising wave of scandals showed that Wall Street's money managers were more concerned with making fortunes for themselves than with helping customers.

The FBI warned in September of 2004 that the greatest wave of financial fraud since the 1920s was underway, but its fraud staff was cut back and assigned to anti-terrorist duties in the wake of 9/11.[2] Banks lent money on increasingly reckless terms, selling the loans to customers who believed that the creation of sophisticated options trading meant that risk no longer existed. The reality was that risk was transferred to the proverbial suckers who lacked sufficient training in mathematical statistics to realize that someone would have to bear the loss from loans that could not be paid.

The gains that were envisioned had been called "fictitious" or "fictive" capital in the late 19th century. From Karl Marx on the left of the political spectrum to Henry George on the right, these terms were commonplace to describe stock market and allied financial manipulations. A century of classical economists defined economic rent as an extractive means of gaining wealth. But economic models no longer draw the distinction that a century of classical economists had emphasized between productive and unproductive labor and investment. Financial gain-seeking is deemed as productive as building factories and investing in public infrastructure.

Along with changing analytic concepts has come a change in the language of economics. Today's writers use jargon terms such as "zero-sum activity" and "transfer payments" to distinguish rent seeking from real wealth based on producing tangible consumer goods and capital goods.

This change reflects the fact that economies now aim at different objectives from those of the classical economic critics and reformers. Instead of allying itself with industry, banking has found its major market in real estate, the rent-yielding oil and mining sectors, and monopolies. I wrote another cover story for *Harper's* in 2006 on the mortgage bubble, warning that the financial sector was making most people so much more indebted that a real estate crash was about to occur, leaving a debt overhang in place that would deplete the economy.[3]

It was at this point that I again tried to publish *The Fictitious Economy* to show how debts tend to grow more rapidly than the underlying economy. My aim was to revive the classical distinction between market prices and intrinsic value, to show how different making fortunes in the Finance, Insurance and Real Estate (FIRE) sector was from the "real" economy of production and consumption. But following the guideline that readers do not want to hear "bad" economic news until *after* the break occurs, publishers told me that they preferred a how-to-do-it book to profiteer from the coming financial collapse, if and when it occurred. Readers wanted to know how to get rich, not how their bubble gains would leave them and the overall economy debt-wracked.

Many investors saw that the bubble could not go on forever. Their main concern was indeed to calculate how they could make money off the coming collapse. John Paulson bet that junk mortgages would default, and got Goldman Sachs to package and sell them to gullible clients, who lost their shirts while he and Goldman made a billion dollars. But this was not the kind of investment opportunity that I wanted to promote.

An otherwise favorable academic publisher proved unable to get my book through the peer review process when one of the referees, who claimed to have taught Adam Smith's economic thought for years, wrote that he could find no evidence of any intent to bring market prices in line with the cost of production (real value). If that reviewer's claim were true, it would mean Smith was not really interested in freeing economies from land rent and monopoly rent.

I found this ignorance shocking. More than a century of classical economic thought aimed precisely to distinguish between market price and the necessary costs of production, so as to isolate land rent and monopoly rent as unearned income paid to an unnecessary *rentier* class. This was the essence of the economic and political reforms advocated from 18th-century France, Scotland and England through the Progressive Era. The focus of classical economics was to free society from rent seeking and exploitative prices being charged, not to celebrate these as investment opportunities. But that body of analysis and reform-minded thought has been airbrushed from the academic curriculum. The history of economic thought rarely is taught anymore. The prospective publisher wrote me: "I suspect that the sort of book you want to write is just not one that will get through the screening process that all academic presses have to carry out. I'm sorry about this, as I think that your original idea (how neoliberals have betrayed Enlightenment ideals) is a brilliant one."

My analysis of the relation between tax policy, money and credit creation prompted another university press reviewer to call my book proposal "populist in the monetary heterodox ('crank') tradition. It also endorses the Henry George Single Tax tradition." The writer evidently wanted to take an easy shot at the Henry George cult, which lacks the value and price theory on which Adam Smith, John Stuart Mill and dozens of other classical economists based their advocacy of taxing economic rent. It's easier to attack a popular journalist like George than to cope with the rent and value theory of Smith, Mill, Alfred Marshall, Simon Patten, Thorsten Veblen *et al*.

As for Modern Monetary Theory (MMT), developed primarily by my colleagues at the University of Missouri, Kansas City (UMKC), it is now becoming accepted as the alternative to neoliberal austerity. Yet so strong is the ideological demand for balanced budgets – and actually a surplus (as the Clinton administration ran at the end of the 1990s) – that those of us who developed an alternative analysis were called "cranks" just a few years ago. But as the saying goes, "cranks turn wheels, and wheels make revolutions."

Our monetary and fiscal alternative rejects the balanced-budget "deficit hawk" policy that is deflating the U.S. and European economies with fiscal drag. Running a budget surplus means raising taxes and/or cutting public spending, taking money *out* of the economy to pay off bondholders. Paying down the public debt sucks money out of the economy, just as paying debt service to banks causes debt deflation. We argue that just as commercial banks create money (deposits) electronically simply by making loans, governments can do the same thing. Government budget deficits spend money *into* the economy – and this is not inflationary when labor and resources are unemployed.

That is why UMKC Economics Department chairperson Stephanie Kelton calls us "deficit owls," to contrast us with the "deficit hawks" currently holding sway. By explaining the linkage between fiscal and monetary policy, Modern Monetary Theory provides an alternative to today's neoliberal Junk Economics, which rationalizes austerity, to be followed by bank bailouts when their disastrous policies inflate financial bubbles that benefit their constituency of bankers and bondholders. MMT views money and credit as a public utility, not as a private monopoly of commercial banks. MMT accordingly urges central banks or treasuries to monetize budget deficits by creating money to spend into the economy. The government's budget deficit is (by definition) the private sector's surplus. (See the MMT entry in the A-to-Z Guide in this book for more discussion.) So the alternative to junk economics turns out to be MMT "crank" economics.

There *Is* An Alternative to Mainstream Economics

It is time to throw down the gauntlet and accuse the *rentier* financial class deceptions of being what they are: economic fictions.

To help draw the lines between "Reality Economics" and the current neoliberal fad, my editor and book producer in the United States, Lynn Yost, suggested in 2013 that my web manager, Karl Fitzgerald in Australia, post the original draft of my dictionary on my website (*michael-hudson.com*). He had the good idea of making each letter follow the "A is for Adam Smith; J is for Junk Economics" format. The definitions were quickly picked up by *Naked Capitalism* and other e-sites.

When my book, *Killing the Host: How Financial Parasites and Debt Destroy the Global Economy* came out to good reviews in 2015, Ms. Yost urged me to expand the A to Z dictionary, add an interview on *Killing the Host,* and a few other select articles as a companion guide. They are as follows:

(1) "The 22 Most Pervasive Economic Myths of Our Time" summarizes today's economic fictions. It is my attempt to demonstrate how today's vocabulary of Orwellian Doublethink and Newspeak dominates the mainstream media, the teaching of economics and even the statistical representation of how the economy works – as if there is no exploitation, barely any economic rent (unearned income), and no quantification of capital gains derived from asset price inflation, despite the fact that these are the main aim of real estate and financial investors.

(2) My most reprinted essay is "Economics As Fraud," which characterizes the methodology of today's deceptively mathematized economic theory.[4] The first draft of that essay was published in 2000 for a German conference on mathematical economics. The World Economics Association (formerly the Post-Autistic Economics group) then anthologized it with other articles that I had contributed to their organization.[5]

(3) Since writing "Economics as Fraud" criticizing the desert-island methodology of individualism, I have come to realize that the contrast between reality economics and junk economics is much broader. My new essay, "Economic Methodology is Ideology, and Dictates Policy," describes how methodology determines content. It shapes the scope, mathematics and even the statistics defined by today's mainstream. The essence of Junk Economics is a narrow conceptualization of "the economy" in terms only of "the market," which merely means the status quo. The resulting economic models exclude the political, environmental and legal ramifications of debt in today's *rentier* economies.

(4) I also include an article I wrote for the Catholic magazine *Commonweal* in 1970 – "Does Economics Deserve a Nobel Prize?" – when it became apparent that creation of the so-called Nobel Economic Prize was a public relations campaign mounted to promote neoliberal junk economics of the Chicago School variety.[6]

(5) The Hudson Bubble Model provides an accounting format to trace how asset-price inflation leads inexorably to debt-strapped economies and austerity programs (formulas and charts included). The analysis first appeared in my book, *The Bubble and Beyond: Fictitious Capital, Debt Deflation and Global Crisis* (2012).

These five articles show the extent to which economics is taught as a pseudo-science of assumptions without regard for reality or history. We are living in a world in which the *rentier* censorial motto has achieved dominance: "If the eye offends thee, pluck it out."

Acknowledgments

As a first step toward the needed reconstruction of economics and rescue of its vocabulary, I owe by far my greatest debt to the forgotten – indeed, expurgated – classical economists, from François Quesnay and Adam Smith to E. Peshine Smith, John Stuart Mill and Karl Marx to Michael Flürscheim, Simon Patten and Thorstein Veblen. While each had his own political aim, they shared an abhorrence of unearned income and parasitic wealth. Their analytic tools and world-view have been consigned to an Orwellian memory hole by lobbyists for the predatory interests who have taken control of economic thought and government policy.

I also owe a debt to the living. Without the loving support of my wife, Grace, this book would not have been completed. Susan Charette, David Kelley, Bertell Ollman and most of all my editor Lynn Yost have made suggestions that have greatly enhanced the substance of this book. Four proofreaders in Australia and the U.S. volunteered to copy edit the original version in 2015: Amy Castor, Brent Grisim, Ben Hughes and Richard Mallard. Also thanks to Dave Yost, Karl Fitzgerald and to Steven Lesh for their final reading and comments. Their changes and corrections showed me that writers should never try to be their own proofreaders.

ENDNOTES

[1] "The $4.7 trillion Pyramid: Why Social Security Won't Be Enough to Save Wall Street," *Harper's*, April 2005, pp. 35-40.

[2] William K. Black, "Control Fraud and the Irish Banking Crisis," *New Economic Perspectives*, June 12, 2011. http://neweconomicperspectives.org/2011/06/control-fraud-and-the-irish-banking-crisis.html.

[3] "The New Road to Serfdom: An illustrated guide to the coming real estate collapse," *Harper's*, May 2006, pp. 39-46. Both *Harper's* articles are reprinted in *The Bubble and Beyond*, along with the model of how the Bubble Economy was being financialized, which I presented in Kansas City at its Eighth International Post-Keynesian Workshop in June 2004 ("Saving, asset-price inflation and debt-induced deflation," published in 2006).

[4] "The Use and Abuse of Mathematical Economics," *Journal of Economic Studies* **27** (2000), pp. 292-31.

[5] *Finance as Warfare* (World Economics Association, 2015).

[6] "Does Economics Deserve a Nobel Prize?" *Commonweal* **93** (December 18, 1970).

Introduction:
Social Naming Disorder and the Vocabulary of Deception

> . . . the decline of a language must ultimately have political and economic causes ... It becomes ugly and inaccurate because our thoughts are foolish, but the slovenliness of our language makes it easier for us to have foolish thoughts. The point is that the process is reversible. ... If one gets rid of these habits one can think more clearly, and to think clearly is a necessary first step toward political regeneration.
>
> — George Orwell, "Politics and the English Language" (1946)

> You can fool some of the people all of the time. Those are the ones you should concentrate on.
>
> — George W. Bush (2001)

Confucius taught that social disorder begins with the failure to call things by their appropriate names. The first step to reforming a malstructured world therefore is "rectification of the names." To Confucius this meant restoring the original meaning of words.

Today's economic terminology is in obvious need of such renovation. Rejecting the classical economics of Adam Smith, John Stuart Mill and their contemporary critics of landlords and monopolists, defenders of unearned income have blurred and obscured economic terminology into euphemisms to deny that there is any such thing as a free lunch. The terms *rentier* and usury that played so central a role in past centuries now sound anachronistic and have been replaced with more positive Orwellian Doublethink.

As advertisers know, naming a product shapes how people perceive it. A vast public relations operation has been engineered to invert the meaning of words to make black appear white. Nowhere is this tactic more political than in the promotion of economic ideology. Today's vocabulary of wealth and the lapse into a rent-and-usury economy is euphemized as progress toward a leisure society, not debt serfdom. Financial bubbles that inflate prices for buying a home or a specific retirement income plan are called "wealth creation," not debt-leveraged asset-price inflation, while downsizing and breaking up industrial companies is called "value creation," not looting.

Economic vocabulary is defined by today's victors – the *rentier* financial class

In Lewis Carroll's *Through the Looking-Glass*, Alice learns that the definition of words depends on who is in control. "'When I use a word,' Humpty Dumpty said, in rather a scornful tone, 'it means just what I choose it to mean – neither more nor less. … The question is, which is to be master – that's all.'"

Just as history is written by the victors, so the vested interests sponsor academic spokesmen and journalists to mold the media's vocabulary in ways that depict Wall Street as playing a productive role. The more predatory its behavior, the more necessary it becomes to shape popular opinion by abusing language, duly awarding prizes for explaining how "free markets" work without government "interference" taxing or regulating wealth.

Today's neoliberal Washington Consensus reverses classical liberalism by favoring predatory rent extraction, regressive tax policy and deregulation. "Reform" now means undoing what in the 20th century was considered to be reform. Anti-labor policies to reduce union power and workplace protection are labeled reform, as is the rewriting of bankruptcy laws reversing the long trend of more humanitarian treatment of debtors.

Nowhere is the Doublethink vocabulary more blatant than in the financial conquest of Greece by the Eurozone "troika" – the European Central Bank, European Commission and IMF. James Galbraith, an advisor to Greek finance minister Yanis Varoufakis, was asked whether "the institutions (the IMF, the EC and the ECB) will have to rescue Greece indefinitely." He answered:

> There is no "rescue" going on here. There is no "rescue," there is no "bailout," there is no "reform" going on. I really need to insist on this, because these words creep into our discourse. They are placed there by the creditors in order for unwary people to use them, but there is nothing of the kind taking place. What is going on is a seizure of the assets owned by the Greek state, by Greek businesses and by Greek households. There is no

sense that this has anything to do with the recovery of the Greek economy or with the welfare of the Greek people. On the contrary, the policy is utterly indifferent to those considerations.[1]

A vocabulary depicting the *rentier* financial class as productive

Every special interest claims to be fair and equitable. Bankers and landlords naturally prefer a vocabulary that depicts them as productive rather than predatory. Today's anti-classical vocabulary accordingly re-defines "free markets" as ones that are free *for* rent extractors. To deter regulation, taxation or nationalization – and even to gain public subsidy and government guarantees – lobbyists for the Finance, Insurance and Real Estate (FIRE) sector depict rent and interest as reflecting their recipients' contribution *to* wealth, not their privileges to *extract* economic rent *from* the economy.

Seemingly empirical National Income and Product Accounts (NIPA) follow this linguistic turnabout by reporting interest and rent as "earnings," as if bankers and landlords produce Gross Domestic Product (GDP) in the form of credit and ownership services. This practice is at odds with John Stuart Mill's definition of land rent as what property owners are able to make "in their sleep," by charging access fees for sites created by nature and given value by the community's overall prosperity. To depict this charge as "earnings" for providing an economic "product" is to pretend that rent extraction reflects real output, as if it is a useful service.

At issue is the classical definition of economic rent as unearned income – the excess of price over real cost-value – a property claim or privilege that does not reflect a necessary cost of production. Such costs ultimately are reducible to payment for labor. Indeed, the Labor Theory of Value was refined as a means of isolating economic rent. By rejecting classical value and price theory, today's literally value-free economics is based on the assumption that *no* activities are unproductive or extractive.

This inversion of language misrepresents what the leading classical economists stood for. Adam Smith and his fellow reformers are claimed to have favored "free markets" and opposed government "interference." What they actually opposed were governments controlled by the landlord aristocracy dominating tax policy, *e.g.* by the power of Britain's House of Lords to tax labor and industry instead of land and finance. Smith criticized military adventures and colonialism for running up war debts, issuing government bonds to be paid by taxing basic consumer goods.

By the late 19th century, reform movements were gaining the upper hand. Influenced by Darwin, nearly everyone saw industrial capitalism evolving into what was widely called socialism. From Christian socialism to the "Ricardian socialism" of Mill, and from utopian socialism to the libertarian socialism of Henry George, the term "socialism" had a broad variety of constructs. Marxist socialism described capitalism as being revolutionary in leading inexorably to stronger pubic ownership and direction of the economy, often via nationalized banking systems.

Surprising as it may seem today, classical ideas of creating a free market were to be achieved by "socialist" reforms. Their common aim was to protect populations from having to pay prices that included a non-labor rent or financial tax to pay landlords and natural resource owners, monopolists and bondholders. The vested interests railed against public regulation and taxation along these lines. They opposed public ownership or even the taxation of land, natural monopolies and banking. They wanted to collect rent and interest, not make land, banking and infrastructure monopolies public in character.

Today, neoliberals and their libertarian mascots seek to make governments too weak to fulfill the classical program of taxing land and natural resources, regulating or preventing monopolies, or providing basic financial and economic services by public infrastructure investment. Denigrating regulation as "central planning," the effect is to leave planning to the world's financial centers from Wall Street to the City of London, Frankfurt and the Paris Bourse, all of which lobby on behalf of their *rentier* clients. What calls itself libertarian thus has become a financially sponsored counter-Enlightenment against democratically empowered governments.

Free markets, liberty and the antidote to "false sight"

Denis Diderot (1713-1784) organized the writing of the *Encyclopédie* as a project of the French Enlightenment. Published in installments from 1751 to 1772, it contained a map of human knowledge along lines that defined the Enlightenment's political program: "The good of the people must be the great purpose of government. By the laws of nature and of reason, the governors are invested with power to that end. And the greatest good of the people is liberty. It is to the state what health is to the individual."

Diderot's "greatest good of the people" has come to be reversed by today's economic mainstream to refer to wealth and output that accrues mainly to the *rentiers*, whom France's Physiocrats and fellow reformers set out to tax. Today's anti-classical reaction re-defines liberty to connote freedom for predators *from* government sanctions against socially destructive behavior. Reversing the classical aim of freeing markets *from rentiers*, neoliberals deem the regulation of monopolies and interest rates, public investment in infrastructure, and taxation of landed property and finance to be an encroachment on liberty. This is antithetical to the liberty of populations *from* debt dependency on credit to obtain access to housing, education, medical care and other basic needs.

Voltaire's *Philosophical Dictionary* (1764) was closely associated with the *Encyclopédie*, written in a more aphoristic style with his usual wit and irony to make it a sarcastic and biting critique of the Roman Catholic Church, the nobility and royal palace. Voltaire in his own way made a similar point to that of Orwell by describing the character of False Minds:

> We have blind men, one-eyed men, squint-eyed men, men with long sight, short sight, clear sight, dim sight, weak sight. All that is a faithful enough image of our understanding; but we are barely acquainted with false sight. … Why do we often come across minds otherwise just enough, which are absolutely false on important things? Why does this same Siamese who will never let himself be cheated when there is question of counting him three rupees, firmly believe in the metamorphoses of Sammonocodom? …The greatest geniuses can have false judgment about a principle they have accepted without examination. … All that certain tyrants of the souls desire is that the men they teach shall have false judgment.

Refering to a fakir (no doubt to avoid censorship by citing the virgin birth and resurrection), Voltaire noted that "the more subtle his mind, the more false is it, and he forms later minds as false as his." Such individuals "will reason crookedly all their lives." My own dictionary criticizes today's neoliberal "free market" economists of similar crooked reasoning based on false assumptions, immune to empirical common sense.

The most typical way that a false mind reasons, Voltaire explained, was "by not examining if the principle is true, even when one deduces accurate consequences therefrom." That is the method of today's mathematical economics, national income statistics, and especially international trade and monetary theory. (I provide a repertory of quotations by Nobel Economics Prize winners along such religiously anti-scientific lines in my article on "Economics as Fraud" in this book.)

Neoliberal "free market" economics today plays the role that religion played in Voltaire's day. But in academia the warning that Voltaire provided his readers remains true: "It is dangerous to be right in matters where established men are wrong." Perhaps that is why economic graduates put their doubts aside when embarking on a tenure-track position at today's respectable universities.

Euphemistic terminology is used to popularize otherwise unpopular policies, or at least to buy time by confusing some of the injured parties. If the aim is to break labor unions, roll back wage levels and reduce workplace protection, the appropriate public relations tactic is to try to co-opt labor by calling the program "labor capitalism" as General Pinochet did in Chile after his 1973 military coup, or "popular capitalism" as his admirer Margaret Thatcher did in Britain after her 1979 Conservative victory. To likewise confuse matters by crafting a false vocabulary to complement false history, lobbyists for privatization have characterized public regulation and protection of consumers as "interference," and indeed as what

Frederick Hayek called *The Road to Serfdom* in 1944 – as if neoliberalism is not the road to neoserfdom and debt peonage.

The academic curriculum has been hijacked to replace classical political economy with a seemingly de-politicized but actually pro-*rentier* ideology. Mathematical symbolism is given the sanctifying role once afforded by Latin. Aping the natural sciences, economists take refuge in abstruse modes of expression. The more complex the math, the more simplistic and banal the postulated relationships and conclusions tend to be. Most of the math refers to choices between different "menus" of goods and services, without much analysis of how these come to be produced, or the long-term economy-wide consequences of buying on credit instead of cash.

Economic theories that focus on the exchange of goods and services without discussing the means of acquiring control over wealth divert attention from examining what is most important in shaping the economy. Ultimately at issue is whether what economic jargon calls the "real" economy of production and consumption more real than the claims of finance and property.

It is not possible to bail out the banks and somehow enable debtors to pay. One side or the other must lose. That is why the economic problem is ultimately one of insolvency, not merely temporary illiquidity. The major economic problem is whether the economy's debts should be downsized to reflect the ability to pay, or growth and living standards should be sacrificed to preserve the value of creditor claims.

The classical distinction between *earned* and *unearned* income

There is false history as well as true history. Factual history rarely is the version promoted by the "victors" (or would-be victors – the fight is not yet over). The same is true of economic theory. There is only one economic reality, so in principle there should be only one body of economic theory: reality economics. But special interests (today's victors) promote deception and outright exclusions in order to depict themselves as economic heroes, as if their predatory gains are those of society at large. Their self-congratulatory image characterizes what passes for mainstream economics.

Acting on behalf of financial, real estate and monopoly interests to defend deregulation and untaxing of their gains, neoliberals have kidnapped the classical economists as part of their pantheon. They brag about Adam Smith, while diverting attention from what he and his classical followers actually said. Their rewriting of the history of economic thought treats Smith's critique of *rentiers* and debt financing as heresy.

For two centuries the classical economists fought against the vested *rentier* interests that survived from the post-Roman law codes and subsequent warlord feudalism. But progressive reform was aborted after World War I. An anti-classical reaction began to emerge in the Gilded Age of the 1880s and 1890s, and gained strength after World War I ended the trend toward the socialization of industrial capitalism (*e.g.*, public health and pensions, public investment in infrastructure and education) and the mobilization of banking to finance industry, which had flowered most of all in Germany.

Anglo-American banking practice emerged as the norm, in alliance with real estate and monopolies instead of the formerly expected triad of industrial capitalism, banking and government. The struggle between what seemed to be the waves of the future – "state socialism" and Marxian socialism – were swept aside by a financialized *rentier* economy. With it came a new set of economic concepts and definitions, whose aim was to deaden resistance to what is now a full-blown Counter-Enlightenment.

The victorious *rentier* interests recognize that as long as they can capture the minds of politicians and the public to shape how people view the economy's dynamics, there is no need to spend money bribing or fighting them. As long as the One Percent can control the educational curriculum to teach that we are at The End of History and that There Is No Alternative (TINA), they will deprive voters of the ability to conceptualize an alternative (see hypocognition below). They promote the idea that austerity – and the economic polarization that goes with it – are our epoch's natural destiny, not a reversal of civil society's forward momentum.

It is not necessary to re-invent the wheel to replace the current malaise with a more realistic analysis. My economic model aims to lay the groundwork for creating a more realistic accounting format for national income and product accounts by excluding the burden of *rentier* overhead from "product." Rent is income *without* product, "empty" price without value. When unearned income is paid to the FIRE sector and monopolies, it is at the *expense* of wages, industrial profits and taxes.

This book therefore is meant as an antidote, starting with a renovation of the language used to describe how our economy works (or doesn't work). The A to Z entries in the vocabulary section illustrate this distinction from the historical and political as well as methodological standpoint.

Hypocognizant democracy: our newest political oxymoron

When I was an undergraduate in the 1950s, the Sapir-Whorf approach to linguistics was the standard. Benjamin Lee Whorf described how the vocabulary and semantics of language shape the way in which speakers conceptualize the world around them.

Anthropologist Robert Levy's 1960s studies of Tahitian suicide rates observed that they rose when unfortunate events made people sad. But their language had no word for "sad" or "depressed." They said "sick" or "strange," and blamed themselves for the way they felt. Much like other vocabulary-poor groups, they attributed their feelings of grief or frustration to a demonic presence that seemed to be taking over their life. To describe this phenomenon, the linguist George Lakoff coined a term, hypocognition, to describe a condition in which "the words or language that need to exist to frame an idea in a way which can lead to persuasive communication is either non-existent or ineffective."[2] In his 2004 book, *Don't Think of an Elephant! Know Your Values and Frame the Debate*, he accuses libertarian "free market" doctrines of personal responsibility and the concept of "less government" as suffering from "massive hypocognition." Lacking appropriate economic concepts to understand what is making people poorer, the ideology of personal responsibility leads people to blame themselves for not being able to avoid being trapped in a system of debt peonage.

The following A-to-Z guide aims at providing the vocabulary and concepts for a more effective diagnosis of today's economic (and by extension, psychological) depression, by thinking in terms of compound interest, debt peonage, *rentier* economies, unearned income, zero-sum activities and economic parasitism. Without such concepts in the forefront of one's mind, today's neoliberalized economies are prone to succumb to the virus of Orwellian Doublespeak.

Junk Economics and its euphemistic vocabulary aim to limit the tools of thought by distracting attention from the causes – and hence, the needed remedy – by trickle-down economics weaving a cloak of semantic invisibility around the phenomena of *rentier* parasitism. The lives of many debtors seem to be taken over by a demonic cloud or presence, an economic personification of Dracula sucking their livelihood. Politicians blame immigrants or other minorities for taking their jobs, while lobbyists try to convince wage earners and the middle class that what keeps them so debt-strapped is not the high cost of housing, education and living financed by mortgages, student loans and credit-card debt. The blame is shifted onto government for taxing the One Percent too much and "over-regulating" business with bureaucratic conditions, above all regulations to promote clean air, healthy food and honest accounting.

Mathematical illiteracy is a precondition for widespread failure to understand this exponential growth in the financial sector's claims on the economy, while Junk Economics fails to attribute today's economic polarization to the predatory dynamics of debt deflation. Debt is absorbing almost all economic growth in countries such as Greece. When the volume of debt has grown as large as national income or GDP, and when it bears an interest rate (typically 5%) above the economy's rate of growth (typically just 1% to 2%), then all the growth in national income is taken by the creditors.

Without widespread understanding of how our economy has become financialized and its income and wealth pledged to creditors, there can be no real economic democracy in which voters elect representatives who will save them from depression and what Martin Luther called the demon Cacus (a personification of exponential growth of debt). Any nominal democracy lacking such economic understanding is an oxymoron – that is its internal political contradiction.

Rewriting economic history by redefining the meaning of words

History is written by the victors, and today's victors are the resurgent vested interests. Just as truth is the first casualty of war, the past is rewritten as if it had to lead inexorably to the present. Rewriting the history of economic thought, lobbyists for the *rentiers* have created a false pedigree of what a classical free market is all about. The aim is to make it appear that all economists awarded status in the intellectual pantheon endorse today's view that wealth and income are fairly distributed, and that the financial elites are mainly responsible for creating it.

In this new view Winston Smith has replaced Adam Smith. In Orwell's *Nineteen Eighty-Four* the Anglo-American superstate Oceania employed Winston Smith to rewrite the past. His job at The Ministry of Truth was to continually update history to fit Big Brother's ever-changing party line. The Ministry's slogan was: "Who controls the past controls the future. Who controls the present controls the past."

Linguistics has become as much a casualty as has history. So one can say that who controls language controls how people perceive the world around them. As Michael Lewis described in *The Big Short*: "The subprime mortgage market had a special talent for obscuring what needed to be clarified." He elaborates:

> Language served a different purpose inside the bond market than it did in the outside world. Bond market terminology was designed less to convey meaning than to bewilder outsiders. … The floors of subprime mortgage bonds were not called floors – or anything else that might lead the bond buyer to form any sort of concrete image in his mind – but tranches. The bottom tranche – the risky ground floor – was not called the ground floor but the mezzanine … which made it sound less like a dangerous investment and more like a highly prized seat in a domed stadium.

The science fiction writer Ursula LeGuin, in *A Wizard of Earthsea* (1968), describes wizards trained by a "Master Namer, a teacher who knows the *true* name for everything." A modern social critic comments on LeGuin's idea: "The true name is different from the common, public name. When you learn the true name of something, you are able to take back any power it has over you. We need to do that with the system in which we live."[3]

This true naming is blocked by financial lobbyists and their public relations strategists, who have crafted the vocabulary used by the mainstream popular media to discuss the economy. The aim is to deflect attention from how the world actually works, creating a fairy tale view in which there is no extractive income and no free lunch – while the actual economy is all about how to obtain a free lunch.

To preserve their special privileges, the vested interests must convince the world that they earn their fortunes by contributing to the common weal. They depict the Progressive Era reforms and subsequent economic regulation and social programs as a relapse into autocracy on the road to debt serfdom, not an escape *from* the legacy of feudal *rentier* interests. And when their self-serving policies plunge economies into austerity, they lobby to persuade governments to absorb their financial losses.

Steering civilization along this destructive path is an absurd detour from the tradition of classical political economy. But as Voltaire famously noted: "People who believe in absurdities commit atrocities." The absurdities of today's mainstream economics have led to the atrocities of austerity in Greece, depopulation in Latvia, and the post-Soviet dismantling of Russian and Baltic industry since 1991. The soaring wealth of the One Percent is achieved by imposing austerity on entire national economies and stripping their assets.

Applause for this asset stripping and for the bubble economy as a business model – along with tolerance for debt deflation – is now holding the world in a deepening depression while endowing a *rentier* over-class to become this century's neofeudal lords.

The pretended opposition of "free markets" to serfdom/Communism

Beyond a language's vocabulary, thought is shaped by social metaphor and group psychology. In his 1928 book *Propaganda*, Sigmund Freud's nephew Edward Bernays (1891-1996) described the then-new discipline of public relations (his euphemism for propaganda) as a form of "invisible government" to manipulate voters and consumers by playing on their hopes and fears. "If we understand the mechanism and motives of the group mind, is it not possible to control and regiment the masses according to our will without their knowing about it?"[4] The key technique, the "engineering of consent"[5] as Bernays later explained, was for public relations strategists and their designated opinion-makers to mobilize the "herd instinct" and create an "us versus them" mentality to channel the self-interest of voters and consumers to act against their actual interests.

Having campaigned for Woodrow Wilson to promote American entry into World War I as a fight against the "German Hun," Bernays helped make smoking acceptable and even chic for women in the 1920s, calling cigarettes "torches of freedom." Further down the road, he supported the United Fruit Company's overthrow of Guatemala's democratically elected president Jacobo Arbenz in 1954 by calling him a Communist.[6] The new junta's U.S. sponsors depicted a reversal of the nation's land reform and of liberation from rural debt slavery as restoring free markets.

That is how today's neoliberals frame their policies to gain public acquiescence. "Freedom from Communism" ("them") is channeled to mean free markets ("us"), defined as opposing progressive taxation and other social democratic policies in the actual interests of voters and consumers. Much like the cigarette companies that trotted out doctors to assure consumers that smoking was healthy (and slenderizing!), today's One Percent parades Nobel Economics Prize winners to promote trickle-down economics and tax breaks for the rich.

A logical extension of Bernays' approach was that of Leo Strauss, a German émigré who became a University of Chicago professor (1949-69). The way to mobilize people behind a policy, Strauss taught, was to appeal to their group identity in the "us" versus "them" way that Bernays had explained. A set of myths was needed to shape public opinion, much as Plato's *Republic* described a "noble lie" (*gennaion pseudos*): "a contrivance for one of those falsehoods that come into being in case of need – some noble one"[7] to gain acceptance for the rule of elites as "golden souls." This is what Greek oligarchs did when they called themselves aristocracies ("the best"), claiming that their actions protected the city-state from "brass souls" (populist reformers demonized as "tyrants") who might rise to the office of guardianship, annul debts and redistribute the land.

Another Strauss colleague at Chicago (1950-1962), Frederick Hayek, lumped Progressive Era social programs, Communism, Nazism and fascism together as intrusions on "free markets" and hence as "the road to serfdom." His rhetoric aimed to reverse the drive by classical economists to end *rentier* privileges and thus free economies from the actual legacy of serfdom: a hereditary landlord class, and bankers who allied themselves with other rent-extracting interests.

Why neoliberals backed neoconservative imperialists

Anti-government ideologues call public investment in infrastructure to prevent private-sector rent extraction "the road to serfdom," not away from it. Geopolitics plays a role, as U.S. investors seek control of foreign rent-yielding natural resources and public monopolies. This drive for control unites neoliberal economists with military neoconservatives pressing for "regime change" of countries seeking to protect their markets, public domain and banking systems to promote their own growth and well-being. Strauss's neoconservative followers twisted "intelligence" into knots of sophistry that have shaped America's Cold War ideology.[8] His fellow Chicago professor (1964-80) Albert Wohlstetter served as dissertation advisor to the

Cold Warriors Paul Wolfowitz and Zalmay Khalizad, an Afghan immigrant who mobilized U.S. support for the Taliban against the secular regime allied with Russia, enflaming fundamentalist military groups to overthrow Near Eastern governments seeking autonomy from U.S. control. Wolfowitz and Khalizad mounted a smear campaign against Saddam Hussein much like that of Bernays against Guatemala, claiming that Iraq was sponsoring Al Qaeda and had weapons of mass destruction.[9]

Neoliberals have created an us-versus-them "noble lie" by appropriating Adam Smith, John Stuart Mill and other classical economists as having endorsed untaxing and deregulating finance, real estate and other rent-extracting sectors. This is the opposite of what they actually advocated in their refinement of rent theory to measure and tax away unearned income.

Such "noble lie" sophistry is depicts pro-financial economic and tax policy as a democratic bulwark against governments strong enough to check the power of high finance and its allied rent-extracting interests. The One Percent aims to create a mythology of tradition, a Stockholm Syndrome dependency, and a pseudo-Darwinian historical inevitability to steer the public to support the One Percent as the universal "we," while demonizing advocates of the interests of the 99 Percent as "them."

This Junk Economics of deception promotes neoliberal treaties as "reforms" to laws, tax and trade rules, reversing the real reforms of the Progressive Era. "Experts" (corporate lobbyists) are adorned with the badges of prestigious academic appointments to redefine "progress" as if there is no rational alternative to shifting economic planning out of democratic government hands to the world's financial centers. This ideological New Cold War is administered by the IMF, World Bank and World Trade Organization under U.S. control. Countries enacting policies that do not serve Wall Street and its financial satellites are deemed to follow the road to unfreedom – that of "the other." This reversal of what was thought to be progress a century ago is a travesty of freedom and an ignoble lie – as are most "noble lies," when one thinks about it.

ENDNOTES

[1] James Galbraith and J. Luis Martin, "The Poisoned Chalice," *Open Democracy*, September 1, 2015. https://opendemocracy.net/can-europe-make-it/james-galbraith-j-luis-martin/poisoned-chalice

[2] George Lakoff, "Women, Fire and Dangerous Things," March 27, 2013, cited in Rebecca J. Rosen, "Millions of Americans are facing a serious financial problem that

has no name," *The Atlantic*, May 7, 2016. See also Robert I. Levy, *Tahitians: mind and experience in the Society Islands* (Chicago: 1975).

[3] Anne Wilson Schaef, *When Society Becomes an Addict* (Harper, San Francisco, 1987) p. 10.

[4] Edward Bernays, *Propaganda* (1928), p. 47.

[5] "The Engineering of Consent," *Annals of the American Academy of Political and Social Science* **250** (March 1947), pp. 113–20.

[6] The details are told in Stephen Schlesinger and Stephen Kinzer, *Bitter Fruit: The Story of the American Coup in Guatemala* (1999), pp. 78-90.

[7] Plato, *Republic*, Book 3, 414b-415d.

[8] Seymour Hersh, "Selective Intelligence," *The New Yorker*, May 12, 2003.

[9] Jim Lobe, "Leo Strauss's Philosophy of Deception," *Alternet*, May 18, 2003. http://www.alternet.org/story/15935/leo_strauss'_philosophy_of_deception. "Like Thomas Hobbes, Strauss believed that the inherently aggressive nature of human beings could only be restrained by a powerful nationalistic state. 'Because mankind is intrinsically wicked, he has to be governed,' he once wrote. 'Such governance can only be established, however, when men are united – and they can only be united against other people.'" See also Scott Horton, "Will the Real Leo Strauss Please Stand Up?" *The Harpers blog*, July 31, 2016. http://harpers.org/blog/2008/01/will-the-real-leo-strauss-please-stand-up/

is for
Adam Smith,
Asset-Price Inflation
and Austerity

Accounting: Like markets, accounting began in the public sector. The root of the term "statistics" is "state," originally referring to data describing the condition of the national economy. Accounting always has been a tool of economic control, and this means hierarchical authority. Someone is reporting to a superior – an overseer, planner or tax collector. (See **Balance Sheet** and **Economic Forecasting**.)

First attested in Sumer's temples c. 4000 BC to keep track of food and other raw materials in workshops and other enterprises, account keeping requires a common standard of value. By the third millennium BC accounting was used to standardize the flow of resources with an eye to cutting costs and squeezing out an economic surplus in Mesopotamian temples and palaces. Because temple (and later, palace) taxes, fees and returns were paid in the form of grain or imported silver, these commodities became the prototypical money. (See **State Theory of Money**.)[1]

Today, accounting has been used increasingly for tax avoidance and to misrepresent the state of the economy. The Federal Reserve publishes notoriously misleading statistics understating the value of land relative to that of buildings (to avoid showing real estate's "free lunch" land-price gains), while the National Income and Product Accounts (**NIPA**) depict FIRE sector revenue as reflecting real output instead of **overhead**. (See **Junk Economics**.)

*Words in **boldface** are cross-referenced to other entries. Additional words and terms can be found in the mini index at the back of this book.*

Corporate accountants use **"over-depreciation"** and other tax loopholes that make FIRE sector income virtually tax-exempt, while "Hollywood" accounting shows no profits owed to outside investors. At the other extreme, Enron's accounting fraud was based **"mark-to-model"** practices like those that facilitated the WorldCom fraud. This led to the demise of the Arthur Andersen accounting firm, and it turned out that the other major U.S. accounting firms were indulging in much the same practice. Deregulation of public oversight has led to accounting fictions based on overstated cash flows that reached their apogee in the Ponzi Scheme perpetrated by Bernie Madoff.

Adam Smith (1723-1790): Traveling to France and meeting with the Physiocrats, Smith adopted their advocacy of a land tax: "Landlords love to reap where they have not sown, and demand a rent even for its (the land's) natural produce" (*Wealth of Nations*, Book I, Ch. 6, §8). Landownership privileges "are founded on the most absurd of all suppositions, the supposition that every successive generation of men has not an equal right to the earth ... but that the property of the present generation should be ... regulated according to the fancy of those who died ... five hundred years ago," that is, the Norman conquerors (Book III, Ch. 2, §6). Driving home the point, he adds: "The dearness of house-rent in London arises ... above all the dearness of ground-rent, every landlord acting the part of a monopolist" (Ch. 10, §55). Yet free market economists have tried to appropriate Adam Smith as their mascot, stripping away his critique of groundrent and monopolies to depict him as a patron saint of deregulation and lower property taxes.

Regarding monopolies, Smith observed that almost every private interest represents its gains as a public benefit, as when CEO Charles Wilson proclaimed that what's good for General Motors is good for the country. But in reality, Smith noted: "People of the same trade seldom meet together, even for merriment and diversion, but the conversation ends in a conspiracy against the public, or in some contrivance to raise prices ... though the law cannot hinder people of the same trade from sometimes assembling together, it ought to do nothing to facilitate such assemblies; much less to render them necessary" (Book I, ch.10, §82). (See **Invisible Hand** for more of Smith's observations along these lines.)

Opposing the wars resulting from empire building and colonialism, Smith urged that the American colonies be liberated so as to free Britain from the costs of wars financed by public debts that taxed consumer essentials to carry the interest charges. (See **Dutch Financing**.)

Affluence: Literally a flowing in. Early British and French affluence came from colonialism and financial conquest. American affluence has come largely from immigration, foreign investment and monetary support (the dollar standard of international finance). Domestically, an affluent class siphons up income and appropriates property from the public domain (*e.g.*, America's great fortunes in land, railroads and natural resources) – and from debtors. (See **Exploitation** and **Parasite**.)

Affluenza: A legal defense to exempt the wealthy from prosecution. The word was coined by psychologist Dick Miller for a lawsuit in which teenager Ethan Couch excused his killing four people while driving without a license by claiming that he was too rich to have a sense of ethics. Psychologists, sociologists and philosophers have confirmed that wealthy individuals are brought up without a social conscience teaching them to distinguish right from wrong.[2]

This is not a new phenomenon. The Greeks called it *pleonexia*, **wealth addiction**, the greedy compulsion to obtain more and more wealth, and specifically what belongs to others. As in the case of *hubris*, the effect is to injure others, because *pleonexia* is essentially adversarial to society as a whole. Hence, Plato argued (*Republic*, Book I), a just society would constrain such drives. Socrates suggests that the unjust person "will strive to get the most he can for himself and from everyone" (349c). Unrestrained self-interest thus is opposed to justice. (See **Too Big to Jail/Fail**.) But much as today's neoliberals define attempts to regulate the market as being unjust "interference," so Thrasymachus in Plato's dialogue claims that restraints on aggressive self-interest and wealth-seeking are unnatural. "Justice is nothing other than the advantage of the stronger" (*Republic* 338c).

Rentiers and their supporters justify their predatory behavior as if it follows natural law. They claim that it is not unfair to extract rent and monopoly income at other peoples' expense, and that they are not committing a crime when they impoverish the economy around them. Having been spoiled and deprived of moral values, their narcissistic upbringing is intensified by today's de-regulatory philosophy. Neoliberal economists encourage their belief that their self-enrichment counts as real wealth creation rather than being at society's expense. Society's permissive *caveat emptor* ("buyer beware") attitude saves bankers, for instance, from having to admit they are doing anything wrong when they indulge in financial fraud and predatory junk mortgage lending. Obtaining wealth in predatory ways is merely doing what is applauded as normal.

When the U.S. Congress discussed closing the "carried interest" tax loophole that protects speculative financial gains from normal taxation, Blackstone's Steve Schwarzman cried that trying to tax his wealth was like Hitler invading Poland. Wall Street's hubris and wealth addiction runs so deep that taxing it at the same rate as labor and industry must seem like throwing them into the gas chambers.

Such affluenza is contagious, thanks to the influence wielded by the **One Percent** over universities, non-profit organizations and even churches to shape social values. Former U.S. Labor Secretary Robert Reich told an MSNBC interviewer that he was asked to talk at a religious congregation about inequality: "And just before I began, the minister who headed the congregation whispered to me and he said, 'don't talk about changing the estate tax and don't in any way attack the rich because we are dependent – you know, we're dependent on them.'"[3]

As Prof. Bill Black (former Director of the Institute for Fraud Prevention) has summarized: "Political scientists' research has revealed the crippling grip on power that the Wall Street billionaires have in practice and the fact that the wealthy have, on key public policies, strikingly different views than do the American people. In particular, the One Percent are exceptionally hostile to Social Security and anything that protects the weak from predation by the wealthy. They are also stunningly unconcerned about problems such as global climate change while they are paranoid about debt, deficits, and inflation even during the depths of the Great Recession."[4]

Agio (a money-changing fee): Medieval Europe banned **usury**, but the Churchmen saw the need for financing foreign trade and transferring money from one country to another, *e.g.*, to go on Crusades or wage royal wars on behalf of the papacy. They permitted a money-changing fee (*agio*) for borrowing money in one currency or country to be paid back in another. In practice this exchange rate fee incorporated an interest charge. Creditors soon found a loophole in the "dry" exchange (occurring only on dry land), which pretended to involve foreign payments although no goods or money actually were imported or exported.

One effect of this *agio* loophole was to channel European banking along the lines of trade financing and discounting bills of exchange until the 19th century, prompting bank strategists such as David Ricardo to back free trade.

American School of Political Economy: The northern economists who focused on protective tariffs, infrastructure investment and a national bank to promote industrial and agricultural technology before and after the Civil War (1861-65). Mathew and Henry Carey, Henry Clay and William Seward among the Whigs and, after 1853, the Republicans, provided the economic policy that enabled America to industrialize and overtake England. They also emphasized the positive effect of rising wage levels and living standards on the productivity that made the American economic takeoff possible. Every major Northern politician and region was associated with a major economist: Alexander Everett for Daniel Webster and other Bostonians; Calvin Colton for Henry Clay; the Carey's for Pennsylvania industrialists; and E. Peshine Smith for Seward and the Republicans. They developed the logic for tariff protection as opposed to Ricardian free-trade theory, and for government-sponsored internal improvements and a national bank to finance industry and achieve monetary independence from Britain.

It is testimony to the censorial power of subsequent free-trade ideology that these writers make no appearance in histories of economic thought. Historians also have ignored them, focusing on the Democratic Party (which meant mainly the South seeking to add slave states). At issue was whether the United States would suffer deflation and monetary and trade dependency on Britain, or would become independent. The American School opposed westward expansion and Manifest Destiny, and also opposed the Anglophilia of free traders and slave owners. The latter demanded monetary deflation to prevent industrialization so as to keep food prices low (and hence the cost of feeding slaves).

When the Civil War brought the Republicans to power, the American School found that the most prestigious colleges – founded originally to train the clergy – simply taught mainstream British free trade economics (largely because New England and southern seaboard schools favored free trade). The path of least intellectual resistance was to create a new set of schools – business schools and state land-grant colleges.

A central tenet of the American School was technological optimism in contrast to the Dismal Science of Ricardo and Malthus based on diminishing returns in agriculture and overpopulation leading to poverty. Also central was the Economy of High Wages doctrine: "It is not by reducing wages that America is making her conquests, but by her superior organization, greater efficiency of labor consequent upon the higher standard of living ruling in the country. High-priced labor countries are everywhere beating 'pauper-labor' countries."[5]

By the late 19th century nearly all the major American economists studied in Germany and followed the Historical School. Returning to America, they developed the Institutionalist School to explain why the United States should follow a different economic path from free-trade Britain. They continued to elaborate the logic for the protective tariffs that were nurturing American industry, as well as for public support for internal infrastructure improvements so as to create a low-cost competitive U.S. economy. Most notable was Simon Patten, the first professor of economics at the Wharton School at the University of Pennsylvania. He taught protectionist trade theory and led economists into the discipline of sociology to analyze what he called the Economy of Abundance that resulted from the increasing returns in industry and agriculture.

When the United States achieved world industrial and financial dominance after World War I, it deterred other countries from protecting their own industry and agriculture – while continuing to protect its own. This about-face emulated British experience in urging free trade on other countries so as to make them dependent. This free-trade logic remains the buttress of today's financial austerity and privatization policies imposed on debtor economies by the United States, the World Bank, and the International Monetary Fund. These policies are the opposite of America's own protectionist takeoff, the Economy of High Wages Doctrine and the Economy of Abundance that powered its rise to global economic supremacy. The lessons of the American School of Political Economy provide a more realistic model for other countries to emulate.

Apex Predator: The predator at the top of a food chain, *e.g.*, killer whales in the ocean or lions in the jungle. In the economic jungle, banks and bondholders stand at the top, followed by real estate moguls, the oil and mining sectors, and infrastructure monopolists in telecommunications and information technology. Along with chemical, pharmaceutical and health care monopolies, these rent-seeking sectors make money by establishing choke points enabling them to appropriate the income and wealth created by labor and industry. (See **Parasite** and *Rentier*.)

Alienation: The result of an exploitative relationship in which labor is not in control of the products it creates or the working conditions of how its products are made. Such relationships have existed since the Bronze Age, in modes of production where labor is dependent and its product is appropriated by an employer, slave-owner, feudal lord, absentee landlord or creditor. The common denominator in such alienation is the loss or deprivation of personal control (see **Choice**) over one's life, working conditions, affordability of ownership of one's domicile, and ultimately the loss of one's status in society.

From the Bronze Age through classical antiquity, getting someone into debt was the main lever forcing such alienation. Debtors pledged themselves – or their slaves, wives or children – in bondage to creditors. That was one of the most ancient means of obtaining dependent labor.

As a legal term, alienation means the transfer of property. Pledging one's subsistence land rights meant losing the family's means of self-support, by forfeiture or forced sale. This meant loss of economic freedom and ultimately, citizenship rights. With the rise of industrial capitalism the main object of sale became one's labor power to employers for wages. Such labor was nominally free in the sense of being able to decide just whom to work for. But it no longer was free to support itself on its own land.

Karl Marx discussed alienation in his 1844 manuscripts and unpublished *Grundrisse* notes before writing *Capital* (where the term does not appear, although the basic concept is there.) His focus was on how wage labor is not in control of its own life. The wage relationship between capitalist and employee separates workers from control over their products and how these are produced. By thwarting what Thorstein Veblen called the Instinct of Workmanship – in which labor is able to express its personality and creativity as part of the production process – the drudgery of industrial labor and exhausting working hours leads to emotional alienation. Employers are in charge of what labor produces, under conditions of dependency in an economic process that is often impersonal.

Capitalists themselves are drawn into this impersonal dynamic as production increasingly is financialized in a dynamic focused on making money as an end in itself. (See **Greed** and **Affluenza**.) Alienation tends to become so ingrained that employers as well as labor are unable to recognize its dynamics. On the broadest social scale, nature's ecological balance is violated by the drive for profits and to carry an exponentially expanding debt load.

"As If" Argument: The simplest way to distract attention from how economies are unfair is to treat economic theory as a purely abstract logical exercise. (See **GIGO**.) A parallel universe is presented as a set of assumptions. As in novels, the key is to get observers to suspend disbelief. Mainstream economics, for instance, reasons as if all wealthy individuals earn their income by playing a productive role and put their savings in banks or the bond market – which are assumed to increase prosperity by lending these savings to entrepreneurs to build factories and employ labor. *Rentier* income, junk mortgage lending and corporate takeover loans play no role in this "as if" picture. Defining the economy's problems narrowly in this hypothetical way facilitates a tunnel vision that Thorstein Veblen called "trained incapacity" – an inability to understand how economies actually work or how financialization leads to systemic problems. (See **Learned Ignorance**.)

Asset-Price Inflation: Despite the fact that most money and bank credit is spent on assets, not on goods and services, the **Quantity Theory of Money**, **MV=PT**, relates money creation only to commodity prices, not asset prices. The reality is that banks don't lend for new direct capital investment, and only a small proportion is lent for consumer goods. Banks lend mainly against assets in place – real estate (about 80% of commercial bank loans), bonds and stocks. This credit for buyers of real estate, stocks and bonds inflates debt-leveraged windfall gains (euphemized as **capital gains**; see **Wealth Creation**).

Assets are worth as much as banks will lend new buyers. Housing prices, for instance, are inflated by steering mortgage credit into real estate, lowering interest rates so that higher mortgage debts can be carried. Also, loosening the terms of mortgage lending reduces the down payments needed.

A related financial phenomenon contributing to asset-price inflation is the corporate practice of borrowing more while using earnings for stock buybacks and higher dividend payouts to raise short-term stock prices. Fiscal policy contributes by shifting taxes off of financial and real estate income and capital gains onto labor. (See **Bubble**, **Great Moderation** and **Tax Shift**.)

The working assumption is that higher asset prices increase net worth, as long as the rise in market prices outpaces the growth of debt. But rising property prices increase living costs by panicking homebuyers to buy now to avoid seeing the rise in property prices outstrip wage gains. The economy polarizes as higher prices for homes oblige families to go further into debt to obtain housing. When prices rise as a result of greater debt leveraging, the resulting carrying charge (interest) diverts income to the financial sector, away from being spent on goods and services. The "real" economy slows, giving way to "Stage 2" of asset-price inflation: **debt deflation.**

Asset Stripping: When corporate raiders take over companies, they cut back research and development spending along with business lines that do not produce short-term returns. They also downsize their labor force in order to make the remaining employees work harder to pick up the slack and cut back defined benefit pension plans. These practices are euphemized as wealth creation when their effect is to improve reported earnings. This raises stock prices over the short term, but undercuts long-term production and competitiveness.

Privatization is a program of stripping the public domain. Debt-strapped countries are obliged to rely on neoliberal planning by the International Monetary Fund (IMF) and World Bank. As a precondition for obtaining the credit needed to service their foreign debts and avoid currency destabilization, governments are obliged to sell off the "crown jewels" of their public domain – mineral rights, public land, forests and buildings, and enterprises long held in the public sector as natural monopolies such as communications, utilities and transportation (see **Commons**, **Conditionalities**, **Privatization** and **Washington Consensus**.) For further discussion see my book *The Bubble And Beyond* (2013).

Austerity: Imposed by the **International Monetary Fund (IMF)** since the 1960s on debtor countries (and since 2008 on Ireland, Latvia, Greece and other Eurozone countries), the assumption is that squeezing out a high tax surplus from labor will "free" more output to be exported, enabling countries to pay foreign debt service.

This theory underlay Allied demands for German reparations in the 1920s. The actual result is to shrink domestic markets and the economy by **fiscal deflation**, adding to unemployment and forcing capital flight and population emigration. (See

IMF Riots and **Stabilization Program**.) Austerity programs lead to economic shrinkage and even deeper **debt dependency**, requiring yet more "monetary medicine" from the IMF in a downward spiral.

Austrian School of Economics: Emerged in Vienna toward the late 19th century as a reaction against socialist reforms. Opposing public regulation and ownership, the Austrian School created a parallel universe in which governments did not appear except as a burden, not as playing a key role in industrial development as historically has been the case, above all in Germany, the United States and Japan.

Carl Menger developed an anachronistic fable that individuals developed money as an outgrowth of barter, seeking a convenient store of value and means of exchange. The reality is that money was developed by cost accountants in Bronze Age Mesopotamian temples and palaces, mainly as a means of denominating debts. (See my forthcoming book, *The Lost Tradition of Biblical Debt Cancellations*.) Few transactions during the crop season were paid in money, but took the form of personal debts mounting up to fall due on the threshing floor when the harvest was in. Mercantile trade debts typically doubled the advance of merchandise or money after five years.

Most of these advances were initially made by temple or palace handicraft workshops, or collectors in the palace bureaucracy. Menger's Austrian theory ignored the fact that weights and measures were developed in the temples and palaces, and that throughout antiquity silver and other metals were produced in standardized purity by temple mints to avoid private-sector fraud. This history has been expurgated, **as if** enterprise only occurs in the private sector, needing no public role or regulation.

Also not appearing is the exploitation of labor by industrial capitalists. Austrians developed the idea of "time preference." Profits were attributed to the fact that capital-intensive ("roundabout") production took time, so profits were simply a form of interest built into nature. (For the Austrian School's **Blame The Victim** theory of interest, debt and saving, see **Impatience**.)

ENDNOTES

[1] For details see Michael Hudson and Cornelia Wunsch, eds., *Creating Economic Order: Record-keeping, Standardization, and the Development of Accounting in the Ancient Near East* (2004).

[2] See Paul K. Piff, "Wealth and the Inflated Self: Class, Entitlement, and Narcissism," *Personality and Social Psychology Bulletin* **40** (2014), pp. 34–43, and also Paul K. Piff, Daniel M. Stancato, Stéphane Côté, Rodolfo Mendoza-Denton and Dacher Keltner, "Higher social class predicts increased unethical behavior," PNAS (Proceedings of the National Academy of Sciences of the United States of America), 2012. http://www.pnas.org/content/109/11/4086.full.

[3] Quoted in Gaius Publius, "Money uses money to neuter Democrats and enable Republicans," *Down With Tyranny*, January 25, 2016. http://downwithtyranny.blogspot.mx/2016/01/robert-reich-money-and-left-political.html

[4] Bill Black, "Wall Street Declares War Against Bernie Sanders," *New Economic Perspectives*, January 25, 2016, citing Benjamin I. Page, Larry M. Bartels, and Jason Seawright, "Democracy and the Policy Preferences of Wealthy Americans," *Perspectives on Politics*, March 2013 (Vol. 11, #1), pp. 51-73. http://faculty.wcas.northwestern.edu/~jnd260/cab/CAB2012%20-%20Page1.pdf.

[5] U.S. Labor Secretary Jacob Schoenhof, *Wages and Trade in Manufacturing Industries in America and in Europe* (New York, 1884), p. 19. I provide a detailed analysis of the American School in *America's Protectionist Takeoff: 1815-1914*.

is for
Bubble and the
Bailout that follows

Bad Debt: Any debt that is defaulted on is called bad – at least for the creditor. But many debts are the result of predatory lending practices. In such cases the term "bad loan" is more appropriate. This is especially true of **NINJA loans,** subprime home mortgage and auto loans, payday loans, and high-interest credit card debt, as well as student loans and hospital loans in default.

As economies sink deeper into debt (usually by following policies demanded by creditors), more debts cannot be paid – that is, paid without destroying the debtor's economic viability. In such cases what is *bad* are demands for payment that strip debtors of their homes, or force entire economies into a downward spiral.

Exploitative loans beyond the reasonable ability of borrowers to pay should be forgiven. What is *good* for such individuals (or national economies) is *not* to pay such debts. It is the bad creditor or vulture bondholder who should bear the moral opprobrium for acting against social norms of equity. The response to a bad debt should be a good writeoff. (See **Bankruptcy** and **Clean Slate**.)

Bailout: A transfer of wealth to creditors, to save them from losing on loans gone bad when the financial bubble burst in 2008. U.S. creditors demanded public bailouts by Congress and the Federal Reserve (and in Europe by the European Central Bank and IMF), as if they were victims rather than the victimizers. Creditors were bailed out, and the bad debts left in place. (See **Junk Mortgage** and **NINJA Loans**.)

Somebody has to lose when banks make bad loans or bondholders over-lend. Bailouts usually save creditors at public expense. Reimbursing bankers, uninsured creditors and speculators to save them from loss preserves economic control in the hands of the financial sector (see **Rentier**, **Oligarchy** and **Who/Whom**). As Federal Deposit Insurance Corp. head Sheila Bair explained regarding the 2008 bailout: "It's all about the bondholders." Banks were saved from being nationalized or socialized to save their bondholders and large uninsured depositors.

The aim of such bailouts is to enable the financial sector to pursue its impossible dream that the miracle of compound interest can keep exponentially increasing society's debt burden without crashing the economy. In the United States the Federal Reserve provided banks with more than $4 trillion of reserves by pretending that the crash was only a temporary illiquidity problem. In Europe, taxpayers were obliged to make up the loss, imposing deep depression on Ireland and Greece.

Balance of Payments: The technical term is "balance of international transactions," because many transactions do not involve payments abroad. U.S. foreign aid is extended "in kind" (*e.g.,* food dumping and military "aid" in the form of weapons), or loans to governments to pay their debts to U.S. banks. The payment never leaves the United States. So what seems at first glance to be an outflow (grants and advances to foreign governments) generates an offsetting credit – and indeed a dollar *inflow* for the United States as foreign countries pay back their "aid" debts.[1]

The balance of international transactions is subdivided into Current Account (trade, interest and dividends, services and immigrants' remittances) and Capital Account (loans and investments). It would be helpful if government budgets and the U.S. National Income and Product Accounts were organized this way, to distinguish asset transactions from current production and consumption.

Military spending accounted for the entire U.S. payments deficit from the time the Korean War pushed the overall balance into deficit in 1951, through the Vietnam War decade of the 1960s. Settling the "balance" consisted of gold sales, until the United States finally was forced off gold in 1971. Since then, U.S. deficits have been settled by a run-up of Treasury debt to foreign central banks. For most other nations, the typical payments (im)balance is foreign debt service, leading to a loss of international reserves (formerly gold, now mainly U.S. Treasury IOUs).

The United States is almost alone in being able to settle its payments imbalances on military, trade and investment accounts in government IOUs denominated in its own fiat currency – U.S. Treasury bonds payable in dollars – without constraint. Other debtor countries are obliged to sell off their public domain, and let U.S. diplomats and the IMF dictate their economic policy. (See

Austerity, Conditionalities, Dollar Hegemony, Privatization and **Washington Consensus**.) This dollar hegemony has turned the euro and Japanese yen into satellite currencies of the dollar, holding their international reserves in the form of loans to the U.S. Government. In effect they are paying for the costs of their own military encirclement by the U.S. "indispensable economy."

Balance Sheet: More than just a bookkeeping concept, balance sheets are a way of viewing the economy as a system, in which every asset has a corresponding liability. Assets and liabilities always go together in an existential binary relationship. One party's saving is another's debt. The basic balance is:

Assets = Liabilities + Net Worth

Money, credit and debt would be more clearly understood if teaching economics started by thinking about the economy in terms of balance sheets. Bank checking and savings accounts are a liability by banks to their depositors. But not all monetary debt is expected to be paid. Paper money, for instance, is technically government debt, and appears on the liabilities side of the public balance sheet. To pay it off would require retiring the money in the private sector's pocket. (See **Modern Monetary Theory**.)

Bank credit is created almost exclusively to purchase assets (real estate, stocks and bonds). The effect is to increase debt/equity ratios for households and industry. In the early stage of the business cycle, asset prices tend to rise faster than the buildup of debt. But rising ratios of debt (liabilities) to net worth make the economy more fragile (see **Hyman Minsky** and **Ponzi Scheme**), while raising the break-even cost of living and doing business, because interest must be paid. (See **Compound Interest** for the problems that ensue.) In time a crash occurs, leading to negative equity (when debts exceed the market price of assets). When that point is reached, governments must decide whether to bail out the banks or save the economy by annulling the debts. (See **Clean Slate**.)

Balance Sheet Recession: A term coined by Nomura Holdings economist Richard Koo to describe how Japan's private sector became so debt-strapped that it did not borrow even at zero interest rates after the bubble burst in 1990. Families and businesses were obliged to pay down debt, leaving less to spend on goods and services, deflating the "real" economy and causing a recession. Property prices fell steadily, and the domestic market shrank as right-wing governments raised taxes on consumer goods.

An alternative term to characterize the post-2008 downturn is **debt deflation**. The plunge in real estate prices led the value of bank mortgages to decline as default rates mounted. These mortgages were the main assets backing bank liabilities to their depositors, bondholders and other counterparties. This shortfall of assets behind liabilities prevented banks from extending new credit. For homeowners, the decline in real estate prices wiped out most of their net worth that had been built up by asset-price inflation leading up to 2008. Payback time had arrived, and the economy stalled. It must continue to stall until the volume of debt is brought back in line with the ability of income and assets to cover what is owed.

Balanced Budget: Most people aggree that individuals should avoid going into debt – and indeed, should get *out* of debt by saving what they can. But governments are different. They create money and spend it into the economy by running budget deficits. When they do *not* run deficits, the economy is obliged to rely on banks – which charge interest for providing credit. When President Clinton ran a budget surplus in the late 1990s, this policy sucked revenue *out* of the U.S. economy. (See **Modern Monetary Theory**.)

Bankruptcy: Financial legislation is a tug of war between creditors and debtors over whose rights should come first. Creditors want to foreclose on as much of the debtor's property as possible. Debtors seek to make a fresh start with as much as they can retain. In archaic and medieval law this included basic means of survival. Gradually, debtors were permitted to keep their personal freedom (see **Bond**) as bankruptcy law became increasingly humanitarian. But in 2005, U.S. banks and credit card companies lobbied successfully to tighten the terms of bankruptcy, increasing their claims on the future earnings of debtors.

For workers and homeowners, bankruptcy leads to forfeiture of property to foreclosing banks or other creditors. Wage earners also lose when corporations use bankruptcy (or the threat of bankruptcy) to shed or scale back pension obligations to pay their bondholders and senior creditors. Only a **Clean Slate** amnesty would wipe out debts without transferring homes and other basic needs to foreclosing creditors.

Banks, Bankers, Banking: See **Finance**, **Financial Sector** and **FIRE Sector**.

Bankster: Often attributed to Franklin D. Roosevelt, the term emerged from the Pecora hearings in 1932, when Senator Burton Wheeler of Montana likened bankers to Al Capone and referred to them as "banksters" to combine banker and gangster.

Banksterism: The bankster-subsidized ideology of a financial free market – free from regulation (see **Regulatatory Capture),** letting banks siphon off income for themselves and leave depositors, clients and the government bearing the risk. (See **Rent Seeking**.)

Barter: Austrian theory depicts barter as the first stage of market exchange (see **Carl Menger** and **Money**). The idea is that individuals preferred metal bullion as the chief barter commodity and savings vehicle since Bronze Age Mesopotamia.

The reality is that metallism always has been associated mainly with payments by and to governments (see **Accounting**) with foreign trade, not individuals exchanging shoes for cabbages or other consumer goods. Anthropologists and historians have not found any "barter stage." Instead, barter appears in the breakdown stage of financialization – for instance as the Roman Empire dissolved into the Dark Ages. Money payments occurred mainly as the top of the economic pyramid (especially for luxuries and to pay soldiers), while the population at large lapsed into self-sufficient Church communities on the land.

Today's rising investment in gold likewise reflects a distrust in the ability of central banks to manage the economy well. Modern governments used bullion to settle balance-of-payments deficits until gold convertibility of the dollar was ended in 1971. But as national financial systems are becoming debt-ridden and unstable, more individuals are turning to gold as a vehicle for saving. As Herman Kahn of the Hudson Institute (no relation) quipped, gold coins are for bribing border guards to get out of countries in a state of collapse.

Today's breakdown of the international payments system is leading governments outside the United States to insist on settling trade deficits with barter deals, and once again are building up their gold reserves. The dress rehearsal for such arrangements occurred in the 1960s and 1970s for bilateral trade with the Soviet Union. The Soviet trade office negotiated barter deals of Russian oil for Finnish consumer goods, and for transactions with the West when access to dollar currencies was politically blocked.

In economies plagued by disruptions and shortages, payment "in kind" (barter) is how families and businesses survive – from butchers to repair shops. But that is a process of breakdown, not how economies started out. Such breakdowns see a revival of subsistence food production, such as gardens at Russian dachas and World War II "victory gardens" as economies revert to a subsistence level.

But the main example of barter occurs in economic textbooks as a way of thinking (or rather, avoiding thought) about money and debt. All exchange is treated as barter, without discussion of how money payments lead to debt buildups that end up crashing the monetary system.

Big Government: Europe's 1848 revolutions by the bourgeoisie against Europe's royalty, landed aristocracies and their allied vested interests sought to transfer power away from government bodies controlled by these classes (*e.g.,* Britain's House of Lords). Subsequent democratic reform movements favored progressive taxation, consumer protection and general economic regulation. These original liberals fought to tax special interests, not to free them from taxation. The thrust of parliamentary reform since the 19th century accordingly has been to make governments strong enough to tax rent extractors such as landlords, high finance and monopolists.

These *rentiers* have fought back by wrapping themselves in the rhetoric of individualism. Accusing politicians of corruption and insider dealing, populist demagogues assert that government is by nature incompetent as compared to private management – which turns out to be giant Wall Street corporations and trusts. The effect (indeed, the lobbying aim) of downsizing democratic government is to turn the economy over to the financial sector and its allied *rentiers* to administer in their own interest. The wealthy are all in favor of Big Government when it is oligarchic.

Trickle-down economists accuse social spending programs of leading to budget deficits that are inherently inflationary, but applaud tax cuts and bank bailouts that benefit primarily the FIRE Sector. Their lobbyists craft a demagogic rhetoric to attack progressive taxation, regulation, and social spending programs by insisting that public management is inherently inefficient as compared to private ownership of basic infrastructure, banking and health care. Claiming that public services are not a proper function of government, they advocate privatization of state-run enterprises, roads and the post office. (See **Planning** and **Political Economy**.)

Frederick Hayek's *Road to Serfdom* (1944) argued that public planning to subsidize basic needs or regulate "the market" (rent extractors, banksters and fraudsters) to protect consumers and employees leads to socialist or fascist autocracy. His libertarian followers insist that government regulation violates their personal rights to charge whatever the market will bear. (See **Affluenza** and **Greed**.) Their oligarchic alternative to big government is to roll back democratic **reforms** by attacking social spending programs, replacing progressive taxes with a low flat tax and sales taxes that fall on labor/consumers; abolishing minimum wage protection, Social Security and other public services; and privatizing public infrastructure to turn it into feudal-style **rent-extraction** opportunities. The aim is to un-tax the FIRE sector (mainly the One Percent) and eliminate the consumer protection and labor reforms put in place in the early 20th century Progressive Era. The meaning of the word "reform" has been inverted, using libertarian-style language coined in the late 19th century against Big Government under the control of aristocrats and other *rentiers*.

The real question is thus whether governments will be democratic or oligarchic. Will they subsidize the economy and undertake public infrastructure investment, or will they tax the population at large to subsidize the FIRE sector and other special interests?

Blair, Tony (1953-): British Prime Minister (1997-2007) who used the Lab
to further Margaret Thatcher's privatization policy and untaxing the One
Fighting bitterly in 2015-2016 to block the Labour Party from returning to
economic policies under Jeremy Corbyn, Blair played on voters' hopes that they
could get rich if they worked hard enough. "Hard-working families don't just want
us to celebrate their hard work; they want to know that by hard work and effort they
can do well, rise up, achieve. They want to be better off and they need to know we
don't just tolerate that; we support it."[2] (See **Labor Capitalism** and **Trickle-Down
Economics**.)

Blame the Victim: Defenders of Ponzi schemes and kindred frauds claim that they
would have continued if only critics hadn't destroyed "confidence," a euphemism
for gullibility by the public. In the run-up to the 2008 junk mortgage crash, New
York Federal Reserve President Tim Geithner announced that the main danger to the
economy was not junk mortgages or other debt leveraging, but economists warning
the public to get out of the market. "There is nothing more dangerous in what we're
facing now," he accused, "than for people who are knowledgeable about this stuff to
feed these broad concerns about our credibility and about the basic core strength of
the financial system."[3] It's as if the Bubble Economy could have continued to inflate
asset-prices with new debt creation *ad infinitum* if only doubters had not pointed to
how mathematically impossible this was. He blamed reality economics, not his
financial mismanagement on behalf of the Fed's Wall Street constituency.

Bond: From the verb meaning "to bind," originally referring to the shackles by
which creditors kept debtors in bondage. Since debtors' prisons have been outlawed,
the term has connoted the purely legal shackles by which debtors are bound to pay
their creditors. This state of affairs prompted Ambrose Bierce to describe debt as "an
ingenious substitute for the chain and whip of the slave driver."

Entire governments and their populations are now being reduced to financial
bondage. In eurozone countries this reflects the political choice by **client
oligarchies** to refrain from monetizing public spending, obliging governments to
borrow from creditors at interest (and subject to **Conditionalities**) to finance budget
deficits.

Bourgeoisie: The bourgeois aim is to live without working, by accumulating
enough wealth to live off interest, rent or capital gains. This fantasy sounds
appealing, but for most people the hope of rising into the *rentier* or capitalist class
through hard work and saving is illusory and reflects a loss of class consciousness.
(See **Middle Class** and **Tony Blair**.)

Bubble: All bubbles are financial in origin, and are promoted by governments, usually to extricate themselves from public debt by puffing up the stock market. The basic strategy is to replace public debt (which is difficult to write down) with private corporate debt or equities, whose price can be left to plunge so that gullible investors will bear the loss. The South Sea Bubble of the 1710s enabled Britain's government to convince its bondholders to exchange their holdings for stock in the South Sea Company, which had a monopoly in the slave trade. France's Mississippi Company had the same objective. Once the government bonds were swapped for shares in these companies, the market was permitted to collapse, enabling Britain and France to blame the madness of crowds for believing the forecasts that political insiders had made.

In 2006, George W. Bush's administration hoped that a similar strategy would help privatize Social Security. The plan was for employees to channel their compulsory FICA wage witholding (currently over 15% of wages) to buy mutual funds instead of relying on government payouts. Social Security contributions would flow into the stock market in a financial tsunami, inflating prices and enabling retirement income to be paid out of capital gains. The problem is that in due course more retirees would draw funds out of the stock market than contributors were paying in, causing stock prices to plunge. (See **Pension Fund Capitalism**.) Fortunately, the stock market plunged before politicians were able to persuade Americans to participate in this tactic, which would have generated huge management fees for Wall Street firms.

After the stock market's dot.com bubble burst in 2000, Federal Reserve Chairman Alan Greenspan flooded the economy with easy credit, lowered interest rates and deregulated the banking system to finance the junk-mortgage bubble. Prospective homebuyers were panicked into buying real estate on credit (that is, debt) before prices soared even further out of reach, and speculators borrowed in hope of getting rich. (See **Great Moderation**, **Junk Mortgage** and **NINJA Loans**.) The legacy of such private-sector debt-leveraged bubbles is debt.

Bubble Economy: An economy trying to get rich and pay pensions simply by **financial engineering**. The dream is that inflating asset prices for real estate, stocks and bonds on credit "creates wealth." But it actually is based on debt **pyramiding**. Bank credit raises access prices for housing, stocks and bonds (increasing the cost of buying a given retirement income as price/dividend ratios rise). At the corporate level, a stock market bubble based on stock buybacks is often elaborated into an economy-wide business plan. (See **Ponzi Scheme** and **Wealth Creation**.)

A bubble economy **polarizes** creditors and debtors as the One Percent holds the 99 Percent increasingly in debt (see **Debt Serfdom**), while prices for property rise relative to wage levels and the goods that labor produces. In due course, bubble economies degenerate into debt-ridden depressions (see **Debt Deflation**), increasing unemployment while shrinking consumption and production.

Bubble Illusion: The idea that rising housing prices (see **Asset-Price Inflation**) reflect real wealth creation. The main bubble illusion is in the real estate market where most bank credit is concentrated.

For example: Suppose Mary Smith owns a $100,000 home free and clear of debt. Suppose that a year or two later, Jane Doe buys a similar home next door, but easier bank credit has led mortgage bankers to offer such large loans that the market for the home rises to $250,000. To outbid other buyers, Jane must take out a $100,000 mortgage.

Who is in a better financial position? On paper Jane has a $50,000 equity advantage ($150,000 after her $100,000 mortgage), as compared to Mary's $100,000 equity (and no mortgage). But Jane only owns 60% of the home's value, and must pay her bank $600 a month – payments that Mary does not have to make, but which a new buyer of her home would have to pay as the financial bubble gains momentum.

If and when the bubble bursts, housing prices in the neighborhood fall back to the $100,000 range. At that point Jane would have no equity (except for the principal value that she has paid down, unless she took out an interest-only loan). But she must continue to pay off the mortgage that now absorbs the property's entire market valuation.

Home buyers near the peak of the bubble think that the debt-leveraging that bids up real estate prices is a force of nature, not lax policy. Many blame themselves for not achieving the prosperity they had hoped for. Journalists refer to the proverbial "madness of crowds" – blaming the victim – as if bubbles are not sponsored mainly by governments and financial insiders.

Meanwhile, the Internal Revenue Service refuses to tax rising land prices to slow financial bubbles, letting the gains be pledged to the mortgage lenders. After 2008 the Federal Reserve lowered interest rates by Quantitative Easing to revive the Bubble Economy, aiming to enrich Wall Street once again, by indebting the economy at large yet more deeply.

Business Cycle: The term "cycle" suggests a natural tendency to recover in due course, as if the economy were a celestial astronomical cycle. This approach fosters an illusion that economies will recover from "recessions" by self-adjusting "automatic stabilizers," not needing political intervention to alleviate the rising debt overhead. This ignores the buildup of debt deflation from one business upswing to

Financial Crisis vs. Business Cycle

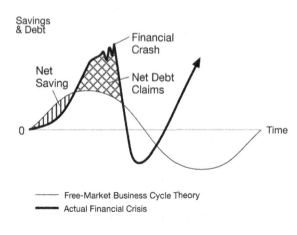

Free-Market Business Cycle Theory
Actual Financial Crisis

the next, leading to stagnation if governments fail to intervene.

Modern depressions ultimately oblige governments to intervene to promote recovery, *e.g.*, by Keynesian-type (see **John Maynard Keynes**) public spending to re-inflate the economy. That political act from "above" the market is by no means automatic. But an anti-government ideology gained momentum early in the 20th century to minimize public policy.

As post-classical economics came to focus on the concept of automatic self-stabilizing **equilibrium**, Wesley Clair Mitchell at the National Bureau of Economic Research depicted "business cycles" in terms of a sequential rise and ebb of business, with leading, coincident and lagging "indicators." (See **Economic Forecasting**.) The result was much like a sine wave of economic activity at a steady frequency, as Joseph Schumpeter depicted in his 1939 book *Business Cycles*. But crashes occur more rapidly than upswings in the actual course of business. As economies become more debt-ridden, each recovery is slower, because it has to carry a heavier debt overhead.

Mainstream business cycle theory fails to explain the exponential buildup of debt from one recovery to the next, and hence fails to see the ultimate crisis. Anti-labor, anti-government neoliberals have hijacked "business cycle" theory by depicting downturns as being caused by rising wages and raw-materials prices as full-employment and full-capacity operations are reached, cutting into profits so that growth tapers off (see **S-Curve**). But the key factor spanning business cycles is the growth of debt and rising interest charges that stifle profits. Debt service absorbs the income hitherto spent on new direct investment and consumption, so employment and production fall off.

The buildup of debt pollution is much like environmental pollution. To assume that the overgrowth of debt is merely temporary and will be "automatically" reversed is much like claims that global warming is merely a weather cycle that will cool down in due course – as if there is no underlying buildup of carbon dioxide, ozone and other products of our modern carbon-based energy-driven society. In both cases, economies are left "under water." In the face of falling asset prices, the collateral held by banks and other debtors fails to cover their liabilities. This ends in a panic as assets are liquidated to pay debts falling due or called in.

Such downturns and crises may be delayed by inflating a **bubble economy**, flooding it with enough credit to enable debtors to borrow the interest falling due (see **Ponzi Scheme**). This simply adds the accrual of interest to the debt balance, so that the debt grows exponentially, making the subsequent crash sink all the more deeply into debt deflation. There is little way to recover without a debt writedown (see **Bankruptcy** and **Clean Slate**) and changes in the economic and legal environment, but this is deemed to be "exogenous" to business cycle theory.

ENDNOTES

[1] I explain the offsets in: *A Payments-Flow Analysis of U.S. International Trans-actions, 1960-1968*. NYU Graduate School of Business Administration, *The Bulletin*, Nos. 61-63 (March 1970).

[2] Tony Blair, "Labour must be the party of ambition as well as compassion," *The Guardian*, May 9, 2015.

[3] Gretchen Morgenson, "A New Light on Regulators in the Dark," *The New York Times*, February 23, 2014, summarizing transcripts of the March 18, 2008 FOMC meeting at the New York Fed.

is for
Casino Capitalism and
Client Oligarchy

Capital: From Latin *caput*, "head," as in heads of cattle. The term is used ambiguously. On the one hand it refers to physical means of production in the form of tools, machinery and buildings. This is the kind of capital referred to by the term capital formation. In Marxian terms industrial capital is wealth that is used to employ wage labor. Such capital earns profits as distinct from rent and interest. But post-classical usage of the term "capital" has been extended to refer to land, mineral rights or legal privileges for rent extraction.

Finance capital consists of the *rentier* claims *on* these means of production and their revenue. Its dynamics tend to *strip* the means of production via interest-bearing debt and other financial claims in excess of the ability to pay out of current income and production.

Capital Flight: Global finance capital and **client oligarchies** tend to be extractive, moving profits and rents offshore via tax havens, ultimately to the United States, Britain or other financial centers. Russia lost an average $25 billion annually during the 1990s as its kleptocrats moved their takings abroad.

Emigration of labor typically accompanies capital flight as the economy shrinks. Argentina is reported to have lost a million workers during the balance-of-payments crisis of 2002-2003 in which a decade of IMF austerity programs led to capital flight. (See **Asset Stripping** and **Washington Consensus**.)

Capital Formation: The full term is "fixed capital formation" or "real capital formation," which the United Kingdom's National Accounts define as "investment in tangible assets." This category "consists of gross domestic fixed capital formation and acquisition of stocks and work in progress. ... Gross domestic fixed capital formation is defined as expenditure on fixed assets (buildings, plant and machinery and dwellings) which either replace existing assets that are no longer productive or increase the availability of productive assets." However, the valuation of such capital formation tends to include the purchase of legal privileges for rent extraction. And industrial capital tends to fall prey to finance capital seeking to bleed companies and strip their assets by failing to maintain or modernize plant and technology to stay competitive.

Capital Gain: Machinery and other physical capital wears out and obsolesces (see **Depreciation**), but prices for real estate, monopoly privileges and other rent-yielding assets and financial securities (stocks and bonds) tend to rise over time. These price gains are taxed at much lower rates than industrial profits (if at all). Heavy campaign contributions to compliant politicians have succeeded in getting the U.S. tax rate on capital gains reduced to just half the normal income-tax rate. (They originally were taxed as normal income when the income tax law was passed in 1913.) Many countries do not tax capital gains at all, or even measure them.

What is not measured has less chance of being taxed. The National Income and Product Accounts (NIPA) do not include capital gains, nor do these appear in the Federal Reserve's Flow of Funds statistics. Yet for the economy at large, capital gains are now the main objective of investors seeking **total returns**, defined as current income (profits, rents or interest) *plus* asset-price gains.

Low taxes on capital gains create a vested interest in a bubble economy in which finance capital masquerades as real industrial capital. In an economy of **asset-price inflation** the objective of investors and speculators is to buy real estate, stocks and bonds whose price is being inflated by debt leveraging. The arbitrage strategy is simply to borrow at a lower interest rate than the rate at which prices are rising. The Fed's $4 trillion in Quantitative Easing since 2008 aimed explicitly at re-inflating real estate prices. This policy of "creating wealth" by financially engineering price gains is different from earning profits on industrial investment. Although lobbyists pretend that capital gains reward innovation and enterprise, most occur passively in real estate. In the corporate sector, financial managers seek short-term gains in their companies' stock prices by using earnings for stock buybacks and cutting *back* innovation.

Capitalism: Popularized by Werner Sombart in *Das moderne Kapitalismus* (1909), the term "capitalism" was used to describe the social system based on promoting industrial capital accumulation. Long used as a term of invective (although Karl Marx never used the word), it has now become glorified by neoliberals, referring mainly to finance capitalism and wealth creation via rent extraction and asset-stripping. Yet in classical terms this *rentier* phenomenon is pre- or post-capitalist, not part of industrial capitalism's close linkages between large industry, government protection and public spending on basic infrastructure.

Capitalism, Casino: See **Casino Capitalism.**

Capitalism, Crony: See **Public-Private Partnership.**

Capitalism, Finance: See **Finance Capitalism.**

Capitalism, Money Manager: See **Money Manager Capitalism**

Capitalism, Pension Fund: See **Pension Fund Capitalism.**

Capitalism, Pentagon: See **Pentagon Capitalism.**

Cash Flow: The modern acronym **ebitda** stands for earnings before interest, taxes, depreciation and amortization (but not **capital gains**). This revenue is available for new direct investment or to pay creditors or stockholders. Under finance capitalism it is absorbed increasingly by interest charges, on which companies do not have to pay taxes (in contrast to earnings paid out as dividends). (See Hudson Bubble Model later in this book for a discussion of cash flow.)

Casino Capitalism: A late or even the final stage of finance capitalism, based on financial engineering rather than industrial engineering. No tangible investment is involved in betting that some financial securities will rise or fall relative to others, based on applying probability theory and correlation to stock and bond markets or foreign exchange rates. Just as casinos benefit from the edge in probability (the 0 and 00 slots on a roulette wheel), investment bankers benefit from their rake-off of commissions and interest paid by the arbitrageurs for credit in the financial casino.

The Wall Street casino has gained more rapidly than almost any other sector. This does not mean that it is a victory by the most productive and fittest economic policies. "When the capital development of a country becomes a byproduct of the activities of a casino," wrote John Maynard Keynes, "the job is likely to be ill done."

Causality: Economists typically start from a policy conclusion – free trade or

protectionism, creditor-oriented rules or more humanitarian treatment of debtors –
and reason backwards to define a set of economic relationships that would lead
logically to it. Such sophistry is designed to produce an illusion of causality, while
depicting alternative policies as causing "bad" results.

When looking at any model of an economy, one therefore should always start
with its policy implications. That will indicate how the lines of causality are selected
to promote specific interests, even when academic supporters seem unwitting of
these and imagine their teaching to be purely objective and scientific. (See **Learned
Ignorance**, **Nobel Economics Prize** and **Thorstein Veblen**.)

Neoliberals and conservatives, for instance, attribute every problem to
government regulation, taxation and public ownership (in short, a mixed economy).
To defend their position, they create a logic that defines economies in ways that
categorize regulations, taxes and public enterprise as an overhead burden, not as
productive or playing a catalytic role or maintaining a fair and balanced allocation
of wealth and income. Fraud and crime by banks and business do not appear in such
models, so all wealth and income are portrayed as being earned as a result of
contributing to GDP. In such cases the methodology that is selected will imply the
policy solution.

The narrower the degree of self-interest, the narrower the selection of cause and
effect. The aim is to avoid looking at the broad economy-wide dynamics at work.
(See **X and Y Axes**.) Free trade theory leaves out of account structural problems
leading to chronic trade deficits, food and trade dependency, non-cost-related
rakeoffs such as economic rent, emigration as a result of poverty, war and the effects
of financing trade deficits by running up interest-bearing debt and losing domestic
political autonomy to international financial institutions.

Central Bank: A semipublic (although initially nominally privately owned) institution,
administered by the largest commercial banks to operate on their behalf. Starting with
the Bank of England (1694) and followed by other countries (the U.S. Federal Reserve
Bank was founded in 1913), the most recent central bank is the European Central Bank
(1998). In contrast to a national treasury, whose aim is to finance or monetize
government budget deficits for spending into the overall economy, central banks aim to
provide banks with liquidity in times of stringency, and most recently simply give them
money or a free line of credit. (See **Regulatory Capture**.)

The response to the 2008 financial crisis was to provide enough credit to keep
inflating the financial bubble at a rate intended to save major debtors from
defaulting. (See **Quantitative Easing**.) This delayed real estate and stock market
loans from going bad and threatening the solvency of commercial banks. But the
debts were kept in place, subjecting the real economy to debt deflation. The

European Central Bank has become notorious for insisting on taxpayer bailouts of bad bank loans in Ireland, Spain, Greece and other eurozone countries.

Central Bank Reserves: Since gold was phased out of settling balance-of-payments deficits in 1971, central bank reserves have consisted mainly of U.S. Treasury debt. The United States spends dollars into foreign economies by running deficits, which result largely from its global military spending. The lion's share of central bank reserves thus represents a monetization of this U.S. geopolitics.[1] The BRICS (Brazil, Russia, India, China and South Africa) have moved to free themselves from dollar dependency by shifting to their own inter-governmental credit denominated in their own currencies.

Chartalism: A technical term for the **State Theory of Money**. As Henry Liu has described: "When the state issues fiat money under the principle of Chartalism … behind it is the fulfillment of tax obligations. Thus the state issues a credit instrument, called (fiat) money, good for the cancellation of tax liabilities. By issuing fiat money, the state is not borrowing from anyone. It is issuing tax credit to the economy."[2] (See **Modern Monetary Theory**.)

Chicago Boys: After the Kissinger-Pinochet 1973 military coup in Chile, University of Chicago economists were brought in to give away public enterprises to the junta's supporters. To silence criticism of Chile's privatization of social security, to let corporate owners loot pension plans, to end public subsidies and to break labor union power, they shut down every economics department in Chile except that of the Catholic University where the Chicago School had gained control. (See **Labor Capitalism**, **Privatization** and **Washington Consensus**.)

These anti-government ideologues recognized that their brand of "free markets" and giveaway of the public sector required that no economic alternative be permitted or even discussed, but could only be imposed at gunpoint with totalitarian political control. Their neoliberal version of "free markets" is akin to medieval conquerors appropriating the land and basic infrastructure by force of arms. The aim is to privatize economic rent, and weaken the power of communities by rolling back democracy. This is typically done by establishing client oligarchies and economic dukedoms.

Chicago School: Named after the University of Chicago's Business School where Milton Friedman and other monetarists established a beachhead. The University was founded by John D. Rockefeller, prompting Upton Sinclair to call it the University of Standard Oil (*The Goose Step*, 1923). The essence of their ideology is that government has no positive role, but is only a deadweight burden. Euphemizing their doctrine as "free market," they advocate deregulation, claiming that "rational markets" will steer the economy. They also support a tax shift off property onto labor, while denying that their policies create a free lunch for *rentiers*. The result is to centralize planning in the financial centers – short-term planning that finds debt pyramiding and asset stripping the most lucrative activities. (See **Market Fundamentalism** and **TINSTAAFL**.)

Choice: The idea that everyone is free to choose their economic fate is a euphemism for **blaming the victim** for not being sufficiently affluent. Real economic choice is limited by a having to pay banks and the FIRE sector in order to obtain housing, health care, education, oil and other basic needs. To obtain home ownership, buyers must take out mortgages at prices inflated by debt leveraging. Homebuyers can decide which bank to borrow from, but must spend most of their working life paying between 25% and 40% of their income to the mortgage lender. This leaves freedom of choice mainly in the sense that Anatole France quipped: "The poor man has as much right to sleep under a bridge as a rich man." My analysis of disposable personal income shows that after paying the monthly "nut" of taxes and FIRE sector obligations "off the top," only about 25% to 30% of wage-earner paychecks remains available for spending on the goods and services that labor produces.

Circular Flow: The earliest model of circular flow was the *Tableau Économique* by the royal surgeon and founder of **Physiocracy**, François Quesnay. Inspired by the circulation of blood in the human body, he traced the flow of receipts and payments among landlords, industrialists, labor and government. His followers urged that land rent be used as the tax base, influencing Adam Smith.

Most economic models since J. B. Say have focused on the reciprocal flow of income between producers and consumers. Malthus and Ricardo, for instance debated over just how landlords spent their rent – on consumer goods, imported luxuries and payments to servants and other labor. Under **Say's Law** equilibrium is maintained when income paid for production is matched by consumption, enabling the economy to keep growing. Employers pay their workers, who spend their wages to buy what they produce. That is why Henry Ford paid them the then-towering $5 a day, so that they could afford to buy his automobiles.

However, the economy's debt overhead grows from one business upswing to the next, diverting a rising proportion of income from production and consumption to pay interest charges. This reduces spending on current output, draining the circular flow much like bleeding the body.

Such growth in debt service may be offset by new lending. But post-2008 Federal

Reserve and Treasury credit to Wall Street has not been for business investment. It has taken the form of bank bailouts, which have been used largely for **casino capitalist** arbitrage. This central bank money creation circulates only within the asset and debt markets, not through the "real" economy of production and consumption.

Clark, John Bates (1847-1938): U.S. economist who spearheaded the rejection of classical rent theory and sought to refute socialist claims that labor was exploited. Clark depicted *rentiers* – landlords, financial magnates and monopolists – as earning their income by adding to output. He maintained that everyone earned precisely what they contributed to production, so that no exploitation existed and there was no such thing as **unearned income**. "It is the purpose of this work," he wrote in the introduction to his 1899 *Distribution of Wealth*, "to show that the distribution of the income of society is controlled by a natural law, and this law, if it worked without friction, would give to every agent of production the amount of wealth which that agent creates." This stripped away the concept of economic rent from mainstream theory. As Simon Patten wrote: "According to the economic data he presents, rent in the economic sense, if not wholly disregarded, at least receives no emphasis. Land seems to be a form of capital, its value like other property being due to the labor put upon it."[3]

Clark's whitewashing of real estate, banking and monopolies was so appreciated by Wall Street that the American Economics Association – gatekeepers of mainstream economics in the United States – created the John Bates Clark Medal in 1947 to award economists under the age of 40 judged to have made significant contribution to economic thought and knowledge in Clark's tradition. It is a tradition in which *rentiers* appear to play a productive role. The award provides an incentive for young economists to depict an economy in which unearned income and exploitation do not appear. (See my chapter "Methodology is Ideology" for how methodology determines content.)

Clash of Civilizations: A term of invective coined by the neoconservative Samuel Huntington in 1992. He depicted Communism, Islam, and government ownership and regulation as enemies of U.S.-centered globalism – the "free market" for Wall Street investors that he deemed to be the culmination of Western civilization. (See **End of History**.)

"The West" is Huntington's inflated euphemism for Wall Street finance capitalism and the military-industrial complex. His bellicose celebration of U.S. unilateralism from NATO to the Pacific helps distract attention from the West's oligarchic war to reverse the Enlightenment's reforms that aimed at freeing industrial capitalism from rent seeking and financialization. In his book *From Plato to NATO* (1998), David Gress traces how this neoliberal view led to a rewriting of history: "The Cold War depicted itself as a war of the West – embodying civilization and progress itself – against the Soviet Union, as earlier it had been World War II against Germany and World War I against the German Hun." The University of Chicago's curriculum of monetarism and "free markets" traces Western civilization only back to an idealized image of Greece and Rome.[4]

The actual origin of Western economic enterprise lies in Mesopotamia's palace-centered mixed economies. This Bronze Age origin has been replaced by a travesty of history in which a new civilization of Indo-European-speaking individualists spontaneously created markets and political democracy. It is as if the westward migration of Near Eastern innovations after 1200 BC did not culminate in oppressive oligarchies in Greece and ultimately Rome as credit was privatized and the traditional clean slates gave way to harsh creditor-oriented laws. So what is thought of as Western civilization is in large part the removal of credit and **markets** from their archaic contexts to benefit a landed financial oligarchy.

Today's civilization stands at a crossroads similar to that of Rome in its violent civil war between creditors and debtors from 133 to 29 BC, giving way to a Dark Age of mass poverty under concentrated proto-feudal property ownership. Once again, a clash *within* "Western" civilization is occurring over whether a creditor oligarchy will reduce vast populations to peonage. This seems to be an eternal problem of all civilizations.

Class: Classical economists defined "class" in terms of the source of income – land ownership, labor or capital. Landlords charge rent, workers earn wages, and capitalists employ wage-labor to produce commodities to sell at a profit. As the American economist, Simon Patten noted over a century ago:

> The older thought assumed that for each kind of income there was a social class which was interested in its defense. The social condition of England at the time economic theory was formulated favored this concept. The aristocracy held the land, the so-called middle or industrial class owned the capital, while the great mass of unskilled and politically unprotected laborers did the work. The essence of the Ricardian [David Ricardo's] economics was an opposition to the aristocratic landlords, and it succeeded so well that an imputation of being unearned was put up on their income. In America, however, while we have rent, we have no landlord class. The income from rent and interest is so diffused that all income-receivers form one class. ... Profit holders blend with the holders of rent and interest and think of themselves as a social unit. All get profits, rent and interest in their income.[5] (See **Middle Class**.)

Not all income is a return to a factor of production. Banks or other creditors lend out money or savings at interest, but money is not a means of production. The banking and financial class is empowered to create credit or lend out wealth as "silent partners."

Along such lines it is helpful to distinguish the FIRE sector (finance, insurance and real estate) from the "real" economy of production and consumption (whether capitalist or socialist). One cannot really speak of a saver or creditor class as such, because all classes tend to be both savers and debtors simultaneously. But *rentiers* derive income from ownership and legal privileges to charge rent for access to land, interest for credit, and monopoly rent for trade and goods or services.

Landlords, bankers and monopolists do not play a direct role in production. A class approach focusing on production relates only to one part of the economy, which is wrapped in a network of taxes and public spending, as well as credit and debt. So one can speak of the banking and monopoly class and, in the 20th century, the managerial class. Milovan Djilas described the Soviet government bureau-cracy in *The New Class* (1957).

Class Consciousness: This term traditionally has been associated mainly with the working class, but the elites may have an even stronger feeling of solidarity as a cohesive class. Their view of their place in the economy is much like that of England's Norman conquerors, who extracted rental and tax tribute. The medieval Arab historian Ibn Khaldun attributed the conquests by pastoral nomads such as Genghis Kahn and Turkish tribes moving into Europe to the binding force of *asabiyyah* (*asabiya*), or social cohesiveness. His *Muqaddimah,* an introduction to a history of the world published in 1377, explained the rise and fall of nations and empires as reflecting the degree to which marauding tribes held together as an ethnic unit, whose mutual aid and shared goals spanned economic classes. Today's financial class is cosmopolitan rather than ethnic or nationalist, absorbing client oligarchies into its ranks. (See **Company**.)

What is needed for economic success as a class is self-consciousness of common interests. Labor has won concessions from industry, but has not deterred finance from exploiting wage earners via mortgage lending, personal debt and **pension-fund capitalism**. Wealth is concentrated at the top of the economic pyramid as banks and bondholders gain control of industry and move to take over governments. Their political aim is to shift taxes off finance and its major clients, and to force taxpayers to pay interest to private bondholders. (See **Neoliberalism** and **Washington Consensus**). It seems as if today's working class (**The 99 Percent**) does not realize that a class war is being waged against them – or that as Warren Buffett said of his own One Percent, "we are winning it."

The financial strategy in this class war is to popularize "identity politics" prompting voters to think of themselves as women, ethnic or racial minorities, or sexual categories (LBGTQ) instead of economic categories such as wage earners, debtors and/or renters. True identity politics should *begin* with economic class consciousness, solidarity and mutual aid. There can be little promotion of group self-interest without this.

Class Struggle: The 19th century's characteristic class conflict saw industrialists fight to keep profits high by keeping money wages low. This was to be achieved by promoting free trade so as to buy food and necessities more cheaply abroad – and by taxing landlords instead of labor and its necessities. Ricardian value theory assumed that raw manual labor would earn mere subsistence wages in any case. So lower prices for food and necessities would mean that industrialists could pay lower money wages to hire workers. Importing low-priced food would therefore save employers money, as money wages would fall to subsistence levels.

The main political struggle accordingly was between capitalists and landlords, with capitalists aiming to minimize economic overhead in the form of land rent and monopoly rent. The class struggle by the industrial capitalist class began as a fight against landlords who sought protective agricultural tariffs (Britain's Corn Laws) to keep food prices (and hence, subsistence wages) high. After the bourgeois revolutions of 1848, the fight against the landlord class was well on its way to being won, giving way to the class struggle against labor unions and socialists over wages and working conditions.

Class conflict has always been concerned with whether the tax burden should fall on land rent (landlords), business profits or consumer spending. But now that the banking and financial sector finds its major source of business in real estate (accounting for 70% to 80% of bank loans) – followed by mining and other privatized natural resources and public monopolies such as water, power and communications – interest is paid more out of **economic rent** than out of industrial and business profits. The financial sector accordingly has joined forces with real estate, natural resource extraction and other monopoly **rent seekers**. These *rentier* sectors now struggle jointly agains labor.

Classical Political Economy: The body of economic analysis emerging from 18th-century Enlightenment moral philosophy by François Quesnay and the **Physiocrats** in France, **Adam Smith** in Scotland, **David Ricardo** and **Thomas Malthus** in England, **John Stuart Mill** and his fellow "Ricardian **socialists**" culminating with **Karl Marx**, linking politics with economics because of its social policy implications. The common denominator of these writers was the **labor theory of value**, used to isolate **economic rent** as unearned income (see **Free**

Lunch and **Privilege**) so as to free society from the *rentier* legacy of feudalism: a landlord class, predatory banking and the monopolies that bondholders convinced governments to create as means of paying off national war debts. As unearned income, such rents are either to be taxed away or otherwise socialized under democratic political reform. (See also **Rent Theory** and **Socialism**. For the reaction against classical political economy and rent theory, see **John Bates Clark**.)

Clean Slate (AKA debt forgiveness): Originally a royal practice in Bronze Age Sumer and Babylonia to annul debts so as to save society from being torn apart by transferring land and personal liberty to creditors. This became the core of Judaic Law as the **Jubilee Year**. Modern debt cancellations are limited to personal or corporate bankruptcy on a case-by-case basis. Exceptions include the moratorium declared on Inter-Ally World War I debts and German reparations in 1931, and the Allied Monetary Reform of 1948 that cancelled most domestic German debts. (See **Economic Miracle**.)

In contrast to ancient society's idea of circular time – with clean slates to restore economic order when debts grew too burdensome – today's concept of linear progress treats the debt build-up as cumulative and *irreversible*. The result is that without debt cancellations economies evolve into oligarchies that claim their takeover is "natural" and thereby morally justified.

Client Academics: "Useful idiots" teaching that the status quo is a product of the evolutionary struggle for existence, reflecting the success of the most productive and hence richest individuals. This implies that we live in the best of all possible worlds, as if any economy is in equilibrium and inequality is an act of nature, not the result of bad policy. (See **Chicago School, Austrian School, Idiot Savant, Lobbyist, Alan Greenspan** and **Neoliberal**.)

Client Oligarchy: A country's ruling class co-opted to serve U.S. and European finance capital by agreeing to IMF and World Bank "conditionalities," permitting capital flight ("free capital movement") and un-taxing monopoly capital and other property. (See **Offshore Banking Centers**.)

Cognitive Dissonance: Disbelief in facts that do not conform to one's preconceptions (see **Denial** and **Truthiness**). Thorstein Veblen's concept of trained incapacity describes the inability of economists to understand why austerity programs make countries poorer and more debt-ridden instead of helping them recover, or to see how cancelling debts may preserve economic order instead of causing the anarchy of debt deflation.

alism: A policy whereby a mother nation underdevelops its periphery by
ing its own homeland industry, food self-sufficiency and high technology,
wime co-opting local **client oligarchies** whose loyalty and identity lie mainly with
the mother nation. The aim is for colonial dependencies to provide raw materials
and products made by low-wage manual labor that their colonizers choose not to
produce at home.

A less formal colonialism is now achieved by using debt as a diplomatic lever,
forcing dependent countries to relinquish democratic control to the IMF and World
Bank unelected central planners. (See **Dollar Hegemony** and **Underdevelopment**.) Most client oligarchies are now hereditary banking and financial
elites, who increase their power by privatizing public infrastructure (see **Commons**)
Pinochet-style or post-Soviet-style.

Commons: Public assets (land, water, mineral rights, airwaves and other public
infrastructure). As natural monopolies, they are best administered in society's
long-term interest via government or a community, not monopolized by *rentiers*
as the ultimate takeover objective of finance capital.

It is an old story. Medieval rulers seeking war loans were obliged to pledge
public assets to their creditors. The Habsburgs forfeited the royal mercury mines
in Spain to the Fugger financial family. Britain's government created royal trade
monopolies such as the South Sea Company and Bank of England to sell off to
bondholders. Today's tactic to pry away the public domain is still to get
governments into debt to bondholders. Under neoliberal IMF or World Bank
programs, Greece and Third World debtors have been forced to privatize their public
domain resources. (See **Kleptocrats**.) Claiming to be more efficient than public
management, rent seekers use spurious junk economics (see **Tragedy of the
Commons**) to depict government bureaucracy as always an evil to be eliminated, so
as to justify privatizing the public domain.

Company: From "companion," literally those who break bread together, reflecting
their origin in antiquity as sanctified cults with their own patron deities and hierarchy
of officials. By medieval European times the typical "company of men" took the
form of marauding bands seizing lands and subduing their populations. The
narrowing of this term to mercantile commerce retains the idea of a closed band.

A limited liability **corporation** (LLC) is a legal filter protecting businessmen
from economic liability for their actions. The environmental and social costs of
conducting business are shifted onto society at large. (See **Externality**.)

Compound Interest: The exponential rate (geometric growth) at which the accrual of interest doubles the debt. Any rate of interest implies a doubling time of the savings/debt principal as creditors recycle their receipt of interest into new loans, or simply add interest accruals onto the debt principal. (See **Rule of 72**.)

Any illusion that today's debt overhead expanding at compound interest is sustainable over time should be expelled by the illustration of doubling times in the chart on the next page, which demonstrates its unfeasibility (from "The Miracle of Compound Interest: How Debt Doubles" from my book *Killing the Host*, Ch. 4).

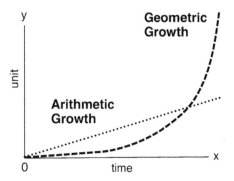

Comparison of geometric growth (exponential growth of compound interest) versus arithmetic growth (simple interest).

The phenomenon was known already in the Old Babylonian period c. 2000 BC by the term "interest on interest" (*mash mash*). However, loan contracts were for a specified duration, and when they expired the creditor had to draw up a new contract to receive further interest. Personal agrarian debt was frequently cancelled by royal clean slates. But modern mainstream economics treats interest only on a microeconomic level, as a contract between borrower and creditor in which everyone gains and debts always are able to be paid – as if there were no inherent tendency for debt to grow beyond the ability to be paid.

The reality is that interest-bearing debt grows exponentially, extracting revenue from the economy at an accelerating pace. The ensuing debt deflation slows economic growth, which tapers off in an S-curve – making it harder to carry and pay off debts, culminating in a debt crisis.

The bankers' ideal is to keep their loans multiplying *ad infinitum*. That is the essential principle of **Ponzi** finance. Before 1972 it was normal for international banks to lend Latin American countries the interest charges falling due on their foreign debt each year. Then came the collapse, when Mexico said it could not pay the exponential debt accrual. In the United States, by 2005 this bank practice of adding the interest onto the debt characterized more than 20% of reported U.S. home mortgage loans. "Freeing" debtors from having to pay down the principal left their debts to mushroom exponentially instead of being paid off.

When indebted economies or their governments (or homeowners) cannot pay (see **"Debts that can't be paid, won't be"**), foreclosure time arrives. This causes the crises that distinguish modern business cycles. In the past they wiped out savings along with the bad debts. But after 2008 savings were not wiped out. The debts were left in place. That is why there has been no normal recovery. The One Percent have

"The Miracle of Compound Interest"
— How Debt Doubles

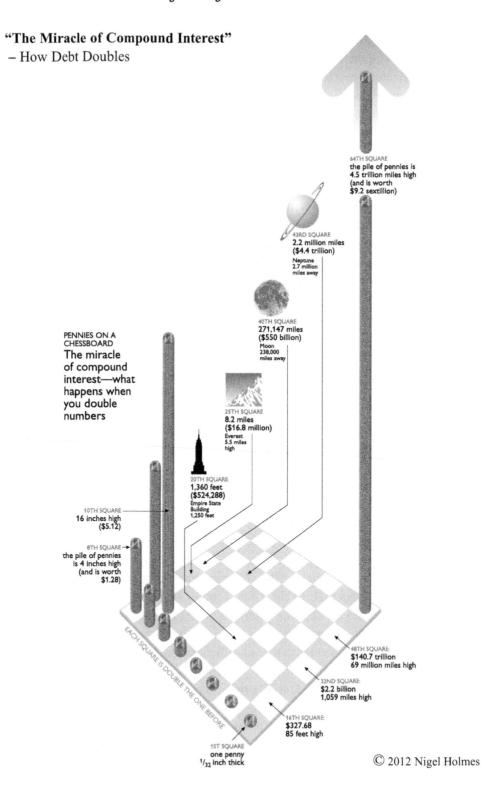

PENNIES ON A
CHESSBOARD
**The miracle
of compound
interest—what
happens when
you double
numbers**

64TH SQUARE
the pile of pennies is
4.5 trillion miles high
(and is worth
$9.2 sextillion)

43RD SQUARE
2.2 million miles
($4.4 trillion)
Neptune
2.7 million
miles away

40TH SQUARE
271,147 miles
($550 billion)
Moon
238,000
miles away

25TH SQUARE
8.2 miles
($16.8 million)
Everest
5.5 miles
high

20TH SQUARE
1,360 feet
($524,288)
Empire State
Building
1,250 feet

10TH SQUARE
16 inches high
($5.12)

8TH SQUARE
the pile of pennies
is 4 inches high
(and is worth
$1.28)

EACH SQUARE IS DOUBLE THE ONE BEFORE

48TH SQUARE:
$140.7 trillion
69 million miles high

32ND SQUARE:
$2.2 billion
1,059 miles high

16TH SQUARE:
$327.68
85 feet high

1ST SQUARE
one penny
1/32 inch thick

© 2012 Nigel Holmes

gained financially from central bank quantitative easing to reinflate th
bond markets, but the "real economy" of production and consumptior
from debt deflation, which is getting more severe.

The coming political fight will be over whose interests will be sacrificed in the
face of the incompatibility between the financial expansion path of debt and the
economy's ability to grow. No matter how well banks are managed at any given
moment of time, a debt crisis is inevitable because of the inherent mathematics of
compound interest. At issue is whether debts will be left on the books to burden
economies with mathematically untenable overhead, or be written down by
legislating a Clean Slate. A debt amnesty is necessary at the point where the economy
becomes so over-indebted that new investment and employment dry up.

Conditionalities: The requirement by the **IMF** and **World Bank** that indebted
governments impose austerity programs of the sort forced on Latin American and
other debtors in the 1970s and 1980s. Debtor countries are told to shift taxes off
property and finance onto labor, privatize the commons (public assets and
enterprises) and deregulate their markets (see **Washington Consensus**). In
exchange, creditor nations refrain from wrecking the banking systems of debtor
countries or overthrowing their governments with regime change.

Conditionalities often involve currency devaluation, lowering the international
price of labor while raising import prices and hence living costs. Local client
oligarchies are enabled to protect their fortunes by capital flight, subsidized by IMF
currency support long enough to enable bondholders and other elites to sell off.
These conditionalities exacerbate the debt problem, polarizing the economy and
requiring even steeper conditionalities in a chronically deepening dependency crisis
that pushes victimized nations into debt bondage.

Conservatives: People seeking to conserve the status quo and power of the vested
interests. In the 19th century they fought to preserve the legacy of feudalism by
blocking parliamentary reform and its seeming evolution toward democratic
socialism. In the United States, Republican Jim DeMint of South Carolina spelled
out the conservative political strategy in a nutshell when he left the Senate to head
the Koch-backed Heritage Foundation: "Obstruct, obstruct, obstruct" to stop so-
called big government from enacting changes that would favor the 99 Percent. One
could add "privatize, privatize, privatize" and "delay, delay delay" to round out their
political strategy. That is the spirit of conservatism through the ages.

Consumer: The media's preferred euphemism for wage earner, viewed in terms of
"free choice" for how to spend wages – without reference to having to work for a

living (see **Middle Class**). Most consumers are obliged to be debtors merely to survive. On their road to debt peonage, their obligatory payments to the FIRE Sector leave less and less truly disposable personal income. But the word "consumer" implies that paying debt service, housing costs and similar charges is like buying the commodities that labor produces, not paying compulsory tribute to *rentiers*. (See **Circular Flow.**)

Consumer Demand: A patronizing euphemism to promote the idea that the "consumer is king" with the power to "demand" what they want, telling producers what to sell – as if advertisers and mass-market producers do not shape consumer tastes with a take-it-or-leave-it choice.

Statistically, consumer spending is much less than the official measure of disposable personal income (net of taxes, wage withholding for Social Security, health care and pensions). Actual consumption is also net of monthly debt service (but *plus* new borrowing) and housing charges. This available residual shrinks as the economy succumbs to debt deflation.

Consumer Price Index (CPI): A measurement of typical current retail prices for goods and services paid by consumers, to show the effect of inflation on their purchasing power.

Corporation (Limited Liability Company, LLC): A legal vehicle to free a business owner from personal liability for debts incurred by the company, or for penalties for its lawbreaking. The responsibility of shareholders is depersonalized. Unlike real people, a corporation is too impersonal to jail. However, the 2010 U.S. Supreme Court ruling, Citizens United v. the Federal Election Commission, gave corporations freedom of expression to contribute to political campaigns backing their favored candidates on the ground of personal free speech. Republican Presidential candidate Mitt Romney told a questioner who urged him to raise corporate taxes in 2011: "'Corporations are people, my friend.' Some people in the front of the audience shouted, 'No, they're not!' 'Of course they are,' Romney said. 'Everything corporations earn ultimately goes to people. Where do you think it goes?'"[6] Mostly it goes to the One Percent, euphemized as "people," using corporate shells.

Corvée Labor: Long before economies were monetized, civilization's most archaic tax took the form of labor time to work on public projects, and (even today) to serve in the armed forces. That is how ancient palaces, city walls, pyramids and public monuments were built. Land tenure originally was assigned to kinship groupings (probably already in the Neolithic Age) in proportion to the seasonal labor they could provide for public building projects and to serve in the army.[7]

Corvée taxes thus presupposed property rights for citizens supporting themselves on the land. The labor was hard, but all citizens were obliged to participate – and these public projects were major occasions for feasting, with abundant supplies of beer and meat. Rulers are depicted as ceremonially carrying baskets of earth, and high-status individuals as well as men and women from the free land-tenured population joined in what seems to have been the defining socializing projects of their epoch. Antiquity's great monuments (including Egypt's pyramids) were built by this free labor, not by slaves.[8]

Gradually, land ownership came to be divorced from corvée obligations. In Babylonia c. 1800 BC, creditors would obtain the land and its crop usufruct (net product) from debtors, but the latter still had to perform the corvée labor attached to the land they worked. By 17th-century France, the landowning nobility was obliged to provide service in the armed forces (mainly the cavalry), but it was their serfs or tenants who bore the liability for providing the hard labor with which the French palace built roads and other public infrastructure.

Cost: See **Value**, contrasted with **Economic Rent**.

Creative Destruction: For Joseph Schumpeter, the motive force of industrial capitalism: innovations that undersell and hence replace earlier production technologies, causing obsolescence of existing fixed capital. Destruction is less creative when it is not associated with rising productivity, as when the term was applied to the "shock therapy" imposed on the Soviet Union after 1990 – pure destruction with no therapy, leading to demographic collapse. It destroyed Russia's industrial viability, turning the economy into a raw materials supplier to the West. The "creativity" at work was to disable resistance to privatizing the commons.

Credit: The act of establishing a **debt** on the part of a loan recipient, customer, or taxpayer. Debts are recorded statistically as the creditor's saving, so credit and debts rise and fall together. (See **Accounting**.) An economy's volume of debt is equal to the initial advance of credit (including unpaid debts) plus accrued interest. So the self-expanding volume of debt increases "savings" on the other side of the **balance sheet**. Today, the purchase of housing and education is financed on credit. The question is, what will rise faster: the asset's market price, or the debt attached to it? (See **Bubble**.)

Archaic economies operated on the basis of gift exchange and, by the Neolithic, of cultivators running up debts during the planting season, to be paid at harvest time on the threshing floor in kind. Little exchange until after 2000 BC was paid in cash (money), because income came in periodic or seasonal lumps (*e.g.,* the harvest or the return of a voyage). Export goods were advanced to merchants on credit, to be paid (with interest) upon the successful completion of the voyage. (If unsuccessful, the debt was cancelled.)

The "credit stage" of economic development is thus the original and major stage in the "three stage" evolution of exchange. Governments developed a money economy as a means of allocating resources and collecting taxes and public fees that built up during the harvest year. Money is a form of credit, initially issued by public institutions and now created by commercial banks. But as empires seized and looted precious metals, their economies later collapsed into barter as in the post-Roman Dark Age.

Crime: Honoré de Balzac observed that most great fortunes originate from theft, corrupt insider dealing or property grabs whose details are so lost in the mists of time that they have become legitimized. Heading the list of hereditary power elites are the real estate families, railroad barons, oil and natural resource lords, and privatizers of monopolies. As crime becomes larger and more successful, it becomes financialized and decriminalized. Victims and reformers who protest are prosecuted.

An example of how unthinkable it is to include crime along with other rent-seeking activities is shown by the fact that in 2014 the Ig Nobel Economics Prize (on contrast to the "real" fake Nobel) was awarded to the Italian government's National Institute of Statistics (ISTAT) for complying with an EU regulatory mandate to include revenue from illegal drug sales, prostitution, smuggling, etc. in its measure of GDP. Neoliberal economics logically treats what used to be viewed as crime as part of the free market – which is why Wall Street banks are treated as adding to GDP instead of prosecuting their managers for fraud and *subtracting* their takings from GDP.

Crime, Financial: See **Too Big To Fail/Jail**.

Criminal: Someone who steals or cheats on too small a scale to afford the legal or political protection needed to avoid prosecution. It is a matter of scale and the degree to which one is a political insider. St. Augustine wrote in *The City of God* of what a pirate said when captured by Alexander the Great: "Because I do it with a little ship only, I am called a thief; you, doing it with a great navy, are called an emperor."

Regarding political and legal theft, the greatest seizures are from the public domain by insider dealing, as capsulized in a 17th-century folk rhyme:

> The law locks up the man or woman
> Who steals the goose off the common,
> But leaves the greater villain loose
> Who steals the common from the goose.

As Franklin Roosevelt explained in announcing his Second New Deal in October 1936: "Government by organized money is just as dangerous as government by organized mob," meaning the Mafia crime mob. But instead of jailing malefactors, civil fines are only levied against their companies, to be borne by their stockholders. Today's emperors of finance have achieved a status above the law, having warned the legal authorities that they will crash the economy if deceptive lending practices are prosecuted.

Crony Capitalism: See **Privatization** and **Public-Private Partnership**.

ENDNOTES

[1] I describe this phenomenon in *Super Imperialism: The Economic Strategy of American Empire* (1972, new ed. 2002).

[2] Henry Liu, "Dollar Hegemony Against Sovereign Credit," *Asia Times*, June 24, 2005. For a historical discussion see L. Randall Wray (ed.), *Credit and State Theories of Money: The Contributions of A. Mitchell Innes* (Edward Elgar, 2004), and also my article "The Chartalist/Monetarist Debate in Historical Perspective," in Edward Nell and Stephanie Bell eds., *The State, The Market and The Euro* (Edward Elgar, 2003, pp. 39-76.

[3] Simon Patten, "Ethics of Land Tenure," *International Journal of Ethics* **1** (April 1891), p. 356. See also Patten, "The Conflict Theory of Distribution," p. 219. I discuss this view in "Simon Patten on Public Infrastructure and Economic Rent Capture," *American Journal of Economics and Sociology* **70** (October 2011), pp. 873-903.

[4] J. G. Manning and Ian Morris describe the Chicago School's rewriting of history going back to Greece as a brand-new civilization in *The Ancient Economy: Evidence and Models* (Stanford University Press, 2005).

[5] Simon Patten (1891) "Ethics of Land Tenure," *loc. cit.* (n3).

[6] Philip Rucker, "Mitt Romney says 'corporations are people,'" *Washington Post*, August 11, 2011.

[7] For details see Michael Hudson and Cornelia Wunsch, eds., *Creating Economic Order: Record-keeping, Standardization, and the Development of Accounting in the Ancient Near East* (2004).

[8] See Michael Hudson and Piotr Steinkeller, eds., *Labor in the Ancient World* (2015).

is for
Debt Deflation and
Debt Peonage

Debt: One party's debt is another's saving or credit. A bank deposit is a debt to the depositor. Money is a government or bank debt. (See **Accounting** and **Balance Sheet**.) Most debt is owed to the One Percent, who account for most of the saving, receiving interest from the 99 Percent. For a discussion of corporate, foreign, household, government and real estate debt, see my book *The Bubble And Beyond: Fictitious Capital, Debt Deflation and Global Crisis* (2012).

Debt Cancellation/Clean Slate: From Sumer in the third millennium BC down through Egyptian practice (*e.g.,* the **Rosetta Stone's** trilingual inscription in 197 BC), it was normal for new rulers to proclaim Clean Slates to annul personal debts owed to the palace, its collectors and other creditors. Humanitarian treatment of debtors was the norm from ancient Mesopotamia through Solon's reforms in Greece (594 BC), Judaism's Mosaic law, Jesus's announcement that he had come to restore the **Jubilee Year** (Luke 4), and Islamic *sharia* law banning the charging of interest.

The essence of Clean Slates from the royal proclamations of Hammurabi's Babylonian dynasty in the second millennium BC to the Biblical Jubilee Year (Leviticus 25) was threefold: to wipe out personal debts (but not commercial debts, e.g., for trade ventures), liberate bondservants to return to their families, and restore land and crop rights that had been forfeited to creditors.

The most notable modern Clean Slate is the 1948 Allied Monetary Reform in Germany wiping out domestic debts except for basic working bank balances and

by employers to their work force. This was politically acceptable because
ere owed to former Nazis. It inaugurated the German **Economic Miracle**,
_..ing a market free from debt overhead.

Debt Deflation: The financial stage following debt-leveraged **asset-price inflation**, which leaves a residue of debt once new lending stops and repayment time arrives. The term was coined in 1933 by Irving Fisher to explain how bankruptcies and the difficulty of paying debts wiped out bank credit and hence the ability of economies to invest and hire new workers.[1] Paying debt service diverts spending away from consumer goods and new business investment.

Debt Dependency: When countries rely on the IMF and other creditors for loans to avoid defaulting on payments owed to their bondholders, the **conditionalities** include austerity programs, privatization sell-offs, and replacement of elected officials with financial technocrats to act on behalf of creditors. The ostensible "cure" to pay off debts leaves these countries even more debt-strapped.

Debt Drag: Akin to fiscal drag, the rate at which income earned in the production-and-consumption sector is diverted ("leaked") to pay to creditors.

Debt Leveraging: The ratio of assets one can buy with a given amount of one's own money (equity). A 90% debt-leveraging ratio means that one has to put down only 10% of the purchase price to buy a home or stock. The risk involved is that a 10% decline in the asset's market valuation wipes out the equity investment. But if the asset's price rises by just 10%, one doubles one's equity money. In a more extreme example, a 99% ratio means that one has to put up only 1%. This means that a fall of 1% wipes out the equity. But if the asset's price increases by just 1%, one doubles the equity down payment.

Buying entirely on credit is 100% debt leveraging – an invitation to speculation. Any decline at all leaves the 100% debt-leveraged investor owing money to the creditor. But any gain is a free lunch.

The tendency of asset-price inflation to inflate capital gains far in excess of interest rates explains the attractiveness of financial bubbles – and also why these end in bankruptcy.

Debt Overhead: The cost of carrying debts (and hence, the economy's volume of savings). The direct cost includes interest and dividends, amortization and other financial charges. Late fees and penalties now absorb nearly as much as interest charges for U.S. credit card companies. This overhead grows exponentially at compound interest. But creditors euphemize this as wealth creation, focusing on the mirror-image asset ("savings") side of the balance sheet. This debt salesmanship works as long as the increase in debt inflates asset prices at a faster rate.

Debt Peonage: The obligation of debtors to provide their own labor (and/or that of family members) to creditors to carry the debt and its interest charges. *The Columbia Encyclopedia* describes debt peonage as spreading from Spanish America after its independence from Spain in the 1820s:

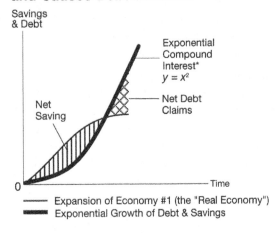

How the Rise in Debt Overhead Slows Down the Business Cycle and Causes Debt Deflation

Savings & Debt

Exponential Compound Interest*
$y = x^2$

Net Debt Claims

Net Saving

0   Time

— — Expansion of Economy #1 (the "Real Economy")
▬▬ Exponential Growth of Debt & Savings

* All compound interest is exponential.

> To force natives to work, the plantations got them into debt by giving advances on wages and by requiring the purchase of necessities from company-owned stores. As the natives fell into debt and lost their own land, they were reduced to peonage and forced to work for the same employer until his debts and the debts of his ancestors were paid, a virtual impossibility. He became virtually a serf, but without the serf's customary rights. ... By 1910 [U.S.] court decisions had outlawed peonage, but as late as 1960 some sharecroppers in Southern states were pressured to continue working for the same master to pay off old debts or to pay taxes, which some states had levied to preserve the sharecropping system.

Debt peonage in today's postindustrial economy takes the form of obliging homebuyers, student debtors and others to spend their working lives paying off their mortgages, education loans and other personal debts, which typically must be taken on in order to survive.

Debt Pollution: Much as environmental pollutants such as DDT disturb nature's environmental balance and causes die-offs, so the buildup of debt stifles economic growth. Interest and amortization charges prevent the economy's surplus from being used to expand the means of production and raise living standards. (See **Environment, IMF, Parasitism** and **Pollution.**)

"Debts that can't be paid, won't be": Over time, debts mount up in excess of the ability of wide swaths of the economy to pay, except by transferring personal and public property to creditors. (For the mathematics of why financial polarization occurs, see **Compound Interest** and my *Bubble Economic Model* article in this volume.)

The volume of debt owed by businesses, families and governments typically is as large as gross domestic product (GDP) – that is 100%. If the average interest rate to carry this debt is 5%, the economy must grow by 5% each year just to pay the interest charges. But economies are not growing at this rate. Hence, debt service paid to the financial sector is eating into economies, leaving less for labor and industry, that is, for production and consumption.

Greece's debt has soared to about 180% of GDP. To pay 5% interest means that its economy must pay 9% of GDP each year to bondholders and bankers. To calculate the amount that an economy must pay in interest (not including the FIRE sector as a whole), multiply the rate of interest (5%) by the ratio of debt to GDP (180%). The answer is 9% of GDP absorbed by interest charges. If an economy grows only at 1% or 2% – today's norm for the United States and eurozone – then any higher interest rate will eat into the economy.

Paying so much leaves less income to be spent in domestic markets. This shrinks employment and hence new investment, blocking the economy from growing. Debts cannot be paid except by making the economy poorer, until ultimately it is able to pay only by selling off public assets to rent extractors. But privatization raises the economy's cost of living and doing business, impairing its competitiveness. This process is not sustainable.

The political issue erupts when debts cannot be paid. The debt crisis requires nations to decide whether to save the creditors' claims for payment (by foreclosure) or save the economy. After 2008 the Obama Administration saved the banks and bondholders, leaving the economy to limp along in a state of **debt deflation**. Economic shrinkage must continue until the debts are written down.

Debt Crisis: A crisis is literally an intersection of trends. A debt crisis occurs when families, businesses and/or public bodies owe debt service in excess of their net revenue. They must default unless they can borrow the interest falling due (see **Ponzi Financing**). Productive business lending would avoid such crises, by providing borrowers with the means to pay their debts. But that is not the case with personal credit or most loans to government. Unproductive lending requires debtors to pay back loans out of what they can earn elsewhere, not from assets or enterprise financed by the loan. Such lending is usurious inasmuch as it typically ends with debtors losing their means of self-support and solvency, while governments are forced to relinquish their public domain.

Decline of the West: The first decline occurred with the collapse of the Roman Empire under the debt burden that stripped its capital and reduced most economic life to the Dark Ages of local self-sufficiency (see **Feudalism**). Market exchange and money survived almost exclusively for the One Percent (whose luxury trade has prompted economic historians to chirp that the Dark Ages may have been not so dark after all). A new Dark Age for the 99 Percent threatens to recur today as a result of the financialized economy's debt deflation and asset stripping.

Decontextualization: Taking markets and business behavior out of their social, institutional and historical context excludes the effect of finance and property ownership on production and general economic welfare. For neoliberals, **"the market"** is synonymous with the entire economy. (See **Chicago School**, **Austrian School**, **Neoclassical Economics** and **X and Y Axes**, and contrast with **Externality** and **Systems Analysis**.)

Deflation: Most people think of deflation as declining consumer prices for goods and services, and falling money wages. But by far the most volatile price declines occur in the real estate and financial markets for bonds and stocks in the aftermath of debt-leveraged **asset-price inflation**. Net worth declines, debt ratios rise and the economy shrinks in a downward austerity spiral. (See **Debt Deflation** and **Monetarism**.)

Demagogy: The post-democratic role of politicians is to deliver their constituencies to their campaign contributors, headed by oligarchs and local *rentier* interests. Demagogues who can deliver the largest support base are the preferred recipients of campaign financing. They typically exploit identity politics – emphasizing voting for one's own identity as one-issue voters – dividing them into ethnic, racial or sexual categories. The aim is to distract attention from their anti-labor economic policies.

The essence of subordinating democratic politics to today's oligarchic policies is to draw up two columns: Column A listing what voters say they want, and Column B listing what campaign contributors and lobbyists want. The rhetorical trick is to wrap each covert commitment in oligarchic Column B in a positive label tested on focus groups made up of people from Column A.

As a "hope and change" presidential candidate in 2008, for instance, Barack Obama promised to write down mortgage debts and bring them in line with the ability to pay. His political language was populist while his actual policies were oligarchic and aimed to prevent the changes that his supporters wanted. Once elected, he called his Wall Street backers to the White House and reminded them that: "My administration is the only thing between you and the pitchforks."[2]

Democracy: In Aristotle's theory of the 3-stage political cycle, democracy is the stage preceding oligarchy, into which it tends to evolve. The term is now applied to any pro-American regime supporting the Washington Consensus, regardless of its political stripe. Such regimes typically are run by a client oligarchy that owns the TV stations, magazines and other media to shape public opinion along neoliberal lines. Vested interests join hands in subverting democracy at home and abroad by shaping voting patterns through their control of these mass media via direct ownership and advertising to sustain and increase their privileges.

Democratization of Credit: Getting the population willingly (even eagerly) to take on debt. The ideal is for debtors to pay all their revenue over and above subsistence needs to the FIRE sector. As of 2015, U.S. Government agencies guarantee mortgages absorbing up to 43% of family income. Student debt may absorb another 10% or so. The result is debt peonage on a widening scale, euphemized as an opportunity to join the middle class by buying a home and an education by mortgaging one's future income. (See **Debt Deflation** and **Road to Serfdom**.)

Denial: Reluctance to acknowledge a systemic problem, such as imagining a debt-ridden economy to be in a viable state. Evidence doesn't matter; it is simply denied. Examples of psychological denial include eating disorders and narcissism. In the economic sphere, denial characterizes wealth addiction and also debt addiction.

Equilibrium theory promotes the belief that debts can be paid without tearing society apart with financial polarization creating a creditor oligarchy. To encourage denial of this dynamic, creditor lobbyists in academia and the popular media ignore the buildup of debt. Neoliberal true believers deny that there is any such thing as **unearned income** or a **free lunch** (see **John Bates Clark** and **TINSTAAFL**), and such unpleasant facts as debt and financial crime.

Neoliberals have an aversion to confronting such unpleasant reality as debt, *rentier* free lunches and financial crime. The first step is to minimize the problem. Deniers may concede that debt defaults do occur, but dismiss them as not being serious enough to call for a debt writedown, much less for jailing crooked junk-mortgage bankers.

Neoliberals may admit that these problems are indeed serious, but claim that nobody could have foreseen them. Or, evidence that contradicts their denial or ideology is rationalized away, often by an alternative reality shifting the blame elsewhere, *e.g.,* onto a decline in the pace of technological breakthroughs, or rising mechanization causing unemployment. But blame is denied for financial asset-stripping.

Most denial is associated with addiction. The cure for financial addiction is said to be *more* credit, such as the Quantitative Easing by the Federal Reserve and European Central Bank after the 2008 debt crisis – as if the economy could "borrow its way out of debt" at lower interest rates to save matters by spurring more asset-price gains.

Dependency: A loss of **choice** – often to creditors today, and in times past to the landed aristocracy monopolizing farming and housing space. The Washington Consensus aims to minimize the ability of economies to choose policies not deemed to be in the interest of the United States. Debt leverage is wielded to make foreign countries accept IMF conditionalities and depend on U.S. dollar credit, food exports and essential technology, while selling the "commanding heights" of their infrastructure to mainly U.S. investors. Democratic voters are to relinquish politics to the central banks, which are to be run preferably by alumni from Goldman Sachs, Harvard or other neoliberal institutions. (See **Dollar Hegemony** and **World System.**)

Depreciation: An accounting charge deducted from reported earnings to write off the cost of capital investment and buildings, equipment or technology. Depreciation is a return *of* capital, not a return *on* capital (profit). The depreciation rate is supposed to reflect the rate at which machinery or buildings wear out or become technologically obsolete as a result of being less productive than new higher-productivity equipment or other capital.

Depreciation was first added to value theory by Karl Marx. Criticizing Quesnay's *Tableau Économique*, he pointed out that Quesnay had neglected the portion of the agricultural crop that had to be set aside as seed-grain to maintain the capital stock for the next year's planting. (See **Falling Rate of Profit.**)[3]

At first glance it would seem to follow that real-estate investors should be allowed to recapture their original outlay for buildings and other capital improvements without having to pay income taxes. However, lobbyists for the **FIRE sector** have transmuted this seemingly logical conclusion into a depreciation allowance loophole that has made absentee-owned real estate free of income taxation. The lifetime of most commercial buildings tends to be almost permanent as a result of ongoing maintenance and repairs (which of course are tax-deductible). Meanwhile, the replacement cost of buildings tends to rise, increasing their market price, while their site value (rent of location) rises even more rapidly. So real estate owners receive a windfall, indeed, over-depreciation when they are allowed to write off the entire building's cost for tax purposes *each time it is sold to* *a new absentee owner.* (Homeowners are not permitted to claim depreciation on their own homes, only on rental properties.)

Deregulation: The proper role of government is to set rules for economic and social behavior. Deregulation represents undoing this power. The effect in today's economies is to shift planning to financial managers, while *rentier* interests take the lead in dismantling anti-monopoly rules and safeguards against fraud and other predatory behavior. (See **Crime** and **Planned Economy**.)

It would be wrong to treat such deregulation as synonymous with a classical free market. Adam Smith warned – with specific regard to bank regulation – that the

> exertions of the natural liberty of a few individuals, which might endanger the security of the whole society, are, and ought to be, restrained by the laws of all governments; of the most free, as well as of the most despotical. The obligation of building party walls, in order to prevent the communication of fire, is a violation of natural liberty, exactly of the same kind with the regulations of the banking trade which are here proposed. (*Wealth of Nations*, Book II, Ch. 2, §94).

Derivatives: The often opaque financial instruments such as credit default swaps or cross-option bets created by investment bankers euphemized as "risk management." Sales to gullible pension fund managers and others played a key role in the 2008 financial crisis. (See **Casino Capitalism, Efficient Market Hypothesis** and **Too Big To Fail**.)

Diminishing Returns: The idea popularized by David Ricardo that food production becomes increasingly costly as population grows and forces recourse to less fertile (and more distant) soils. The effect would be to increase prices for grain and other food crops to reflect the highest-cost margin of cultivation, increasing economic rent on the more fertile soils already cultivated. Ricardo used this assumption to warn that unless Britain repealed its Corn Laws (its protectionist agricultural tariffs) and imported its food freely from abroad, the rising price of feeding domestic labor would push up wage levels until there was no more room for industrial employers to make a profit. The Corn Laws were duly repealed in 1846, favoring industrialists and their bankers (who focused mainly on financing exports and imports) over landlords.

Ricardo wrongly asserted that even if soil fertility were to be chemically increased, the relative "original and indestructible powers of the soil" would maintain soil differentials. He voiced this ill-grounded agricultural pessimism just as Justus von Liebig, Albrecht Thaer and other chemists and scientists were contributing to a revolution in fertilizers that would increase agricultural productivity, while agriculture was being mechanized. Contra Ricardo, Thomas Malthus argued that landlords would increase farm productivity by investing their rising rents in capital improvements.

Ricardo made no mention of how rising rent-of-location increases differential land rent. As Heinrich von Thünen pointed out in *Die isolierte Stadt* (1826), this was especially the case as urban land prices for housing and commercial purposes rose to far outstrip prices for agricultural land. Britain seemingly inadvertently created a loophole for farmland in the 1930s by making it exempt from the inheritance tax and hence a vehicle for tax avoidance.

Ricardo also made no mention of how the price of land was affected by lower interest rates and easier bank credit creation. What actually increases a financialized economy's cost structure is not physically diminishing returns, but the rise in debt overhead coupled with lobbyists blocking of local or national government from taxing the rise in land rent as the basic source of public revenue. This pro-*rentier* policy leaves the land's rent to be pledged to bankers as interest. Land prices have been increased by extending bank credit on increasingly loose debt-leveraged terms, culminating in the junk mortgage bubble that burst in 2008. This rising debt overhead is the dominant economic phenomenon of our time. Yet it plays no role in mainstream models, although Steve Keen's "Minsky Model" has introduced it.

Discretionary Income: Income that recipients can spend at their own discretion *after* meeting non-discretionary obligations, headed by debt service, rent and mortgage payments, and for basic necessities such as food, essential communications and transportation. (See Hudson Bubble Model in this book for a more detailed discussion.) Government budgets classify interest payments and military spending as non-discretionary, while social welfare and other long-term programs are categorized as discretionary – meaning that they can be cut back, being subordinate to financial claims by bondholders.

Dismal Science: A term coined by Thomas Carlyle (1795-1881) to describe the discipline of the two leading principles of classical economics: Thomas R. Malthus's (1766-1834) blaming poverty on the alleged tendency for population to grow faster than the supply of food (thereby keeping wages down), and David Ricardo's (1772-1823) assumption of diminishing returns to soil, implying a rise in food prices and hence the cost of living over time. Both concepts were controverted by the American School of Economists (E. Peshine Smith, Henry Carey *et al.*). Advances in agricultural chemistry were vastly increasing crop yields, and wage levels in the United States were rising as a result of productivity gains from cutting costs in agriculture as well as industry. Alfred Marshall found increasing returns to be characteristic of industrial production, and Josef Schumpeter cited this increase as the mainspring of capitalist development in the form of creative destruction.

Despite the real world's increasing returns, economics textbooks continue to base equilibrium price and income theory on the assumption of diminishing returns. Only by that assumption can economists derive a singular mathematical solution to their academic exercises. Increasing returns lead to much more complex results – and neoliberals abhor complexity.

Disposable Personal Income (DPI): National income statistics (see **NIPA** and Hudson Bubble Model) define DPI as what wage earners take home after deduction of state and local income taxes (20% to 30%) and FICA paycheck withholding for Social Security and Medicare (currently more than 15%). This measure logically should include property taxes, as well as sales taxes and on what consumers buy.

What remains is far from being freely disposable for discretionary spending on the goods and services that labor produces. A number of expenses must be paid "off the top," mainly to the FIRE sector. These expenses are headed by housing charges for mortgage payments (up to 43% of personal income) or rent, plus debt service (interest and fees) to banks or other creditors (about 10%), plus non-public pension and health care set-asides. When banks scaled back their lending and credit card exposure, most households were obliged to pay down the debts they had taken on. Such quasi-saving is squeezed out of family budgets, not available for discretionary spending. These payments to the government and the FIRE sector leave only a quarter to a third of wages really disposable for spending on goods and services.

If tax policy treated labor like capital, only this net after-expense income would be taxed. Basic living expenses are the household equivalent of business operating costs – and businesses are able to deduct all their operating costs (and more!) from their taxable income. Taxing personal income as measured *before* netting out these basic expenses such as businesses are allowed to deduct imposes a much heavier burden on labor, adding to its cost of living – while shifting the tax burden off the *rentier* sector.

There is no measure of disposable personal income that reflects household "total returns" – income plus capital gains or losses (*e.g.,* the rise or decline in the market price of homes and financial securities). Such a measure would have shown prices for homes falling after 2008, offsetting the Bubble Economy's earlier gains. The balance sheets of the most recent homebuyers were left in negative equity (debts exceeding the market value of their assets).

Dollar Hegemony: Political control or influence via the U.S. dollar, as exemplified by America's ability to run a balance-of-payments deficit on military operations, imports and buyouts of foreign assets without constraint. The guiding principle is that U.S. military spending, consumer spending and investment spending should serve as the "engine" that drives global production. This transforms **Say's Law** (that production spending drives consumption) into a circular flow in which the U.S. militarized balance-of-payments deficit ends up as foreign central bank reserves. The BRICS countries are attempting to free themselves from this dollar hegemony so as to avoid having to pay the cost of their own encirclement by the U.S. military.

Dollar Standard: An arrangement in which central banks hold their reserves in the form of loans to the U.S. Treasury instead of in gold or other assets. U.S. military spending accounts for most of its balance-of-payments deficits, pumping excess dollars into foreign economies.

Doublespeak: A term coined by George Orwell in his novel *1984* to signify part of Big Brother's **Newspeak** euphemistic vocabulary obscuring an ugly reality. Mainstream economics calls rising debt pyramiding wealth creation, while deregulation of the financial sector is called a free market. Conversely, demagogues call public regulations to protect populations from exploitation and debt peonage a road *to* serfdom, not away from it.

Doubling Time: The time it takes for an interest-bearing loan, savings deposit or debt (or other rate of increase, such as price inflation) to double. (See **Compound Interest** and **Rule of 72**.) At 5%, the doubling time is just over 14 years ($72/5 = 14.4$).

Dutch Disease: The curse of rich natural resources, especially oil. *The Economist*, which coined the term in 1977, explained:

> Large gas reserves had been discovered in 1959. Dutch exports soared. But …from 1970 to 1977 unemployment increased from 1.1% to 5.1%. Corporate investment was tumbling. We explained the puzzle by pointing to the high value of the guilder, then the Dutch currency. Gas exports had led to an influx of foreign currency, which increased demand for the guilder and thus made it stronger. That made other parts of the economy less competitive in international markets.[4]

This definition might equally well apply to Australia during its boom in iron ore exports. In both cases the added liquidity spilled over into a real estate bubble, discouraging industrial competitiveness by increasing the cost of living to new homebuyers.

"The curse of oil" applies above all to non-industrial economies. Their oil and gas subsidize economic self-indulgence, not unlike the case of trust-fund children inheriting enough wealth so that they never have to work and take control of their own fate. (See **Affluence** and **Neoliberal Disease**.) "Free" natural resource rent encourages dependency on nature instead of industry. The curse is political as well as economic, supporting kleptocracies and autocratic rulers in control of natural resources, most notoriously in Saudi Arabia and neighboring Oil Gulf states. Such regimes tend to be client oligarchies of the major international oil and mining corporations (and hence of the U.S., British and French governments).

Dutch Finance: A derogatory 18th-century term for Britain's policy of paying for wars by borrowing (mainly from the Dutch). Debt financing makes the cost of war less visible to the population, by stretching out its expense over time. Adam Smith opposed this policy, urging parliaments to force governments to tax their population on a pay-as-you-go basis, which would make them feel the war's real cost and hence presumably oppose it. Smith opposed Britain's military adventures and colonial rivalries that led to this public debt, documenting how interest charges on each new war borrowing were paid out of a proliferation of new taxes levied on essentials. Even winning a war left the nation higher-cost with a combination of debt drag and fiscal drag.

Today, of course, governments outside of the eurozone can finance budget deficits simply by monetizing their debts instead of having to borrow from bondholders. Such deficits are self-financing when they are for productive investment in basic infrastructure to lower the cost of living and doing business. The tax rate need not rise, because taxes are paid out of higher economic activity.

Dystopia: A social system that leads to economic polarization and shrinkage, held together by authoritarian or imperial policies. (See **Neoliberalism** and **Washington Consensus**.)

ENDNOTES

[1] Irving Fisher, "The Debt-Deflation Theory of the Great Depression," *Econometrica* (1933), p. 342.

[2] I provide a technical discussion in "Saving, Asset-Price Inflation and Debt Deflation," in *The Bubble and Beyond*, ch. 11 (ISLET, 2012), pp. 297-319, first published in L. Randall Wray and Matthew Forstater, eds., *Money, Financial Instability and Stabilization Policy* (Edward Elgar, 2006), pp. 104-124. See also my

book, *Killing the Host*, ch. 11, "The Bubble Sequence – From asset-price inflation to debt deflation."

[3] For additional analysis of depreciation, see "The Real Estate Bubble at the Core of Today's Debt-Leveraged Economy," chapter 8 of my book, *The Bubble And Beyond* and "Real Estate and the Capital Gains Debate" (with Kris Feder), The Jerome Levy Economics Institute of Bard College, Working Paper No. 187 (March 1997).

[4] "What Dutch disease is, and why it's bad," *The Economist*, November 5, 2014. http://www.economist.com/blogs/economist-explains/2014/11/economist-explains-2

is for
Economic Rent and
"Euthanasia of the *Rentier*"
who extracts it

Ebitda: An acronym for Earnings Before Interest, Taxes, Depreciation and Amortization. (A more colloquial term is **cash flow**.) That portion of **total returns** which consists of of current income over operating expenses (but not including capital gains). This explains the aim of *rentiers*:

(1) Minimize taxes (t) by using loopholes and also offshore banking enclaves in tax-avoidance centers

(2) Maximize tax-deductible depreciation and amortization writeoffs (d and a), a largely fictitious non-cash, tax-deductible expense in the case of real estate

(3) Pay out the remaining cash flow as tax-deductible interest (i)

(4) Obtain asset-price gains, acheived mainly by debt-leveraging

Closing these subsidies for *rentiers* would oblige the One Percent to pay a larger share of taxes.

An analogous measure of ebitda for wage-earners is how much personal income is disposable after wage withholding for Social Security and medical care (over 15%), income and sales taxes (t, perhaps 15% to 20%) and pension set-asides, as well as the monthly "nut" of interest and housing (rent or mortgage 30% to 40%), other credit card and bank debt (i, up to 10%), leaving only about 30% available for actual consumer spending. Most marginal income growth since 1980 has been for rent, interest and other debt service, not for spending on goods and services. (See **Debt Deflation** and **Disposable Personal Income**.)

Charting these components of the National Income and Product Accounts (NIPA) shows that a rising proportion of income growth since 1980 has been for rent, interest and other debt service.

Earned Income: Wages earned by labor, and profits on business capital investment for producing goods and services, but not economic rent or interest, which are paid *out of* profits and wages, leaving less to spend on consumption and tangible capital investment instead of being recycled as depicted by **Say's Law**.

Economic Forecasting: Much as the U.S. Government has a Council of Economic Advisors to forecast the future (always promising better times ahead under the ruling party), the Babylonian palace in the second and first millennia BC had what might be called a Department of Divination (mainly looking at astral phenomena) backed up by a Department of Extipacy to examine sheep livers for omens. The methodology was much like that used by today's National Bureau of Economic Research's "leading and lagging indicators": tabulate many diverse time series of statistics and hope that a meaningful correlation pattern will emerge.

Babylonian forecasters looked at the major celestial cycles much as today's economic advisors look at business cycles, but their logic was in many ways more politically realistic. The royal Astrological Diaries (starting in the late 7th century BC and continuing to the start of the modern era) correlated movements of the planets with the weather, water levels (affecting irrigation) and grain prices, as well as with political happenings.

Today's business cycle theory assumes that recovery is *automatic*, as a result of built-in stabilizers that are supposed to return economies to stable equilibrium when disturbed. It is as if equilibrium is a norm as the economy grows at a steady pace, like a river flowing calmly with an ebb and flow of waves on the surface – a smooth sine curve chart, as in Joseph Schumpeter's book *Business Cycles*. This idea that a recession or even a financial crisis sets in motion self-stabilizing forces implies a *laissez faire* policy requiring no political intervention by the government.

Modern forecasting models fail to take into account the all-important fact that debt tends to expand steadily from one business upswing to the next, causing imbalances that tend to intensify. Babylonian accountants were taught how debts tend to grow exponentially. Mathematical training exercises from c. 2000 BC asked students to calculate the doubling times of loans and debts at interest, and also to calculate how herds of animals tend to taper off in an S-curve. It was well known that crops occasionally failed, causing debt arrears to mount up when cultivators could not pay the grain they owed for public fees, services and other debts. That perception led new rulers to start their reign by restoring economic balance and liberty for their citizens by proclaiming a clean slate to wipe away the accumulation of back taxes and other fees and personal debts that had mounted up.

The contrast between exponential financial growth and that of the "real" economy is at the core of business cycles or, as they were called more accurately in the 19th century, financial crises. The contrast is between what Thomas Malthus's 1798 population theory characterized as "geometric" growth and linear "arithmetic" growth. That contrast already was familiar to his audience in the distinction between simple and compound interest popularized by the actuarial accountant, Richard Price (1723-1791). Emphasizing how debts grow at compound interest, Price suggested that governments save money in a sinking fund to pay off their war debts by reinvesting the interest annually. He did not realize that creating a budget surplus would extract so much revenue from the economy that it would impose austerity and stagnation. It is easy to forecast economic crises that result when bondholders and banks persue the same exponential mathematics.

Today's "free market" forecasters believe that normal growth can be resumed without a debt cancellation. There is no recognition that debt ratios grow steadily, extracting more interest charges and transferring more property to creditors, giving them political as well as economic control. Without this perception there is no emphasis on the need to write down debts in order to restore economic balance.

Economic Miracle: Germany's post-1948 Economic Miracle was catalyzed by the Allied monetary reform that *cancelled* most of Germany's domestic debts, leaving the economy relatively debt-free and hence low-cost. (See **Clean Slate/Debt Cancellation**.) The antithesis is debt deflation, as when German leadership persuaded the European Union and IMF not to write down Greek debts in 2015, plunging the economy into austerity.

Economic Rent: Price *minus* **Value** (P – V). The excess of market price over intrinsic cost (value). Rent was the classical term for income that has no counterpart in necessary costs of production. Rent recipients have no out-of-pocket costs for supplying land or monopoly "services" for what basically are **transfer payments**.

In David Ricardo's model, landlords owning the most fertile soils receive the largest groundrent, a free lunch paid out of crop prices set at the high-cost margin. As in the case of monopoly rent, reducing such rent does not lead a production input such as land to be withdrawn, because it is supplied by nature or otherwise extraneously to its recipient's own efforts.

In industry, the British economist Alfred Marshall (whose 1890 book *Principles of Economics* was the dominant economic textbook in England for many years) described quasi-rents as accruing to innovative producers with lower costs of production, under conditions where market demand enables prices to be set by the older higher-cost producers. (See **Monopoly Rent**, *Rentier*, **Rent Theory**, **Free Lunch** and **Unearned Income**.)

Economics: The linguistic roots of the word "economics" stem from Aristotle's Greek terms *oikos* (house or household) and *nomos* (rule). This often is trivialized as self-sufficient "household management," in contrast to *chrematistics*, making money by market exchange and money lending. But economic organization and markets always have been wrapped in a political context as mixed economies. The paradigmatic "household" was the Mesopotamian "large house" (Sumerian and Babylonian *é.gal*), the temples and later the palaces in which accounting, weights and measures (including the origin of money), standardized interest and wage rates are first documented.[1] Most merchants in Mesopotamia's takeoff occupied official status in the royal bureaucracy, adopting management techniques from the large institutions. Prices were denominated for accounting purposes and for payment of debts to these large institutions, but were free to fluctuate outside of the city gates and outside of the temple and palace sector.

It thus is a travesty to narrow the study of economics to "markets," defined simplistically as private sector households earning and spending their income on goods and assets. All markets operate in the context of public regulation, taxation and government spending. To provide basic services, including those of the military and religious infrastructure.

Economic theory in modern Europe started as Political Arithmetic for royal management. The key concerns were money, taxes, and the trade policy needed to obtain silver and gold. James Steuart (1713-1780) called the latter "money of the world" and related it to population growth and immigration, colonialism and export production. **Classical political economy** shifted the focus of economics to domestic **value**, **price** and **rent** theory with a view toward political reform to check the power of landlords and other rent extractors.

Economist: Originally, a member of the Physiocratic School *(Les Économistes)* founded by François Quesnay (1694-1774) who developed the *Tableau Économique*, the first formal national income statement. The *Économistes* worked with other reformers to check the aristocratic and royal *rentiers* by replacing France's proliferation of excise and income taxes with a land tax (*l'impôt unique*).[2]

This became the aim of subsequent British political economists from Adam

Smith to John Stuart Mill and the "Ricardian socialists." But toward the end of the 19th century the *rentiers* fought back. (See **John Bates Clark**.) Objecting to accusations that their rent, interest and monopoly income was unearned, they sought to denigrate **government** taxation and regulation as wasteful. (See **Austrian School** and **Privatization**.) Today's post-classical neoliberalism thus inverts the original spirit of public economic policy, by taking a landlord's-eye or banker's-eye view focusing on "the market," taking political and institutional structures for granted instead of as the subject for reform as in classical political economy (see **Institutionalism**). To paraphrase Oscar Wilde's definition of a cynic, a modern mainstream economist knows the price of everything and the value of nothing. Wilde wrote that quip (in *Lady Windermere's Fan*) in 1892, when the distinction between value and price was still central to economic theory, but was coming under attack.

Education: H. G. Wells optimistically wrote: "Human history becomes more and more a race between education and catastrophe." But two American writers, Thorstein Veblen and Upton Sinclair (1878-1968) held a view later expressed by Ivan Illich (1926-2002): "School is the advertising agency which makes you believe that you need the society as it is." (See **Client Academic** and **Learned Ignorance**.) Under a curriculum of Doublespeak, confusing the distinction between earned and predatory income, education and economic catastrophe may now go together. (See also **Student Loans**.)

Efficient Market Hypothesis: A tunnel-visioned view that what is bought and sold in financial markets realistically reflects overall economic conditions. The political aim is to free the economy from government regulation. "**The market**" is treated as an efficient economic planner, optimizing production and resource allocation. The practical effect is to leave the economy steered by banks, monopolists and other *rentiers*. (See **Planned Economy** and **Race to the Bottom**.) It seems that a precondition for joining the staffs of finance ministries and central banks is to fervently believe that interaction among the market's participants will bring prices in line with their intrinsic value, reflecting the "real" economy's prospects.

Banks and brokerage houses, gamblers and fraudsters, pension funds and other institutional investors are assumed to interact in a way that produces a realistic valuation of stocks, bonds, bank loans, packaged mortgages, and financial casino bets on derivatives. In this view, crashes are always unexpected. If markets always know what is happening, there would have been no junk mortgage bubble or widespread bank fraud leading up to the 2008 crash. Newspaper reports would not incessantly be writing about "surprising" bad statistics and "unexpected" crises. There would have been no need for Queen Elizabeth to have asked: "Why didn't anyone see this coming?"

The costs of polluting the environment, global warming or rising debt overhead are deemed to be "external," that is, irrelevant to stock and bond investors, whose time frame is short-term, and to the NIPA, whose economic range is limited to market activities.

What is deemed "efficient" from the financial sector's vantage point: its ability to demand bailouts "or else" – or else, it may create a crisis and close down the ATMs. "Efficient Markets" are not so efficient for the economy at large. High finance holds the power to make its loss bring down the financial system, frightening populations with losing their savings, pensions and jobs. What Wall Street managers did know in 2008 was that they had bought control of politicians, so their institutions would be bailed out. (See **Regulatory Capture**.) Yet this financial control makes little appearance in today's economics discipline and its treatment of "the market."

End Of History: A term reflecting neoliberal hopes that the West's political evolution will stop once economies are privatized and public regulation of banking and production are dismantled. Writing in the wake of the collapse of the Soviet Union, Francis Fukuyama's *The End of History and the Last Man* (1992) coined the term "liberal democracy" to describe a globalized world run by the private sector, implicitly under American hegemony after its victory in today's **clash of civilizations**.

It is as if the consolidation of feudal lordship is to be restored as the "end of history," rolling back the Enlightenment's centuries of reform. As Margaret Thatcher said in 1985: "There is no alternative" [TINA]. To her and her neoliberal colleagues, one essayist has written "everything else is utopianism, unreason and regression. The virtue of debate and conflicting perspectives are discredited because history is ruled by necessity."[3]

Fukuyama's view that history will stop at this point is the opposite of the growing role of democratic government that most 20th-century economists had expected to see. Evidently he himself had second thoughts when what he had celebrated as "liberal democracy" turned out to be a financial oligarchy appropriating power for themselves. In 1995, Russia's economic planning passed into the hands of the "Seven Bankers," with U.S. advisors overseeing the privatization of post-Soviet land and real estate, natural resources and infrastructure. Russian "liberalism" simply meant an insider kleptocracy spree.

Seeing a similar dynamic in the United States, Fukuyama acknowledged (in a February 1, 2012 interview with *Der Spiegel*) that his paean to neoliberalism was premature: "Obama had a big opportunity right at the middle of the crisis. That was around the time *Newsweek* carried the title: 'We Are All Socialists Now.' Obama's team could have nationalized the banks and then sold them off piecemeal. But their whole view of what is possible and desirable is still very much shaped by the needs of these big banks." That mode of "liberal democracy" seems unlikely to be the end of history, unless we are speaking of a permanent Dark Age in which forward momentum simply stops.

End Time: The Biblical End Time was the time of troubles leading to apocalyptic turmoil. It was to culminate in a grand **Jubilee Year**, a new start in which personal debts were annulled and everyone would be restored to their idealized original state of liberty.

Jesus had a long Judaic and earlier Babylonian tradition to draw on when he announced that he had come to proclaim the Year of the Lord – the "good news" (gospel) that personal debts were to be annulled (Luke 4). Today, Christianity and Judaism have dropped their original focus on debt relations and the Jubilee Year that formed the basis for social reform. Only marginal palliatives, such as more government spending or charity, are being discussed to cope with today's financial polarization between creditors and debtors.

What is ending today is the long arc of industrial capitalism that promised to raise productivity and living standards to usher in a leisure economy of abundance. Instead of enjoying shorter work weeks, families are having to work longer just to carry the debts they need to take on to buy a home of their own, an education and to meet other basic needs. The result is today's counterpart to medieval serfdom – a looming epoch of debt peonage for entire economies. The new hereditary lordship class is headed by the financialized One Percent holding the 99 Percent in deepening debt, much as occurred in ancient Rome and Greece.

Today's End Time is a similar tumultuous transition period, driven by the burden of debts exceeding the ability to be paid, and continuing to grow rather than being written down. Deepening austerity and poverty produce an apocalypse of disease, environmental disaster and collapse of the old order.

Enlightenment: The thrust of classical British and French political economy was to free society from incomes resulting from inherited privilege rather than labor and enterprise. Society was to be remade along technologically optimum lines, by stripping away the "artificial" political institutions bequeathed from feudalism: a privileged landowning aristocracy, hereditary royalty and wealth, and religion as opposed to science. In the words of French philosopher Denis Diderot (1713-1784), the Enlightenment's program of restoring the "natural order" would occur "when the last king was strangled with the entrails of the last priest."

By the mid 19th century it seemed that democratic political reform would succeed in turning parliamentary political and lawmaking power over to majorities instead of privileged lords of the land and emperors of finance. Classical liberals hoped that the oppressive and extractive state supporting hereditary *rentier* property and predatory finance would be replaced by a regime of fair laws and regulations. What made Karl Marx so radical was his conclusion that industrial capitalism was revolutionary in seeking to free itself from the legacy of feudal privileges and monopolies. Within this classical tradition, and along with most economists of his day, he thought it logical to expect that industrial capitalism would evolve toward socialism. This seemed to be taking hold as European and American governments played an increasingly productive role inexpanding industrial infrastructure. He found the logical conclusion of classical political economy to be that the working class majority should govern in its own interest. Before this could occur, industrial capitalism had to clear the way by eliminating the unnecessary overhead costs of supporting an unproductive *rentier* class (absentee landlords, bankers and monopolists).

These Enlightenment aims have been rolled back over the past century. One twist has been that the major revolution in the name of Marx occurred in 1917 in Russia, not in the advanced industrial economies of Germany or England. Lenin argued that inasmuch as workers were too busy working to obtain the managerial skills necessary to govern a revolutionary socialist country, a dictatorship of the Bolshevik party was needed to govern on their behalf. The party leadership evolved into a managerial bureaucracy (Stalinism), culminating in post-Soviet privatization by kleptocrats after the dissolution of the Soviet Union in 1991 guided by the neoliberal Washington Consensus version of neofeudalism.

Environment: The context within which trends unfold. Much as the ecological environment is deteriorating as a result of global warming and pollution, the legal and political context of economies is becoming more unbalanced – the distribution of wealth and income, savings and debt. In contrast to the over-simplified assumption underlying correlation analysis of trends – that the environment remains constant – there is an ongoing self-transformation as a result of feedback between the economy, its social context and the natural environment. (See **Externality** and **World System**.) **Equilibrium** theory ignores these relationships. For instance, the financial analogue to environmental pollution and rising sea levels is debt pollution as the deluge of compound interest submerges the economy's balance sheets under water. (See **Economic Forecasting**.)

Equilibrium: Mainstream economics teaches that the status quo is self-stabilizing. Any disturbance is supposed to set in motion feedback adjustments to establish a new stable balance, in which each factor of production receives its fair economic value. If this really were true, there would be no serious structural problem – and no need for governments to "interfere" by redistributing income or wealth.

Such tautological models seem irrelevant once it is recognized that a man falling on his face is in equilibrium at the point where his head hits the ground. Death is a state of equilibrium – as is each moment of dying. Global sea levels 20 or 30 feet higher would be another equilibrium. By this logic, any economy and any status quo seems to be in a state of equilibrium at any given point in time.

Most "market equilibrium" analysis deals only with small marginal changes. This way of thinking makes equilibrium theory an anti-reform ideology, because it do not recognize structural problems that need to be cured by government intervention from "outside" the economy, such as running "Keynesian" budget deficits to restore employment. Falling wages are supposed to do the trick. (See **Efficient Market Hypothesis**.) Yet most economic dynamics are exponential and therefore are polarizing, headed by compound interest.

A third-world debtor economy is deemed to be in equilibrium under conditions where it suffers capital flight and emigration and must sell off the pubic domain to pay foreign creditors. Mainstream equilibrium theory ignores such structural environmental effects as being "off the balance sheet," that is, not part of "the market." Short-term investors simply don't care!

It therefore is necessary to ask just what is supposed to "adjust" to what, and how the adjustment process affects the distribution of income and wealth. For example, when a leading British economist, William Nassau Senior, was told in 1845 that a million Irishmen had died in the potato famine, he replied that this was not enough! The famine "would not kill more than one million people, and that would scarcely be enough to do any good," being insufficient to bring the Irish people's ability to live in keeping with their ability to spend, given the ownership of their land by British landlords.[4] Rising inequality is blamed on "the market," not on vested interests pushing economies out of balance.

International trade theory is an especially egregious application of equilibrium theory. Abolishing protective tariffs to "buy in the cheapest market" is supposed to make all economies richer. No long-term consequences are recognized, because equilibrium theory applies only to the short run. It implies that countries will converge internationally, not explaining why the global economy is polarizing.[5]

Instead of basing economic analysis on equilibrium theory, the mathematical economist Steve Keen emphasizes complex instability. "Not only is equilibrium no longer necessary, the continued use of the construct of equilibrium by economists is, without doubt, the major barrier to progress in the field. ... even more so than the weather, the economy is a complex system, and it is never in equilibrium."[6]

When an economy gets out of balance, especially as a result of financial dynamics, self-reinforcing tendencies push it further out of balance. Systems analysis calls this positive feedback. By becoming disruptive, economic dynamics force a political decision to be made. But this is deemed an "externality," which is "exogenous" to equilibrium models (see **Externality**). Although economists define their discipline as allocating scarce resources among competing ends, when resources really get scarce they call it a crisis and turn matters over to the politicians.

Errors and Omissions: This euphemism for short-term foreign exchange movements not recorded elsewhere in the IMF's *International Financial Statistics* refers mainly to the hot money of drug dealers, officials and local oligarchs embezzling export earnings by using false invoices, usually in cahoots with offshore banking centers.

Euphemism: The substitution of a nice-sounding term for an unpleasant reality. News reports call declines in the stock market "profit taking" or a "buying opportunity" instead of a loss. Running into debt to ride a wave of asset-price inflation is called "wealth creation." The junk economics profession has become a public relations office creating euphemisms for finance capitalism and the Washington Consensus, leading the public to perceive rent-seeking and similar exploitation in a positive light. In the process of distracting attention, euphemism tends to become elaborated into a full-fledged cover story. Among the most egregious such euphemisms are **capital gains**, **free market**, **labor capitalism** and **reform**. (See **Doublethink** and **Newspeak**.)

European Central Bank (ECB): Enforcer of austerity on Eurozone debtor countries, withdrawing credit lines and causing a crisis (as in Greece in 2015) if governments balk at surrendering to conditionalities that reduce pensions, cut back social programs, privatize public assets, and replace democratically elected officials with technocrats whose policies favor banks and bondholders.

"Euthanasia of the *rentier*": A phrase coined by **John Maynard Keynes** in his *General Theory of Interest, Employment and Prices* (1936), reflecting his belief that economies would be better off without policies that favor stockbrokers and creditors over debtors. Keynes sought to free society from reliance on the financial class by reducing its main taproot, high interest rates (*e.g.,* "euthanasia" of the sources of *rentier* income, not a revolution). He saw that without low interest rates and direct public investment, the economy would end up smothered in debt with low employment. That is now happening at an accelerating pace. Instead of "euthanasia of the *rentier*" phasing out the financial sector's free lunch, we are seeing the middle class being euthanized.

Exploitation: The term implies one party gaining at another's expense, in an exchange characterized by an unequal power relationship. One form of exploitation is monopoly rent, charging a price over and above the necessary cost of supplying land and real estate to renters or credit to debtors. (See **Economic Rent**.)

Classical exploitation of industrial labor reflects coercion and dependency – the worker's need to get a job to survive. But labor is being exploited increasingly in post-industrial ways, by financial and kindred rent-extracting charges imposed from outside the production process. Most such exploitation occurs via the FIRE Sector, in the form of interest and fees for access to credit, medical insurance and other compulsory payments to health care monopolies, and access charges to obtain housing (rent or mortgage interest).

It is natural for exploiters to embrace John Bates Clark's insistence that no exploitation exists. (See **Denial**.) Employers depict themselves as providing a livelihood for their workers, saving them from the ranks of the jobless. Banks advertise that borrowers can rise in status by going into debt to buy homes that may rise in price, or to take on student loans to get a better-paying job. An illusion is fostered that instead of setting them along the road to debt peonage, buying real estate or an education ("human capital") on credit makes them capitalists in miniature in a financialized economy. (See **Labor Capitalism** and **Middle Class**.)

Exponential functions: See **Compound Interest, Doubling Time**, and **Rule of 72**.

Externality: An impact affecting society at large but not recognized by the bottom line of business sales and profits. Mainstream free-market models distract attention from the adverse side effects of business behavior by deeming these "external" (or "exogenous") to the subject matter of economics, narrowly defined. These effects include pollution, health problems for employees, and political corruption stemming from economic polarization. (See **Environment**.)

The guiding motive in such tunnel vision seems to be that what is not discussed or acknowledged has less chance of being taxed or regulated. That is why the oil industry denies global warming, and why banks oppose analysis of the effects of how debt deflation shrinks economies and spurs emigration and a demographic crisis. (See **Decontextualization** and **Systems Analysis**.)

Extractive Economy: A *rentier* economy in which industrial growth is stifled by what Thorstein Veblen called the vested interests extracting land rent, natural resource and monopoly rent, interest and financial fees. When the economy shrinks, *rentier* lobbyists blame labor for being paid too much. Their solution is austerity for consumers and labor, as if wage and pension cuts – and cutbacks in public social spending – will overcome the high prices imposed by such exploitation, by enough to make the economy competitive despite its *rentier* overhead.

The aim of this blame-the-victim ideology is to leave more economic rent available to be paid to the FIRE Sector. (See **Asset Stripping** and **Race to the Bottom**.) The end stage occurs when FIRE sector managers take the money and run, leaving behind them an empty shell deeply in debt. (See **End of History**.)

Extremist: A term of invective applied by beneficiaries of inequality and polarization to reality-based critics who explain that economic dynamics are exponential and tend to polarize societies to inequitable and unsustainable extremes. The real extremism is that of "free market" theory pretending that the economy will settle at a happy equilibrium in which everyone (especially the wealthy) gets what they deserve. What actually polarizes the economy to extremes is passivity in the face of the assumption that *rentier* unearned income reflects an addition to real output instead of being merely an exploitative transfer payment.

ENDNOTES

---

[1] See Michael Hudson and Cornelia Wunsch, eds., *Creating Economic Order: Record-Keeping, Standardization and the Development of Accounting in the Ancient Near East* (Bethesda, 2004).

[2] The French Jesuit Abbot Augustin Barruel wrote in his *Memoirs, Illustrating the History of Jacobinism* (1789) that the French Revolution resulted from the efforts of three groups "atheists, Encyclopaedists and *Économistes*." But a century later the economic reformer and journalist Henry George derided economics as "a science which…seems but to justify injustice, to canonize selfishness by throwing around it the halo of utility." (*Science of Political Economy* [1898], p. 6).

[3] Manuela Cadelli, "Neoliberalism is a species of fascism," *Defend Democracy Press*, July 11, 2016.
http://www.defenddemocracy.press/president-belgian-magistrates-neoliberalism-form-fascism/

[4] I review the false assumptions of such theorizing in detail in my *Trade, Development and Foreign Debt* (2009).

[5] Nassau Senior, "The Relief of Irish Distress," *Edinburgh Review*, January 1849.

[6] Steve Keen, "Olivier Blanchard, Equilibrium, Complexity, And The Future Of Macroeconomics," *Forbes*. October 4, 2016.
http://www.forbes.com/sites/stevekeen/2016/10/04/olivier-blanchard-equilibrium-complexity-and-the-future-of-macroeconomics/6/#38c4352d18be.

is for
Fictitious Capital and the
FIRE Sector

Factoid: An idea that reflects popular opinion, regardless of whether it is true or not. When a seemingly plausible story appears on the Internet or in a "respectable" publication such as *The New York Times*, people accept it as fact, even after a retraction is published. A famous example: Iraq's fictitious weapons of mass destruction. Among the most egregious factoids on which junk economics is founded are the ideas that all forms of income and wealth are earned by contributing to production (*e.g.,* there is no such thing as unearned income), so that there is no such thing as predatory zero-sum activities. (See **Fallacy, Economic**; **Implanted Memory**; **Mathiness** and **Truthiness**.)

Factor of Production: This much-abused term often refers indiscriminately to the major **classes** receiving income: labor, landlords and capitalists. The post-classical pretense is that everyone's income reflects their role in production, not a non-production charge or privilege such as hereditary land rents and legal monopoly power.

Finance is traditionally excluded, having no direct role to play in the production process as such. Its rising extraction of interest and fees is an **externality** eating into the circulation of income between producers and consumers (see **Say's Law**). Yet today's mainstream economists treat the financial sector's revenue as a cost of doing business, and hence include if in measures of GDP as if it reflects a contribution to actual output.

Despite the all-important role played by public infrastructure investment, it rarely is cited as a factor of production. But as the American economist Simon Patten described, public improvements such as the Erie Canal and roads are a "fourth factor of production." Their return is not measured by the profit they generate, but by the degree to which they lower the economy's overall cost of living and doing business.

Labor and capital are the two basic factors of production, creating value. (The value of a capital good is the labor needed to produce or, more accurately, reproduce it.) Although some economists have treated land as a factor of production, it is actually a property right – the privilege to extract groundrent. Like air, water and fire, land is needed as a *precondition* for production, but nature provides it without cost. Being free (or supplied freely by the public sector), it does not produce value, but simply provides opportunities to extract economic rent. Land's rent-yielding privileges result from legal claims permitting landlords to charge for access to a given site. Their only cost of production is that of securing such legal or physical tollbooths.

Failed State: A nation whose government has been taken over by neoliberals and/or kleptocratic oligarchy and its public domain privatized. Such economies impose rent extraction and austerity to squeeze out more revenue for the FIRE Sector. The resulting economic shrinkage forces governments to borrow from bondholders, making them dependent on the financial cartel administered by the IMF in support of the *rentiers*. (See **Washington Consensus**.) The ensuing social chaos leads to a neofeudal economy. (See **End of History** and **Polarization**.)

Fallacy, Economic: Economic fallacies are promoted by lobbyists or client academics to shape how people view reality. Seemingly bland characterizations can stultify generations of economic thought. S. Dana Horton pointed out in *Silver and Gold* (1895): "The fallacies that lurk in words are the quicksands of theory; and as the conduct of nations is built on theory, the correction of word-fallacies is the never-ending labor of Science." (See **Factoid**.)

Examples include the idea that privatized ownership is more efficient than public management. Another misleading idea is that if the Gross Domestic Product (GDP) grows by, say, 2%, then the 99 Percent must be that much better off – even when all the economic growth is monopolized by the One Percent. Such confusion often is backed by awards of academic prizes to the most successful popularizers of perspectives favored by *rentiers*.

Falling Rate of Profit: **Karl Marx** expected production to become increasingly capital intensive, leading **depreciation** and amortization (a return *of* the original cost of capital goods) to rise relative to profit *on* capital. This rising proportion of depreciation in overall **cash flow** (**ebitda**) leaves less remaining taxable profit. It does not mean that the *overall* return to capital (the rate of surplus value) falls, but simply that the rate at which capital goods are used up or became obsolete rises. Regarding obsolescence, Joseph Schumpeter called rival cost-cutting technology creative destruction, as it required existing machinery to be scrapped when priced out of the market.

Under finance capitalism, nominal profits fall because of the rising debt-leveraged character of production as more corporate cash flow is paid as interest (which is tax deductible), leaving less available as profit (which is taxable). The tendency of debt service to "crowd out" profit thus leads to debt deflation and fiscal crisis.

False Correlation: An unwarranted linking of two phenomena as if there is a causal relationship. (See **Economic Forecasting**.) A notorious example is the relationship between money creation and commodity prices. The Chicago School opposes deficit spending by governments, claiming that central bank monetization of budget deficits is inflationary (or as they like to say, hyperinflationary) rather than helping employment and output grow. This false correlation is in contrast to Keynesian recognition (going back to John Law and other 18th-century economists) that when labor is unemployed and overcapacity and unemployment exist (as in economic downturns), government spending and money creation enable markets and employment to expand without raising prices.

A related problem is a *failure* to correlate causal dynamics. Banks create credit-money by creating debt, mainly to transfer the ownership of assets (mortgage lending, corporate takeover loans via debt leveraging and stock market credit), and only marginally to spend on goods and services or increase their prices. The recent Bubble Economy that crashed in 2008 saw bank credit inflate real estate, stock and bond prices, but not wages and commodity prices.

Federal Reserve System (the Fed): The U.S. central bank, established in 1913 (six years after the 1907 financial panic) to shift monetary authority from the Treasury to the commercial banking system, and to rescue banks with public bailout money (euphemized as "more flexible credit") to maintain the solvency of debtors and the banks to which they owe money.[1] As long as central banks are run by and for commercial banks (see **To Big to Fail/Jail**), they will limit this money-creating power to helping creditors, imposing fiscal austerity instead of saving the economy's 99 Percent by financing real economic growth.

In the 1920s, Fed Chairman Benjamin Strong flooded the economy with low-interest credit to encourage U.S. lending to German cities and other borrowers. The indirect aid was to provide Germany's central bank with enough hard currency to pay its reparation debt to the Allies. This enabled England and other Allies to turn around and pay their World War I arms debts to the United States. This easy-money (that is, easy-debt) policy fueled a domestic U.S. financial and stock market bubble, leading in due course to the 1929 crash and subsequent 1931 write-down of German reparations and Allied debts.

In 1951 the Fed reached an Accord with the Treasury to settle the implicit conflict of interest between the government, seeking to borrow at the lowest possible interest rate – and banks, which wanted high rates (euphemized as "fighting inflation"). Bank lending was deregulated under Alan Greenspan's Chairmanship (1987-2006), fueling a financial bubble that gained momentum after 1992, flooding the economy with low-interest mortgage credit after 2001 to inflate the real estate bubble. (See **Ponzi Scheme**.)

When junk mortgages collapsed in 2008, the Federal Reserve provided the leading banks with over $4 trillion of low-interest reserves at only 0.1% interest (a tenth of one percent) to help them recover. The aim was to re-inflate prices for real estate and other assets, saving bank balance sheets from negative equity. This episode illustrates how central banks can create money electronically without causing consumer price inflation rather than taxing populations to pay for government budget deficits. (See **Modern Monetary Theory**.)

Feudalism: A power relationship between lord and serf based on land ownership, collection of groundrent and the mobilization of armies. The expansion path was achieved by manning armies for conquest of new lands and seizure of natural resources. Productivity was measured by population growth, not by rising output per serf or other dependents. Increasing public taxes or borrowings were spent on outfitting armies – and luxury trade for the aristocracy and royalty at the top of the social pyramid.

FICA (Federal Insurance Contributions Act): A regressive U.S. tax law requiring employers to withhold taxes from wages paid to employees for Social Security and Medicare. No contributions are required for interest, capital gains or other non-labor income, or for individuals earning more than $116,000 (as of 2016), except for a modest Medicare surtax.

Fictitious Capital: By the late 19th century the term "fictitious" or "fictive" capital was used across the political spectrum from Karl Marx to Henry George to describe debt claims and property privileges ("rights") that have no real cost of production (value), except for payments to lawyers and politicians to obtain special privileges to siphon off a flow of *rentier* payments.

What ultimately makes such claims for payment fictitious is the inability of tangible capital investment or real wages to keep pace with what is owed or demanded. A typical view was voiced in the 1920s by the banker Paul Warburg: "The world lives in a fool's paradise based upon fictitious wealth, rash promises, and mad illusions. We must beware of booms based on false prosperity which has its roots in inflated credits and prices."[2]

Frederick Soddy (1877-1956) called such financial claims **virtual wealth,** because they are claims *on* "real" wealth and income.[3] But there is nothing fictitious about the corrosive real-world effect of financial and other *rentier* claims. Creditors gain legal priority over tangible property ownership when bankruptcy proceedings and foreclosures transfer real estate and industrial companies to them. Wealth obtained in this way enables financial interests to gain control of government and its lawmaking power, public enterprise and infrastructure. As a result, financialized economies are characterized by asset prices bid up relative to the price of labor (real wages) by debt leveraging and extractive rent seeking.

Rising asset prices for real estate, stocks and bonds may give an illusion of growth (see **Bubble** and **Great Moderation**), but must give way to debt deflation, euphemized as "secular stagnation" to avoid placing the blame specifically on the financial sector and the economic fictions it sponsors. Yet today's anti-classical reaction has led the term "fictitious capital" to all but disappear from usage.

Fictitious Costs: Charges over and above wages and normal business profits. (See **Economic Rent**.) The main examples are interest on debt to leverage one's investment (*e.g.* on corporate buyouts), stock options, management and underwriting fees, and the watered stock printed and given to cronies and political insiders by railroad barons and emperors of finance around the turn of the 20th century.

Fiduciary Responsibility: The guideline that professional financial advisors should put the interests of their clients before their own personal gain or that of their employers. The post-Enron prosecutions brought by New York Attorney General Eliot Spitzer provide a compendium of stratagems that money managers, banks, insurance companies and stock brokers have used to "stretch the envelope" of fiduciary responsibility. Money managers typically look at their clients in much the way that a lawyer does: "How much money does this person have, and how much can I make off them?" To maximize their take, money managers seek to minimize legal restraints on transferring risk and losses onto clients and counterparties. Many insurance-company managers and brokerage houses unload bad securities onto their clients, or simply "churn" their accounts to generate trading fees.

Even quicker money is now made by negotiating derivative straddles almost guaranteed to wipe out clients. Such opportunities increase as local municipalities and pension funds become desperate to take risks to meet their budgetary shortfalls resulting from untaxing finance and property.

Finance Capitalism: A term coined by Bruno Hilferding in *Finance Capital* (1910) to signify the evolution of industrial capitalism into a system dominated by large financial institutions, usually in conjunction with government (especially military spending) and heavy industry. To the extent that Wall Street managers take control of industry, their policy typically is to bleed profits to pay interest, dividends and other financial charges instead of investing in new capital formation and hiring. Today's finance capitalism thus has become antithetical to the needs and dynamics of industrial capitalism. (See **Money Manager Capitalism**.)

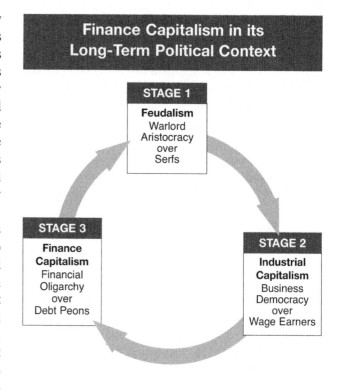

Finance capitalism is defined by the relationship between creditors and debtors, and speculation for financial gains not related to tangible capital investment or production. The aim is to to extract interest and financial fees by indebting labor, industry, real estate and government. Mortgage bankers aim to absorb all the net rental cash flow (ebitda).

The culmination of this dynamic is the point at which the expanding debt overhead siphons off all net discretionary personal income and business profits. For loans to governments, the aim is to absorb the net tax revenue, and then to strip away the public domain in payment (*e.g.,* as in eurozone loans to Greece since 2010).

To increase its gains, the financial sector promotes (indeed, demands) the creation of legal monopolies and privatization of land ownership and public infrastructure, to be sold on credit. This builds interest charges into the break-even cost of doing business, increasing the economy's overall cost structure. In the **Bubble** stage of finance capitalism, the measure of financial productivity is total returns: interest plus capital gains. These gains on stocks and bonds are engineered by debt leveraging. Homebuyers, real estate speculators and corporate raiders pay their current income as interest, hoping that prices for assets bought on credit will rise at a faster rate.

These gains appear to be "saving" with interest being paid for expectations of capital gains. (See **Ponzi Scheme**.) This economic and political dynamic of finance capitalism following feudalism and industrial capitalism (see chart above), ends in debt peonage and a plunge of asset prices as the economy succumbs to debt deflation. The effect is a kind of neofeudalism.

Financial Engineering: Raising stock prices by purely financial means – debt leveraging, stock buybacks and higher dividend payouts – instead of new capital investment to hire more workers to produce more goods. Financial engineering raises earnings per share by reducing the number of shares outstanding, not by selling and earning more. Corporate managers use earnings to raise their stock price by paying out a higher proportion as dividends, and even go into debt to buy back their shares.

These financial strategems are more extractive than productive, and raise debt/equity ratios. They go hand in hand with asset stripping as financial managers "bleed" companies to improve short-run earnings by cutting back research, development and projects requiring long lead times to complete.

Financialization: The degree to which debt leveraging accounts for an asset's market price, and hence for debt service as a proportion of income (ebitda). These ratios tend to increase until a crisis wipes out debt, converts it into equity, or transfers assets from defaulting debtors to creditors. But until a crash occurs, debt leveraging makes money by producing asset-price gains. The effect of mortgage loans is to bid up real estate prices.

Bank lending and an expanding bond market – replacing equity with debt – is the main dynamic of financialization. Bank credit is not used to finance tangible industrial investment to expand production, but is extended to buyers of real estate, and stocks and bonds already issued. Asset prices reflect whatever banks will lend against them, so easier credit terms (lower interest rates, lower down payments and longer amortization maturities) increase the amount that a bank will lend against a given rental value or income earmarked to pay interest. The resulting debt leverage inflates prices for real estate and corporate stocks. Most of the interest that banks receive from this lending thus is paid out of property rents and monopoly rents. To leave as much of this revenue as possible "free" to pay for more bank loans or stock issues, the financial sector defends tax benefits for its major customers, recognizing that whatever the tax collector relinquishes is available to be paid as interest on loans for credit to buy rent-yielding assets. These loans create debt-leveraged "capital" gains, which receive favorable tax treatment compared to profits and wage income.

When corporate managers earnings divert earnings to pay dividends or buy back shares, growth slows. But by that time, today's managers will have taken their money and bonuses and run. That is the result of paying managers according to how much they can raise their companies' stock prices in the short run.

The income from these assets ends up in the hands of banks, which do not spend it back into the economy but try to recycle the interest. Creditors recycle the interest they receive by making more loans. That is how economies become debt-ridden. This increases the debt overhead, reducing income available for consumer spending and new direct captial investment.

On the household level, buying a home with a 25% down payment leaves the home 75% financialized. That was the normal rule of thumb for mortgage lending in the 1960s. Another rule of thumb was for interest and amortization charges to absorb no more than a quarter of the buyer's income. But today (2016), homebuyers can put up as little as 3% down payment for a mortgage guaranteed by Freddy Mac (and 3.5% for an FHA-insured mortgage), leaving homeowners with 97% financialization. The U.S. Government guarantees home mortgages absorbing up to 43% of the buyer's income to pay debt service. Student loans, auto loans, credit cards and other bank debt may absorb another 10% of the debtor's income. The combination of financialization and the tax shift off the FIRE sector onto wage earners/consumers (via FICA wage witholding, income and sales tax) thus may absorb as much as 75% of the income of indebted consumers. (See **Debt Peonage**.)

Financializing real estate has shifted economic control from the hereditary landed aristocracies to bankers. Instead of serfs paying part of the crops to the landlord (and supplying labor days each month), the population at large is now obliged to go into debt to buy homes, and even to get an education. That is what "rising" into the middle class means in financialized economies. Its dynamics are concentrated in the FIRE sector, diverting income away from personal consumption and tangible new investment to pay creditors.

This debt overhang has become an economic dead weight since the 2008 crash. Markets have shrunk, and new investment and hiring have not recovered as profits and wages have stagnated. The asset-price inflation that seemed to be making the economy richer has turned into debt deflation, leaving many households strapped to meet their monthly "nut." In due course, the growing volume of debt exceeds the economy's ability to produce a large enough surplus to pay it back. This makes a financial breakdown inevitable, as well as increasing the inequality of wealth and income.

The breaking point can be sustained by new credit to enable borrowers to pay the interest charges. (This is what Hyman Minsky called the **Ponzi** phase of the financial cycle.) The problem with this "solution" is that lending debtors the money to pay the interest falling due causes debt to rise at compound interest. The dynamic ends in a transfer of property from debtors to creditors, unless debts are written down (see **Debt Forgiveness**). In 2008, banks convinced governments to "solve" the debt problem by taking bad bank debt onto the public balance sheet. That is what bailed out the banks – and their bondholders. (As FDIC head Sheila Bair wrote in her memoir, "It was all about the bondholders.")[4] But the government did not bail out the debtors.

A government bailout or IMF loan may enable creditors to jump ship, shifting the burden onto the government – mainly to be borne by taxpayers if the central bank refuses the money that is needed. The resulting financial austerity forces governments to cut back spending in areas other than paying bondholders – or to raise taxes to transfer income from taxpayers to bondholders.

So far, governments have chosen not to save the economy at large, but to save bondholder and banking claims *on* the economy. This policy is transfering property to creditors – including privatization by debt-strapped governments. Financialization thus has become the major dynamic causing economic polarization in today's world.

FIRE Sector: An acronym for the symbiosis of Finance, Insurance and Real Estate. This sector comprises the banking, property and debt superstructure that is wrapped around the production-and-consumption economy (see **Two Economies**). It accounts for most of the economy's unearned income, "capital" gains from asset-price inflation, and in due course debt deflation.

Much of the ostensible value added by property rights, credit and insurance merely add overhead charges. As Bertrand Russell noted already in 1934:

> Every improvement in industry, every increase in population of cities, auto-matically augments what the landowner can exact in the form of rent. While others work, he remains idle; but their work enables him to grow richer and richer.
>
> Land, however is by no means the only form of monopoly. The owners of capital, collectively, are monopolists as against borrowers; that is why they are able to charge interests. The control of credit is a form of monopoly quite as important as land. Those who control credit can encourage or ruin a business as the their judgment may direct they can within limits, decide whether industry in general is to be prosperous or depressed. This power they owe to monopoly.
>
> The men who have most economic power in the modern world derive it from land, minerals and credit, in combination.[5]

Instead of producing a real product, the FIRE sector extracts transfer payments *from* the economy in the form of rent, interest and dividends. (See **Rentier.**) Most consumer price inflation is caused by the FIRE sector, led by housing (rising rents and/or mortgage debt service), healthcare costs (insurance fees and rising costs, including monopoly products such as pharmaceuticals) and bank debt (including student loans, which have made education part of the FIRE sector).

The effect is to raise prices above the costs that would characterize socialist economies. For these reasons the FIRE sector should be treated as a subtrahend *from* Gross Domestic Product (GDP; see **NIPA**). It does not produce real output, but is an extractive zero-sum activity. This perception is blurred by FIRE sector lobbyists using part of that sector's gains to sponsor neoliberal deregulatory policy and deception to dull public opposition to the sector's rising overhead burden.

Fiscal Surplus (AKA Fiscal Drag): Most governments run Keynesian-type budget deficits, spending more money than they collect in taxes and user fees. By contrast, running a budget surplus does the reverse: It takes money *out* of the economy. (See **Modern Monetary Theory [MMT].**) The effect is fiscal deflation, shrinking economies and leading to future budget deficits as the ability to pay taxes shrinks. (See **Debt Deflation**, **State Theory of Money** and **Treasury**.)

Flat Tax: The antithesis of progressive income taxation, it reduces taxes on the wealthy by pretending that it is equitable for everyone to pay the same percentage, from billionaires to their cleaning ladies. First imposed by neoliberals on Russia and other post-Soviet states, it is the oligarchic dream policy to widen economic inequality in the United States and other financialized countries. The aim of U.S. Republicans, such as would-be presidential candidate Steve Forbes in 1996 and 2000, has been to exempt "capital" gains altogether, and to maintain tax loopholes for other financial returns.

Forced Saving: Since 1982, U.S. wage withholding has been steeply increased to prepay Social Security and medical insurance instead of managing these programs (and pensions) on a pay-as-you-go basis as in Germany. (See **Labor Capitalism** and **Sinking Fund**.) The **FICA** program's fiscal surplus enabled the Republican Congress to cut taxes for the higher income brackets. Making it a user fee instead of funding it out of the overall budget via progressive taxation makes this forced saving part of a tax shift benefiting the wealthy. And saving for pensions – pre-paying for retirement – became a major factor pushing up stock market prices. (See **Pension-fund Capitalism** and **Financialization**.)

Foreclosure: A transfer of property from debtors to creditors – the opposite of Debt Forgiveness. Yet JP Morgan Chase CEO Jamie Dimon euphemized bank foreclosure as "debt relief to people that really need it."[6] If the relief really were for debtors, they would be able to keep their homes. Foreclosure deprives them of home ownership, the main criterion of membership in the middle class. Yet Dimon claimed that homeowners "are probably better off going somewhere else, because they get relieved almost 100% of the debt through foreclosure." The real "debt relief" is to the banks, by letting them foreclose on homes – and also letting them collect back interest and even higher penalties and legal charges from the government for guaranteed mortgages when shortfalls occur.

Fragility: The term popularized by Hyman Minsky for financial markets becoming more debt-leveraged. Financial fragility increases as the volume of debt service expands on its way to the ultimate point where it exceeds the ability to pay. A crash may be postponed by lending the debtor the interest that is due (simply by adding it onto the debt balance; see **Ponzi** financing). That is how Latin American countries rolled over their foreign debt until the overhead became so obviously unpayable that charade imploded in 1982 with Mexico's insolvency. Rising debt leverage ended in a break in the chain of payments, leaving a backwash of debt deflation.

Free Lunch: A popular term for economic rent, transfer payments or prices that have no counterpart in the actual or socially necessary costs of producing goods or services. Most business ventures seek such free lunches not entailling actual work or real production costs. To deter public regulation or higher taxation of such rent seeking, recipients of free lunches have embraced Milton Friedman's claim that There Is No Such Thing As A Free Lunch (**TINSTAAFL**). (See also **Chicago School**, **Parasitism** and **Windfall**.)

Even more aggressively, rent extractors accuse governments of taxing their income to subsidize free loaders, pinning the label of "free lunchers" on public welfare recipients, job programs and the beneficiaries of higher minimum wage laws. The actual antidote to free lunches is to make governments strong enough to tax economic rent and keep potential rent-extracting opportunities and natural monopolies in the public domain.

Free Market: To the classical economists, an economy free of land rent, usurious banking practices and monopolies in private hands. But as finance capitalism has superseded industrial capitalism, it has inverted "free market" rhetoric to mean a market free *for* rent extractors to obtain land rent, natural resource rent, monopoly rent and financial gains "free" of government taxation or regulation. This inverted re-definition depicts a free market as one free for the financial and propertied classes to subject the economy to a network of extractive tollbooth fees. Such a "free market" has become a doublethink term for the path to neo-feudalism, financialization and kindred *rentier* policies. (See **Free Lunch**, **Kleptocrats** and **Road to Serfdom**.)

Free Trade: The stage of trade policy that followed mercantilist and protectionist success in raising first Britain and then the United States and Germany to industrial and financial dominance. Pulling up the ladder, these leading industrial nations demand that other countries open their markets to lead-nation exports and investment instead of protecting, subsidizing and modernizing their own industry and agriculture. Such "free trade" has become a euphemism for centralizing industrial, agricultural and financial power in the United States, while offshoring employment to the low-wage countries.

Academic rationalization of this kind of globalization is based on short-term **equilibrium** theory that excludes consideration of how protectionist policies may support capital investment to raise productivity over time. Also ignored are "off balance sheet" costs borne by society to clean up environmental pollution and global warming. For further discussion of protectionism, see my book *America's Protectionist Takeoff: 1815-1914* (2010).

Friedman, Milton (1912-2006): The most prominent Chicago School advocate of financial and fiscal austerity, Friedman popularized the monetarist theory that changes in the money supply are reflected in proportional changes in consumer prices, commodity prices and wages. His failure to understand that bank money is spent mainly to buy real estate, stocks and bonds blocked him from understanding asset-price inflation or its sequel, debt deflation. He was awarded the 1976 Nobel Economics Prize for his neoliberal depiction of government as pure overhead and "interference," while distracting public attention from the asset-price gains resulting from bank credit. (See **"As If" Argument, Junk Economics** and **TINSTAAFL.**)

ENDNOTES

[1] I give the historical details in "How the U.S. Treasury avoided Chronic Deflation by Relinquishing Monetary Control to Wall Street," *Economic & Political Weekly* (India), June 2016.

[2] Quoted in Ron Chernow, *The Warburgs: The Twentieth-Century Odyssey of a Remarkable Jewish Family* (Vintage [Kindle Locations 4558-4561]).

[3] Frederick Soddy, *Wealth, Virtual Wealth and Debt. The solution of the economic paradox* (George Allen & Unwin, 1926).

[4] Joe Nocera, "Sheila Bair's Bank Shot," *The New York Times Magazine*: July 10, 2011. This was the interview she gave upon stepping down from the FDIC.

[5] Bertrand Russell, *Freedom and Organisation* (1934, chapter 19, p. 186).

[6] CNBC interview, January 11, 2011. "Giving debt relief to people that really need it, that's what foreclosure is." http://video.cnbc.com/gallery/?video=1737074353

is for

Grabitization and the Groundrent that is its main objective

George, Henry (1839-1897): A self-taught American journalist who attacked railroads, landlords and other *rentier* interests. His writings helped inspire a generation of muckrakers to expose the oil and railroad monopolies and their insider dealings. His main point was that most land is not produced by labor, and hence yeilds unearned income. Treating property claims for land rent as fictitious capital because rent was merely a transfer payment from renters to owners, George distinguished "value from obligation" from "value from production."[1] His view was kindred to that of Adam Smith and David Ricardo, as opposed to John Locke's view that most land incorporated labor-intensive improvements with little "free lunch."

George's *Progress and Poverty* (1879) urged a **Single Tax** (see **Land Value Tax**) on land rent, claiming that no other taxes were necessary. He claimed that it was merely necessary to tax away its rent, leaving ownership in private hands. (See **Henry George Theorem**, a somewhat misleading term coined by Joseph Stiglitz. Lacking a value and price theory, George had no concept of classical economic rent, but only a journalistic perception that unearned income was bad.)

George's position led to a libertarian stance increasingly opposed to the socialist advocacy of nationalizing land. Fighting socialists more than the landlords, his followers ended up as sectarians on the right wing of the political spectrum.

German Economic Miracle: The Allied Monetary Reform of June 20,1948, freed Germany's economy from some 90% of the internal debts inherited from the Nazi era. Domestic debts were annulled, except for designated minimum working balances and employer debts to workers. This created a largely debt-free and hence low-cost economy. The 1952 London Agreement on German External Debts further scaled back what Germany owed from before and after World War II. These debt cancellations created the ensuing **Economic Miracle**.

By contrast, to support their hard line against writing down debts by the Greek and other governments, today's creditor interests have sought to wipe out any memory of Germany's **debt cancellations**, attributing its economic resurgence simplistically to "free markets," abolition of price regulations and tax reductions. What has been forgotten is that Germany was given freedom from debt overhead.

GIGO (Garbage In, Garbage Out): Originating in the field of information technology, this acronym refers to the fact that when computers are fed nonsensical input data ("garbage in"), they produce correspondingly useless output ("garbage out"). (See **"As If" Argument, Junk Economics** and **Monetarism**.)

Facts in themselves are not worthless ("garbage"), but the tendency to impose ideological preconceptions on what is a classical source of error. Giving a perverse meaning to the motto "Seek, and ye shall find," today's monetarists blame every downturn on labor's wages, government spending, and taxes being too high. Much as astrologists correlate the planetary movements with human events and assume a causal connection so that coincidences will be repeated, economists feed large numbers of variables into a computer, hoping that a pattern will emerge among the correlations. (See **Economic Forecasting**.) In place of realistic causal connections, policy ideology is substituted.

GINI Coefficient: A ranking by percentiles (or 10% aggregations) to measure the degree to which wealth, property ownership or income is concentrated. Charting how much is controlled by the top One Percent of the population shows the economic polarization that has occurred in nearly every country since 1980. This post-1980 period was euphemized as the Great Moderation because bank lending enabled the 99 Percent to survive in the face of widening inequity by running deeper into debt to the top One Percent – imagining that all this was natural and fair.

Gold: Domestic money is created by governments accepting it as payment for taxes.

(See **State Theory of Money** and **Taxation**.) But "gold bugs" make a fetish of the metal, and oppose the idea of government creating credit to spend into the economy on infrastructure and social programs. Their advocacy of "hard money" – keeping the price of gold or foreign exchange rate constant – would result in monetary deflation. This increases the power of money and wealth over labor by causing unemployment and holding down wages. That was the aftermath of Britain's bullionist policies following the Napoleonic Wars, of America's "crucifixion on the cross of gold" after the Civil War, and France's economy after World War I. Today's eurozone is now imposing a similar monetary straitjacket, with the tight supply of euros playing the "hard money" role that gold used to play.

Gold's main surviving monetary use today has been to settle balance-of-payments deficits. The alternative is for central banks to hold bonds of other countries. These bonds are issued mainly for war making, which always has been the major cause of balance-of-payments deficits – and also of government budget deficits, and hence of public debt. By comparison, a gold-exchange standard limits the ability of nations to finance military adventures, which forced the dollar off gold in 1971.

Gold need not be the only form of international money. A global central bank could create "paper gold" as a means of settling balance-of-payments deficits. But that cannot be done fairly unless all nations agree on the purposes for which such global money should be created. Under current arrangements, IMF Special Drawing Rights (SDRs) are lent to the United States to finance its global military spending. That is what most central bank dollar reserves are now used for. It is to create an alternative to the U.S. Treasury-bill standard or similar paper money under U.S. control that other countries are now building up their official gold stocks.

Government: From the Greek root *cyber*, meaning "to steer," this social control function historically has been provided by public institutions at least ostensibly for the general welfare. Sovereign states are traditionally defined as having the powers to levy taxes, make and enforce laws, and regulate the economy. These planning functions are now in danger of passing to financial centers as governments become captive of the vested interests. The FIRE sector and its neoliberal supporters (see **Chicago School** and **Free Market**) seek to prevent the public from regulating monopoly rent, and also aim to shift the tax burden onto labor and industry. (See **Big Government**, **Oligarchy**, **Postmodern Economy** and **Tax Shift**.)

The recently proposed Trans-Pacific Partnership (TPP) agreement and its European Counterpart, the Transatlantic Trade and Investment Partnership (TTIP), would compel governments to relinquish these powers to corporate lawyers and referees appointed by Wall Street, the City of London, Frankfurt and other financial centers. (See **Regulatory Capture**.) The non-governmental court would oblige governments to pay compensation fines for enacting new taxes or applying environmental protection regulations or penalties. The fines would reflect what companies would have been able to make on rent extraction, pollution of the environmental and other behavior usually coming under sovereign government regulations. Making governments buy these rights by fully compensating mineral and other rent-extracting businesses would effectively end the traditional role of the state. (See **Neoliberalism**.)

Grabitization: The Russian term for **privatization** after Boris Yeltsin dissolved the Soviet Union in 1991 and accepted American advice to turn over existing enterprises and natural resources to Red Directors and the banks they hastily organized. Cold War neoliberals applauded this as a free market, recognizing that the only way that the post-Soviet appropriators could turn their takings into cash and keep it free from future taxes and clawbacks was to sell their shares to U.S. and European buyers, holding most of their proceeds in London and other hot-money centers.

The neoliberal cover story was that managers acting in their own interest would make industry more productive than would be the case under state ownership. In practice the result was **asset stripping** and **insider dealing** (see **Kleptocracy**). The new factory owners stopped paying for employee benefits, and went for long periods without paying employees at all. This turned Russia and other post-Soviet economies into financially polarized oligarchies, with much less progressive taxation than was applied in the West – typically a flat tax that fell only on labor and consumers, not on property and financial income or asset-price gains. Russian stocks listed on the New York and London exchanges became the leading gainers leading up to the 1997 Russia-Asia financial crisis, yet between 1990 and 2015 Russia suffered capital flight and losses of about $25 billion a year – over half a trillion dollars.

Great Moderation: Not originally meant to be a sarcastic term, this was the **Bubble Economy** period of Alan Greenspan's tenure at the Federal Reserve, 1987-2006. During these two decades the wealth and income of the One Percent pulled far ahead of the 99 Percent as prices for real estate, stocks and bonds were inflated on credit. (See **Asset-Price Inflation**.) While wealth soared at the top of the economic pyramid, wages stagnated and GINI coefficients reached their highest degree of polarization in a century. Greenspan deemed these gains "moderate" because workers went so deeply into debt that they were afraid to strike and complain about working conditions (the "**traumatized worker syndrome**.") Financial fraud flourished as bank lending was deregulated and lenders inflated the **junk-mortgage bubble** (see **NINJA Loans**). Banks lent homeowners and other borrowers enough money to keep current on their debt service. (See **Ponzi Scheme**.) The lending that financed asset-price inflation left a residue of debt deflation, coupled with a tax shift onto wage earners that "moderated" the rise in consumer prices.

Greed: "All for ourselves and nothing for other people, seems, in every age of the world, to have been the vile maxim of the masters of mankind," wrote Adam Smith (*Wealth of Nations*, Book III, Ch. 3). Yet subsequent mainstream economics has shied away from confronting the dynamics of greed. The supply and demand curves of late 19th-century utility theory were based on the hypothesis of diminishing marginal utility: The more food, clothes or other consumption goods one has, the less pleasure each additional unit gives. If money and property were like bananas and other food, this would mean that instead of the One Percent tapering off their demand for wealth, they would become satiated, leaving the path open for less rich individuals to catch up.

But as the ancients knew, the principle of diminishing marginal utility does not apply to money and property. The more one has, the more one wants. Wealth is addictive, sucking its possessors into a compulsion to accumulate. Gilded Age economists ignored the seemingly obvious tendency for wealthy people to strive to increase their fortunes in ways that injure the economy. (See **Affluenza**, **Hubris**, **Wealth Addiction** and **Zero-Sum Activity**.)

The proper task of democratic and fair societies is to keep this compulsive acquisitiveness in check. Low-surplus economies dependent on mutual aid tend to have peer pressure sanctions against the accumulation of money or other personal wealth, especially where the main way of obtaining it is at someone else's expense. Such communities need to maintain a self-supporting population, if only for military defensive purposes. Disenfranchising citizens would mean fewer army members, leaving the community more prone to being conquered by rivals. For example, only as the Roman world grew rich enough to hire mercenaries was it possible for restraints on greed to be loosened to indebt and disenfranchise the citizen armies.

Greenspan, Alan (1926-): A follower of Ayn Rand, the Austrian School and the Chicago School, he said that he didn't believe the financial sector would risk its reputation by behaving in an unethical way – as if its bubble economy fortunes did not stem largely from fraud and deception. As Federal Reserve Chairman (1987-2006), he blocked the central bank from stopping the junk-mortgage bubble's pervasive fraud.

Describing the "traumatized worker syndrome," Greenspan explained why wages remained stagnant despite the remarkable rise in labor productivity and money creation. Workers had become so deeply indebted with such large monthly carrying charges that missing a credit card or public utility payment would bump up interest charges to around 29% penalty rates, while missing a mortgage payment would endanger their home ownership. As a result, workers were afraid to strike or even to risk being fired by complaining about low wages or abusive working conditions.

Groundrent: The portion of rent paid to hereditary owners for use of a specific site. After the Norman Invasion of 1066, England's landlords charged groundrent in the form of leases. This is separate from what the property users pay for buildings or other capital improvements.[2] (See **Adam Smith, Economic Rent, Henry George** and **John Locke**.)

Over and above statutory hereditary groundrent is the land rent set by the market – mainly in the most urbanized or commercial areas. Most such urban land rent today is created by public infrastructure investment, amenities and prestige creation. In high-status neighborhoods with good transportation, schooling and communications, this site rent-of-location reflects public infrastructure investment and the general level of prosperity. (See **Thorstein Veblen**.) Such locations bear a property tax that should be basically a user fee to reimburse the public sector for its contribution to site valuation. But today's property taxes only capture a small portion of the full land rent.

The full **rent-of-location** thus stems not only from nature (such as soil fertility), but also reflects the infrastructure services provided by society. Privatization of rent thus appropriates not only nature but also the value of public investment and overall prosperity. The real estate market determines the level of land rent over and above the landlord's capital investment in buildings and kindred improvements.

ENDNOTES

[1] Henry George, *Progress and Poverty* ([1879] (New York: 1981, pp. 39f.): "Increase in land values does not represent increase in the common wealth, for what landowners gain by higher prices, the tenants or purchasers who must pay them will lose." The result is a zero-sum *transfer* of wealth and income. See also the *Science of Political Economy* (New York, 1980, pp. 259-63, first published posthumously in 1898).

[2] The British aristocracy still owns a third of all land area (mainly rural) in the U.K. See Tamara Cohen, "Look who owns Britain: A third of the country STILL belongs to the aristocracy," *Daily Mail*, November 10, 2010. The largest hereditary holding is the Kensington area of London, whose value reflects the general level of prosperity and rent-of-location from public infrastructure and neighborhood.

is for
Hyperinflation

Half-life: In physics, the time it takes for half the mass of a radioactive element to decay into the next-lower isotope or element, typically ending in stable and inert element such as lead. By analogy, the time it takes for an economic theory or ideology to lose half its influence, *e.g.*, as Karl Marx's value theory (50 years), Henry George's Single Tax (15-20 years), John Maynard Keynes multiplier theory (40 years), Milton Friedman's Chicago School monetarist theory (20 years) and, most recently, neoliberalism (which hopes to last forever as the **End Of History**).

Have-nots: People who have debts instead of wealth. (See **Debt Peonage** and **Neo-Serfdom**.)

Haves: The One Percent that holds the 99 Percent as debt hostages, while aiming to monopolize the rise in income and wealth. (See **Affluence** and **Oligarchy**.)

Henry George Theorem: A term coined in 1977 by Joseph Stiglitz for the principle that public spending on roads and other transportation, parks, schools and other basic infrastructure increases local rent-of-location and hence property valuations by at least an equal amount.[1] The theorem is named after Henry George, apparently for his claim that a **Single Tax** on the rental value of land would be enough to defray public expenses for basic needs. But these two phenomena are not the same thing.

In London it cost £3.4 billion to extend the Jubilee tube line to the Canary Wharf financial district – while raising the valuation of land along the route by over £10 billion. Taxpayers bore the cost, but "land owners contributed nothing towards the increased value that accrued to their assets."[2] The entire cost of public construction could have been defrayed out of site taxes on the land's increased valuation. (See **Economic Rent** and **Groundrent**.) This would have been preferable to taxing wage income and profits.

Heinrich von Thünen earlier had attributed land prices mainly to location, in contrast to Ricardian soil fertility. But the site value for location is largely a result of public amenities – in addition to transportation, the proximity to schools, parks, public institutions, communication, visual landscaping, access to water and so forth. Neither von Thünen nor George related rental value explicitly to public infrastructure investment. George attributed the rising price of land simply to its increasing scarcity in the face of population growth.

Thorstein Veblen made the point that urban politics and civic improvements were mainly concerned with projects to promote real estate by land speculators. The "law" thus would better be called the **Thorstein Veblen theorem** – except that from the vantage point of the financial and real estate sectors that dominate American politics, the aim of public infrastructure spending is indeed to increase land prices. But real estate developers and their pet politicians try to keep all the land-price gains for themselves, not for the public purse to tax these asset-price gains.

Stiglitz evidently found it more innocuous to cite George as intellectually non-threatening, although George's proposals went further than Stiglitz's term suggests. George's early writings urged that basic infrastructure such as railroads and even banking be kept in the public domain. But after becoming a libertarian politician, George differentiated himself from socialists by opposing strong government. Neither his followers nor Stiglitz's neoclassical mainstream school took the trouble to calculate just how large land rents were, or the degree to which they rose as a result of public investment as distinct from general prosperity, bank credit or "nature." Such a calculation would make the fairness of taxing the full **rent of location** that public spending creates all too obvious.

Veblen's analysis of country towns applies equally well to specific neighborhoods:

> The location of any given town has commonly been determined by collusion between 'interested parties' with a view to speculation in real estate, and it continues through its life-history (hitherto) to be managed as a real estate 'proposition.' Its municipal affairs, its civic pride, its community interest, converge upon its real-estate values, which are invariably of a speculative character, and which all its loyal citizens are intent on 'booming' and 'boosting,' – that is to say, lifting still farther off the level of actual ground-

values as measured by the uses to which the ground is turned. Seldom do the current (speculative) values of the town's real estate exceed the use-value of it by less than 100 per cent.; and never do they exceed the actual values by less than 200 per cent., as shown by the estimates of the tax assessor; nor do the loyal citizens ever cease their endeavours to lift the speculative values to something still farther out of touch with the material facts. A country town which does not answer to these specifications is 'a dead one,' one that has failed to 'make good,' and need not be counted with, except as a warning to the unwary 'boomer.'[3]

Veblen was too trenchant a critic of neoliberal economics to be safely acknowledged by today' mainstream. His focus on land prices went beyond merely capitalizing (financializing) *current* rents into mortgage loans, emphasizing real estate sales promotion and advertising.

Any theorem purporting to relate rising land prices to tax policy and public infrastructure thus must look at the overall economy as a system centered on banking and the real estate sector. Banks, for instance, provide the mortgage credit that enables new buyers to bid up real estate prices. The rule of thumb is that rent is for paying interest, which tends to capitalize the rising rental value. So banks end up with the main benefits of land-price gains resulting from public investment.

The aim of politicians orchestrating these price gains is to leave them in private hands, keeping local governments from recapturing the gains that their infrastructure investment creates. My own version of the relevant "theorem" is therefore that *increases in public infrastructure expenditures raise land prices by the extent to which the increased rental site-value is capitalized into bank loans.* The aim is for further such debt-leveraged "capital" gains.

Host Economy: A nation that lets its land, natural resources, public infrastructure and industrial production be privatized, especially by foreign investors (financed with foreign bank loans) in alliance with client oligarchies. I elaborate the extractive character of such intrusion in my book, *Killing The Host: How Financial Parasites and Debt Destroy the Global Economy* (2015).

Hudson Bubble Model: I describe how bubbles evolve from the **asset-price inflation** stage to **debt deflation** later in this book. For the basic concepts see **Bubble, Compound Interest** and **Economic Forecasting**.

Hubris: A Greek term meaning overgrowth or proliferation, an addiction to power and wealth, typically involving abusive behavior toward others, above all by creditors against debtors. (See **Affluenza, Greed** and **Wealth Addiction**.)

In Greek drama, acting arrogantly toward others was to be punished by Nemesis, the goddess of justice, who represented the oppressed and their spirit of equality. Corporate scandals sent Ivan Boesky and Michael Milken at Drexel-Burnham, Bernard Ebbers at WorldCom, and Enron executives to jail for the personal greed that caused injury to their victims.

Hyperinflation: Nearly all hyperinflations have stemmed from trying to pay foreign-currency debts far beyond an economy's ability to earn enough foreign exchange by exporting (see **Balance of Payments**). (An exception is the case invoked by today's budget-deficit scaremongers: Zimbabwe's practice of simply printing domestic money without taxing it back.)

John Stuart Mill explained in 1844 how paying foreign debt service (or military spending as occurred during Britain's Napoleonic Wars) depreciates the currency. This makes imports more expensive and increases the debt burden as measured in gold or "hard currencies" against domestic currency.

After World War I, Germany was obliged to pay reparations beyond its ability to export. The Reichsbank simply printed marks to sell on foreign exchange markets to obtain the dollars, sterling and other currencies needed to pay the Allies. The plunging exchange rate that ensued raised the price of imports, and hence domestic price levels.

This phenomenon later became a chronic condition for Third World debtors, most notoriously in the hyperinflations of Chile and Argentina to pay for their trade deficits and ensuing foreign debt treadmill. The resulting currency depreciation invariably involves paying extractive foreign debt, not spending public money for domestic social programs or to increase employment. (See **Implanted Memory and Inflation**.)

Hyperinflation can be stopped by new borrowing (as in the case of U.S. loans to German municipalities in the 1920s and Third World bond-buying in the 1970s), but the cure ultimately requires a Clean Slate to write down debts that exceed an economy's ability to pay. That is what occurred in 1931 with the moratorium on German reparations and inter-ally debts, and again with Argentina's default in 2002 and subsequent debt write-downs.

Hypocognizant: A term coined by the American linguist George Lakoff to describe how a lack of vocabulary leads to the inability to think in a critical way about history, current events, or problems in general. Vocabulary-poor groups can be manipulated to believe (and vote for) what is not in their best interests. The term "hypocognizant democracy" describes today's lack of popular understanding of political and economic problems. This prevents them from being worked out thoughtfully and rationally. Avoiding the relevant terms and concepts enables neoliberalized economies to sidetrack populations that consider themselves "free" and detour them onto the road to serfdom and debt peonage, believing that this is how a "free market" naturally works (see **Blame the Victim)**.

ENDNOTES

[1] Richard J. Arnott and Joseph E. Stiglitz, "Aggregate Land Rents, Expenditure on Public Goods, and Optimal City Size," *Quarterly Journal of Economics* **93** (November 1979), pp. 471–500.

[2] Fred Harrison, *Ricardo's Law* (London: 2006), p. 83.

[3] Thorstein Veblen, *Absentee Ownership and Business Enterprise in Recent Times* (1923), pp. 142ff.

is for
Inner Contradiction and
Invisible Hand

Ideology: A moral perspective on how the world works, with a set of values promoting either acceptance or rejection and reform of how society is organized and what is fair.

As sponsored by the vested interests, the mainstream ideological frame of reference is defensive of the status quo. Its beneficiaries tend to view society as limited to "the market," defined as the existing pattern of supply and demand, asset ownership and debt relationships. The intent is to create a mindset in which debtors and labor will feel responsible for their economic condition (see **Blame the Victim**) and see their powerlessness as the result of natural law. The existing order is depicted as a product of natural selection, and hence is the best of all possible worlds. Conversely, this ideology characterizes public regulation to make economies more equitable as inefficient and hence burdensome, and even as the road to serfdom.

"Free market" ideology (an example of what Antonio Gramsci called cultural hegemony) depicts the One Percent as earning their economic rent and "capital" gains by creating jobs and promoting the well-being of their employees and customers (the 99 Percent). Predatory activities are treated as anomalies to the customary pretense that most fortunes are made by adding to social well-being, not exploitation, insider dealing and fraud. **Neoliberal** trickle-down economists portray the One Percent as investing profits in new tangible capital formation to raise productivity and output. The policy conclusion is to untax and deregulate the wealthy, on the assumption (not empirically verified) that they will use their income and wealth to raise output and living standards.

Individualists go so far as to argue that there is no such thing as society (see **Margaret Thatcher** and **Clash of Civilizations**). The inference is that the 99 Percent deserve no support from government, but must pay out of pocket for consumer safety protection, public education and health care, and indeed for most infrastructure. Checks and balances to regulate the potentially predatory activities of the One Percent are accused of adding to economic overhead and hence to the prices that consumers must pay, not as preventing monopoly prices and rent extraction.

Socialist ideology opposes these dynamics by advocating more productive, sustainable and fair economic relations. This requires demonstrating how ideology tends to reflect class interests. Unrealistic assumptions and tunnel vision rarely gain widespread popularity without sponsorship. Some interest group is almost always eager to elaborate economic error as a self-serving deception. Lobbyists for these special interests recruit useful **idiot savants** to provide a rationale for deceptive economic logic – trickle-down economics, free trade and free capital movements (*i.e.*, capital flight), austerity, balanced budgets or surpluses – as if society at large benefits instead of high finance and monopolists.

Idiot Savant: A "learned idiot" with a quick mind but not much worldly judgment. Many tunnel-visioned individuals are adept at mathematics or abstract logic, but lack grounding in what to be smart *about*. (See **Learned Ignorance**.)

Client academics are the proverbial "useful idiots" defending the status quo, as if any economy is in natural market equilibrium, with its inequality being an act of nature, not the result of bad policy or debt deflation. Many of the economists most applauded by the **vested interests** speculate by *a priori* axioms about a world that *might* hypothetically exist, but lacks reference to current reality or history. They depict the status quo as a naturally fair and equitable product of the struggle for existence, implying that we live in the best (or at least the most inevitable) of all possible worlds. (See **Austrian School, Chicago School** and **Neoliberal**.)

Ignorance: Socrates argued that the ultimate source of evil was ignorance, because nobody knowingly commits evil. But the financial and property sector willingly acts (often with violence) to pursue its own narrow interests, destroying the social organism as collateral damage in its greed. (See **Affluenza**.) Promoting ignorance as a means of disabling popular opposition to financial interests and monopolists is the essence of evil. Predatory corporate practice has become a combination of the

Ken Lay "Enron" defense of executive ignorance (Lay claimed that he didn't know what was going on) and the Nuremburg defense by subordinates ("We were only following orders").[1]

Such assertions of ignorance (see **Denial**) almost always are lies, as when individuals who are accused in court answer every incriminating question with, "I do not recall." The reality is that chief executives are paid millions of dollars in salaries and tens of millions of dollars in bonuses and stock options precisely to know what is going on. Yet when fraud is discovered, they pretend that they were fooled by scheming subordinates. (See **Client Academic, Idiot Savant** and **Learned Ignorance**.) Their companies pay the civil fines while the executives are allowed to keep their accumulated takings – bonuses and stock options.

IMF Riots: A popular response to the **austerity** programs imposed by the International Monetary Fund. Democratic opposition arises not only against the ensuing economic and fiscal collapse, but by World Bank and Washington Consensus demands for privatization sell-offs to pay foreign bondholders. A recent examples is the summer 2015 demonstrations in Greece against the European Central Bank/IMF austerity and privatization program.

The rioters were protesting the junk economics underlying these programs. The IMF pretends that austerity will enable economies to pay – if only labor's wages and pensions are cut enough. This monetarist fallacy has been disproven ever since the German reparations crisis of the 1920s. The pretended "stabilization program" only locks debtor economies further into dependency on foreign finance capital, intensifying their internal **class struggle** and immiseration. The "riots" are thus the only democratic outlet for populations to oppose the **client oligarchies** imposing the austerity programs.

Immiseration: Economic impoverishment to benefit an **oligarchy**. "Progress" under a regime of **trickle-down economics** breeds deepening poverty, most recently by a regressive **tax shift** onto labor and consumer spending (via a Value Added Tax or flat tax) and privatization. (See **Asset Stripping, Chicago School, Class Struggle, Colonialism, Debt Peonage, Dismal Science, Dystopia, End of History, Forced Saving, Greed, Neo-Serfdom, Privilege** and **Race to the Bottom**.)

Impatience: The **Austrian School's "blame the victim"** excuse for why economies become so debt-ridden as they polarize between creditors and debtors. According to Eugen von Böhm-Bawerk, the reason why so many people are poor and so deeply in debt is that they choose to consume *now* (impatiently) instead of deferring consumption by saving and earning interest to get rich enough to consume more later.

Böhm-Bawerk's explanation is framed on the purely personal level between individual savers and borrowers. He claimed that the only reason wage-earners take on debt is that they are impatient to consume in the present. This does not take into account the social and financial dynamics that drive populations into debt in order to survive with the basic necessities. In this Austrian view, paying debt service, taxes, rent or housing expenses, to get an education and meet medical emergencies or other basic needs seems to be a matter of **choice** and "impatience." This is very difficult for people who will starve if they don't eat now.

Savers and creditors are deemed to deserve interest by being more patient, not because of inheriting fortunes, special privileges or predatory rent seeking. The Austrians described the rate of interest as being set by what consumers who chose to live in the short run and business owners were willing to pay "patient" individuals who choose to forego current consumption in order to obtain more later. (See **Junk Economics**.) There is no acknowledgement that banks have the privilege of money creation, and simply create credit to lend out "by a stroke of the pen" *without* requiring prior saving by "patient" individuals.

The reality is that the lower income brackets, driven most deeply into debt at the most extortionate interest rates (payday loans and credit-card debt), tend to be the *most* patient, simply to survive. Labor unions defer current income by negotiating lower wage gains in the present in exchange for pensions to be paid upon retirement. The major hope for advancement of one's family members is to take out student loans to obtain a good education. The way to enter the middle class is to take out a mortgage loan that absorbs the largest share of one's income for the entirety of one's working life.

These financial arrangements are not the result of impatience. The foresight of such individuals, even as a class, leaves them little alternative except to run into debt. That has become the financial price to be paid for pursuing one's livelihood, raising a family and trying to rise into the middle class by buying a home on credit.

It is the wealthy, and above all bankers and financial managers (see **FIRE Sector**, *Rentiers* and **Affluenza**) who are most impatient (see **Greed**). That is the problem with financial management. Its scope is short-term. Financial managers spend corporate cash flow increasingly on stock buybacks and higher dividend payouts to create spurts in their stock price, and hence on their bonuses. Bankers for their part do not lend for the future to create new means of production, but create credit against collateral in place: real estate (mortgage credit), companies (debt-leveraged buyout loans to financial raiders) or lend against firmly established income streams. Banks and bondholders thus seek to avoid the "patience" and risk that the Austrians cite to justify interest charges.

Upon gaining control of government, financial planners run the economy as an asset-stripping exercise. Financiers then cut and run, leaving debt-ridden husks in their wake. This behavior (indeed, strategy) enables financial managers to threaten to wipe out pension benefits promised to employees – who were patient enough to take deferred income security – by declaring bankruptcy unless labor agrees to replace these contractual promises with "defined contribution plans." In the latter, all that contributors know is how much is docked from their paychecks to turn over to Wall Street money managers.

The end of this financial short-termism is a convulsion of corporate bankruptcy, not long-term growth. On the economy-wide level this leaves debt-ridden workers and consumers unable to buy what they produce (see **Debt Deflation**). This mindset is a result of impatience and greed, siphoning off wealth in extractive ways that polarize economies, not help them invest and grow.

Imperialism: The first and most brutal form of imperialism was military conquest. The object was to seize land and natural resources. The next step was to tax the population and extract land rent, turning the conquered territory into a colony, raising money to pay by producing exports desired at home – especially raw materials. Britain's colonial system is the classic example. It aimed to achieve imperial self-sufficiency in raw materials and money, while making colonies and other countries dependent on the resources it provided.

But empire building costs money, and colonialism implies war. Wars drain gold, and force mother-country governments into debt to bondholders – who traditionally have sought to convert their loans into monopoly privileges. Britain created the East India Company and other monopolies to sell to Dutch investors and other holders of their gilt Exchequer bonds. So colonialism's military overhead ends up making imperial countries financially dependent on a global cosmopolitan class.

Modern imperialism is largely financial. Armies are no longer needed to appropriate foreign real estate, natural resources or public infrastructure. Financial dependency makes debtor countries subject to IMF and World Bank "conditionalities" imposing austerity that forces them to pay creditors by selling off their public domain.[2] This transfers assets to the United States and other creditor powers, while avoiding overt colonialism's expensive military overhead.

U.S. diplomats seek to consolidate American financial power by sharing gains with local client oligarchies that remain in the dollarized financial system and adopt neoliberal Washington Consensus policies. Pinochet-style "regime change" is mounted against countries that try to protect their political and financial independence by creating or joining rival currency blocs and banking systems (*e.g.,*

Libya and Syria). But like militarized colonialism, monetary imperialism tends to overplay its hand. When U.S. strategists imposed trade and financial sanctions against Russia and Iran to block their steps toward monetary autonomy, the effect was to drive them together with China and other BRICS countries to break free by creating their own trading and currency clearing area. (See **Independence**.)

Implanted Memory: A false memory of the past, a **factoid** implanted to manipulate public opinion. Germans are told that their hyperinflation of the 1920s resulted from their central bank's money creation to finance budget deficits, as if this resulted from domestic spending rather than paying the reparations that collapsed the currency. Germany's post-1948 Economic Miracle is attributed to free market policies, not to the Clean Slate that cancelled domestic debts or the 1953 writedown of its foreign debt. Historical reality is replaced with a false fiscal and financial mythology popularized by "hard money" creditor interests.

Increasing Returns: Increasing returns normally characterize economies as production costs decline in agriculture, industry and services. By the late 19th century it seemed that rising productivity would usher in what Simon Patten called an Economy of Abundance. What such expectations left out of account was that the exponential growth of compound interest (and hence, society's debt overhead) tends to outstrip productivity growth, forcing the real economy to taper off in an S-curve. (See **Business Cycles** and **Economic Forecasting**.) Such incompatibility between financial and economic trends results in mathematically indeterminate solutions. Economists shy away from such problems on the ground that any solution must be political from "outside the system," and hence seems less "scientific" than Dismal Science approaches that give wrong answers to the decimal place.

Independence: Under colonialism, mother countries took responsibility for the military defense and basic support of their colonies. Granting colonies nominal political independence provided an opportunity for imperial powers to shed their fiduciary responsibility. This enabled the former mother countries to rule via client oligarchies while making former colonies debt-dependent. Haiti, for instance, was obliged to pay reparations to France for its independence. The former American colonies remained dependent under British free-trade imperialism and British banking. And ever since Greece achieved independence in 1832, the country has remained debt-strapped.

Since World War II, nominal political independence has been overridden by the IMF and World Bank to apply globalized creditor leverage. (See **Austerity**.) By

2015 this had developed to the point where German financial officials could tell the Greek finance minister that the election supporting anti-austerity simply did not matter. The financial troika of the IMF, European Central Bank and European Union would set Greek austerity policy regardless of democratic choice. The alternative, Greece was warned, would be economic chaos – something like closing the ATM machines for consumers, but on a national scale. (I devote three chapters to Greece in *Killing The Host*.)

Individualism: An anti-government ideology that rationalizes the right of creditors and other wealthy individuals to deprive consumers, debtors and renters of economic choice and liberty. Like marginalism, economic individualism idealizes an economy free of government and isolated from society. (See **Austrian School**, **Junk Economics** and **Margaret Thatcher**.) This ideology is based on a view of economies "as if" they consist only of rational, moral and ethical individuals seeking to maximize their consumption ("utility") by working ("disutility") and saving, with no unearned income or inherited wealth.

Debt is viewed as a contract between consumers paying for being enabled to consume now rather than later (see **Impatience**), or businessmen seeking to make a **profit**, without taking note of the rising debt overhead accruing from one cycle or generation to the next. (See **Neoliberalism** and *Rentier*.) Public regulation of fair pricing to reflect the actual costs of production is mischaracterized as being deadweight overhead, along with taxes and even infrastructure investment. Government borrowing appears to produce no economic return in this accounting format.

Inflation: The word "inflation" refers to consumer or wholesale prices, and implicitly to wage gains. Price inflation for stocks, bonds or real estate assets is euphemized as "appreciation," or even more confusingly, "wealth creation" instead of debt-leveraged asset-price inflation raising the cost of buying a home, education or the stocks and bonds whose dividends and interest provide pension payments for retirees.

As a cover story for reducing wages, central banks claim that monetary austerity – cutbacks in public spending and high interest rates to deter new industrial investment and hiring – will save consumers from inflation and restore budget surpluses. The reality is that higher interest rates are factored into prices. So "fighting inflation" with austerity is counter-effective. Its effect is to shrink markets. (See **Inner Contradiction**.) The economy is sacrificed to increase the power of financial wealth and the One Percent over labor. That result actually is the objective of monetarist junk economics.

Inner Contradiction: A principle emphasized by Karl Marx, emphasizing how actions and policies in one direction create antitheses leading to a new synthesis (which is not necessarily knowable in advance). For instance, debt-leveraged asset-price inflation sets dynamics in motion that lead to debt deflation. The principle of security for private property is used to promote the sanctity of debt claims, leading to bankruptcy, financial foreclosure and hence expropriation leading ultimately either to revolution or stagnation. (See **Law of Unintended Consequences.**)

Innocent Fraud: A term coined by John Kenneth Galbraith in *The Economics of Innocent Fraud: Truth for Our Time* (2004) as a polite way of pointing to the leading misconceptions that politicians use to distract people from understanding who gains or loses from the way today's economies are organized. Warren Mosler's *Seven Deadly Innocent Frauds of Economic Policy* (2010) points out that most such intellectual frauds are self-interested, not innocent. The financial class depicts its credit creation as invariably productive and useful, while government or central bank money creation is said to be the first step toward Zimbabwe-style hyperinflation if governments do not "live within their means." They are told to tax their population and borrow from foreign or domestic bondholders instead of monetizing their budget deficits (see **Modern Monetary Theory**). Such fraud is never really innocent, but is at best sanctimonious by depicting itself to be all in the public interest.

Insanity: Following the same policy repeatedly, believing or hoping that next time the outcome will be different. In economics, pursuing austerity programs in the belief that they will provide more tax revenue and growth out of debt, despite the reality of widening budget deficits and shrinking economies leading to yet more debt defaults.

While victims of neoliberalism and the Washington Consensus thus suffer from repetition compulsion, the authors of austerity – bondholders and the One Percent – are not really insane, unless we count greed and affluenza as forms of insanity. They simply have wrapped their self-serving austerity doctrine in a persuasive propaganda imagery of "as if" junk economics.

Institutionalism: A primarily American school of economics that studies **property**, **financial** and legal relationships, especially regarding **rent-seeking privileges.** (See **Vested Interests**.) Major institutionalists were **Thorstein Veblen** and the discipline of sociology encouraged by German-trained economists such as **Simon Patten**.

Production technology tends to be common to most economies at any given point in time, but the ability to charge prices in excess of cost-value is social and political in character. Nations evolve in different ways, and **economic rents** account for most wealth and who owes debts to whom.

Despite the fact that the success or failure of economies depends mainly on their institutional structure, *rentier* advocates exclude the study of rent-seeking and the study of property and finance from the sphere of "pure" economics. Neoliberal logic argues that institutionalism is devoid of theoretical content because it does not deal with universals. Being regulated by society, such institutions are political, not "natural." Hence the institutions of economic rent and monopoly privileges are deemed not to be part of **"the market."** This tunnel vision limits the scope of "scientific" economics to markets as they would exist in a "pure" system in which unearned income, exploitation, governments and social policy make no appearance. The argument against institutionalism is thus basically against classical political economy.

Insurance, Insurers: See **FIRE Sector**.

Interest: Antiquity had no word to distinguish interest from **usury**. Medieval Churchmen drew that distinction in order to contrast commercially productive loans and foreign currency transfers with usury. Their logic was that commercial creditors shared in the risk ("interest") of profit-making business ventures. In such cases interest was supposed to cover the creditor's cost of doing business, plus compensation for risk. Recognizing this distinction provided church-approved credit to finance foreign trade and currency transfers (see **Agio**).

What legitimized the charging of interest most of all was borrowing at the top of the social pyramid, by the nobility to finance their treks on Crusades, and kings to pay Peter's Pence to the papacy and to wage the wars it sanctified – and in time wars of colonial conquest.

The ancient term usury has become largely vestigial, and is now limited to interest charges *in excess of the legal maximum*. This upper limit has been raised steadily over time, and by the 1980s usury limits were removed altogether after interest rates peaked at 20%.

Interest, compound: See **Compound Interest**.

Interest, mortgage: Mortgages account for 70% to 80% of bank loans, and hence for most interest charges in the U.S. economy. Debt service on this lending absorbs most of the land's site rent and otherwise taxable profits for commercial real estate, leaving only the property tax available for the tax collector. In the United States and many other countries, that tax is only 1% or less – far below the amount of interest that is paid on the property.

To avoid paying income tax (thus leaving more rental income available to pay bankers as interest), absentee real estate owners are allowed to claim "book losses" by pretending that their buildings depreciate and hence lose value (see **Over-depreciation**). Real estate investors can use this fictitious loss to offset income taxes on revenue from their other operations. Coupled with the tax-deductibility of mortgage interest, these special loopholes push the tax burden onto labor via higher sales taxes and income taxes.

Investment: Only a part of what colloquially is called "investment" represents tangible capital formation in the means of production to produce industrial profit (see **Industrial Capitalism**). Most investment aims at *rentier* income and "capital" gains on stocks and bonds, whose dividends and interest payments derive from extracting economic rent from real estate to natural resources, licensed monopolies and patents.

The word "investment" also means occupation by an enemy force. This occurs when finance capitalists occupy the industrial sector and government. Tangible capital formation appears on the asset side of the corporate and overall economic balance sheet, while debts, stocks and bonds appear on the liabilities side. Frederick Soddy called such financial claims and other *rentier* overhead "virtual wealth."

Investor: The trickle-down self-image of investors is that they create means of production. But a rising number are *rentiers* buying tollbooth rights and patents in order to charge **economic rents** for access to the *preconditions* for production: land, water, raw materials and energy, proprietary technology, patents and access to credit. This proliferation of rent seeking and capital gains motivation for "investment" does not make economies more prosperous; it creates a rent-wracked economy. It thus is a travesty for investors controlling such choke points to euphemize this phenomenon as "wealth creation."

Invisible Hand: The term dates back to Adam Smith's *Theory of Moral Sentiments* (1759) postulating that the world is organized in a way that leads individuals to increase overall prosperity by seeking their own self-interest. But by the time he wrote *The Wealth of Nations* in 1776, he described hereditary land ownership, monopolies and kindred rent seeking as being incompatible with such balance. He pointed to another kind of invisible hand (without naming it as such): insider dealing and conspiracy against the commonweal occurs when businessmen get together and conspire against the public good by seeking monopoly power. Today they get together to extract favors, privatization giveaways and special subsidies from government.

Special interests usually work most effectively when unseen, so we are brought back to the quip from the poet Baudelaire: "The devil wins at the point he convinces people that he doesn't exist." This is especially true of the financial reins of control. Financial wealth long was called "invisible," in contrast to "visible" landed property. Operating on the principle that what is not seen will not be taxed or regulated, real estate interests have blocked government attempts to collect and publish statistics on property values. Britain has not conducted a land census since 1872. Landlords "reaping where they have not sown" have sought to make their rent seeking invisible to economic statisticians. Mainstream orthodoxy averts its eyes from land, and also from monopolies, conflating them with "capital" in general, despite the fact that their income takes the form of (unearned) rent rather than profit as generally understood.

Having wrapped a cloak of invisibility around rent extraction as the favored vehicle for debt creation and what passes for investment, the Chicago School promotes "rational markets" theory, **as if** market prices (their version of Adam Smith's theological Deism) reflect true intrinsic value at any moment of time – assuming no deception, parasitism or fraud such as characterize today's largest economic spheres (see **FIRE Sector**).

"It's not what you make, it's what you net": Nominal after-tax wages are termed **disposable personal income (DPI)** in official statistics, but this measure does not really leave wage earners with much to spend on goods and services after paying their monthly "nut" for housing, debt service, public utilities, transportation, and compulsory health care or pension plan contributions. By far the largest portion of wage income is passed on to the FIRE sector, not being freely available for discretionary spending. (See "Hudson Economic Model" later in this book.)

ENDNOTES

[1] Bill Black, "The High Price of Ignorance," *Naked Capitalism*, November 7, 2011. http://www.nakedcapitalism.com/2011/11/bill-black-the-high-price-of-ignorance.html.

[2] I describe the dynamics of this financial empire building in *Super Imperialism: The Economic Strategy of American Empire*, and my essays in *The Bubble and Beyond*.

is for
Junk Bonds,
Junk Economics and
Junk Mortgages

Jubilee Year: In Judaic Law (Leviticus 25) a **Clean Slate** to be proclaimed every 50 years to annul personal and agrarian debts, liberating bondservants to rejoin their families, and returning lands or crop rights to debtors who had forfeited them to creditors or sold them under duress. (Nothing was said about commercial "silver" debts owed by merchants trading abroad or at home.) Long accused of being merely a utopian ideal, the policy has now been traced back to royal proclamations issued and legally enforced as a normal and regular event in Sumer and Babylonia in the third and second millennia BC.[1] (See **Liberty Bell**.)

The Hebrew word used was *deror*, cognate to Babylonia's royal *andurarum* proclamations that annulled personal debts and payments owed to royal collectors for fees and taxes. The aim was to restore economic balance and personal solvency. Debt bondage was supposed to be only temporary, and bondservants were released when rulers decreed Clean Slates that annulled the backlog of debts.

The obvious reason for avoiding such destruction was that survival depended largely on the size of the free population. Depriving the citizenry of land and liberty would destroy the ability to field a citizen army. Classical Judah and Rome liberated debt servants and even slaves in times of military attack so that they could fight to defend their communities.

The Jubilee year was introduced from Babylonia after the Jews returned from exile and codified their Bible. No economic records survived from the ensuing centuries. Jesus's adversary, Rabbi Hillel, introduced the *prosbul* clause by which debtors waived their right to the Jubilee Year. It was against this Pharisee circumvention of the Jubilee Year that Jesus delivered his first sermon (Luke 4) announcing that he had come to proclaim the Jubilee "Year of our Lord." (I describe this and its Near Eastern background in *The Lost Tradition: From Pre-Biblical Debt Cancellations to the Jubilee Year* (forthcoming in 2017.)

Junk Bonds: High-interest bonds whose issue was escalated in the 1980s primarily by Michael Milken at Drexel Burnham, most notoriously to finance corporate raiders, mergers and subprime borrowers. The damage caused to other buyers of such bonds included widespread bankruptcies of savings-and-loan associations (S&Ls). Mr. Milken was sent to jail for securities fraud along with his client Ivan Boesky, and Drexel was disbanded as a result of its insider trading scandals linked to debt takeovers.

The fiscal ruling that makes junk bonds so remunerative – and increased debt leverage so fiscally disastrous – is that interest-payments are tax-exempt, in contrast to dividends paid to stockholders *after* paying corporate income tax. At the 50% income-tax rate typical in the 1980s, companies could pay twice as much of their pre-tax income as interest to bondholders than they could pay as dividends to stockholders. So by replacing equity (stocks) with bonds and bank debt, the financial sector gained at the expense of the tax collector. This contributed to the sharp rise in U.S. public debt in the 1980s.

Another destructive effect of junk bonds is that bondholders often are paid by downsizing the labor force, outsourcing it, breaking up companies and selling their parts off piecemeal. This has turned the junk-bonding of American industry into a smash-and-grab exercise. Companies whose cash-rich position and low debt make them prospective targets are obliged to avoid being raided by resorting to poison pills, loading themselves down with so much debt (or initiating their own mergers and acquisitions or buying up their own stock) to make it uneconomic for raiders to borrow to take them over, because no uncommitted cash flow is left to strip away.

Junk Economics: A public-relations exercise promoted by **vested interests** to depict their behavior in a positive light instead of as exploitative zero-sum rent seeking. (See **Neoliberal** and **Neoclassical Economics**, **Monetarism**, **Parasitism** and **Washington Consensus**.) Junk economics is a kind of **"as if"** science fiction with assumptions appropriate to a utopian parallel universe in which *rentiers* are the heroes. Much as a good novel or play must have characters that act consistently, the criterion of this economic pseudo-science is merely the internal consistency of its assumptions, not worldly realism. Many of the most applauded economists reason logically by *a priori* axioms about a world that might hypothetically exist. (See my essay *Economics as Fraud* later in this book.)

The trickle-down strategy of financial populism is to convince the public that the economy's bottom 99 Percent are best served by pursuing policies that favor the top One Percent. This requires erasing the classical concept of rent distinguishing between productive and predatory activity. (See **TINSTAAFL**.)

Free-market economics such as the **Chicago School's** "rational market" theory, **Laffer Curve** and **marginalism** ignore the long run to focus on the short run, and ignore the large economic picture to focus on the individual. Debt is treated as a contract by impatient consumers to pay for being able to consume now rather than later, or by businessmen seeking to make a profit by borrowing for a long-term capital investment. This frame of reference has no room to analyze the rising overall volume of debt passed on from one business upswing or generation to the next as banks create new credit/debt. (See **Business Cycle** and **Economic Forecasting**.)

Public infrastructure spending also plays no role, so government borrowing appears simply as a tax without an economic return – a deadweight overhead. Government spending is assumed only to increase consumer prices, not increase employment or lower the cost of infrastructure services to businesses and families. "Sound money" is supposed to be only created by banks, not governments. The aim of such assumptions is to capture monetary policy and mainstream economic thought, weaponizing it for class warfare purposes.

When persistent error achieves broad success, one always finds a special interest behind it. (See **Idiot Savant**, **Neoliberal** and **Neoclassical Economics**, **Monetarism**, **Parasitism** and **Washington Consensus**.) On the broadest level, Karl Marx observed: "Scientific bourgeois economics … was no longer a question of whether this or that theorem was true, but whether it was useful to capital or harmful, expedient or inexpedient … In place of the disinterested inquirers there stepped hired prize fighters; in place of genuine scientific research, the bad conscience and evil intent of the apologetic."[2]

Just Price: Anticipating a line of analysis that would become the **labor theory of value**, Church theologians in the 13th century listed the elements of income that were morally justified. It was deemed moral for bankers and merchants to earn enough to support their families in the normal style appropriate to their status, but not to charge such extortionate rates as to live extravagantly. Bankers were allowed to charge *agio* fees to compensate for risks such as non-payment and other loss of their money. The concept of *interest* reflected their shared risk with debtors regarding mutual gain in commercial enterprise, mainly foreign trade and what was, in effect, a mode of shipping insurance. The focus was on the socially necessary costs of providing banking services.

Junk Mortgage: A bank loan to a subprime borrower without regard for the ability to pay (see **NINJA Loans**), typically with "exploding" interest rates that rise sharply after three years. Federal Reserve Chairman Alan Greenspan recommended such loans to consumers on the factoid that the average American family moves every three years, and therefore would be able to sell their homes (making a price gain in the process) before the higher interest rates came into effect.

Homeowners who stayed in place, Chairman Greenspan suggested, could refinance their mortgages by borrowing even more as the real estate bubble continued its seemingly *ad infinitum* upward trajectory. He also assured people that there was no national real estate bubble, only localized problems. To back this falsehood he stifled pressure from within the Federal Reserve Board by Ed Gramlich (a then-governor of the Federal Reserve who died in 2007) to clamp down on rampant junk mortgage fraud.[3] The resulting wave of junk mortgages was the immediate cause bringing down the U.S. and European economies in 2008.

ENDNOTES

[1] See my *Debt and Economic Renewal in the Ancient Near East* (ed. with Marc Van De Mieroop) (CDL Press, Bethesda, 2002).

[2] Marx, "Afterword" to the 2nd German edition of *Capital* (Vol. I, [1873], London, 1954), p. 25.

[3] See *e.g.* Sewell Chan, "Greenspan Criticized for Characterization of Colleague," *The New York Times*, April 10, 2010.
http://www.nytimes.com/2010/04/10/business/10gramlich.html

is for
Kleptocrat

Keynes, John Maynard (1883-1946): In the 1920s, Keynes became the major critic of World War I's legacy of German reparations and Inter-Ally debts. Against the monetarist ideology that prices and incomes in debtor countries would fall by enough to enable them to pay virtually any given level of debt, Keynes explained that there were structural limits to the ability to pay. Accusing Europe's reparations and arms debts of exceeding these limits, Keynes provided the logic for writing down debts. His logic controverted the "hard money" austerity of Jacques Rueff and Bertil Ohlin, who claimed that all debts could be paid by squeezing a tax surplus out of the economy (mainly from labor).

Modern Germany has embraced this right-wing monetarist doctrine. Even in the 1920s, all its major political parties strived to pay the unpayably high foreign debt, bringing about economic and political collapse. The power of "sanctity of debt" morality proved stronger than the logic of Keynes and other economic realists.

In 1936, as the Great Depression spread throughout the world, Keynes's *General Theory of Employment, Interest and Prices* pointed out that **Say's Law** had ceased to operate. Wages and profits were not being spent on new capital formation or employing labor, but were hoarded as savings. Keynes viewed **saving** simply as non-spending on goods and services, not as being used to pay down debts or lent out to increase the economy's debt overhead. (Banks had stopped lending in the 1930s.) He also did not address the tendency for debts to grow exponentially in excess of the economy's ability to carry the debt overhead.

It was left to Irving Fischer to address debt deflation, pointing to how debtors "saved" by paying down debts they had earlier run up. And it was mainly fringe groups such as Technocracy Inc. that emphasized the tendency for debts to grow exponentially in chronic excess of the economy's ability to carry its financial overhead. Emphasis on debt has been left mainly to post-Keynesians, headed by **Hyman Minsky** and his successors such as Steve Keen and **Modern Monetary Theory (MMT),** grounded in Keynes's explanation of money and credit as debt in his *Treatise on Money* (1930).

Kleptocrat: Members of Russian President Boris Yeltsin's "family" and other *biznezmen*, typically Red Directors and Soviet-era officials who appropriated public enterprises and natural resources for themselves after the demise of the Soviet Union in 1991. Advised (or at least abetted) by U.S. **neoliberals**, the Communist Party leadership turned over real estate and and other assets to managers drawn from the Communist youth groups, cooperatives and gangs that created banks to coordinate their operations.

The population was issued "vouchers" convertible into corporate shares on the pretense that this would make them part owners of society's capital. (See **Labor Capitalism**.) But most vouchers were sold to wholesale buyers who registered assets in their own names or those of banks they created. The major giveaway was capped by the 1994-1995 loans-for-shares scam. (See **Privatization** and **Washington Consensus**.) The term "kleptocrat" is now used broadly worldwide as asset grabs are spreading in the wake of foreign debt burdens.

is for
Labor Capitalism and
Learned Ignorance

Labor Capitalism: First popularized by Chile's "free market" dictator Augusto Pinochet (1973-1990), the term was adopted by British Prime Minister Margaret Thatcher as a populist label for her anti-labor privatization policy of selling shares in British Telephone and other large public companies at giveaway prices to consumers to make quick stock-market gains. (Most gains were taken by the big investors and privatization underwriters who issued the stock.)

The aim is to make workers think of themselves as capitalists in miniature, so that they will acquiesce in policies that help the stock market by increasing profits, even when this achieved by policies that are against their interests and that of society at large. Employees and their representatives are not permitted to use their nominal share ownership to vote on management policies, but remain passive investors.

As refined by Pinochet's Chicago Boys, labor capitalism is a perverse variety of pension fund capitalism. Wages are set aside for pension plans to be channeled into the stock market, or into Employee Stock Ownership Plans (ESOPs) for employers to invest in their own stock or lent to their affiliates. (Most Chilean companies simply looted their plans, leaving them bankrupt by the end of the 1970s, claiming that this was all part of the free market.)

Labor's relation to labor capitalism is like that of a lamb to a lamb-chop. It is the exploited party, in ways beyond the Marxian sense of being hired to produce goods for employers to sell at a profit. "Labor capitalism" exploits labor financially, first through debt (mortgage debt, student loan debt, credit-card debt, auto loans, payday loans, etc.); second via compulsory saving to pre-pay for Social Security and medical care as part of the tax shift off profits and rents onto labor and consumers; and third, by using labor's compulsory saving to bid up stock prices for their employers (in ESOPs) or the general stock market (as in pension fund capitalism).

Instead of paying pensions and Social Security out of the overall public budget, retirement income has been financialized. Pensions and 401(k) retirement accounts are to be paid out of **asset-price inflation**, earning returns arbitrarily assumed to be a wildly optimistic 8% or more, so that only a minimum of savings needs to be set aside for old age. The working class is told to think of itself as rising into the **middle class** by saving and investing in the stock market and buying homes on credit to make capital gains. The reality is a predatory money manager capitalism that is squeezing labor's take-home pay and leaving most of the capital gains to insiders. The end game is to be capped by a blame-the-victim rhetoric when workers fail to obtain labor capitalism's promised retirement income.

Since Chile's era of military free-market terrorism ended, subsequent politics have been shaped by popular opposition to the widespread employer theft of ESOPs and the rip-offs by fund managers brought in by the Chicago Boys.

Labor Theory of Value: An analytic tool to isolate the elements of price in excess of intrinsic value, which ultimately is reducible to the cost of labor effort. The non-labor components of prices are headed by rent extraction and financial charges. This non-production overhead has been left mainly to muckrakers to expose and classical economists and institutionalists to analyze. (See **Economic Rent** and **Just Price**.)

Laffer Curve: Originally drawn on a table napkin by Republican advisor Arthur Laffer in 1974, the hypothetical correlation shows an inverse relationship between tax rates and tax revenues. As tax rates are reduced, tax collection is supposed to rise instead of falling – **as if** lower tax rates will give less incentive for tax avoidance and more incentive to invest in production and hire more employees. The logic is that taxes stifle business investment, reduce earnings and hence income-tax payments. The deeper the tax cuts, the more tax revenue is supposed to be collected – seemingly without limit. (See **Junk Economics** and **Reaganomics**.) The actual result in the Reagan-Bush administration (1981-92) was a massive budget deficit and a quadrupling of U.S. public debt.

Laissez Faire: Coined by the French Physiocrats, *Laissez faire* meant "let us be," free from the royal taxes shifted onto labor and industry. The Physiocratic alternative was the Single Tax (*L'Impôt Unique*) falling on the land held by France's hereditary aristocracy and royal family. Adam Smith advocated such a tax on Britain's (absentee) landlords, and subsequent economists extended it to include *rentier* income in general.

Today's right-wing **libertarians** have reversed this original idea of *laissez faire* to mean freeing the *rentier* class *from* taxes. This shifts the fiscal burden onto labor and consumers – the reverse of what the Physiocrats, Adam Smith and other classical economists meant. Libertarian anthropologists draw pictures of a mythical age in which no public sector existed with no palace or temples to regulate economies and levy taxes or fees for basic public services. Such junk archaeology about a "natural" or "primordial" society provides a faux-historical rationalization for junk economics.

Land: Physically, an area of soil or urban site. But ownership of land rights to its crop surplus or other rental yield is a social construct, not a function of nature. Economically, land is a property right (see **Privilege**).

Such rights originated in a communalist context in the Neolithic when land was the primordial source of subsistence. It was the source of the community's surplus labor, initially corvée labor supplied by citizens. Land tenure rights were granted to clan groupings in exchange for labor service on public works and for serving in the army.[1] Land rights were defined by this labor obligation reflecting estimated crop yield or, in time, monetary tax-paying ability.

Down to the eve of the modern era, landholding was a precondition for citizenship. Archaic land tenure initially was kept within clans, and was transferred only with difficulty. After about 2000 BC in Babylonia, debt foreclosure became the main means of "free" land acquisition. To do this, creditors had to be adopted into the debtor's family in order to obtain land upon the debtor's death in accordance with custom. But the new "outsider" owners (creditors) sought to shift responsibility for the land's corvée tax onto the former heirs-become-renters.

In today's economies, land is a vehicle for property claims to a site or natural resource (including subsoil mineral rights). In agriculture the site consists of the soil. In most real estate, "land" is the location's area and zoning rights, which play a role similar to that which fertility plays in determining the rent and market price of agricultural land. (See **Rent of Location**.) By extension, the concept of land may extend to water and even air rights as these become bought and sold, creating legal chokepoints to access, enabling rent extractors to put tollbooths in place. (See **Privatization**, **Rent** and **Rent Theory**.)

Land ownership and its rent today is no longer limited to citizens, and is freely transferable. But most buyers require bank loans to obtain it. Land is worth whatever banks will lend against it – and a rising proportion of rental value is absorbed by interest charges, leaving a shrinking portion available to be paid in taxes. The effect of giving special tax breaks to real estate owners reverses the original creation of land tenure to reflect the land's ability to yield taxes (originally paid in corvée labor and crops, and in the obligation of landholders to serve in the army, as noted above). As real estate has been financialized, land rent has passed out of the hands of the public and of landholders, to mortgage lenders.

Landlord: The original term for the land's conquerors. After the Norman Conquest of Britain in 1066, the victors sanctified themselves (and hence their heirs and subsequent owners) as lords of the land. Initially they owed its yield to the king in the form of military and fiscal obligations. After the Revolt of the Barons in the 13th century, the landed aristocracy privatized the land for themselves, and levied groundrent on its occupants and users.

The term "landlord" now refers to real estate owners in general, of whom Adam Smith said: "Landlords love to reap where they have not sown." But since land has became freely marketable, its rent is paid to the mortgage bankers instead of to the tax collector, capitalizing (financializing) the rental income that has been "freed" from taxes into mortgage interest payments. The more taxes are cut, the more rental income is available to pay mortgage interest. In effect, receipt of land rent has passed from the public sector to hereditary landed aristocracies to mortgage bankers. (See **Economic Rent.**)

Land Rent contrasted to Monopoly Rent: See **Monopoly Rent contrasted to Land Rent**.

Land Value Tax (LVT, AKA Land Valuation Tax): A means of keeping down mortgage debt (and hence, housing prices), by taxing the rental valuation of land, so that it will not be available to be pledged as interest payments to banks for mortgage loans. (See **Groundrent**, **Rent** and **Rent Theory**.) To classical economists, land is provided by nature and hence has no cost of production and hence no value as such (see **Factors of Production**). But it does have a market price, reflecting mainly rent of location, largely from civic improvements (see **Commons** and **Public Domain**), and the willingness of banks to lend against it.

The higher the yearly tax charge is, the lower the land price becomes, because less income is available to be capitalized (financialized) into a bank loan and paid as mortgage debt service. (See Myth #15 and #16 in "The 22 Most Pervasive Economic Myths of Our Time" later in this book.) A Land Valuation Tax thus acts as a counterweight to mortgage debt – which is why banks oppose property taxes, realizing that what is not paid to the tax collector can be paid to themselves as interest. (See **Henry George Theorem** and the contrast between a **Single Tax** and a **Flat Tax**.)

Law of Unintended Consequences: The solution to every problem tends to create new and unanticipated problems, whose magnitude frequently exceeds that of the original problem. (See **Inner Contradiction**.) However, the adverse consequences of many seeming failures, especially debt bubbles and IMF austerity programs, are indeed intended, although public relations handouts to the press assure the public that "nobody could have foreseen" how bad these consequences would be. When special interests gain and the economy suffers, the perpetrators always claim innocence (see **Innocent Fraud**), on the ground that the austerity and breakdown were unintended. But the emergency bailouts to the One Percent and emergency privatization sell-offs demanded by IMF conditionalities are indeed put in place well in advance! The "unintended" consequences are rarely innocent, although **idiot savants** may be trotted out from the ranks of mainstream economists to provide a cover story.

Learned Ignorance: A term coined by the medieval philosopher Erasmus to describe unworldly or gullible book knowledge. In his 1672 play in *Les Femmes Savants*, Moliere quipped: "A learned fool is more foolish than an ignorant one." **Thorstein Veblen's** *Higher Education in America* (1918) called the tunnel-visioned logic that was coming to plague post-classical economics as "trained incapacity": the condition of being trained not to recognize the important **causal** factors at work. (See **Education** and **Idiot Savant**.)

"Educated incapacity often refers to an acquired or learned inability to understand or even perceive a problem, much less a solution," Herman Kahn elaborates. Veblen "used it to refer, among other things, to the inability of those with engineering or sociology training to understand certain issues which they would have been able to understand if they had not had this training."[2] The phenomenon occurs especially "at leading universities in the United States – particularly in the departments of psychology, sociology, and history, and to a degree in the humanities generally. Individuals raised in this milieu often have difficulty with relatively simple degrees of reality testing."

A precondition for high administrative public position is *not* to understand how the financial and debt creation system works. (See **Nobel Prize.**) The problem is greatest in neoclassical, monetarist and neoliberal economics, which train observers to overlook the most important and also most disruptive dynamics: financial and property relationships.

Liberal: From Latin *liber*, meaning "free." Originally an advocate of free trade or *laissez faire* (loosely, "leave us alone") from government regulation. Britain's Liberal Party urged taxation of groundrent to free the economy from its post-feudal landlord class. The aim was to create a classical free market economy, although it left a *rentier* overhead paid to banking and financial interests and monopolies.

As governments were democratized, especially in the United States, liberals came to endorse welfare spending on behalf of the poor and disadvantaged, and government intervention in general to provide basic infrastructure so that it would not be monopolized in private hands. This led the term "liberal" to be associated with big government programs, Pentagon Capitalism and a salvationist military policy abroad. By the 1960s, liberal Vice President Hubert Humphrey aggressively supported the war in Southeast Asia that led to budget deficits and stagflation. By the early 21st century, liberalism came to depict the United States as the world's "indispensable nation," entitled to install neoliberal governments by force under R2P as "Responsibility to Privatize," not its Progressive Era democratic roots.

Liberal Democracy: See **End of History.**

Libertarian: Anti-government advocates of deregulation to disable the public ability to tax and govern finance, real estate and other rent-seeking. The effect is to centralize planning in the hands of the financial sector – Wall Street and its satellites in the City of London, the International Monetary Fund (IMF) and the European Central Bank (ECB). The aim of libertarian planning is privatization, leading to economic polarization, oligarchy, debt peonage and neofeudalism.

What the libertarian (that is, financialization) argument leaves out of account is that taxing land rent and other unearned *rentier* income requires a strong enough government to rein in the vested interests. Opposing government has the effect of blocking such public power. Libertarianism thus serves as a handmaiden to oligarchy as opposed to democracy.

Liberty Bell: America's Liberty Bell is inscribed with a verse from Leviticus 25: "Proclaim liberty throughout all the land, and to the inhabitants thereof." The biblical Hebrew term translated as "liberty" was d'r'r (*deror*). This was a cognate to Babylonian *andurarum*, used by rulers to annul the citizenry's personal and agrarian debts, liberate bondservants and restore self-support lands to citizens who had forfeited them to foreclosing creditors or sold them under duress. The imagery can be traced back to Hammurabi raising the "sacred torch" to signal the royal **Clean Slate** proclamations that evolved into the **Jubilee Year**, which Jesus announced in his first sermon (Luke 4) that he had come to proclaim.

Liquidate: To destroy (by selling). Debtors are obliged to liquidate their assets to pay their creditors. (See **Privatization** for the liquidation of the public domain by indebted governments.) Corporate raiders make a killing by carving up companies and liquidating their assets in corporate breakups.

Liquidity: The amount of credit that banks will extend against a given asset, making it "liquid," meaning saleable. The easier the credit terms, the more credit banks create to capitalize (financialize) an asset's income stream into a flow of interest payments. As the supply of credit mounts up and banks seek new markets, the range of assets that are liquid (that is, bankable) widens, at rising prices.

Liquidity Trap: A term coined by **John Maynard Keynes** to describe how low interest rates may *not* spur new investment in situations where markets are shrinking (which he blamed on over-saving). In 2009-2015 the Federal Reserve found the trap difficult to escape from, because the debt overhead was left in place, shrinking markets. **Quantitative Easing** keeps interest rates low, but fails to stimulate new investment as debt deflation spreads globally. (Japan suffered the same problem after its own bubble crashed in 1990.) Failure to write down debts (see **Debt Forgiveness**) makes it difficult to escape from the liquidity trap.

Lobbyist: Hired by special-interest groups to plead their case for tax favoritism, subsidy and protection by government, lobbyists are the political counterparts to client academics. (See **Idiot Savant** and **Chicago School**.) Their task is to weave a web of economic deception, well described by Adam Smith (*Wealth of Nations*, Book I, Ch. 11):

> The proposal of any new law or regulation of commerce which comes from [business], ought always to be listened to with great precaution, and ought never to be adopted till after having been long and carefully examined, not only with the most scrupulous, but with the most suspicious attention. It comes from an order of men, whose interest is never exactly the same with that of the public, who have generally an interest to deceive and even to oppress the public ...

Locke, John (1632-1704): Developed a labor theory of property, justifying land rent only as a return for the landlord's labor and out-of-pocket costs, not for what nature provides freely. The subsequent Labor Theory of Value isolated land rent as morally unjustified to the extent that it does *not* reflect actual labor costs, and hence is not really *earned* by landlords but belongs to the community. (See **Economic Rent** and **Groundrent**.)

ENDNOTES

[1] I survey the emergence and evolution of land tenure in the Neolithic and Bronze Age in *Labor in the Ancient World* (ed. with Piotr Steinkeller, ISLET, 2015) and *Urbanization and Land Ownership in the Ancient Near East* (ed. with Baruch Levine, Cambridge, Mass: Peabody Museum, Harvard, 1999).

[2] Herman Kahn, "The Expert and Educated Incapacity," *World Economic Development: 1979 and Beyond* (Westview Press, 1979) pp. 482-484.

is for
Marginalism and
Money Manager Capitalism

Makers and Takers: A campaign slogan used by Republicans Mitt Romney and Paul Ryan in the 2012 U.S. Presidential election. The term reverses the thrust of the classical labor theory of value, which describes labor as making commodities, while rent seekers and exploiters are "takers" that do not play a direct role in production but are merely extractive. Republicans turned the tables by describing the One Percent as "makers" (a.k.a. "job creators") and the rest of the population – recipients of Social Security, Medicare and other government support, and users of public services as well as the unemployed seeking work – as "takers." This language reflects the oligarchy's interest in promoting a flat tax and a value-added tax (VAT) on consumers instead of taxing finance and property. The spirit is that of Thomas Robert Malthus, blaming labor for its poverty (see **Blame the Victim**), not exploitation by landlords, loan sharks and oppressive employers.

Malthus, Thomas Robert (1766-1834): Economic spokesman for Britain's **landlord** class, his *Principles of Political Economy* (1820) countered Ricardo's critique of **groundrent** by pointing out that landlords spent part of their revenue on hiring servants and buying luxury products (coaches, fine clothes and so forth), thus providing a source of demand for British industry, while investing part of their rents on capital improvements to raise farm productivity. This emphasis on consumption and investment endeared Malthus to John Maynard Keynes. However, it did not deter Ricardo's banking class and manufacturing industry from pressing to repeal the Corn Laws in 1846, freeing trade in grain to minimize domestic food prices, and hence labor's subsistence wage (as well as agricultural rents).

Matters have not worked out in a way that either Malthus or his adversaries anticipated. Most rent ends up being paid as interest to mortgage bankers. (Buying on credit is the only way that most families can afford homes.) This has led bankers to reverse their opposition to land rent, and to view real estate and monopolies as their largest loan market. There is no longer agitation that higher site-value rents impair profits, because the focus of wealth-seeking has shifted to the FIRE Sector and asset-price inflation. Political pressure is now brought mainly to *lower* real estate taxes, leaving more rental value to be paid to banks as interest and thus raising property prices with yet *more* credit/debt.

Malthus is best known for his population theory. The contrast between compound and simple rates of growth was already familiar from debates over the expansion path of interest-bearing debt and whether Parliament should establish a **sinking fund**. Malthus used this contrast to blame the victims (the poor) for their poverty, by warning that they would respond to higher wages simply by having more children. Their tendency toward "geometric growth" (see **Exponential Functions**) would keep their wage levels down. In reality, the normal response to rising incomes has been *falling* reproduction rates as families spend their income on elevating the educational, living and housing standards of their children (usually on credit).

Marginalism: An approach to economics that takes the institutional and financial environment as given, focusing on small changes that do not affect the economy's policy structure. Marginally diminishing returns are viewed as forcing up prices, while marginally higher productivity and output reduce them. In contrast to classical political economy and institutionalism, this approach avoids making policy and social reform the major focus of economic analysis. (See **Structural Problem**.) Lenin noted that Hegel and Karl Marx opposed marginalism: "Leaps! Breaks in Gradualness! Leaps! Leaps"[1]

Marginal Utility Theory: In the 1870s classical political economy began to be replaced by British and Austrian theory focusing on small changes in pleasure or "pain" resulting from small quantities added or subtracted from consumption. Such marginalist analysis views economic relations in terms of a crude supply-and-demand schedule of psychological satiation, ignoring the wealth addiction that characterizes *rentier* income, as well as what Thorstein Veblen called conspicuous consumption. Joan Robinson (*Economic Philosophy,* 1964) noted the circular reasoning involved:

"utility is the quality in commodities that makes individuals want to buy them, and the fact that individuals want to buy them shows that they have utility."

Market: See **"The Market."**

Market Bolshevism: The shock therapy (no real therapy, only shock) that enabled Boris Yeltsin's "family" of allied **kleptocrats** to seize power and overrule the Duma parliament in ways reminiscent of Lenin's Bolshevik coup in 1917. (See **Grabitization**.) Public utilities and natural monopolies were turned over to insiders, who "cashed out" by selling their takings on the New York and London stock exchanges. Subsequent economic advisor Sergei Glaziev noted the lesson for Russia from this disastrous **neoliberal** experiment: "if the state does not regulate the market, then the market is occupied by monopolies, speculators, and God knows whom. The role of the state is to create the most advantageous conditions for the increase in the investment and economic activity…. people saying that the state should stay out of the economy are working in the interests of those who want to control the market."[2] In other words, an **oligarchic** "free market" is as centrally planned as a Keynesian or socialist economy, but its objective is to financialize economic rent.

Market Economy: Every economy is planned in one way or another. The question is, how are exchanges and markets shaped and regulated? Is the center of planning more in the public sector or in the private sector? The most viable and stable economies are mixed public/private economies with appropriate checks and balances (see **Government, Mixed Economy** and **Regulation**). In today's economies, governments absorb between 30% and 40% of GDP.

Every economy has rules of exchange, and in that sense can be thought of as a market economy in one way or another. Three modes of market relationships typically co-exist: 1) gift exchange in a system of reciprocity (on credit); 2) redistributive exchange at allocated prices (originally on credit, not direct payment); and 3) flexible unregulated price-setting markets, which may or may not involve sales on credit.

Anti-government ideologues claim that attempts to regulate prices are inherently futile. Of course, standardization of prices and quality always has been a public regulatory function. The earliest documented prices are found in Mesopotamia in the third millennia BC. The palaces and temples administered a stable set of price equivalences for key commodities, salary and interest rates by for their transactions with the economy at large. These administered prices provided a stable context for the population to pay debts in grain, silver, copper, wool or other basic products. (See **Money** for references to early Mesopotamian royal price proclamations and the Laws of Hammurabi.)

Market Fundamentalism: A lobbying effort to deregulate an economy. Epitomized by Margaret Thatcher's declaration that "there is no such thing as society," it claims that public regulation to enforce honest dealing or pricing "distorts" economic behavior. The effect is to promote a *rentier* oligarchy. (See **Chicago School** and **Free Market**.)

Market Price: What pharmaceutical companies charge for patented drugs, what kidnappers demand as ransom, or what MacDonald's temps work for. Typically a power relationship when it comes to basic essentials such as housing, health care and food. Masquerading as a voluntary exchange, the prototypical market bargain is "Your money or your life," or "My kingdom for a horse." Cost-value is not the determining factor in such situations.

Market Socialism: Under market socialism, government agencies subsidize prices for basic infrastructure services (transportation, communications and power) to minimize the economy's cost of living and doing business (see **Public Domain**). The ultimate aim is to provide basic resources freely, starting with roads, education and health care. Incomes and wage levels are supported to assure that families can afford basic needs whose prices are freed from the watered costs, interest, monopoly rent and other economic rent characteristic of privatization and its associated financialization.

Mark-to-Model Accounting: Junk accounting (also called Enron accounting) that enhances a balance sheet by valuing assets as if they will make fantastic returns, while assigning debts and other liabilities to a separate entity in a footnote. The aim is to maximize a company's credit lines and stock price, and hence the bonuses of its managers. (See **Accounting, Fictitious Capital** and **Junk Economics**.)

Governments and IMF projections use mark-to-model fictions to pretend that the overall economy can grow fast enough to pay its soaring mortgage debt, student debt, public debt and kindred financial claims that are the assets ("savings") of banks and bondholders. Pension funds unrealistically project their assets as growing steadily at more than 8% annually. (See **Compound Interest** and **Ponzi Scheme**.) Instead of acknowledging the need for debt forgiveness as an alternative to austerity, junk economics is mobilized to back this mark-to-myth optimism, leaving entire economies as hopelessly indebted as Enron was.

Marx, Karl (1818-1883): Marx was the last great **classical political economist**. Embarking on a study of political economy after he earned a doctorate in philosophy in 1841, his sense of political and economic justice led him to participate as a radical journalist in Europe's 1848 revolutions by the bourgeoisie against royalty and the aristocracy. But he criticized the bourgeoisie for stopping short of raising labor's wages and improving working conditions. Going beyond the mainstream economic reform movement that aimed primarily at reducing the power of landlords and monopolists, he defined industrial profits as being exploitative of wage labor, which he found to be the distinguishing feature of industrial capitalism.

Commissioned by the International Communist League, Marx wrote the *Communist Manifesto* with Frederick Engels, published in English in London in February 1848. He defined the historical task of industrial capitalism to be to maximize efficiency and free economies from the unnecessary costs (*faux frais*) of production inherited from feudalism. That was the class war of his day, by the industrial bourgeoisie against landlords and bankers who extracted groundrent and interest at the expense of industrial profits. Marx said that a further political revolution would be needed to socialize property ownership, freeing labor from industrial capital.

To outline the economic logic of implicit in this looming class conflict, Marx defined profit in terms of the price markup at which capitalists sell labor's products over and above the wages they pay. He pointed out that under the labor theory of value, "labor" has two types of cost: (1) the wages paid by employers, and (2) the price at which its products are sold at a profit. Wage labor does not receive the full value of its product, leaving it unable to buy what it produces. Capitalists may use their profits to invest in new means of production, but the system is prone to increasingly severe economic and financial crises as a result of its internal contradictions.

This interpretation of the labor theory of value led the *rentier* and industrial interests to reject the value, price and rent theory developed by Adam Smith, David Ricardo and John Stuart Mill that led logically to Marx's theories. In its place, mainstream economics adopted marginal utility theory, Austrian School individualism and the post-classical economics of John Bates Clark, which did not recognize the phenomena of exploitation or unearned income. The interests of industrialists, landlords and bankers found a common ground in turning what had been political economy narrowed into "economics."

Extending the scope of economic reform to the social and cultural sphere, Marx described **alienation** as separating wage workers from their status as human beings in control of their lives (see **Choice**), working conditions and product, and also over their relationship with others and, collectively, over society as the ultimate human product. To save labor from this fate, Marx defined the aim of socialism as being to free labor from capital owned by the property classes, and hence from the state that industrial capital was in the process of prying away from the landed aristocracy. This fight would lead ultimately to the communist ideal of abolishing the state as an exploitative apparatus.[3] Juxtaposing the class struggle to what was becoming the mainstream trickle-down ideology of his day proclaiming a harmony of interests to exist between labor and capital, Marx expanded the idea of equality of rights and mutual aid beyond the nobility to include the hitherto excluded working class. He viewed class consciousness at the bottom of the economic pyramid as aiming to socialize the means of production (land, factories and public infrastructure) and banking.

In Germany, the most advanced country at the time, this seemed likely to occur democratically with the formation of the Social Democratic party. In Britain, the Parliamentary Labor Party was organized, and other countries developed similar parties to promote the interests of labor. But the vested interests pushed back, from the Paris Commune in 1871 to the Pinkerton thugs in America, using force and violence against attempts to fight for workers' rights and better working conditions.

Volume I of *Capital: A Critique of Political Economy* was published in 1867, but Volumes II and III were published by Frederick Engels from notes left behind after Marx's death. These latter two volumes (and also Marx's posthumous *Theories of Surplus Value*, his original draft notes for *Capital*), treat interest-bearing debt as being independent of profit and growth rates, self-multiplying according to the purely mathematical rules of compound interest. But like nearly all economists of his era, Marx expected industrial capitalism to bring banking out of its usurious medieval origins to finance capital investment.

Marx was optimistic in believing that financial, political and other social institutions would evolve to reflect the most efficient mode of production. He viewed the industrialization of banking as part of a broader economic restructuring in which governments were to make a widening range of services freely available, headed by public health, pensions, education and other infrastructure services. Broadly called "socialism," this strategy was widely discussed as the likely future evolution of industrial capitalism. Yet more than any other economist of his time, Marx showed (in Vol. III of *Capital*) that the tendency of interest-bearing debt to grow exponentially led to financial crises. These crises exacerbated the underlying inability of labor to buy the goods it produced. (See **Circular Flow** and **Say's Law**.) Since World War II the global economy has lapsed into a financialized neo-*rentier* economy that neither Marx nor his contemporaries were so pessimistic as to forecast.

Marxism: Variations on the ideas of Karl Marx, usually involving public ownership of land, basic infrastructure and the means of production, political reform (to end control of government by royalty, the aristocracy and the wealthy), and revolutionary tactics (general strikes and takeover of government by force).

Marx had little to say about how the dynamics of socialism would work themselves out, but all such speculation is now labeled "Marxist." This is unwarranted. To conflate Marxism with the detour that followed Russia's October 1917 Revolution is a misrepresentation, despite the fact that its leaders identified themselves as Marxists. Marx doubted that less industrialized countries (such as Russia in his day) were in a position to transition from serfdom directly to socialism. Most Russian leaders viewed their political task to be to follow the lead of more advanced German and other Western European socialist movements.

Instead, Stalin made Russia the focus of the Communist International and self-proclaimed Marxism. German Communists and Social Democrats left a political vacuum enabling Adolph Hitler to seize power. The Soviet Union under **Stalinism** became an authoritarian travesty of Marxism, despite the superficial similarity of state ownership of the means of production.

Subsequent attempts to revive the Progressive Era trajectory – a kind of economy widely called socialism, toward which the West seemed to be moving in the years leading up to World War I – therefore are labeled "Marxist" mainly in adopting his analysis of the interaction of labor, industrial and finance capital. This analysis recognizes exploitation in the working conditions of wage labor, economic rent and interest extracted by the *rentiers*.

Mathiness: British economic journalist John Kay defines mathiness as a "use of algebraic symbols and quantitative data to give an appearance of scientific content to ideological preconceptions." Expressing an idea in mathematical symbols instead of straightforward literary terms helps legitimize it in the minds of many people, thanks to a seeming similarity with natural science. In this respect math is basically a form of numerical rhetoric. "The American economist Paul Romer has recently written of 'mathiness,' by analogy with **'truthiness,'** a term coined by American talk show host Stephen Colbert. Truthiness presents narratives which are not actually true, but consistent with the world view of the person who spins the story. It is exemplified in rightwing fabrications about European health systems – their death panels and forced euthanasia."[4] (See **Factoid**.) Paul Samuelson, for instance, trivialized economics in terms that give the outward appearance of science by being expressed mathematically, even when its assumptions are purely hypothetical (and not all realistic) and there are no quantitative statistics to illustrate its categories. (See **GIGO** and **Nobel Economics Prize**.)

Menger, Carl (1840-1921): Austrian economist notorious for saying that facts don't matter: "even if money did not originate from barter, could it have?"[5] In typical junk-economics fashion Menger insisted that money is a "hard" asset, not a social creation, and that it has nothing to do with government or paying fees and taxes to it. The reality is that historical records document the origin of money as a medium to pay debts to Sumerian temples. But Austrian "individualistic" ideology became the foundation for Ludwig von Mises, Frederick von Hayek and others seeking to impose austerity by blocking public money creation and budget deficits (except to subsidize bankers and bondholders each time they wreck the economy).

Middle Class: Being in the middle income brackets is different from "class" as traditionally understood, *e.g.*, the working class living on wages or the capitalist class making profits. Wage-earners able to borrow enough to buy a home on credit are encouraged to think of themselves as "consumers" rather than as debtors. They are tempted with dreams of becoming capitalists in miniature, as if having a bank account, a pension fund and perhaps a mutual fund qualifies them as members of the financial class instead of being just wage-earners.

At a 2015 protest by New York University faculty against cutbacks in full-time teaching in the face of massive new real estate spending, one professor complained that NYU was treating the faculty like wage labor. From the university's vantage point, that is what they are. So part of the middle-class mentality is the illusion of rising to some higher status.

Labor's workplace rights and wage remuneration are directly tied to its legal status as wage earners instead of the independent self-employed "piecework" businesses. Piecework or "gig" arrangements account for an estimated 20% to 30% of U.S. and European workers. Employers would like to use this as an opportunity to avoid contributing to unemployment insurance and paying for vacation time, health care, minimum wages and other responsibilities put in place over the past century's progressive labor legislation.

Uber, the on-demand taxicab company, has sought to treat drivers as independent "small businesses" in order to free itself from having to offer basic workplace protection. But a London tribunal ruled in 2016 that Uber's 30,000 drivers "are 'workers' entitled to the minimum wage and holiday pay." The British union for Uber drivers, GMB, successfully made its case that "Uber exerts a lot of control over drivers when their [cellphone] app is on: it sets the fee; it does not tell them where customers want to go until after they have been picked up; and it 'deactivates' drivers whose average customer ratings drop too low." The business expenses of fuel, auto maintenance and insurance are offloaded onto the drivers, whose nominal return in Britain averages £16 an hour after paying commissions to Uber. The three-person tribunal's lead judge found that: "The notion that Uber in London is a mosaic of 30,000 small businesses linked by a common 'platform' is to our minds faintly ridiculous." Uber's use of "fictions, twisted language and even brand new terminology, merits, we think, a degree of skepticism."[6]

New York City's Uber drivers won a similar class action suit to qualify for unemployment benefits and other workplace rights. In April 2016, a California court ordered Uber "to pay a $100 million settlement to almost 400,000 drivers in California and Massachusetts, but still classed drivers as freelancers. ... a judge subsequently ruled the sum was inadequate." (See also **Class** and **Labor Capitalism**.) Without owning the means of production such individuals are workers and de facto employees. That is their economic class status.

What really is at issue, of course, is whether such wage or "gig" workers can make enough income to raise their living standards.

In popular language, to be middle class means earning enough to buy a home and to get a college education. This involves going into debt, taking out a student loan whose charges may absorb between 10% and as much as half of the graduate's income. The next step toward middle class debt peonage is to buy a home with a mortgage. U.S. housing agencies now guarantee home loans whose mortgage payments absorb up to 43% of the applicant's income. Credit card debt and auto or appliance debt absorb yet more as wage earners seek a middle-class life style. (See **Bourgeoisie** and **Disposable Personal Income**.)

Banks depict such debt as offering an opportunity to rise in status – by which they really mean a rise in consumption levels. But what really is the key is that most of what workers may earn in wages or salaries is paid to the FIRE sector, especially for housing in better neighborhoods as they move up the social ladder – which turns out to be a debt ladder.

Military Junta: A regime usually associated with **client oligarchies** that impose **neoliberal** policies on countries that reject the **Washington Consensus**. From the Greek "colonels" regime of 1967-74 to Chile under General Pinochet and Hillary Clinton's Honduran coup in 2009, these regimes use military force to cope with IMF riots that result from austerity programs imposed by foreign creditor, and to use police to prevent political alternatives from being enacted.

Military Spending: Governments use a national security umbrella (also called **State Socialism**) to subsidize heavy industry and high-technology research and development via arms manufacture, space exploration and information technology. However, as Seymour Melman explained in *Pentagon Capitalism* (1970), the aim of military-industrial engineering is to *maximize* costs, in order to maximize their cost-plus contractual profits. This cost-plus system of billing severs the link between profit-seeking and economic efficiency. By the 1970s this led less militarized economies such as Japan and Germany to pursue their own cost-cutting engineering practices to underprice U.S. competitors. (See **Pentagon Capitalism**.)

Mill, John Stuart (1806-1873): The son of Ricardian economic journalist James

Mill, his *Principles of Political Economy* (1848) has been called a halfway house from Ricardo's critique of landlord groundrent to the socialism of Karl Marx. In Book V, ch. II §5, Mill described rent-yielding properties as enabling their holders to demand payment from society "without any exertion or sacrifice on the part of the owners ... Landlords ... grow richer, as it were in their sleep, without working, risking, or economizing. What claim have they, on the general principle of social justice, to this accession of riches?"

On this ground Mill and his circle have been called Ricardian socialists. To free society from landlords receiving the unearned increment of rising land prices, he (along with Herbert Spencer and others) urged governments to buy out the landlord class so as to restore land rent as the main source of fiscal revenue. (See **Henry George Theorem**.) However, Mill's policy would simply have transformed landlords into money lords (financiers). Some landlord families did become bankers, and the financial sector has absorbed real estate into the FIRE sector since housing and other real estate holdings in most countries have been democratized and bought on credit.

The upshot is that rent is now paid as interest to the bankers instead of as taxes to the public sector. In that sense our financialized economy is paying a steep price for the failure to take land or at least its rent into the public domain.

Minsky, Hyman (1919-1996): Economist who pioneered **Modern Monetary Theory (MMT)** and explained the three stages of the financial cycle in terms of rising **debt leveraging**:

(1) In the **hedge phase**, most borrowers are able to pay interest as well as principal. This was the case with 30-year self-amortizing mortgages provided from the late 1940s to the late 1970s.

(2) In the **interest-only** phase, debtors are only able to pay interest. This was the case with interest-only mortgages extended in the years leading up to the 2008 junk mortgage crash.

(3) In **"Ponzi" phase**, debtors need to borrow the interest as it accrues, adding it onto the debt exponentially. That is how Latin American countries rolled over their debts in the 1960s leading up to Mexico's 1972 breakdown, which quickly spread throughout the Third World. And it is how real estate mortgages were rolled over until 2008.

When debts grow too far beyond the ability to pay, the "Minsky moment" occurs: a financial crisis. As an alternative, Minsky advocated regulating the credit system to prevent speculative and fraudulent over-lending. He urged central banks to create enough credit to sustain a full-employment economy, in large part by public-works spending, not to bail out banks for their bad loans. Minsky's approach is taught primarily at the University of Missouri (Kansas City) and applied at the Levy Institute at Bard College in Annandale-on-Hudson, New York. The economist Steve Keen has applied Minsky's ideas in his "Minsky mathematical model" of the economy.

Mixed Economy: Every economy is mixed, with public and private sectors co-existing like the DNA molecule's intertwining spiral strands. (See **Market Economy**.) Well-run societies need reciprocal checks and balances to avoid the extremes either of public or private sectors, ranging from Stalinist Russia to neoliberal regimes.

Historically, the basic elements of commercial enterprise – standardized prices and accounting, interest-bearing debt and profit-sharing contracts – first seem to have emerged in Bronze Age Mesopotamian temples and palaces (especially for long-distance trade) and gradually diffused throughout the economy at large. (See **Accounting** and **Government**.) Today's public sectors still play a supporting and **regulatory** role, providing legal and economic infrastructure and military security for the private sector, and creating the money supply.

Wealthy elites tend to gain ascendency via financial dynamics, which typically take over governments as well as real estate and industry. An equally predatory outcome may occur when bureaucracies seek their own self-interest by controlling the flow of revenue and hence the economic surplus. This often leads to insider dealing. In both cases an emerging **kleptocracy** creates an **oligarchy**. Governments tend to be controlled by families at the top of the economic pyramid – going all the way back to the chieftains' households that dominated Mesopotamia's temples and palaces. No society in history seems to have resisted this kind of polarization for long, although popular morality has almost always called for such reforms, checks and balances.

Modernization: Every totalitarian state distorts language by changing the meaning of words. Neoliberalism uses Orwellian Newspeak to deform perceptions of reality by depicting budget cuts to public programs (*e.g.,* health care, education and other infrastructure) as reform, modernization and progress, as if there is no alternative. But this really is retrogression opposing modernity as understood in the Progressive Era a century ago.[7] Back then, it seemed "modern" to free economies *from* special privilege by creating public regulations to guide economies into the modern age of abundance. But today's neoliberal image of the **End of History** turns out to be neofeudalism and austerity under a financial oligarchy.

Modern Monetary Theory (MMT): MMT views money and credit as a public utility.[8] (See **Government** and **Money**.) Money is a legal creation, not a commodity like gold or silver. Creating it costs central banks or treasuries virtually nothing (likewise for banks creating their own electronic credit). Governments give money value by accepting it in payment of taxes and fees.

The folding money in peoples' pockets is, technically, a government debt – but it is a debt that is not expected to be repaid. That debt – on the liabilities side of the government's balance sheet – is an asset to money-holders. This money does not necessarily to lead to inflation when labor and other resources are less than fully employed. By contrast, most bank credit is created to finance the purchase of real estate, stocks and bonds, and thus fuels **asset-price inflation**. That is a major difference between public and private money creation. And just as hydrocarbon fuels lead to environmental pollution and global warming, bank credit to bid up asset prices leaves a residue of **debt deflation** in the economic environment.

Banks promote a market for this debt creation by doing what other advertisers do: They sing the praises of their product, as if running up more debt (created electronically at almost no real cost to the bank) will make people richer (*e.g.*, by asset-price inflation) instead of leaving them more deeply indebted.

A major virtue of MMT is to dispel the illusion that all government spending must come from taxpayers. Not a penny of the $4.3 trillion that the **Federal Reserve's Quantitative Easing** program has provided to Wall Street since 2008 came from taxpayers. Governments do (and should) create money by printing it (or today, creating it electronically), over and above the collection of taxes. Instead of only giving it to the banks at 0.1% interest, the Fed could just as easily have created money to spend *into* the economy for public programs.

MMT urges central banks or treasuries to monetize budget deficits by creating money to spend into the economy in this way. The government's budget deficit is (by definition) the private sector's surplus. By contrast, running budget surpluses (as the United States did for decades after the Civil War, and as it did in the Clinton Administration in the late 1990s) sucks money out of the economy, leading to **fiscal drag**. If public debt-money were to be repaid (by running a fiscal surplus), it would be removed from circulation. That is why budget surpluses are deflationary – and why balanced budgets fail to provide the economy with the money needed to grow and to create jobs.

By *not* running deficits, the economy is obliged to rely on banks for the money and credit it needs to grow. Banks charge interest for providing this credit, leading to debt deflation. Neoliberals want to keep bank credit-money privatized. To keep it as a monopoly, they seek to block governments from creating money. Their aim is for governments to finance public spending *only* by taxing the 99 Percent – which drains revenue from the economy – or by borrowing from banks and bondholders at interest.

The popular illusion that all bank loans come from deposits and savings is kept alive by journalists such as columnist Paul Krugman of the New York Times despite the seemly obvious fact that since 2008 little new bank credit has been supplied by depositors.[9] MMT Economists know that commercial banks can create money simply on their computers, by crediting the borrower's account when the customer signs an IOU for the debt. The basic "service" that banks perform by their credit creation is to create debt, on which they charge interest. (See **Exponential Function** and **Compound Interest** for the problems this causes). *Loans thus create deposits* – while also creating debt. When banks borrow reserves from the Federal Reserve (at just 0.1% interest), they then are able to charge as much interest as they can get their customers to pay.

Money always has been a claim *on* some debtor – a liability either of governments or banks. On the broadest plane, a holder of money has an implicit claim on society at large – which is in effect a collective debtor to the money holder. This private banker's monopoly privilege of money creation can be maintained – and bank profits maximized – as long as they can by preventing a public bank from being created as a public utility to provide the economy with less expensive (and better directed) credit. That is why financial lobbyists try to convince the public that only private banks should create credit-money, instead of governments creating public money by deficit spending.

Monetarism: A view of money as a commodity to be bartered, like coinage whose value is based on its bullion content. (See **Austrian School** and **Gold**.) In contrast to the **State Theory of Money** and **Modern Monetary Theory**, monetarism urges that paper money be created only when backed by hard assets, not government debt and public taxing power. Governments are told not create their own money, but to borrow – as if banks do not simply create their own credit electronically as governments could do just as easily. (See **Modern Monetary Theory**.) Monetarism is thus the natural lobbying position for commercial bankers.

Deflationary monetary policy blocks governments from treating money creation as a public utility. The policy aim is to keep money and credit privatized, with minimal government regulation (which monetarists call "interference"). The result is that monetarism, financial fraud, austerity and debt deflation go together, supporting oligarchies against democracies. Monetarist ideology in Ricardo's day has sponsored postwar price deflations (favoring creditors over debtors) by rolling the price of gold back to pre-war levels in Britain after the Napoleonic Wars ended in 1815. A similar monetary deflation was imposed in the United States from the ending of its Civil War in 1865 through the remainder of the 19th century.

The cover story for such needless monetarist austerity is that government money creation spurs price inflation (as in **MV = PT**, referring only to consumer prices, not asset prices). Milton Friedman and the Chicago School follow Ricardo's Banking School (so-called because its views served the banking sector) in claiming that financial and international imbalances are automatically self-curing, so that debt cannot pose a systemic structural problem. Hence, there seems to be no need for governments to intervene in financial policy – or discourage borrowing in foreign currencies. This tunnel vision led to the junk bond and junk mortgage bubbles wrought by Greenspan, the deregulatory 2008 crash and its sequel, and the post-2008 debt deflation.

Money: Modern governments create paper or electronic money and spend it into the economy by running budget deficits. Paper currency is a government debt, appearing on the liabilities side of the public balance sheet. (It can be a pure token – "equity" or "net worth" money.) This money is a claim by its holder on the government, which the government settles by accepting it as payment for taxes or fees. Governments give value to this liability by accepting it for payments. This willingness by governments to accept it is money's defining characteristic. The modern monetary base is government-backed IOUs, including the paper money in one's pocket. If the government were to pay off this debt-money permanently, there would be no money except for what banks create. The classic analysis is Georg Friedrich Knapp's *State Theory of Money* (*Die Staattheorie des Geldes*, 1904, translated into English in 1924).[10]

Bank money is a claim for payment by the bank, but is accepted by government, which has granted banks the money-creating privilege. Both government and bank money are assets to their holders, but a liability of governments or banks. And in both cases, money's main function is to denominate debts – starting with tax obligations.

Ancient Mesopotamian palaces accepted grain as payment, so grain was money, although obviously not a good means of paying for most transactions, except at harvest time on the threshing floor. Most transactions were settled by running up debts, most of which were to be paid when the harvest was in. Rulers often began their reign by declaring a price schedule for grain or silver accepted as payments to palace collectors. Grain and silver (and also copper and other commodities) were assigned standardized price equivalencies to pay palaces and temples. But a "hard" asset such as silver or gold has never been money as such, unless governments establish its value as a commodity by accepting it as a means of payment for taxes, public fees or tribute levied on conquered populations.

Society outside of government usually follows the government's lead in adopting money that is acceptable as a vehicle to pay the public sector. That is the essence of the **State Theory of Money** (sometimes called **Chartalism**). It finds money first attested in ancient Mesopotamia before 2000 BC, long before coinage was issued. Monetary silver, and later Greek and Roman coinage, was minted by the temples in order to ensure honest purity and weight. (From Babylonian literature through the Bible, private merchants were notorious for counterfeiting and using false weights and measures.) Silver was a store of value mainly saved in the temples, especially in Greece and Rome. It could be melted down in emergencies such as paying mercenaries in war crises.

Today, little bank money is used to increase the means of production or employment. Banks create their money as credit, mainly to buyers of real estate, or for speculation in stocks and bonds, or to raid companies (see **Debt Leveraging**). When bankers write loans on their computer keyboards, this creates a counterpart deposit. Governments may or may not back the banks' ability to pay their liabilities to depositors and bondholders when the market price of assets and collateral in their loan portfolio falls below the level of deposits and loans they back. (See **Quantitative Easing**.)

Money's early role as a commodity or debt payment accepted by public institutions for taxes levied on conquered populations as tribute or to pay soldiers finds its counterpart in today's world. Central bank reserves consist mainly of dollars in the form of U.S. Treasury IOUs, mostly for American military spending abroad. To Europe and other dollar-holding governments, their monetary base is a form of tribute paid as "protection," mainly from American displeasure and the ever-present threat of "regime-change."

Money Illusion: A term coined by Irving Fisher to describe the tendency of workers and consumers to imagine themselves better off when their wages or salaries rise, even when the goods and services they buy also cost more.

But prices and wages rarely rise at the same rate. Wages rose faster during the Vietnam War inflation of the 1960s and 1970s, and inflation makes debts easier to pay out of rising wages. To be sure, creditors seek to counter this benefit to debtors by raising interest rates on new loans. This has the effect of slowing construction and investment and hence the economy.

A kindred illusion is that rising asset prices for housing, stocks and bonds enrich the economy. The actual effect is to increase access prices for buying a home or a retirement income. To the extent that asset prices are bid up with easy bank credit, debt overhead rises for new homebuyers. But financial lobbyists have little interest in drawing attention to this bubble illusion, because debt leveraging is the banker's product, after all. When hard-money "deficit hawks" talk about the money illusion, their actual preference is for deflation and unemployment to keep wages down.

The difference between these two illusions – the money illusion and the bubble's asset-price illusion – is that wage inflation benefits the 99 Percent, while asset-price inflation benefits mainly the One Percent who own most of the stocks and bonds that are rising in price. Asset-price inflation raises the debt level that must be taken on to buy a home, driving the 99 Percent further into debt – and then leaves the economy to languish in debt deflation.

Money Manager: Investment banks, mutual funds, pension funds and insurance companies that charge commissions for managing (or mismanaging) society's savings, organizing mergers and acquisitions (including corporate raids financed by debt leveraging) and privatizing public enterprises. (See **Casino Capitalism** and **Labor Capitalism**.) The common aim of money managers is privatization across the board: money and finance, pension plans, insurance and the health care that seemed on their way to becoming public functions a century ago.

Money managers are now seeking a bonanza of fees from privatizing Social Security's compulsory saving. This would steer funds into the stock market, producing asset-price gains, much as **pension fund capitalism** did after the 1950s. The money manager's objective is to obtain as much of the clients' return as possible in commissions and fees, leaving pension contributors with only a portion of the returns – and with the losses when asset prices decline. An ultimate stock price decline is likely to occur as the population ages and stocks are sold to pay their pensions. Retirees will pull more funds out of the financial markets than new employees are contributing. But by this time, money managers will have taken their commissions and run.

Money Manager Capitalism: The term coined by **Hyman Minsky** for an economy whose economic planning and resource allocation shifts to Wall Street and other financial centers. As Vanguard CEO John C. Bogle has observed: "The agency (or intermediation) society is not working as it should." The **ownership society** is being financialized into "an intermediation society dominated by professional money managers and corporations [that has] not been accompanied by the development of an ethical, regulatory and legal environment."[11] (See **Finance Capitalism**, **Oligarchy** and the **One Percent**.)

Monopoly: The ability to charge more for a product than is warranted by its cost of production (including normal **profit**), as a result of limited competition. (See **Value** and **Economic Rent**.) Monopoly power is maximized by limiting the ability of consumers to choose alternatives (see **Choice**). This is easiest to achieve with natural monopolies such as transportation and communications, and patent-protected products such as pharmaceuticals and information technology.

To prevent such rent extraction, governments long retained basic infrastructure in the public domain. However, finance always has been the mother of monopolies, and it has gained the upper hand, especially since 1980. (See **Margaret Thatcher** and **Neoliberal**.) Today's emerging financial oligarchy seeks to create monopolies by forcing privatization on debt-strapped governments that can be subjected to IMF and World Bank **conditionalities** to pay bondholders with the sales proceeds.

Monopoly Rent contrasted to Land Rent: Both these forms of economic rent represent income that does not reimburse a corresponding cost of production. Land rent is a legacy of medieval conquest of the land by warlord aristocracies, who appropriated the taxable crop surplus for themselves as government's ability to tax this surplus weakened. Monopoly rent emerged via a similar privatization of essential services, with privileges created to pay international creditors instead of warlords. Governments created trading monopolies (such as the East and West India Companies and South Sea Company) to sell to bondholders to reduce royal war debts. Governments also granted colonization privileges, trading privileges and patents as a means of reducing their royal or public debt.

Today, monopoly rent is the main objective of privatization, and is forced mainly on deeply indebted countries. In Greece, the IMF and European Central Bank (ECB) demanded $50 billion in privatizations to pay for the bailout of bondholders in 2010 and 2012 (which finds its counterpart in the $50 billion in the flight capital to Switzerland tabulated in the "Lagarde list"). In the United States, debt-strapped cities are forced to privatize their roads and even sidewalks to raise money to pay bondholders. In this sense rising land rent and monopoly rent go together, a result of anti-classical and pro-financial tax policy.

Moral Hazard: "Socializing the risk" of bad loans (see **Bad Debt**) or gambles via taxpayer bailouts of bankers or bondholders who lose money on bad and even fraudulent loans. There is nothing socialist (although some call it "socialism for the rich") about this particular form of Big Government. A better term for this moral hazard is "oligarchizing the risk." (See **State Socialism**.) Reversing the idea that the role of banks and other financial institutions is to serve the economy, financialization sacrifices the economy to protect the One Percent from suffering losses on its assets and bad loans. The effect of such subsidy to banks **Too Big To Fail/Jail** is to shift assets from the public at large (the 99 Percent, euphemized as "taxpayers," although the Federal Reserve plays the major role) to the financial sector (the non-taxpayers under oligarchies).

For instance, the U.S. Government reimbursed uninsured depositors in high-risk S&Ls in the 1980s, leading to insolvency of the Federal Savings and Loan Insurance Corporation (FSLIC) after a fire sale of assets. In the wake of the 2008 crash Ireland's government likewise bailed out Anglo-Irish Bank depositors at public (taxpayer) expense, plunging the economy into depression. Moral hazard also increased as the bubble economy gained momentum leading up to 2008. under Robert Rubin's gang, Citibank embarked on a series of risky ventures, secure in the knowledge that the Obama cabinet (following Citigroup's recommendations) would bail it out. The alternative, bankers threatened, was to block depositors from access to their banks' ATM machines.

Murabaha Loan: Moslem law bans the charging of interest (**usury**), but permits loopholes that achieve a similar effect in practice (see **Agio**). A *murabaha* mortgage loan is extended without nominal interest to purchase a house or other property, but the borrower pays a rental charge until finally taking ownership, after paying a stipulated amount to the creditor/owner. The rental contract and purchase price are set high enough to incorporate an equivalent interest charge. (See **Sharia Law**.)

ENDNOTES

[1] V.I. Lenin, "Conspectus of Hegel's Science of Logic," *Collected Works*, Vol. 38, p. 123 (written in 1914).

[2] Vladimir Pozner interviews Sergei Glaziev, *The Saker*, October 20, 2015, http://thesaker.is/vladimir-pozner-interviews-sergei-glaziev/

[3] As Terence McCarthy wrote in his introduction to Marx's *A History of Economic Theories* (the first English translation of *Theories of Surplus Value*, New York: 1952), p. xi: "Marx was more of a revolutionary than his enemies have charged because he demonstrated that the thinking of the most respected bourgeois economists who preceded him led logically to socialism."

[4] John Kay, "Economists should keep to the facts, not feelings," *Financial Times*, October 7, 2015.

[5] Karl Menger, "On the Origin of Money." *Economic Journal* **2** (1892), pp. 239–55. For a recent discussion see Pavlina R. Tcherneva, "Money, Power, and Monetary Regimes," Levy Institute Working Paper No. 861 (March 2016). Noting that "Barter

arrangements of course did exist, but they were never a coordinating mechanism for social provisioning in any society," she cites Cambridge anthropologist Caroline Humphrey, "Barter and Economic Disintegration." *Man*, New Series **20** (1985), p. 48: "No example of a barter economy, pure and simple, has ever been described, let alone the emergence from it of money; all available ethnography suggests that there never has been such a thing."

[6] Sarah O'Connor, Jane Croft and Madhumita Murgia, "Uber drivers win UK legal battle for workers' rights," Financial Times, October 29, 2016. In response to Uber's claim "to help drivers 'grow' their business," the panel's lead Judge Anthony Snelson observed: "No driver is in a position to do anything of the kind, unless growing his business simply means spending more hours at the wheel."

[7] Manuela Cadelli, "Neoliberalism is a species of fascism," Defend Democracy Press, July 11, 2016. http://www.defenddemocracy.press/president-belgian-magistrates-neoliberalism-form-fascism/

[8] Modern Monetary Theory is taught primarily at the University of Missouri (Kansas City). Good summaries of the theory are Randall Wray, *Modern Monetary Theory: A Primer on Macroeconomics for Sovereign Monetary Systems* (2012), *Why Minsky Matters* (2015), and *The Rise and Fall of Money Manager Capitalism* (2015). Also helpful for the mathematical models based on MMT are Steve Keen, *Can We Avoid Another Financial Crisis?* (2017) and *Debunking Economics* (2011). Significantly, the UMKC Economics Chairperson, Stephanie Kelton, served as Chief Economist for the Democratic Minority Staff of the Senate Budget Committee chaired by Sen. Bernie Sanders, and was an economic advisor to his 2016 presidential campaign. UMKC's New Economic Perspectives blog provides an ongoing MMT commentary on U.S. financial developments.

[9] See the debate between Steve Keen and Paul Krugman on the orthodox 'Loanable Funds Theory,' at https://www.opendemocracy.net/ourkingdom/steve-keen/keen-krugman-debate

[10] For an explanation of money's evolution created by central authority, see L. Randall Wray (ed.), *Credit and State Theories of Money: The Contributions of A. Mitchell Innes* (Edward Elgar, 2004), L. Randall Wray, *Understanding Money* (Edward Elgar, 1998), and Michael Hudson and Cornelia Wunsch, ed., *Creating Economic Order: Record-Keeping, Standardization and the Development of Accounting in the Ancient Near East* (CDL Press, 2004), as well as Steve Keen, *Debunking Economics* (Pluto Press, 2001).

[11] John C. Bogle, "The Amazing Disappearance of the Individual Stockholder," *Wall Street Journal*, October 3, 2005 and http://www.vanguard.com/bogle_site/sp20051003.htm

is for
Neofeudalism and its
Neoliberal Advocates

National Income and Product Accounts (NIPA): The main source of data on general economic activity in the United States. Seemingly "objective" simply by virtue of being quantified, their conceptual organization follows the anti-classical revolution of the late 19th century, denying that any category of income is unearned. Any activity that is paid for deemed to be "output," except for crime, bribes and extortion, which do not appear in the NIPA despite their economic importance. No attempt is made to distinguish economic rent from profit by specifying land rent or overall rental payments for land, natural resources, monopolies or the financial sector. Yet the mainstream media treat each change in GDP as if it reflects overall welfare. This confuses output with overhead.

François Quesnay (see **Physiocrats**) created the first national income account, the *Tableau Économique* (1758) to focus on the flow of rent to France's landlord class. Its aim was to quantify the land rent available for taxation. (See **Single Tax**.) By contrast, the NIPA make such a calculation convoluted, although they *do* show that the real estate sector has reported almost no taxable revenue since World War II, thanks to the tax-deductability of interest and fictious and over-depreciation.

Natural Monopolies: See **Monopolies, Public Domain** and the **Commons.**

Neoclassical Economics: A term coined by **Thorstein Veblen** for the conservative reaction in the last quarter of the 19th century opposing the socialist tendencies toward which classical economics was leading. The main aims of this post-classical economics were to strip away the characterization of groundrent and other economic rent as unearned income, and to ward off any analysis showing how governments played a productive role as investors in public infrastructure, money creators or regulators. (See **Austrian School** and **John Bates Clark**.) And by taking the existing institutional and property environment for granted, the **marginalist** approach avoided discussion of the structural reforms needed to cope with economic polarization, the economy-wide expansion of debt, and the FIRE Sector's mode of rent-seeking and "virtual wealth." So a more apt term would have been *post-classical economics*, because it rejected the political dimension of political economy.

Neocon (AKA neoconservative): An extension of the neoliberal consensus to the global sphere by military force and covert regime change (coups) to impose the **Washington Consensus**. (See **Dollar Hegemony**.) What is to be "conserved" politically is American's unique economic power inherited from World Wars I and II – the world's "indispensable nation," immune from the constraints of international law and the balance of payments.

What is to be conserved financially are the creditor claims of Americans and client oligarchies on the world's labor, industry and governments. Opposing public regulation of finance and taxation of property income, this unipolar ideology imposes austerity and subordination of democratic politics to a financial oligarchy centered in the IMF, World Bank and NATO controlled by U.S. diplomacy.

Neofeudal Economy: Medieval feudalism's seizure of land and natural resources by military conquest and the extraction of groundrent is achieved today by financial means: debt leverage, foreclosure and privatization. Just as feudalism monopolized access to land for housing and food to force an enserfed population to work for subsistence, today's economies block access to housing and education without paying debt service that siphons off labor's income above basic subsistence levels. Instead of landlords controlling the economic and political system, money lords – the One Percent – are making themselves into a hereditary oligarchy by holding the 99 Percent in debt peonage.

Unlike serfs tied to the land on specific manorial estates, families now are free to live wherever they want. At least two-thirds of North American and European families are nominal owners of their homes, but with shrinking equity relative to their mortgage debt. Wherever they go, they must take on a lifetime of mortgage debt to obtain home ownership, heavy education debt (to get a job to pay the mortgage), auto debt (to afford a car to drive to work) and credit card debt (to shop at the company stores).

Neofeudalism: Much as warlords seized land in the Norman Conquest and levied rent on subject populations (starting with the Domesday Book, the great land census of England and Wales ordered by William the Conqueror), so today's financialized mode of warfare uses debt leverage and foreclosure to pry away land, natural resources and economic infrastructure. The commons are privatized by bondholders and bankers, gaining control of government and shifting taxes onto labor and small-scale industry. Household accounts, corporate balance sheets and public budgets are earmarked increasingly to pay real estate rent, monopoly rent, interest and financial fees, and to bear the taxes shifted off *rentier* wealth. The ***rentier* oligarchy** makes itself into a hereditary aristocracy lording it over the population at large from gated communities that are the modern counterpart to medieval castles with their moats and parapets.

Neoliberal Disease: A term coined by Jan Hellevig to describe the free hand that leaders of the demoralized post-Soviet bureaucracies gave neoliberals to redesign and de-industrialize their economies by creating client **kleptocracies**. "They freed the markets, but only for the criminals. They totally neglected investments to modernize the industry, and let the assets and cash streams be openly or covertly stolen by insiders and the mob. The result was total chaos and the breakup of the Soviet Union."[1]

Neoliberalism: An ideology to absolve banks, landlords and monopolists from accusations of predatory behavior. Just as European fascism in the 1930s reflected the failure of socialist parties to put forth a viable alternative, today's U.S.-centered neoliberalism reflects the failure of industrial capitalism or socialism to free society from *rentier* interests that are the legacy of feudalism.

Turning the tables on classical political economy, *rentier* interests act as plaintiffs *against* public regulation and taxation of their economic rents in contrast to Adam Smith and other classical liberals, today's neoliberals want to **deregulate** monopoly income and free markets for rent seeking, as well as replacing progressive income taxation and taxes on land and banking with a value-added tax (VAT) on consumers.

Endorsing an oligarchic role of government to protect property and financial fortunes (see **Chicago School** and **Moral Hazard**), neoliberalism loads the economy with an exponential growth of debt while depicting it in a way that avoids recognizing the rising *rentier* overhead (rent, interest and insurance) paid to the

FIRE sector. (See **Junk Economics** and **Social Market**.) Neoliberals want to privatize public infrastructure. They defend this grabitization by depicting public ownership and regulation as less efficient than control by financial managers, despite their notorious short-termism. The pretense is that private operators will provide goods and services at lower cost even while extracting monopoly rent, building interest, dividends and high management salaries into prices. (See **Pentagon Capitalism**.)

Neo-Serfdom: A financial mode of economic power based on interest and rent charges expanding to a point that leaves debtors with little or no disposable income above subsistence levels. (See **Debt Peonage**, **Economic Rent**, **FIRE Sector** and **Oligarchy**.)

Net wages: "It's not what you make, but what you *net*" after paying the FIRE sector, basic utilities and taxes. The usual measure of **disposable personal income (DPI)** refers to how much employees take home after income-tax withholding (designed in part by Milton Friedman during World War II) and over 15% for **FICA (Federal Insurance Contributions Act)** to produce a budget surplus for Social Security and health care (half of which are paid by the employer). This forced saving is lent to the U.S. Treasury, enabling it to cut taxes on the higher income brackets. Also deducted from paychecks may be employee withholding for private health insurance and pensions.

What is left is by no means freely available for discretionary spending. Wage earners have to pay a monthly financial and real estate "nut" off the top, headed by mortgage debt or rent to the landlord, plus credit card debt, student loans and other bank loans. Electricity, gas and phone bills must be paid, often by automatic bank transfer – and usually cable TV and Internet service as well. If these utility bills are not paid, banks increase the interest rate owed on credit card debt (typically to 29%).

Not much is left to spend on goods and services after paying the FIRE sector and basic monopolies, so it is no wonder that markets are shrinking. (See Hudson Bubble Model later in this book.)

A similar set of subtrahends occurs with net corporate cash flow (see ebitda). After paying interest and dividends – and using about half their revenue for stock buybacks – not much is left for capital investment in new plant and equipment, research or development to expand production.

Newspeak: An Orwellian term to describe the **doublespeak** language used by totalitarian dictatorships and neoliberals to shape popular attitudes. Newspeak discourages thinking about the content or nuances of words. The U.S. Defense Department (a classic euphemism) uses jargon terminology such as "collateral damage" (civilian casualties) or abbreviations such as "psyops" for psychological operations such as waterboarding and other means of torture used in "enhanced interrogation."

Ninety-Nine Percent (as in "We are the **99 Percent**"): A term coined during the **Occupy Wall Street** protests in 2011 to emphasize that incomes and net worth for the vast majority of the population have not grown since the financial meltdown of 2008. After price adjustments, the average wage has not increased since the mid-1970s, while the minimum wage has fallen steadily in purchasing power. The result has been a growing wealth gap between the **One Percent** (the wealthy elite) and the 99 Percent who are not super-rich. (See **Traumatized Worker Syndrome**.)

NINJA Loans: Acronym for **junk mortgage** loans to borrowers with No Income, No Jobs or Assets. These "liar's loans" (without documented borrower income statements) are euphemized as "Alt-A" mortgages. The liars are mainly the real estate brokers and **banksters** who packaged these loans, aided and abetted by the ratings agencies that sold AAA credit labels to Wall Street loan packagers.

Nobel Economics Prize: A lobbying attempt to legitimize "free market" speculation about how well economies might work if tendencies toward polarization, rising indebtedness and dependency did not exist.

After endowing the Nobel Memorial Prize for Economic Science in 1969 and awarding it to the Scandinavian statistical model designers Ragnar Frisch and Jan Tinbergen, the Swedish Bank awarded the second prize, in 1970, to Paul Samuelson. His Factor-Price Equalization Theorem describes a parallel universe in which wage and profit rates become similar under "free trade," not polarized as occurs as a result of foreign debt and public policies such as subsidies and privatization of infrastructure monopolies. Samuelson defended his tunnel vision by claiming: "In pointing out the consequences of a set of abstract assumptions, one need not be committed unduly as to the relation between reality and these assumptions."[2]

No prizes have been given to explain the reality of the international economy polarizing between creditor and debtor nations, or between protectionist nations such as the United States and Japan, and "free trade" countries where capital controls and public subsidies have been dismantled. No prizes are given for explaining financial polarization or the rise of rent extraction and other predatory economic activity. The ideological aim of the Nobel Prize is to demonize such logic as unscientific, as if institutionalist explanations are merely "anecdotal." Rent seeking is deemed political and hence "exogenous" to the economics discipline.

As 1996 Nobel prizewinner William Vickrey explained: "In any pure theory, all propositions are essentially tautological, in the sense that the results are implicit in the assumptions made."[3] (See **Learned Ignorance**.) Avoidance of any logic endorsing protectionist or socialist policies makes the Nobel's term "economic science" misleading. The economics discipline is not evaluated in terms of how realistic its assumptions are, but merely how logically consistent they are, much as one might criticize a work of literature or science fiction subject to the reader's "suspension of disbelief."

Given mainly to economists of the Chicago School, the Nobel award helps legitimize anti-government "free market" ideology. Milton Friedman received the prize in 1976 for his views on money (relating it only to commodity prices, not asset prices), and Bertil Ohlin in 1977 for his pro-creditor defense of German reparations and free-trade theory. Among the most extreme anti-government ideologues, James Buchanan won the prize in 1986, and Ronald Coase in 1991 for his view that government regulation is mere deadweight and inflates transaction costs. (Coase ignored the FIRE sector's impact on rent seeking and interest charges.) Douglass C. North was rewarded in 1993 for making the same point, defending privatization and denouncing government for adding to "transactions cost" by taxes and regulatory paperwork. Robert C. Merton and Myron S. Scholes won in 1997 for valuing derivatives in short-term marginalist ways that quickly led to the 1998 bankruptcy of their firm, Long-Term Credit Management (which crashed the stock market that year). Robert Mundell won in 1999 for his role in designing the Euro in a way that imposes austerity and forces the Eurozone into chronic depression.

The 2008 financial crash should have dispelled faith in asset markets being fully "rational" with all prices and the status quo justified at any given moment in time. But Chicago's Eugene Fama won the 2013 Nobel for his belief that market pricing of assets needs no public regulation. The list could go on and on. It contains a smattering of non-free market economists as window dressing to give an illusion of objectivity for the badge of pseudo-science awarded mainly to true believers. (See my article: "Does Economics Deserve A Nobel Prize?" later in this book.)

ENDNOTES

[1] Jon Hellevig, "Russian Economy – The disease is not Dutch but Liberal," *Awara*, www.awarablogs.com, March 2, 2016, reprinted in *Johnson's Russia List*, March 3, 2016, #12.

[2] Paul Samuelson, "The Gains from Trade," *Canadian Journal of Economics and Political Science* **5** (1939), p. 205.

[3] William Vickrey, *Microeconomics* (McGraw Hill, 1964), p. 5.

is for
Oligarchy and
Ownership Society

Occupy Wall Street: This protest movement began on September 17, 2011 in New York City, three years after the financial melt-down of 2008 left the U.S. economy stagnating while the **Too Big to Fail/Jail** banks and the **One Percent** gained sharply. Using the slogan "We are the **99 Percent**," a small camp was set up in Zuccotti Park in the Wall Street financial district. The sit-in/sleep-in lasted a number of months before being broken up by a violent midnight police raid that methodically destroyed the possessions of the occupiers and drove them out. But by that time the movement had spread to other cities and even to Europe, and inspired focus groups such as Occupy the SEC and Alternative Banking.

Offshore Banking Center: International "double taxation" treaties enable companies to choose whatever country's tax laws they want to adopt. Preventing "double taxation" thus means in practice "no taxation," leading to a global fiscal **race to the bottom** as companies register trading affiliates in zero-tax countries and pretend that their global profits are made there.

Such tax havens were first established by the oil industry as "flags of convenience" in Liberia and Panama to avoid North American and European taxes. To save tax avoiders from foreign-exchange risks, these psuedo-countries have no distinct currencies of their own, but use U.S. dollars. An oil-tanker affiliate registered in one of these havens can buy crude oil cheaply from the parent company's branch in an oil-producing country, and then sell it to the company's refineries in Europe or North America at a nominal price high enough to leave no profit to be declared to either European or U.S. tax authorities on the capital investment in oil refining. This **transfer pricing** enables oil companies to take their global profits in enclaves that levy no income tax. Official statistics depict the oil industry's huge investment in refineries as a charitable not-for-profit operation.

The U.S. and European governments have a number of motives for permitting such tax avoidance. Oil is America's largest natural resource sector, and is almost equally politically dominant in Britain and France. And in balance-of-payments terms, in the 1960s the United States sought to finance the drain caused by its foreign military spending by replacing Switzerland as the world's major money-laundering haven. The State Department encouraged U.S. banks to establish branches in the tax-avoidance havens proliferating throughout the Caribbean and the South Pacific to attract flight capital from criminals of all stripes, including officials in **client oligarchies**. These offshore bank branches recycled their hot money to their U.S. head offices, providing an inflow into the dollar that otherwise would have gone to Switzerland, London, Luxembourg, Monaco or other such shady enclaves.

Oligarchy: Rule by the few, usually the richest **One Percent**. In Aristotle's political theory, oligarchy is the stage into which democracy evolves, and which ends up becoming a hereditary aristocracy. "The essence of oligarchic rule," wrote George Orwell in *Nineteen Eighty-Four*, "is not father-to-son inheritance, but the persistence of a certain world-view and a certain way of life ... A ruling group is a ruling group so long as it can nominate its successors ... Who wields power is not important, provided that the hierarchical structure remains always the same."

The word "oligarchy" has been applied to Russia's **kleptocrats** who obtained natural resources and other assets under Boris Yeltsin, most notoriously in the 1994-1996 "bank loans for shares" insider deals. It also applies to Latin American and other **client oligarchies** that concentrate wealth in the financial and propertied class at the top of the pyramid. However, U.S. media vocabulary defines any country as a democracy as long as it supports the **Washington Consensus** and U.S. diplomacy.

One Percent, The: Coined during the **Occupy Wall Street** protest movement, this term focuses on the growing wealth gap between the *rentier* elite and the 99 Percent. The statistics collected by Thomas Piketty and Immanuel Saez have documented the widening disparity between the One Percent and the rest of the population since

1980 in nearly all countries. Subsequent reports have described how nearly all growth in U.S. asset values and income growth since the 2008 crash have been monopolized by just one percent of the population, mainly via the **FIRE sector**. This One Percent increases its power by lending money and creating new bank credit to indebt the 99 Percent, extracting a rising flow of interest and other *rentier* income.

Optimum: In model building, a position from which one cannot move to improve his or her situation. Most people think of optimum as representing an ideal situation, but an Abu Ghraib inmate suspended by his hands over a box with electrodes that will shock him if he moves is said to be in an optimum position, in the sense that any move would only make things worse. So an optimum position may mean merely the least bad. For the poor, survival is the prime need. The price of survival typically involves going into debt to pay for necessities, so debt peonage may become the "optimum" choice. (See **Equilibrium**, **Neo-serfdom** and **Quandary**.)

"Other Peoples' Money": A euphemism for bank credit created electronically. The pretense is that banks are only intermediaries recycling savings to borrowers. The reality is that banks create credit freely on their computer keyboards. (See **Central Bank** and **Modern Monetary Theory**.)

Over-Depreciation: A tax credit based on the pretense that buildings lose their value, despite the landlord's outlays on maintenance and repairs, and despite the inflation of property and land prices. U.S. tax law allows absentee landlords (but not homeowners) to recapture their original outlay assigned to buildings or other capital improvements, **as if** their value deteriorates or they become obsolete as is the case with industrial plant and machinery.

In theory, a depreciation tax credit is counted as a recovery of one's investment. But real estate differs from industrial investment. The depreciation tax credit starts afresh all over again each time a property is sold. This enables absentee landlords to claim fictitious book losses, rendering their property free of income taxation. For the U.S. real estate sector as a whole in most years since World War II, the rate of depreciation is set high enough to offset the rental income otherwise taxed. Thus, according to David Kay Johnson, Donald Trump "pays little to no income tax because he does these real estate deals that allow him to take – as a professional real estate developer – unlimited paper losses like depreciation against income he gets from NBC for his show."[1]

The effect is to favor bank lending and investment in real estate over industry – the opposite of classical tax philosophy.

Overhead: The part of national income not necessary for production and consumption to take place. This category includes **economic rent, interest** and **watered costs** – which really are **zero-sum** transfer payments – as well as military spending, government waste and corruption.

Ownership Society: The term coined by the George W. Bush administration for policies aimed at increasing home ownership by extending junk mortgages to NINJA buyers and others who signed mortgages with "exploding" interest rates and balloon payments falling due. Lending to new buyers on recklessly easier credit terms inflated the housing market, increasing the power of finance and property relative to wage income by raising the price (and hence, debt levels) that wage earners had to pay for homes. (See **Asset-Price Inflation**.) Bush sugar-coated the resulting housing bubble on October 15, 2002: "We can put light where there's darkness, and hope where there's despondency in this country. And part of it is working together as a nation to encourage folks to own their own home."[2]

The aim of coining such euphemisms as "ownership society" is to divert attention from the disproportionate share of assets owned by the top One Percent of the population, plunging the economy into debt peonage instead of ownership free and clear of debt.

A related euphemism along these lines is **labor capitalism**, siphoning off wages into Employee Stock Ownership Plans (ESOPs) controlled by employers. The kindred strategy of **pension-fund capitalism** is to bid up prices for stocks, bonds and real estate. The political intent is to make employees feel that although their paychecks are being squeezed, they will gain as stockholders and homeowners. ("Sorry you lost your job. We hope you made a killing on your home.")

ENDNOTE

[1] Quoted in Katrina vanden Heuvel, "Emperor Trump Has No Clothes," *The Nation*, April 22, 2011.

[2] Jo Becker *et al.*, "Bush drive for home ownership fueled housing bubble," *New York Times*, Dec. 21, 2008.

is for
Ponzi Scheme and
Pension Fund Capitalism

Panic: The culminating point in the business cycle when asset prices plunge, forcing property and financial securities to be sold to pay debts. (See **Hyman Minsky**.) Panics pose the political problem of who will bear the losses and who will be bailed out by government and the bankruptcy courts. Since 2008 the banks and bondholders were bailed out by central banks across the world, not the indebted economies at large. From the United States to the Eurozone, the legacy of such panics is **debt deflation**.

Parallel Universe: A hypothetical set of assumptions whose function in the economics curriculum is to create "educated incapacity" (see **Thorstein Veblen**) by distracting attention from how the real world operates. The aim is to turn students into **idiot savants**, not knowing what to be smart *about*. (See **Neoclassical Economics**, **Junk Economics** and **Nobel Economics Prize**.)

Parasite: A **free luncher**. In biology, parasites avoid detection by masquerading as part of the host's body, using enzymes to take control of the host's brain to block it from taking counter-measures to defend itself. Similarly, *rentiers* and monopolists masquerade as contributors to the production process, as if their revenue is earned rather than siphoning off income from the production-and-consumption economy to the FIRE sector in zero-sum activities. (See **Economic Rent**.) Their intellectual enzyme is junk economics demobilizing governments and academic studies.

Among the various parasitic species, the financial class tends to ride on the backs of real estate investors and monopolists, lobbying to un-tax their rent-seeking activities so as to turn their land rent and monopoly rent into interest payments instead of leaving it for governments to tax.

Partial Equilibrium Analysis: A methodological assumption by economic theorists that one variable can be changed and related to just one other without feedback affecting the overall economy as a dynamic system. (See **X and Y Axes**.) IMF austerity programs, for instance, assume that reducing wages will lower production costs proportionally. This neglects the consequences of change throughout the economy as markets shrink, unemployment increases, governments run deficits as tax revenues fall while public social support payments rise. Labor emigrates and capital flees, debt arrears mount up and foreclosures transfer property to creditors. Bondholders then demand that governments privatize their national infrastructure, creating a *rentier* economy with rising prices. Partial equilibrium "two variable" analysis distracts attention from these consequences. (See **Junk Economics**.) The result is disequilibrium in the relationship between the analytic map drawn by neoclassical and neoliberal economic theory and the trajectory of reality.

Patten, Simon R. (1852–1922): The first professor of economics at America's first business school, the Wharton School of Business at the University of Pennsylvania. Appointed because of his protectionist economics in contrast to British free-trade theory, he was trained in classical political economy in Germany with its Historical School economists, as were nearly all major American economists of his day. (See **American School of Economics**.)

Juxtaposing the coming "economy of abundance" to the "economics of scarcity" that still characterizes most academic price theory, Patten emphasized public investment in infrastructure as a "fourth factor of production."[1] He pointed out that unlike private investment, public infrastructure's aim is not to make a profit, but to provide essential services on a subsidized basis or freely, so as to lower the economy's cost of living and doing business, thereby making public/private mixed economies more competitive internationally. His urging of public investment instead of privatization sought to resist John Bates Clark's support for *rentier* income and denial that any income was unearned.

Pension Fund Capitalism: A term coined in the 1950s to reflect **finance capitalism's** mode of exploiting labor by withholding a portion of wages to invest in stocks. The resulting **asset-price inflation** inspired proposals to privatize Social

Security to engineer a similar rise in stock prices, while generating management fees that would absorb a large share of the gains.

In Chile, the Pinochet junta (advised by the **Chicago Boys**) let companies invest pension funds in their own stocks, increasing their equity prices – and then shift their gains to banks controlled by the corporate *grupo*, leaving the industrial employer a bankrupt shell, wiping out labor's pension savings. (See **Labor Capitalism**.)

Pensioners have now replaced **widows and orphans** (living on trust funds invested in financial markets) as fronts trotted out by Wall Street as proxies for the wealth of the One Percent. It is argued that hurting corporate profits would leave pension funds with lower gains, making it harder to pay retirees. Investing pension funds in the stock and bond market instead of financing direct investment leaves pensioners (along with middle-class savers) hostage to the financial sector. Its lobbyists claim that reforms to help consumers by regulating monopoly pricing and product safety, improving working conditions or paying better wages would hurt pension funds by eroding corporate profits and hence stock-price gains.

Pentagon Capitalism: A term coined in 1970 by Seymour Melman, a professor of industrial engineering at Columbia University, to describe the U.S. practice of "cost-plus" military procurement contracts. Basing profits on a fixed commission rate charged on how much a company spends to develop and produce a weapon means that profits are *maximized* by maximizing their production costs instead of cutting costs below that of rivals as under industrial capitalism.

The sector's political lobbying and campaign contributions lead to insider dealing. When Halliburton chairman and CEO Dick Cheney became U.S. Vice President, for instance, he gave his company contracts in the Iraq War without competitive bidding or meaningful public oversight. (See **Grabitization**.) Pentagon capitalism and its bloated budgets thus foster a militarized **kleptocracy** supported by **neoconservative** politicians.

Physiocrats: Followers of French reformer François Quesnay (1694-1774), called *Les Économistes*. Quesnay created the first **national income account**, the *Tableau Économique*. As surgeon to the royal family, his idea of the **circular flow** of income among cultivators, landlords, industry and the government was inspired by the circulation of blood in the human body. (See **Say's Law**.) Arguing that **land rent** – the main domestic economic surplus (*produit net*) in 18th-century France – was not produced by the nobility's labor or enterprise (contra **John Locke**) but by nature, ultimately from the sun's energy, the Physiocrats advocated that the landed aristocracy's **groundrent** be taxed (*l'impôt unique*) instead of labor and industry. (See **Adam Smith, John Stuart Mill** and **Henry George**.)

Planned Economy: Every economy since the Neolithic has been planned in one way or another. That is why calendar keeping and seasonal rhythms based on the weather and the harvest became the foundation of economic **accounting** in the Neolithic and Bronze Age for fiscal and trade policy and for land tenure. (See **Economic Forecasting**.)

At issue in any epoch is who will do the planning and what its aims will be. The ostensible aim of democratic planning is to design tax and regulatory systems to promote economic growth and sustainability, preferably with a fair distribution of income and wealth. For the classical economists this involved taxing or discouraging *rentier* income, and subsidizing socially desirable investment and basic needs.

Today's epoch is seeing financial managers replace rulers and elected government representatives as planners of economies. Financial planning is at least as centralized as government planning, but its aims are different: namely, to concentrate income growth and asset-price gains in the hands of the One Percent.

The financial time frame is short-term and extractive. And fiscally, financial planning seeks to shift taxes *off* unearned income and financial returns *onto* wages and profits. Most fatally, it favors debt leveraging (see **Bubble**), leading ultimately to debt deflation and austerity. (See **IMF** and **Central Banks**.) The main issue in today's planning debate is thus whether democratic politics can recover the classical public steering and regulatory mechanisms that have been relinquished to the financial sector.

Poison Pill: A defense against financial raiders who aim to pull cash reserves out of a company via debt-leveraged takeovers. Potential target companies borrow so much money that interest charges absorb most of their profits, leaving no room for raiders to issue new junk bonds to finance a takeover. (See **Cash Flow/Ebitda**.) A related defensive ploy is to pass a resolution to pay off bondholders immediately in case of an unfriendly takeover. This would deplete the cash reserves that raiders would have targeted. The effect is that un-raided as well as raided companies end up paying heavy debt service, so the corporate sector suffers financialization either way, debilitating companies by diverting profits from being used for real capital investment.

Polarization: The tendency for economies to polarize between the **One Percent** and the **99 Percent**, above all between creditors and debtors. (See **Credit** and **Debt**.) This tends to characterize **bubble** economies. (See **Great Moderation**.) The tendency can be countered by progressive taxes focusing on **economic rent** (unearned income) and **asset-price** gains ("capital" gains); not allowing interest to be tax-deductible; keeping money and banking as a public utility; and creating credit along productive lines instead of to inflate asset prices.

The income distribution chart (above)[2] shows how the One Percent

Distribution of Average Income Growth During Expansions

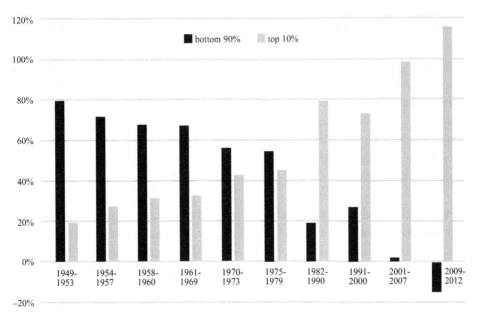

Source: Pavlina R. Tcherneva, analysis of Piketty/Saez data and NBER (including capital gains)

monopolized income growth in the expansion (bubble) leading up to the 2008 meltdown, and further consolidated their position in the post-bubble economy when payback time arrived for the debts that homebuyers and businesses had run up in the hope that credit might make them rich.

Politics: Now part of the market economy as policy-making is put up for sale. Under "pay to play," politicians raise campaign funds from the wealthy One Percent while seeking votes from the 99 Percent. Promising to protect the public interest, politicians vie among themselves to deliver their constituencies to their financial backers. The oligarchy's aim is to keep election discussion away from economic issues by focusing on identity politics such as ethnic minorities, women and LGBTQ.

Pollution: The tendency for a given trend in the climate system or economy to accelerate to the point where it stifles and destabilizes the overall system. Global warming, for instance, is caused by runaway carbon-based fuel emissions. Sea levels rise and weather becomes extreme as glaciers melt, causing the earth to heat up faster as it absorbs more sunlight.

Debt pollution has a similar destructive effect. Increased lending to households, industry and government extracts more interest and fees. This concentrates income and property in the hands of banks and bondholders (see **FIRE Sector**). The economy stagnates as **debt deflation** shrinks markets, deterring new investment and employment.

Assuming that living in this way can continue in a stable trajectory without taking protective counter-measures fails to take into account the self-reinforcing tendencies of instability that accelerate over time. Failure to reverse debt pollution by writing down debts with a Clean Slate is analogous to the failure to stop carbon emissions and reverse global warming. In both cases pollution is caused by living in the short run as the vested interests (the oil industry, banks and bondholders) block counter-measures to restore the system's stabilizing checks and balances and halt the instability.

Ponzi Scheme: A financial operation in which early investors are paid with money put up by new subscribers, not out of actual profits. Investor concerns are allayed by promises of exorbitant returns, often from a hitherto "undiscovered" scheme to make money. The Italian-American confidence man Carlo Ponzi claimed to have found such an opportunity in international postage-stamp arbitrage. Bernie Madoff was widely believed to be making gains by front-running and insider dealing.

On the economy-wide level the term Ponzi Scheme is applied to financial bubbles expanding at an **exponential** rate without earning enough income to remain solvent. (See **Compound Interest** and **Fragility**.) For **Hyman Minsky**, the Ponzi stage of the credit cycle occurs when debtors can avoid default only by borrowing the interest falling due. (Banks often are willing partners in such schemes.) Such Ponzi-type growth necessitates a constant influx of new capital to avert bankruptcy. Collapse occurs at the point where new inflows of funds or public credit creation no longer grow exponentially. (See **Economic Forecasting**.) The U.S. **junk-mortgage bubble**, for instance, was sustained until 2008 by the Federal Reserve and banking system creating enough exponential growth in credit to enable investors to keep on making asset-price gains (euphemized as the **Great Moderation**).

Populism/Populist: The demeaning epithets applied to democratic policies that neoliberals and the One Percent do not like.

Postindustrial Economy: A euphemism to depict *rentier* economies as evolving forward, as if this is progress instead of a lapse back into the extractive pre-industrial usury-and-rent economy of feudalism. (See **Neofeudalism** and **Stages of Development**.)

Postmodern Economy: A century ago the term "modern" referred to Progressive

Era economic policies promoting a less polarized distribution of wealth, headed by progressive income taxation that collected mainly *rentier* income. Today's neoliberal program reverses this trend, backing a regressive tax shift *from* property and finance *onto* labor, and reducing the government's regulatory power except where it transfers income upward to the wealthiest layer of the population. (See **Alan Greenspan**, **Laffer Curve**, **Oligarchy** and **Neofeudalism**.)

Price: See **Just Price**, **Market Price** and **Value**.

Privatization: The word "private" derives from Latin *privatus*, meaning restricted, as in **privilege**, and *privare*, "to deprive" and indeed, "to rob," as in *prevaricate*. Starting with the enclosure of the **commons** – the fencing in of communal grazing land and forests in Britain – the enclosures of the 16th through 18th centuries deprived peasants of their land rights and means of subsistence, driving them into the cities as "loom-fodder" for textile mills and workhouses. (For the Soviet Union's post-1991 carve-up, see **Grabitization** and **Kleptocracy**.)

Since 1980 the main lever of privatization has been financial. Debt-strapped governments are forced to sell off the public domain as a **conditionality** imposed by the IMF in exchange for credit to avoid defaulting on bank debts or foreign debts. (See **Washington Consensus**.) The prime assets being privatized are natural monopolies able to extract economic rent by raising prices for hitherto public services. These rents tend to be paid out as tax-deductible interest to affiliates in offshore banking centers in order to deprive host economies of a public return on their land and natural resource patrimony or their immense capital investment in infrastructure – much of which was financed by foreign debts for which governments remain liable.

Such privatization de-socializes public infrastructure, usually by rent extractors in partnership with government insiders. Access charges may be raised as high as users ("the market") will pay. Junk economics pretends that this will be more efficient than public investment to provide basic services at low prices. The reality is that countries that fail to invest in minimizing the cost of basic services (by avoiding tollbooths for financialized rent extraction) have a higher cost of living and doing business, making them less competitive in global markets.

Privilege: Literally a "private law," granting ownership or rights to charge **economic rent** as an access fee to users of natural monopolies otherwise in the public domain (land, water and natural resources), infrastructure (railroads, roads, communications and other public utilities) or artificial trade monopolies. Such *rentier* privileges are obtained by insider dealings, as spoils of war or by financial leverage and foreclosure. (See **Property**.) Classes living off such privileges include landlords, bankers and monopolists (mainly the financial class).

Productive Loan: A loan that enables the borrower to earn sufficient income to pay the creditor and still emerge with a profit. Adam Smith cited as a rule of thumb that the rate of interest tended to settle at half the rate of profit. That would enable commercial borrowers to split their overall returns 50/50 with their "silent partner" creditors (see **Sleeping Partner**). But rising debt leverage has expanded the volume of today's interest charges to absorb most profits in real estate, and also in corporate takeovers by raiders financing their leveraged buyouts with junk bonds (see **Debt Leveraging**). The aim is to make tax-favored asset-price gains. Real estate investors are willing to pay the entire property income as interest in order to emerge with such capital gains when they sell to the next "greater fool." Such bubble-economy speculation is "productive" only to the extent that asset-price gains outpace the rate of interest. (See **Cash Flow/Ebitda** and **Pyramiding**.) Such bank lending to bid up asset prices adds to the economy's debt overhead without expanding the means of production or earnings.

Personal loans are deemed unproductive because they must be paid out of income earned elsewhere rather than being invested productively to earn an income. Junk education loans sponsored by for-profit colleges are said to be backed by "human capital," but this is a Doublethink euphemism for false promises that their degrees will enable their graduates to earn enough additional income to pay back the loan and its interest charges. The U.S. Government recently recognized the need to write down such debts. These loans are an example of **fictitious capital** – assets on the books of banks (and the government that guarantees such frauds) with no real counterpart in the ability to be paid.

Productive vs. Unproductive Labor: Defining productivity is fairly easy when the measure of output consists of uniform commodities: steel, crops or automobiles produced per man-year. But today's National Income and Product Accounts (NIPA) define the productivity of labor by Gross Domestic Product (GDP) per work-year, regardless of whether it produces commodities, financial "services" or simply makes money by zero-sum speculation.

Goldman Sachs's Lloyd Blankfein has bragged that his firm's partners are the economy's most productive individuals, as measured by the huge amounts of money they make. This reasoning is circular: It claims that people are paid according to their productivity as measured by their wages, salaries and/or bonuses – which are assumed to be paid in proportion to their productivity!

But what about economic activity that is merely extractive and predatory? **Value-free economics** abandons the classical definition of productive labor or investment as that which produces profit on "real" production. At issue is what is real and what is mere overhead.

Adam Smith and his followers defined labor as productive only if it produced commodities for sale. That was in an epoch when most services were performed by servants (maids, butlers, coachmen and other employees of the wealthy) as consumption expenses. This personal employment was deemed to be part of the *rentier* class's overhead. Church officials, government workers, the army, tutors and teachers or other professionals in what today is called the non-profit sector also were deemed unproductive.

To Karl Marx, labor under industrial capitalism was productive to the extent that it produced a profit for its employer. He pointed out that even prostitutes were productive – of a profit, if employed by their madams, just as steel workers were productive of a profit to mill owners. His 3-volume *Theories of Surplus Value* reviewed the classical discussion of productive labor, **value** and **price**.

From the classical vantage point, rent extraction, debt leveraging and related financial overhead is not part of the economy's necessary core, and thus would be viewed as a subtrahend from "real" output and productivity. Post-classical economists stopped distinguishing between intrinsic value and market price so as to avoid the critique of land rent, monopoly rent, and financial and other *rentier* charges as undesirable overhead.

After Russia's 1917 revolution, Soviet statisticians reverted to Adam Smith's definition of physical productivity: material output per worker. Their non-capitalist society had no *rentier* class, and the state did not charge interest or rent, so no implicit rent-of-location or cost of capital was measured in their national income statistics. These exclusions left Russia somewhat naïve when it opened its economy to the West in 1991, not realizing that the main aim of neoliberal investment was rent extraction from natural resources, land and monopolies (see **Rent Theory**).

The postindustrial epoch in the West itself has seen industry turned into a vehicle to extract economic rent and interest, and to make "capital" gains from asset-price inflation as a "total return" on equity. From the classical vantage point of the industrial economy at large, this is an overgrowth of unproductive investment. The quick collapse of Russian manufacturing after 1991 is an object lesson in the effect of replacing industrial productivity with *rentier* asset stripping.

Profit: Classical political economy defined profit as the return to capital invested in plant, equipment and related outlays to hire wage labor. Today's popular language uses "profit" indiscriminately for income, regardless of its source. (See **John Bates Clark**.) The U.S. National Income and Product Accounts (NIPA) report *rentier* income from land or monopoly rights as "earnings," conflating economic rent with profit earned on tangible capital investment.

Progress: Today's word "progress" has degenerated from its 19th- and 20th-century meaning of democratic reform. Every process of social decay euphemizes itself as progress, as if moving forward in time is invariably upward, not retrogressive. (See **Stages of Development**.) So there is "real" progress and false progress. The neoliberal ideology favoring *rentier* income over wages, deregulation, financialization and privatization over public investment is antithetical to classical political economy's definition of social progress as replacing feudal privilege with progressive income tax and regulatory policy promoting greater equality of opportunity and income, mainly by taxing economic rent and windfall to property and financial gains.

Theories of progress treat the debt buildup as cumulative and irreversible, in contrast to ancient society's idea of circular time with periodic financial clean slates to restore economic balance from outside "the market." Without debt cancellations, economies evolve into oligarchies, which depict their takeovers as "progress" and thus as morally justified on the ground of its seeming inevitability. (See **End of History**.)

Progressive Era: The 1890s to 1920s, when leading politicians sought to cure society from the excesses of the Gilded Age. Major changes in public policy included the income tax (Sixteenth Amendment of the U.S. Constitution), direct election of senators (Seventeenth Amendment, to counter government corruption), Prohibition (Eighteenth Amendment against the vice of liquor), and women's suffrage (Nineteenth Amendment, giving women the right to vote). Labor union-ization helped raise wage levels and improve working conditions, promoting the rise of a middle class largely through rising home ownership, better access to education. Socialist parties were formed and gained influence throughout the world, while government investment in basic infrastructure provided a widening range of public services at subsidized prices or without cost.

These progressive moves led to a countervailing response. Creation of the Federal Reserve system in 1913 shifted control of banking away from the U.S. Treasury to Wall Street.[3] And after World War I, banking practice throughout the world shifted away from the German emphasis on industrial banking to the Anglo-American tradition of collateral-based banking and speculative finance.

This reaction sought to justify itself by sponsoring a counter-revolution against classical political economy, rejecting the concept of economic rent as unearned income. Today's junk economics rationalizes privatization and financialization, reversing the tendencies toward the less polarized distribution of income and wealth that underlay economic progress from the 1930s to 1980.

Propensity to Save: To **John Maynard Keynes**, the portion of income an economy does not spend on consumption. This refers to *net* **saving**, which has fallen to zero for the United States, because the **One Percent** lend out their **savings** (and new money creation) to become the **debts** of the **99 Percent** (appearing as debt on the liabilities side of the balance sheet). *Gross* saving remains as high as ever, but it was all lent out leading up to the 2008 crash.

Keynes treated saving simply as hoarding, not as debt payment. But since the 2008 crash, a large number of consumers have been obliged to "save" by paying down their debts. That is why reported net saving rates have risen. For most families this does not mean more available money. Just the opposite: banks have stopped lending and repayment time has arrived. The result of this rising "propensity to save" is **debt deflation**, which occurs when amortization (not to mention interest) paid to the financial sector exceeds new lending.[4]

Property: It was mainly with land in mind that the French socialist Pierre Joseph Proudhon (1809-1865) wrote: "Property is theft." Military conquest has been the traditional lever to privatize land, but as property becomes burdened with debt, foreclosure becomes the main lever for creditors to pry it away. In the past this was achieved by usury on an individual scale, but recently the public domain has been privatized as creditors oblige indebted governments to surrender to IMF conditionalities. (See **Privilege** and **Kleptocracy**.)

Prosperity: The opposite of austerity and the ideology of scarcity as propagated by Junk Economics. (See **Simon Patten** and the economics of abundance.)

Protecting Savings: Banks and bondholders are euphemized as "savers," identifying their interests with those of pensioners and family savings. But if all credit were as productive as is depicted, debtors would be able to pay and there would not be defaults leading to a crash. But the economy's overall volume of savings (other peoples' debts) mounting up at **compound interest** cannot be carried *ad infinitum*. In the end it is an impossible task. Something must give when bankruptcies wipe out borrowers. Governments are called upon to "make savers whole" by compensating banks for losses on their credit creation and bubble lending. (See **Moral Hazard**.)

Protectionism: The policy of imposing tariffs and quotas on imports, subsidizing exports, preferential "buy at home" government spending, and blocked currencies to provide higher returns for domestic industry and agriculture. This has been U.S. policy since the Civil War, while promoting free trade for other countries. (See **American School of Political Economy**.)

The protected sectors claim that higher prices and profits will enable them to invest more in raising productivity. That is how the spokesman for England's landlord class, Thomas Malthus, defended Britain's Corn Laws (its agricultural protectionism) after 1815. But whereas British policy protected land rent, American protectionism supported profits on industrial capital formation. American industrial strategists from Alexander Hamilton through Henry Clay, Henry Carey and E. Peshine Smith argued for tariff protection to serve manufacturing.

Public domain: The **commons**, consisting of land and natural resources, infrastructure and government enterprises. Natural monopolies such as canals, railroads, airlines, water and power, radio and television frequencies, telephone systems, roads, forests, airports and naval ports, schools and other public assets were long kept out of private hands. Their privatization since 1980 has turned them into rent-extracting opportunities for hitherto public services.

Financing their purchase on credit (often at giveaway prices paid to debt-strapped or corrupt neoliberal governments) enables these monopolies to include interest, dividends and high managerial salaries in their cost structure. The most rapidly rising consumer prices in the United States since 2008, for instance, are for health insurance (privatized Obamacare), education and cable service. Privatization and economic polarization thus go together.

Public Investment: Simon Patten called infrastructure investment a fourth factor of production (after labor, capital and land), supplying basic transportation, communication, health services, water and power, and other public services. Investment in such infrastructure is often the largest category of a national economy's capital formation. Unlike private investment, its return is to be calculated not by the profit it makes, but by the extent to which it lowers the economy's overall cost structure. Its aim is to provide services at cost, below cost, or freely as in the case of roads and other basic needs.

Yet Frederick Hayek called public investment the "road to serfdom," a Doublethink term for economies freeing themselves from rent-extracting monopolies. By minimizing the economy's cost structure, public investment and ownership is the main defense *against* such *rentier* tollbooth charges. Its virtue lies in avoiding the profit, interest charges and rent extraction that private investors and their financial backers build into the price of supplying water, roads, transportation, power, communications and other basic needs. By contrast, socialist policy advocates keeping natural monopolies and infrastructure in (or transferred to) the public domain.

Public-Private Partnership: Crony capitalism in which governments guarantee a specified return and absorb the losses on cost overruns (akin to **Pentagon Capitalism**).

Pyramid: Ancient Egyptians devoted their surplus of food, labor and raw materials to building stone pyramids to deify their pharaohs. Each time a pharaoh died, a new monument and its funerary cult removed land and labor from the economy.

Our modern economy devotes its surplus to a debt pyramid. Unlike Egypt's pyramids with their wide base tapering off toward the peak on top, today's debt pyramid is inverted: a narrow base of production and earning power at the bottom with a widening financial overgrowth expanding exponentially at the top, fed by the magic of **compound interest**. Interest and amortization charges on this debt leave less income available for the rest of the economy, making the base more unstable as it grows financially top-heavy, until the debt superstructure tips over and crushes the economic base beneath it. (See **Ponzi Scheme**.)

Pyramiding: Debt leveraging (called "gearing" in Britain) involves using as little of one's own money and borrowing as much as possible, as long as interest rates are less than the rate of profit plus capital gains. For these total returns (income plus asset-price inflation) to continue to exceed the interest rate, an exponential increase in bank credit is required to support enough asset-price gains to enable borrowers to borrow the interest falling due.

The process is inherently self-terminating. The real estate bubble burst in 2008 when banks stopped lending new homebuyers enough to keep bidding up prices fast enough. Existing mortgage debtors were unable to borrow enough new credit to pay their debt-servicing costs once asset-price gains stopped. The analogous Ponzi Schemes end when there are not enough new entrants to finance the pace of cash withdrawals by earlier players.

ENDNOTES

[1] I review Patten's protectionist and sociological views in *America's Protectionist Takeoff: 1815-1914* (ISLET 2010) and "Simon Patten on Public Infrastructure and

Economic Rent Capture," *American Journal of Economics and Sociology* **70** (October 2011):873-903.

[2] Pavlina R. Tcherneva, "Growth For Whom?" Levy Economics Institute of Bard College, October 6, 2014.

[3] I describe this shift in "How the U.S. Treasury avoided Chronic Deflation by Relinquishing Monetary Control to Wall Street," *Economic & Political Weekly* (India), May 7, 2016.

[4] I explain the accounting in "Saving, Asset-Price Inflation, and Debt-Induced Deflation," in L. Randall Wray and Matthew Forstater, eds., *Money, Financial Instability and Stabilization Policy* (Edward Elgar, 2006):104-24.

is for
Quandary

Quandary: A situation where a party cannot change position without making its situation worse. (See **Optimum**.) Unlike a problem (which implicitly has a solution), a quandary has no way out to save matters. Examples include the Federal Reserve's Quantitative Easing policy from 2009 to 2016. Keeping interest rates low helped revive prices for real estate, stocks and bonds, and thus saved the largest and most reckless U.S. banks from insolvency. But these low interest rates also pushed pension funds and insurance companies into shortfalls in the rate of return needed to pay retirees and policy holders. On the other hand, raising interest rates would cause the dollar's exchange rate to soar. It also would raise borrowing costs and hence the cost of debt-leveraging. Speculation would be cut back, rolling back prices for bonds, real estate and stocks, threatening a new wave of insolvency for economies mired in debt. Hence, the policy remained frozen throughout the Obama Administration.

Quantitative Easing (QE): Central bank support for bank credit creation to drive down interest rates and re-inflate real estate and stock market prices. In the wake of the 2008 crash the Federal Reserve and European Central Bank (ECB) promoted new bank lending and arbitrage speculation as an alternative to writing down debts. The hope was that new bank lending would re-inflate the bubble. The European Central Bank's QE ("as much as it takes," said its president, Mario Draghi) lent money and purchased bonds to bail out banks and bondholders for their bad loans and investments. But it did not create money to revive businesses or indebted homeowners and consumers. Focusing only on subsidizing bank balance sheets, its aim was to save the financial sector and the One Percent behind it, not the economy. So QE had little effect in coping with the underlying problem, which was debt deflation. In fact, Eurozone governments imposed austerity, sacrificing national economies by giving priority to creditor claims.

In the United States, the Federal Reserve accepted mortgages and other bank loans at full face value as reserve deposits, enabling banks to meet their capital ratios and create new electronic credit. But the $4.2 trillion U.S. Federal Reserve creation of bank reserves did not increase commodity prices or wages as the Quantity Theory of Money implied it would. Banks engaged mainly in speculation. They bought foreign bonds and currencies, and lent to hedge funds and for corporate share buybacks, mergers and acquisitions. None of this financed new investment. The U.S. and European economies remained debt-wracked and suffered deepening debt deflation.

Without QE the banks would have had to sell their loans in "the market" at falling prices, at rising interest rates – further lowering the price of collateral-backed bank loans, forcing yet further sell-offs. So in the name of saving "the market," the Fed and ECB overruled it in the aftermath of the 2008 junk mortgage crash.

Apart from banks, other sectors of the financial markets suffered along with the rest of the economy – above pension funds and insurance companies. Money managers urged an end to the Federal Reserve's Quantitative Easing policy to hold down interest rates. One argument was that higher interest rates are necessary to support workers in their role as consumers as well as pension plan savers. It was almost as if labor obtains its spending money mainly from bonds and stocks. "In the first place," a fund manager opined in a *Wall Street Journal* op-ed, "the Fed's policy of zero or near-zero interest rates means negligible returns on savings. Consumers thus have less to spend and those nearing retirement need to save more."[1]

This depicts workers/consumers as *rentiers*, not debtors. The trick is to get indebted voters to think of themselves as savers, benefiting from higher interest rates rather than suffering as debtors. "In human terms, the Fed's policy means emergency room nurses in Texas work longer hours to make up for low yields on CDs, dairy farmers in Iowa forgo equipment purchases to save more for retirement, charities for the homeless in Manhattan reduce services as foundations cut grants, and local governments from Albany to Sacramento close libraries to fund pension plan deficits."[1]

The higher retirement savings required by nurses, farmers and charities – for whom widows and orphans are stand-ins – are a result of how the economy has been financialized. Debt service and compulsory savings are owed *by* these nurses on their home mortgages and education debts, *by* farmers on their equipment and mortgage debts, and *by* local governments on their borrowings. Higher interest rates make these charges heavier. What is needed to alleviate their financial squeeze is debt relief (see **Clean Slates**), along with a shift of Social Security and pensions, health care and education back to the public sector, to be financed out of progressive taxes on *rentier* income and wealth as well as public money creation.

Quantitative Easing thus was a policy to save only the banks and bondholders, not the economy at large. The effect since 2008 has been to sharply increase the power of the One Percent over the rest of the economy. In the United States, 95% of the population has seen its real income and net worth decline during 2008-2016, despite the soaring stock and bond markets. And while real estate hedge funds such as Blackstone have made a killing by buying up foreclosed properties, home ownership rates have fallen back from 69% to 63.5%. The decline has been especially sharp for blacks, who were the major victims of junk-mortgage loans, and for individuals under 35 years old, who cannot afford to buy homes as long as they remain saddled with student debts and other obligations in the face of a falling-wage economy. The "easing" in Quantitative Easing has thus been only for the top of the economic pyramid.

Quantity Theory (Tautology) of Money (MV = PT): The myth that monetary and credit expansion inflates consumer and commodity prices. Most bank lending inflates **asset prices**, because most loans are spent on real estate, stocks, bonds and packaged bank loans. Credit creation to finance the 2001–2008 real estate bubble siphoned off a rising swath of income from homebuyers to pay their mortgage debt, leaving *less* income available to spend on goods and services.

Quantum finance: Financial methodology developed by quantum physicists and mathematicians on the basis of correlation analysis ("projecting the past"), applied most notoriously by the Black-Scholes mathematics that drove Long Term Credit Management broke in 1998. (See **Nobel Economics Prize**.) This marginalist approach is based on correlations of small changes. It leads to economic near-sightedness. But to non-mathematicians, the complexity of the formulas became a selling point that made many bad financial instruments of the 2000s appear plausible, precisely because they were opaque when being sold by unscrupulous investment bankers and traders. Wall Street's "smart boys" won huge sums at the expense of pension funds and wealthy "marks."

ENDNOTE

[1] John C. Michaelson, "The High Costs of Very Low Interest Rates," *Wall Street Journal*, August 11, 2010.

is for
Rentiers and the
Race to the Bottom
they sponsor

R2P ("Responsibility to Protect"): A euphemism for "Responsibility to Privatize." The Obama Administration's military hawks used this Orwellian term (see **Doublethink** and **Newspeak**) to destroy countries possessing oil resources or pipeline routes not under American control, or other countries with assets that U.S. strategists sought to pry control away from sovereign governments. At best, the term means "Responsibility to Protect oligarchies and privatizers" adhering to the neoliberal **Washington Consensus**.

Race To The Bottom: The policy of countries trying to increase their exports (and attract foreign investment inflows) by cutting wages levels. Toward this end, **austerity** programs ultimately are self-defeating. Without raising education and living standards, labor productivity can be increased only by working labor more intensively and cutting back health care and pensions. When the state of Alabama cut education and health spending to minimize taxes, ostensibly to attract business, companies pulled out on the ground that the state's labor force was too low-skilled and in bad health. New Jersey's economy and employment likewise suffered when it cut taxes instead of modernizing its transportation and tunnels to New York City.

Reaganomics: The policy of cutting taxes for the wealthy (especially for real estate investors) while increasing the Social Security tax on employees. (See **Alan Greenspan, Laffer Curve** and **Tax Shift**.) The effect was to quadruple the public debt during the 1981-1992 Reagan-Bush administration, while dismantling environmental regulations and **deregulating** finance to produce a wave of Savings and Loan (S&L) fraud, **junk-bond** takeovers and a stock market **bubble**. This was euphemized as "wealth creation," not debt creation.

Real Economy: The **National Income and Product Accounts (NIPA)** define "real output" as all the economy's transactions fit to record (but not crime and fraud). This GDP measure is then deflated by an index number for price inflation of goods and services.

But not all of this is "real" in the sense of actual production, consumption and new capital investment. The essence of the tangible economy is the circular flow in which employers earn profits, which they invest in capital goods and pay their employees, who spend their income to buy the goods they produce. (See **Say's Law**.)

THE "REAL" ECONOMY
(domestic private sector)

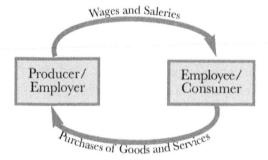

Banks, landlords and monopolists do not make products. Yet the NIPA include the FIRE sector as *part* of the economy, not as a subtrahend diverting wages and business income to pay interest and economic rent. The FIRE sector uses its legal privileges to extract income *from* the economy in a zero-zum *rentier* activity. So "real" does not refer to the actual production, distribution and consumption of goods and services. What turns out to be most "real" – in the sense of being an inexorable burden, to be paid first "off the top" – is the superstructure of debt and credit, monopoly rights and privileges in which the mode of production is wrapped. (See also **Government** and the **Two Economies**.)

Junk Economics conflates this dominant FIRE sector with the production-and-consumption economy at large, refusing to acknowledge its different role, dynamics, and its political and legal levers of control over government policy.

Real Estate: Literally "royal" estate, reflecting the idea that **land** and its **rental income** is held for public purposes and to defray public expenditure (originally to supply fighting men and corvée labor). As land and natural resources have become privatized, they also have been financialized, that is, bought on credit. Seeking debt-leveraged asset-price gains, investors are willing to pay land rent to banks as interest, creating a **debt overhead** for the economy as a whole. Banks thus have ended up with what "originally" was paid to the community or government as taxes.

Real Wages: Economic jargon uses the term "real" in an idiosyncratic way. It refers only to a price adjustment, often applied to concepts that are somewhat unreal to start with. "Real wages" refer to money wages adjusted for the erosion of purchasing power as measured by the rise in the consumer price index (CPI). The adjustment is supposed to reflect the decline in purchasing power of nominal wages when the cost of living rises. This measure shows that there has not been a real gain of annual wages since the 1970s. If annual wages rise by a nominal amount (say, 2% a year), but consumer prices also rise by this much, there has been no real gain. And if the CPI rises faster than wages, wage-earners "really" receive *less*.

But even this measure fails to reflect the errosion of labor's real living standards. In recent years wage-earners have suffered from an much more unpleasant reality. They are not able to consume anywhere near what they are paid, because a rising *proportion* of their household budget must now be paid to the FIRE sector as debt service, rent and other housing costs and insurance, as well as steeper FICA wage withholding. (The "Hudson Bubble Model" later in this book explains the accounting.) So what really is "real" is substantially less than what is reported as real wages. The CPI refers to the *shrinking* proportion of household budgets (perhaps as little as one third) that is spent on commodities. What is missing is the rising carve-out for debt, rent, and other FIRE-sector rake-offs.

Real Wealth: The market price of assets deflated by the rise in the consumer price index (CPI) or a Gross Domestic Product (GDP) price deflator for goods and services. The implication is that wealth is erroded when wages or prices rise. But the wealthy do not spend much of their income on consumption, so this adjustment seems irrelevant.

The way that most of the One Percent makes its fortunes is not "real" in the sense of producing value in the form of goods and services. "Wealth" today refers not only to tangible means of production, but to any bankable asset. A "wealth" fund consists of financial claims *on* society's means of production (in the form of mortgages and other bank loans, stocks and bonds) – what Frederick Soddy called **virtual wealth**, which rightly should appear on the *liabilities* side of the economy's balance sheet.

The problem with confusing real wealth with financial claims is that rising access prices for housing and other basic needs is treated as a gain for "the economy" as a whole. The middle class imagines itself to be growing wealthier as the price of its housing rises – on credit – causing debt deflation for the overall economy and thus slowing *real* wealth creation.

Reform: The aim of 18th-century Enlightenment reform became that of classical political economy: to end free lunches and privilege. But today's post-modern "reform" aims to roll back these goals. The word "reform" is now attached to any policy as an advertising slogan, much like the word "new." Russia's neoliberal "reformers" sponsored kleptocracy. The IMF, eurozone and kindred Washington Consensus demand labor market "reforms" that would reverse the 20th century's workplace reforms and unionization gains. So in today's **Doublespeak**, "reform" means undoing the **Progressive Era's** reforms.

Regressive Taxation: The reverse of progressive taxation: a tax policy that falls on the lower income and wealth brackets instead of on the highest. (See **Tax Shift**.) Examples include replacing income taxes with a **Value Added Tax (VAT)** that falls on consumers, and financing Social Security and health care programs with user fees instead of out of the general budget. (See **Alan Greenspan** and **Laffer Curve**.)

Regulation: From a root meaning *to rule* (as in regal). Every society is regulated in one form or another. Rulers create regulatory systems that in principle (or at least, as a cover story) are supposed to maximize growth and prosperity. When today's governments **deregulate**, they relinquish planning power to the financial sector. The result is as centralized as is public regulation, and favors *rentiers* instead of limiting their power. (See **Planned Economy**.)

Regulatory Capture: Banks and other rent-extracting sectors gain control of public regulatory agencies by blocking nominees who might actually regulate, tax or prosecute the FIRE sector and monopolies. Reversing the classical objective of checks and balances on privatized rent seeking, the neutered agencies act on behalf of the **vested interests** to promote oligarchy. Recent examples include Wall Street pressing to appoint Alan Greenspan as head of the Federal Reserve Board, and to put Robert Rubin's protégés and Goldman Sachs alumni in charge of treasuries and **central banks** in the United States and Europe. The aim is to remove policy making and law enforcement from democratic government to Wall Street, the city of London, Frankfort, and the Paris Bourse.

Rent: A periodic payment of a stipulated amount, as in property rents paid to landlords, or French *rentes* (government bonds) paying interest on a regular calendric basis at a specified rate. As real estate has been transferred from hereditary class ownership to buyers on credit, most of the land's rental value is now paid to mortgage lenders as interest for the mortgage loans needed to obtain property and join the **middle class**. (See **Debt Peonage, FIRE Sector, Groundrent** and **Ownership Society**.)

Rent, Economic: See **Economic Rent** and **Rent Theory**.

Rent, Monopoly: As with all economic rent, monopoly rent is the excess of price over real cost-value. Britain created royal monopolies in the form of **privileged** trading companies, from the East India Company in 1600 to the South Sea Company in 1711. In modern times **privatized** public utilities (such as Carlos Slim's Mexican telecom monopoly) and technology companies such as Microsoft and Apple, obtain monopoly rent – as much as the market will bear, without public anti-monopoly legislation or enforcement – by charging access fees to use their phones or the software installed on computers around the world.

David Buchanan's 1814 notes to Adam Smith's *Wealth of Nations* described groundrent as monopoly rent, resulting from the scarcity of land. (Ricardo attributed land rent solely to the advantage of fertile soils over zero-rent land at the high-cost margin of cultivation.) Monopoly rent and groundrent (including for oil, gas and other natural resources) are the major revenue flows that today's creditors seek to transform into a flow of interest and dividends. So in principle, monopolies should be included in the FIRE Sector, starting with the natural resource sectors (oil and gas, mining, water and forestry).

Rental Income (as distinguished from **Economic Rent**): The overall "house rent" or commercial property rent paid to landlords. This gross rent includes not only land rent but also covers returns for the building's cost-value, plus current operating and maintenance costs. For commercial investors, "rent is for paying interest." When real estate prices are rising (see **Bubble Economy**) their strategy is to put down as little of their own money as possible, using the rental income to carry the bank loan. The aim is to end up with a capital gain when they sell the property.

For the economy at large, this process leaves government with no income tax receipts, only a modest property tax that is just a fraction of what bankers receive from the real estate sector as interest. (Property taxes typically are just 1% of the assessed property value, compared to about 6% for mortgage interest.)

Rent of Location: The rental income resulting from favorable location, which is now the main monopoly character of **land rent**. In his 1826 book *Die isolierte Staat* [*The Isolated State with Respect to Agriculture and Political Economy*], Heinrich von Thünen distinguished this type of rent from Ricardian rent attributed to soil-fertility differentials. Location rent is increased by railroads, subway lines, roads and other transport infrastructure, by better schools and neighboring parks, and by zoning permission to shift land use from agriculture or brownfields to more remunerative commercial or residential use or higher-rise buildings

Rentier: A class of people living on property **rent** and **interest**, sometimes called "the idle rich" or "coupon clippers." An early French government bond was called a *rente*. Bonds used to have coupons attached to them, to be cut out and cashed in at the treasury when interest came due – hence the term *rentier*. Landlords also collect rents at regular calendrical intervals.

In his *General Theory* (1936), John Maynard Keynes said that he looked forward to **"euthanasia of the *rentier*,"** a class that he called "functionless investors."[1] Applying the maxim, "If the eye offend thee, pluck it out," the vested interests have sponsored a post-classical reaction claiming that all income is earned and reflects their supposedly productive role. (See **John Bates Clark** and **Affluenza**.)

Rentier **Income: Rent** and **interest** are obtained without the recipient having to provide labor or enterprise that contributes to the "real economy" of production and consumption. (See **Groundrent, Unearned Income** and **John Stuart Mill**.)

The essence of liberal reform early in the 20th century was to free society from economically needless *rentier* income, as John Hobson expressed: "The under-production and under-consumption of a trade depression are the plain register of certain 'irrational' factors in the operation of the economic system. These irrational factors consist of the rents, surplus profits, and chance gains, which as income not merely are not necessary to evoke or sustain useful human efforts, but which actually repress them."[2]

R. H. Tawney described the parasitic character of *rentier* income: "The greater part of modern property has been attenuated to a pecuniary lien or bond on the product of industry which carries with it a right to payment, but which is normally valued precisely because it relieves the owner from any obligation to perform a positive or constructive function. Such property may be called passive property, or property for acquisition, for exploitation, or for power.... It is questionable, however, whether economists shall call it 'Property' at all, and not rather, as Mr. Hobson has suggested, 'Impropery,' since it is not identical with the rights which secure the owner the produce of his toil, but is opposite of them."[3]

Other terms for *rentier* income were "virtual wealth" (Frederick Soddy), and the late 19th-century's "fictitious" or "fictive" capital. Today's neoliberal ideology is the diametric opposite of this liberalism, aiming at maximizing the FIRE sector's interest and rent extraction. This explains why *rentier* income and its asset-price gains (which Hobson called "chance gains" and **Keynes** called "**windfalls**") are not singled out in the **National Income and Product Accounts (NIPA)**.

Rent Seeking: A **zero-sum activity** in which one party's gain is another's loss, unlike new capital investment and hiring that expand an economy's production and income stream. The classical meaning of "rent seeking" refers to **landlords**, natural resource owners or monopolists who extract **economic rent** by special **privilege**, without their own labor or enterprise.

Neoliberals have diverted attention from the land rent, resource rent or monopoly rent that classical economists associated with the FIRE sector. They have re-defined "rent seeking" to refer only to politicians and labor unions lobbying for "special privileges," such as Social Security, a minimum wage and public programs to meet other basic needs. But these programs have nothing to do with classical rent seeking. They are proper functions of government.

In introducing the term "rent seeking" in 1974, Anne Krueger applied it to import licensing and quotas that she claimed interfere with free trade, and extended the idea to government regulation in general – including legislation setting a minimum wage, claiming that this led to rising unemployment.[4] Gordon Tullock, a follower of Ludwig von Mises (see **Austrian School**), defined rent seeking as lobbying by politicians for special privileges such as higher Social Security payments![5]

As a high-ranking World Bank and IMF official defending free trade, Ms. Krueger opposed agricultural protectionism designed to save foreign economies from food dependency on U.S. farm exports. Conflating rent seeking with subsidies to modernize, her 2012 book *Struggling with Success* (p. 86) accused all government regulations, tariffs and subsidies of being bad and wasteful. "Ultimately, regulation has negative effects on the market in the country imposing the regulation ..." The political effect of such dergulation and non-subsidy is to let "the market" pass by default to financial managers – as if their own major aim is not to seek classic economic rents to empower themselves as monopolists and financial rent seekers!

Nobel Prize-winner James Buchanan's euphemistic "public choice" anti-government philosophy (that government should make *no* choices, except to disappear) goes so far as to claim "that a tax with more excess burden," such as taxing wages or industrial profits (adding to the cost of living and doing business) is better than a more reasonable tax on land rent with *less* burden. His argument is that classical rent theory would work, but that this would increase government power, precisely by being reasonable and economically efficient – "because government, if allowed to tax in the less burdensome way, may get more revenue," which Buchanan opposes.[6]

Such language makes a travesty of economic vocaulary. It strips away the classical association of rent with the FIRE sector, applying it only to the "cost" of government regulations and pretending that only government bureaucrats receive economic rent, not private sector *rentiers*. This leaves out of account the obvious fact that a strong government is needed to overcome opposition from predatory vested interests. The polical effect of "public choice" ideology and its self-proclaimed "libertarian" doctrine is thus to serve as a handmaiden to oligarchy. It relinquishes economic rent to the FIRE sector instead of taxing it.

At the end of this road, imagine everyone paying user fees for everything from fire hydrants to schools, turning every road and parking space into a toll road. Payment for these erstwhile free public services would be made to owners and financiers of these natural monopolies, free from public regulation or other "Big Government" acting to save the economy by preventing predatory fees. In the name of opposing economic rent as "socialism," AKA "the road to serfdom," "public choice" doctrine thus prepares the groundwork for classic rent grabbing, financialization and kleptocracy.

Rent Theory: A central focus of the **classical economics** of **Adam Smith, David Ricardo, John Stuart Mill, Heinrich von Thünen, Simon Patten** and **Thorstein Veblen**. (See **Rent, Unearned Income, Free Lunch** and **Zero-Sum Activity**). Alfred Marshall's *Principles of Economics* (1890) provides charts to demonstrate the mathematics of rent theory. The common aim of these economists was to base the tax system on **land rent**, natural resource rent and kindred **unearned income** instead of taxing wages and industrial profits. (I deal with rent theory's central focus on freeing markets from the legacy of feudal privileges in Chapter 3 of *Killing the Host*.)

Ricardo refined the concept of economic rent to describe how rising land rents ended up being paid by industry and labor. But the post-classical aim has been to free landlords and the FIRE sector in general *from* taxation, and also from public regulation such as anti-monopoly legislation. To avoid being taxed, *rentiers* sought to deny that economic rent is **unearned income** (see **John Bates Clark**), and to exclude its discussion from the academic curriculum (and its magnitude from national income statistics; see **NIPA**).

Politically, *rentiers* oppose the fiscal power of democracies to tax real estate investors and speculators, owners of natural resources (*e.g.,* oil and gas fields), other natural monopolies and financial wealth. To gain popular support, anti-government "libertarians" argue that if governments tax away the economy's land rent, economic rent and other unearned income, they would become "Leviathans," crushing the economy.[7] Grover Norquist's recommendation to "shrink government to a size small enough to drown it in a bathtub" reflects Nobel Economics Prize-winner James M. Buchanan's euphemistic "public choice" theory that rejects a land tax on the ground that precisely by helping the economy become more competitive, it would justify taxation, mainly on the One Percent, while encouraging big government! Leaving economic rent in private hands as an overhead for the economy at large is deemed preferable to taxing away special *rentier* privilege and spending it on public infrastructure (which "free market" advocates insist should be privatized) and social programs (which anti-government ideologues claim is the road to serfdom).

The reality is that land rent, natural resource rent and monopoly rent account for an enormous flow of untaxed revenue, accounting for over a third of national income (if you include capital gains). This revenue has empowered the landlord, financial and monopoly "Leviathan" to turn democracies into financial oligarchies throughout the world (see **Globalization**). To distract public attention from the desirability of taxing this flow of unearned income to finance the legitimate functions of government, the concept of economic rent – and with it the history of economic thought – has been excluded from today's mainstream academic curriculum. It has been replaced by the mathematized tunnel vision of junk economics.

Ricardo, David (1772-1823): A bond broker, Member of Parliament and spokesman (that is, lobbyist) for Britain's financial sector, his *Principles of Political Economy and Taxation* (1817) defined **land rent** as rising when population grew, forcing recourse to less fertile soils and hence increasing crop and food prices. Diminishing returns would provide a **windfall** to owners of lands with higher fertility, but industrial profits would fall as the subsistence wage rose to reflect the higher food prices for crops grown on less fertile soils. (Ricardo denied that fertilizer would make any difference in relative fertility.)

The way to make Britain the workshop of the world, Ricardo explained, was to repeal its Corn Laws (agricultural tariffs) and adopt **free trade** to buy its food and raw materials in the cheapest markets. This served bank strategy, because apart from lending to governments, foreign trade was the major private-sector market for bank credit at that time. (See **Agio**.)

As a Bullionist advocating metallic currency or gold-backed paper currency, Ricardo claimed that foreign borrowing would not worsen balance-of-payments deficits, but would set in motion self-stabilizing adjustments that would enable debts to be paid "automatically." This "debts don't matter" theory is the source of today's **Chicago School** monetarism and **IMF austerity** plans – in which monetary deflation and lower wages are not really automatic but are enforced by political conditionalities.

Road to Serfdom: During World War II, Frederick Hayek wrote *The Road to Serfdom* to accuse the Progressive Era's public regulation as leading inevitably to centralized bureaucracies of the Nazi or Soviet type. The book became an ideological bible for subsequent neoliberals such as Margaret Thatcher to shrink government authority and privatize the public domain. What they failed to recongnize that inasmuch as every economy is planned, such efforts leave a political vacuum, which is filled by giant financial institutions. Their mode of planning imposed by the IMF, World Bank and Washington Consensus has turned out to be the *real* road to serfdom by loading down economies with unproductive debt, imposing austerity on the populace and using the resulting financial crisis to assert dictatorial powers over government at the expense of labor and of debtors, as in Greece in 2015.

Instead of democratic governments leading the world beyond the legacy of feudalism, Hayek's followers are headed by financial planners eager to impose **client oligarchies**, **austerity** and **debt deflation**, leading to neo-serfdom. The financial sector captures control of national treasuries and central banks. (See **Regulatory Capture**.) The result is that in contrast to public planning protecting society from economic rent and similar exploitation and taxing wealth in ways that promote prosperity, Hayek's Wall Street admirers such as Alan Greenspan shift the tax burden *off* wealth onto labor and pursue related anti-labor "reforms." (See **Free Market**, **Labor Capitalism** and **Race to the Bottom**.)

By defining "serfdom" as a government powerful enough to check the power of the property owners and their financiers, Hayek's proposed road to avoid "serfdom" is actually a road to debt peonage. Instead of progressive tax policy and public infrastructure investment aiming to minimize the cost of living and doing business (by bringing prices in line with real cost-value), financial planners aim at *maximizing* prices for real estate, stocks and financial securities, especially relative to wage levels. That is the real road to serfdom – dismantling government and turning its planning over to financial centers to create a neofeudal oligarchy.

Rosetta Stone: Unearthed in 1799, this trilingual translation of an ancient Egyptian **debt cancellation** provided the key for translating hieroglyphics. But its content has been ideologically ignored.

Carved on a chunk of black diorite, it commemorates a cancel-lation of tax arrears and other debts by the 13-year-old pharaoh Ptolemy V Epiphanes in 196 BC. He was indoctrinated by Egypt's priesthood into the ways of former pharaohs who proclaimed

British Museum (© AdobeStock)

amnesties to save the country from over-indebtedness (mainly to royal collectors). (See **Jubilee Year** and **Clean Slate**.) My forthcoming book *The Lost Tradition of Biblical Debt Cancellations* tells the story of these pre-Biblical events in detail.

Rule of 72: A quick way to approximate how long a loan or debt will take to double at a given rate of interest. Dividing 72 by the annual interest rate provides an estimate of how many years it takes for the interest to accumulate as large a sum as the original principal (the amount borrowed or owed) at a compound rate of growth.

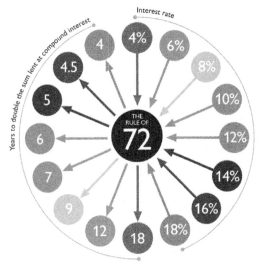

FORMULA

$$\frac{72}{\text{Interest rate}} = \begin{array}{c}\text{Years to double}\\\text{investment or debt}\end{array}$$

The result is fairly accurate up to a rate of 20%. To double money at 8% annual interest, divide 72 by 8. The answer is

9 years. In another 9 years the original principal will have multiplied fourfold, and in 27 years it will have grown to 8 times the original sum. A loan doubles in 12 years at 6%, and in 18 years at 4%. This is of course unsustainable. As Herbert Stein (chair of the U. S. Council of Economic Advisers 1972-1974) quipped: "Things that can't go on forever, don't." (See **Sustainability** and **Compound Interest**.)

ENDNOTES

[1] John Maynard Keynes, *General Theory* (1961 Papermacs edition, p. 376).

[2] J. A. Hobson, "Underconsumption: An Exposition and a Reply," *Economica*, No.42, November 1933, pp.402-427.

[3] R. H. Tawney, *The Acquisitive Society* (1920), Chapter V: "Property and creative work."

[4] Anne O. Krueger, "The political economy of the rent-seeking society," *The American Economic Review* 64.3 (1974): 291-303.

[5] Gordon Tullock applied it specifically to people who secure monopolies or tariffs from government (including, presumably, real estate owners seeking public infrastructure investments and tax breaks to increase the market price of their property) in "The welfare costs of tariffs, monopolies, and theft," *Economic Inquiry* **5** (1967), pp. 224-232.

[6] Mason Gaffney, "The Hidden Taxable Capacity of Land: Enough and to Spare," *International Journal of Social Economics*, Summer 2008, citing James Buchanan, "Constitutional Economics," in Milgate, Murray, *et al.* (eds.), *The New Palgrave, A Dictionary of Economics* (1987), Vol. 1, p. 588.

[7] Geoffrey Brennan and James M. Buchanan, "Towards a tax constitution for Leviathan," *Journal of Public Economics* **8** (1977), pp. 255-273.

is for
Say's Law
and Serfdom

S-curve: The typical shape of growth in nature. Human beings and other living organisms taper off in height and size as they reach maturity. Most business recoveries also taper off as employment, raw materials and resource limits are approached. Profits slow as rents, wages and commodity prices rise while debt and interest charges grow at compound interest, stifling business expansion (usually in a financial crisis). (See **Economic Forecasting**.)

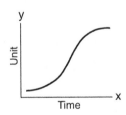

Saint-Simon, Claude Henri de Rouvroy, comte de (1760-1825): French reformer best known for urging that bank lending at interest be replaced with loans taking the form of equity (stock) investment. Following this doctrine the Pereire brothers created the Crédit Mobilier banking company in Paris in 1852, basically as a mutual fund to finance infrastructure development. In practice, this model was pursued most successfully in Germany in the late 19th and early 20th century. Earlier, Saint-Simon sought to abolish inheritance so that people would possess only the fruits of their own labor.

Sanctity of Debt vs. Debt Cancellation: For more than half of recorded history, from 3000 BC to 1000 AD, religions sanctified the cancellation of personal (non-commercial) debt so as to prevent **debt bondage** and widespread forfeiture of self-support land to foreclosing creditors. The Biblical **Jubilee Year** (*deror* in Leviticus 25) was a direct descendent of Babylonian *andurarum* antecedents. (See **Clean Slate**.) Today's neoliberal crucifixion of economies on a cross of debt and **austerity** thus reverses the original economic core of the Judeo-Christian ethic.

Saving (distinguished from **Savings**): To most people, saving means accumulating money in the bank for their retirement, or simply to have on hand as a cushion to draw against. But the reported rise in the U.S. saving rate since 2008 – saving as a proportion of national income or Gross Domestic Product – does not mean that people have more "liquidity" and are building up more of a cushion. Just the opposite: post-2008 is a negation of a negation. Banks reduced their credit card exposure, so the population had smaller credit-card lines to draw on. Banks also scaled back their mortgage lending and home equity lending, requiring people to pay *down* the debts that they had run up. This is called "deleveraging." It is a form of **debt deflation**, because it leaves less income available to spend on goods and services. So not all saving is available for actual spending, or even is voluntary.

When firms "age their bills" by delaying payment, these unpaid debts create statistical "saving" on the part of their hapless suppliers, who accumulate financial claims on the asset side of their balance sheet for unpaid "receivables." The firms not being paid are unwilling savers. For wage labor, the main categories of **forced saving** are Social Security and pension deductions. The **National Income and Product Accounts (NIPA)** treat the amortization payment as "saving," but not the interest and fees that banks syphon off.

John Maynard Keynes viewed saving simply as non-spending. (See **Propensity to Save**.) But one party's savings take the form of other parties' debts (and to a smaller degree, as tangible capital investment). Savings and debts thus tend to grow exponentially together on both the asset and liabilities sides of the balance sheet – with a steady rise in the 99 Percent's ratio of debt to savings.

Alan Greenspan's characterization of taking out a home equity loan as "using your home as a piggy bank" was a false metaphor. A piggy bank has real savings in it. When savers take money out of a piggy bank, they don't run up a debt; they simply have less saving. But in a "home equity" loan, the borrower's equity in his or her home goes *down*, not up. Taking out such loans force people to repay later – by putting money *into* the real-life piggish banks that made the loans and now demand payment, with interest.

Savings (distinguished from **Saving**): Financial securities (stocks and bonds), cash on hand ("hoarding"), and direct investment in real estate, corporate business or even fine art, to the extent that these assets have a market value that banks will lend against, as collateral for potential liquidation purposes.

Net worth is the excess of assets over debts (mainly owed to the One Percent). **Negative equity** is the excess of debts over assets. That is the condition into which homeowners fall when mortgages exceed the market price of their property. It also is the case for banks when financial bubbles crash and bank loans go bad, leaving them unable to cover what they owe their depositors, bondholders and other counterparties.

Say's Law: Named for the French economist Jean-Baptiste Say (1767-1832), this "law" states that "supply creates its own demand" as employees spend their wages on buying what they produce. Payments by companies to their employees thus would equal what employees buy from said companies. If this application of **circular flow** really were the case, there would be no **business cycles** or **depressions**. John Maynard Keynes accordingly devoted a large part of his *General Theory* (1936) to explaining why this circular flow is interrupted, blaming the financial system.

By ignoring the fact that **finance** and **property** (the **FIRE Sector**) are independent from the "real" production and consumption economy, Say's "Law" fails to operate mainly because of rent extraction (the culprit in Ricardo's analysis) and debt deflation (explained most classically by the American economist Irving Fisher). Typical American blue-collar budgets leave only about a third of gross wages available for discretionary spending on goods and services, after paying the FIRE sector and taxes.

Serfdom: The final stage of Rome's imperial breakdown after the creditor oligarchy blocked the government from taxing the wealthy or protecting debtors. A quarter of the population was reduced to debt bondage or outright slavery. Coinage was adulterated as taxes were cut and economic life on the land reverted to barter as the debt overload crashed the economy. Cities were depopulated as Western Europe dissolved into manors under local warlords who became feudal landlords. In the absence of a debt cancellation, their luxury spending was the main monetized activity. Their status became hereditary, while cultivators were tied to the land as serfs. (See **Feudalism**.)

Shareholder Value: An ambiguous term that usually represents a company's "book value" or the cost of having acquired its assets. This measure reflects the prices paid for real estate, monopolies and other *rentier* claims that may have no inherent cost of production in the classical sense (except payments to lawyers and politicians). So meaningful book value is difficult to calculate in practice. A company may carry undervalued real estate at a low outdated price, for instance, making it a takeover target.

Alternatively, stock prices may be established by projecting their income streams, predicting prospective long-term earnings. Fast-growing companies sell at a premium over their current reported income.

But the financial sector lives mainly in the short run. A company's stock price may be raised by financial engineering to pay out corporate cash flow (ebitda) as dividends or used for share buybacks. The aim of today's financial managers is to produce higher stock prices (on which their remuneration is based), not more affordable or better goods and services. Shareholder value is often increased by "cost cutting" – ending pension plans and employer contributions to 401Ks, reducing healthcare support, eliminating staff and product lines, and banking offshore to avoid income taxes. The effect is to reduce long-run production. (I discuss this short-termism in *Killing the Host*, chapters 8 -10.)

Sharia Law: Much as medieval Christian law legitimized charging **agio** and commercial "**interest**," Moslem **murabaha** banking enabled usury to enter through the back door by permitting creditors to take their returns as a proportion of the borrower's gain. A loan for real estate may be structured as a rental until the balance is paid off. Or, a loan to a merchant may be structured as a profit-sharing agreement. Lacking Christian financial law, for instance, Spain's Isabella and Ferdinand structured their investment in Christopher Columbus's voyages of conquest as a *sharia* loan.

Single Tax: A tax levied on the land's **groundrent**, advocated by France's **Physiocrats** and later popularized by the American journalist **Henry George**. Most classical economists urged extending the land tax to fall on all economic rent yielded by natural resources or infrastructure monopolies. George's policy disagreement with socialists was to leave land and key industry in private hands instead of nationalizing and socializing land and natural monopolies into the public domain (providing their services freely or at subsidized prices instead of being privatized). The movement for a single tax evaporated largely because George and his followers had no clear theory of cost-value, price and economic rent, and hence no basis for statistical analysis. Most fatally, their libertarian opposition to big government meant in practice that government would not be strong enough to fully tax land rents and monopoly gains by the vested landed interests and the financial interests behind them. George denounced landlords, but idealized bankers, not realizing that they were becoming the major opponents of a land tax. (He had no coherent understanding of interest.)

Sinking Fund: A fund set aside by Britain's Parliament in the late 18th century to pay off the national debt by investing in bonds and automatically reinvesting their interest. The idea was for the balance to accumulate at **compound interest**, doubling and redoubling until it reached a magnitude sufficient to pay off the entire national debt. But in practice Parliament could not resist raiding the Sinking Fund to wage war. In any case, its financial surplus would have over-burdened the economy with fiscal deflation – the same debt deflation effect as running a fiscal surplus to extract tax revenue via an austerity program.

In the United States, Social Security is organized as a sinking fund to accumulate prepaid user fees and invest them in Treasury securities. In practice, lending this money to the government has enabled it to cut taxes on the higher income brackets. This is like raiding the fund in time of war (in this case, a class war waged by the One Percent). A pay-as-you-go system, financed by progressive taxation and focused on taxing *rentier* income would avoid this problem.

Refusal to collect FICA taxes on wages from well-to-do earners (currently, income more than $117,000 annually) led President George W. Bush to claim in 2005 that Social Security wage set-asides were so low that the system would be insolvent in half a century. He urged its privatization to steer wage withholding into stock purchases. The aim was to inflate a new financial bubble that would pay retirees out of stock market price gains. But as the population ages (and shrinks in response to debt deflation), stock sell-offs to pay retirees threaten to reverse the stock-market run-up and wipe out pension savings, making it a bad idea to privatize Social Security.

Sleeping and Eating: Metaphors traditionally used to describe creditors. Babylonian contracts referred to creditors as "eating" the interest owed them, in an epoch when many debts were paid in grain. Thomas Nast's 19th-century cartoons depicted plutocrats as fat, a sign of gluttony and greed. Werner Sombart (1863-1941), German economist and sociologist, likened the highest status bourgeoisie to globules of fat floating on top of soup.

John Stuart Mill characterized **land rent** as what landlords collect "in their sleep," through no efforts of their own. A "sleeping partner" (a bank or investment firm) advances money to a trader or entrepreneur (the active partner) to make a profit, which is to be shared with the creditor as interest and/or a share of the profits.

Sleeping Partner (AKA silent partner): A creditor who lends to an entrepreneur to make a commercial **profit**, which is split with the creditor as equity and/or **interest**. The essence of such arrangements is that the active parties do the work, not their financial partners. Landlords, bankers, and other *rentiers* are sleeping partners vis-à-vis the economy at large, advancing the credit needed to function and the land or other preconditions for production to take place. This control over money and credit is analogous to feudal landlords' control over land. Today's counterpart to their claiming the crop surplus is the financial sector controlling money and basic infrastructure to charge interest and monopoly rent.

Smith, Adam (1723-1790): See **Adam Smith.**

Smith, E. Peshine (1814-1882): The law partner of Whig and Republican abolitionist and protectionist William Seward, his *Manual of Political Economy* (1853) provided the argument for the economic platform adopted by the newly formed Republican Party from the Henry Clay Whigs: protective tariffs, internal improvements, and a national bank. A follower of Henry Carey, Smith emphasized the environmental cost of free trade monocultures: soil depletion resulting from cultivation of tobacco, cotton and other Southern plantation crops. Smith developed an energy theory of the value of goods and services. The rising efficiency of energy production over time – from animal and human effort to wind and water power, wood, coal and oil – led production costs to fall in keeping with rising energy efficiency.

As the foremost economist in the 19th-century American School of Political Economy, Smith's *Manual* was often reprinted in the United States as a critique of British free-trade theory, and was translated into German, French and Italian. In 1871, Smith capped his career by becoming an advisor to Japan's Mikado, using his position to break up the Chinese coolie trade with Latin America.

Socialism: The term used by 19th-century writers across the political spectrum for how they expected industrial capitalism to evolve. Ricardian socialists believed that taxing the land's rent, buying out the land or simply nationalizing it would free society from feudalism's most burdensome legacy, the extraction of economic rent. Socialist policy advocates that natural monopolies and infrastructure be kept in or transferred to the **public domain**. (The key problem, of course, is to prevent corrupt management, just as in private investment.)

Liberal Parliamentary reformers in Britain as well as Marxian socialists saw a need to gain control of the government to bring prices in line with intrinsic value.

This required being strong enough to overcome the power of the vested interests seeking to protect their special *rentier* privileges.

Many "old" socialist policies have been adopted: pensions and public health programs, progressive income taxation, anti-monopoly regulations and consumer protection to free markets from fraud and lawbreaking. Denouncing such policies as "socialist" thus implies that the free market economics of Adam Smith, John Stuart Mill and kindred 19th-century liberals were actually socialist. The right-wing use of "socialism" as a term of invective – and "reform" to mean the *reversal* of Progressive Era reforms – is an attempt to roll back pensions and public investment. The label "socialism" is applied to any critique of the neoliberal policy of looting pension funds, selling off public infrastructure to pay bondholders, shifting taxes onto consumers and wage earners, and deregulating economies for rent extractors and financializers. (See **Oligarchy** and **Kleptocracy**.)

Soviet Russia's totalitarian state is an entirely different case (see **Stalinism**). Confronted by Western military opposition to force "regime change," it became a war economy under permanent emergency rule. Stalin's forced industrialization without a democratic middle class (indeed destroying the kulaks and bourgeoisie) was the antithesis of early socialism and Marxism. But its traumatic experience threw into question just what socialism and a **planned economy** was all about.

For European socialists, what was planned were to be constraints on privilege, rent seeking and kindred exploitation. Marx even supported free trade with India, on the logic that British industrial imperialism would lead to modernization of backward colonies.[1] Once freed from post-feudal privileges for landlords and bankers, he believed industrial capitalism would evolve toward socialism in the interest of the majority of citizens, the working class. By the 20th century the major political issue of politics in Britain and other countries had become "not socialism versus capitalism, but the forms which socialism shall take and the pace at which it shall be developed." These various forms were "an outgrowth of English classical political economy as was *Capital* itself."[2]

But many nominally socialist parties gaining office today throughout Europe and Latin America have turned into the opposite of the socialism of a century ago. They endorse privatization and austerity, headed by Tony Blair's neoliberal British Labour Party and Greece's PASOK, and indeed the Second ("Socialist") International.

Socialism for the Rich: See **State Socialism**.

Social Market: Margaret Thatcher's euphemism for her anti-social antithesis to socialism: a financialized and neoliberalized anti-labor market. Public investment and government authority are to be dismantled in order to promote *rentier* domination by the FIRE sector. Hitherto public infrastructure is to be privatized and run by financial managers seeking to maximize rent extraction. (See **Chicago School** and **Reaganomics**.)

Society: The "market" is only part of society, which forms the context within which markets operate. When Margaret Thatcher said that "There is no such thing as society," she meant that human and social relationships outside of market pricing should be ignored – the very definition of **alienation**. In practice, her slogan meant that the status quo's dominant players would be "the market" without other parts of society having a say as to tax policy, subsidies, social welfare spending, war or environmental regulation, or workers' rights, human rights or mutual aid.

Socrates (470-399 BC): In Book I of Plato's *Republic* (380 BC), Socrates discusses the morality of paying debts. Cephalus, a businessman living in the commercial Piraeus district, states the ethic that it is fair and just to pay back what one has borrowed.[3] Socrates replies that it would not be just to return weapons to a lunatic. Because of the consequences, paying back the debt would be the wrong thing to do.

   What ultimately is at issue is how this act affects society. If a madman is intent on murder, returning his weapon to him will enable him to commit unjust acts. Likewise, the morality of paying back all debts is not necessarily justice. We need to look at the overall consequences.

   The morality of paying today's bondholders and other creditors is analogous to paying off the madman discussed by Socrates. At issue is what should be saved: wealthy creditors from loss (and the morality that all debts should be paid), or the overall economy from unemployment and misery leading to emigration, worse health and shorter lifespans.

   Also at issue is the selfish and abusive behavior of creditors. Later in the *Republic* (Book VIII, 555d-556b) Socrates talks with Glaucon, pointing to the "negligence and encouragement of licentiousness in **oligarchies**." (See **Affluenza**.) Their **greed**, Socrates explains, inserts the parasitic "sting of their money into any of the remainder who do not resist." The effect is to burden many Athenians with debt, to suffer foreclosure on their land and disenfranchisement, fostering "the drone and pauper element in the state." This leaves the people (the *demos*) to "conspire against the acquirers of their estates and the rest of the citizens, and be eager for revolution." The way to quench this disaster in the making, Socrates suggests, is to enact "a law prohibiting a man from doing as he likes with his own, or in this way, by a second law that does away with such abuses."

   "What law?" asks Glaucon.

   "The law that is next best ... commanding that most voluntary contracts should be at the contractor's risk. The pursuit of wealth would be less shameless in the state and fewer of the evils of which we spoke just now would grow up there."

This obligation of creditors to share in the risk of non-payment is the principle that American economic reformers urged after the 2008 crash. Banks that made junk mortgage loans beyond the ability of debtors to pay out of their normal income should have their recklessly over-mortgaged obligations written down to reflect reasonable rental values and prices instead of letting banks foreclose or profiteer from homebuyers, pushing the U.S. economy into debt deflation.

Sovereign Debt: Debt guaranteed by a government or its central bank, usually denominated in dollars, sterling or euros. These foreign-currency bonds typically are registered in New York or London, and hence are subject to creditor-nation courts, not domestic law.

Under today's global linkages this foreign debt is the main lever to turn democracies into oligarchies. The 2012-2015 crises in Argentina and Greece showed how little sovereignty debtor countries have in the face of the absence of an international court recognizing the ultimate need to write down sovereign debts. Threats by bondholders to cut off credit, cause banking chaos and seize public assets to pay vulture funds and other creditors enable the IMF, the European Central Bank and even vulture funds to override democratic regimes and public referendums. The upshot is that it doesn't matter what voters want or whom they elect. Economic policy is dictated by the bondholders, and they are rapacious in demanding **austerity** and kindred IMF **conditionalities**.

Sovereignty: See **Government** and **Money**.

Stabilization Program: A euphemism for the destabilization caused by IMF conditionalities in the form of austerity. The effect is to deter investment, employment and wage levels, by cutting public investment while raising taxes on consumers. This creates deepening dependency on foreign lenders, leading to yet harsher junk economic demands to "bleed the patient" (with leeches in the form of vulture creditors and privatizers). (See **Inner Contradiction** and **Washington Consensus**.)

Stages of Development: The idea that history has been moving inexorably toward the present distribution of wealth and income, assuming (by tautology) that today's status quo must be the most efficient and hence "fittest." (See **Progress** and **Teleology**.) The hypothesized stages of development usually are arrayed in sets of three, *e.g.*, from agriculture via industrial capitalism to "postindustrial" finance capitalism, culminating in today's dominance by financial planners – as if this is the end of history, not a retrogression to feudalism.

Most concepts of "stages of development" get the actual sequence backward. Headed by the Austrian School, 19th-century monetary theorists speculated that economies evolved from barter via a money economy to a credit system. This misses the fact that the Neolithic and Bronze Age Mesopotamian economies were credit economies. As planting and harvesting developed in the Neolithic, credit became necessary to bridge the time gap for expenses incurred during the crop year (such as ale to drink and agricultural and public services, typically to be paid for at harvest time).

All three "stages" are usually found simultaneously. Economic historian Karl Polanyi's (1886-1964) "three stages" of market development, for instance, distinguish reciprocity (gift exchange) and administered prices from market exchange at flexible prices. Even in today's economies, individuals still reciprocate meals, gifts and other social obligations.

Money developed gradually as a means of denominating and settling crop debts, most of which were owed to the temples and palaces. Rulers set prices for grain, silver, and other key goods and services to enable debts to be paid to these large institutions in these commodities ("in kind").

The volume of debt grew so large under Rome's oligarchy that the fiscal and monetary system broke down for the vast majority of the population. Except for the narrow warlord-landlord layer, economic units were obliged to become locally self-sufficient. The Western Roman Empire deteriorated as silver and gold were drained to the East. Debt deflation, austerity and collapse are thus the final stage of debt-ridden economies. This makes the "credit" or "financial" stage a transition to economic collapse and reversion to barter, unless political decisions from "outside" or "above" the market check *rentier* power to create a more stable and equitable social arrangement. That requires debt cancellations to bring an economy's debt overhead back within the ability to be paid.

Nearly all modern "stages of growth" theories deny the basic principle that defines "the final stage" of financialization: debts that cannot be paid, won't be. Either a clean slate or a lapse into debt serfdom is needed to end the preceding cycle and inaugurate a new takeoff or recovery.

Stagflation: During the Vietnam War years in the late 1960s and 1970s, U.S. prices rose rapidly (along with interest rates) without spurring new investment and employment. (See **Inflation** and **Money**.) The opposite condition is today's stagnating *de*flation: Quantitative easing by central banks lowers interest rates, but fails to induce new investment (what John Maynard Keynes called the liquidity trap) or re-inflate commodity prices or wages. Debt deflation causes economic stagnation, ultimately more serious and persistent than inflation.

Stalinism: The intermediate stage between capitalism and kleptocracy. One could define neoliberalism in the same way, but it concentrates economic planning in the financial centers, not in autonomous state bureaucracies.

State Socialism ("Socialism for the Rich"): Use of government agencies, especially the Treasury and central bank to rescue and subsidize commercial banks, bondholders or other elites. The opposite of genuine socialism, such government spending to support a *rentier* oligarchy should be called corporatism or neo-feudalism. The One Percent euphemize it as a "free market," pretending that their gains (usually capital gains) will trickle down to the 99 Percent.

The key, of course, is just who *controls* the state. Under *rentier* domination there can be no such thing as a real socialist policy. For example, "socialized medicine" under Obamacare is simply a public giveaway to the financial and health insurance sectors and pharmaceutical monopolies – the same kind of oxymoron as Margaret Thatcher's **social market** or **labor capitalism.**

State Theory of Money: Governments give value to money not so much by declaring it to be legal tender as by accepting it in payment of taxes and fees. Given its name by Georg Friedrich Knapp in his *State Theory of Money* (1905, translated from German into English in 1924 at the urging of John Maynard Keynes), recognition of this principle is also known as **chartalism.**[4]

The essential idea was known long before Knapp formulated it in academic terms. Alexander Hamilton wrote in his 1790 *First Report on Public Credit* (Art. 1, Sect. 8, clause 2): "in countries in which the national debt is properly funded, and an object of established confidence, it answers most of the purposes of money. Transfers of stock or public debt are [the] equivalent to payments in specie," that is, metallic coinage.

Banking interests push to get governments out of the picture so that they can control money and credit themselves. In keeping with George Orwell's motto, "Who controls the past controls the present," the **Austrian School's Carl Menger** created a fanciful theory of how money originated without public institutions, temples or palaces playing any role. This ideologically airbrushed view of history speculates that money emerged when individuals **bartered** food and other products, preferring metal for the three mainstream textbook functions:

(1) a compact *store* of value (namely, metal, not grain or cloth);
(2) a *measure* of value, and
(3) a *medium of exchange*, that is, a commodity as a means of payment.

These three functions have always been public (see **Stages of Development**):

(1) **Metal** had to be of a specified purity. To avoid adulteration, silver and gold were minted in temples throughout antiquity, and by governments down through the modern world. Also, metallic coinage has to be weighed, and weights and measures were provided by the temples or palaces (and by governments in the modern world) to avoid the notorious private mercantile cheating.

(2) **Prices first measured by money** were crops, cloth and other handicrafts in which community members paid their debts to ancient temples, palaces or civic governments for public services, products and taxes.

(3) **Debts accrued** and payments were not made on the spot at the time of purchase, they accrued as debts to be settled when the harvest was in (paid on the threshing floor) or when merchants returned from their voyages and paid the temples or other consigners or backers.

All these roles of money involved public institutions, which "free market" economics denigrates by pretending that governments play no role except to impose "overhead" transactions costs, not to save the private sector from fraud and cheating.

What most mainstream monetary theory leaves out of account is the historically most important function of money: to denominate debts. The first formally monetized debts were owed to Mesopotamia's temples and palaces. That is why rulers set price ratios for grain and other commodities serving as money to pay fees and debts to these two large institutions.

Sterile: A **zero-sum** and hence exploitative economic activity that is merely a **transfer payment**, not an addition to real output. In antiquity this was typified above all by usury. (What was "born" from the loan was merely the passage of time, not a product or the means to pay.[5]) Aristotle described money as being sterile, despite interest being charged. Stoic Roman historians used the metaphor of sexual sterility to characterize usurers as aging homosexuals abusing young boys pledged in debt bondage. The medieval French ruler Philip the Fair made use of a similar metaphor in 1306 to prosecute the Templars and seize their wealth, accusing them of conducting abnormal sexual rites.

The Physiocrats viewed industry and commerce as being sterile, on the ground that industry merely worked up the agricultural surplus ("net product") provided by nature. This became a rationale for taxing the landed aristocracy instead of industry and commerce. Adam Smith described industry as well as agriculture as productive, but counted personal services (such as butlers and coachmen) and public bureaucrats as sterile, in the sense of dissipating the economic surplus, not adding to it. The 19th century saw a long debate over the character of productive and unproductive ("sterile") labor and investment, distinguishing industrial profits from rent seeking. The vested interests, especially the FIRE sector, sponsored a value-free reaction by denying the concept of economic sterility or **parasitism**. (See **John Bates Clark**.)

Stockholm Syndrome: A state of demoralization in which kidnapped parties believe they will be safer by identifying with their predator, and urge others to meet his demands as if he were their protector. The economic analogy is a belief by the 99 Percent that the way to recover their lost prosperity is to give more tax breaks and subsidies to the One Percent, hoping that the benefits may **trickle down**. (See **Supply Side Economics**.) The wealthy depict themselves as job creators, needed by the 99 Percent (as in the conservative chestnut, "no poor man ever gave anyone a job").

A kindred example is the belief by debt-ridden populations that they can escape from their quandary by borrowing enough to keep current on their debt service. This financial Stockholm Syndrome leads demoralized voters to support central banks supplying low-interest credit to commercial banks so that they can lend more and enable populations to "borrow their way out of debt." Instead of rescuing the economy, this leads to deeper debt deflation.

A similar syndrome leaves workers and voters to fear that criticizing, taxing, regulating or otherwise offending their employers or the One Percent will lead to unemployment and economic collapse.

Structural Problem: A problem that cannot be resolved by merely marginal reforms, but requires political change. A chronic structural problem is the tendency of debts to grow in excess of the ability to be paid (see **Compound Interest**). Leaving them in place leads to asset stripping as property is forfeited to creditors. Neoclassical and marginalist economists dismiss the resulting austerity and economic stagnation as externalities, that is, external to thier narrow scope of supply and demand within a given institutional structure. This narrow scope is a precondition for their ideology depicting *rentiers* in a positive light – because there seems to be no alternative structure thinkable *without* them.

Student Loans: Just as real estate is worth as much as a bank will lend – and costs more and more as lending terms are loosened – so the price of education is inflated on credit. The larger the government-guaranteed debt leverage, the more colleges are able charge for the sale of degrees – without regard to whether the loan creates the means to pay it off. The volume of U.S. student debt soared to $1.4 trillion in 2016 – more than credit card debt. This debt must be paid regardless of whether students graduate or earn enough to pay off the loans, because it cannot be wiped out by personal bankruptcy under the harshly rewritten recent bankruptcy code. To carry their debt service, graduates often must keep living at home with their parents, deferring family formation. (See **Debt Deflation**.)

The cover story enabling universities to raise their fees is that lending to students finds its counterpart in "human capital" yielding a higher income on educational "capital." But government-guaranteed education loans have led to a proliferation of for-profit diploma mills, whose courses have little linkage

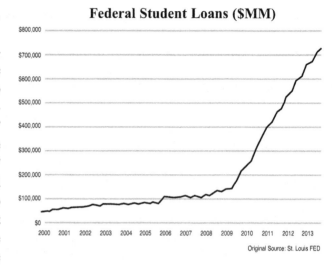

Federal Student Loans ($MM)

Original Source: St. Louis FED

to training of the sort that actually increases income. In any case, most of the increase in earnings by graduates must now be turned over to banks, as interest on their student loans. The fruits of "human capital" thus end up enriching finance capital.

Super Profits: Excessive returns beyond what is necessary to induce capital investment and employment. See **Monopoly Rent** (*e.g.,* in information technology, health insurance, oil and gas).

Supply-Side Economics: A rationale for cutting taxes on finance and property (see **FIRE Sector**). The **Laffer Curve**, named for Republican economic advisor Arthur Laffer, pretends that the deeper taxes are cut, the *more* tax revenue can be collected. The cover story is that high-income recipients will have less incentive to cheat or hide their profits abroad in offshore tax havens – as if their accountants don't always try to keep *every* dollar of profit away from government. The actual result of such tax cuts is a deepening budget deficit, creating pressure to raise taxes on labor and consumers to rebalance the budget.

The pretense is that what needs to be "supplied" to spur economic growth are tax cuts (see **Tax Shift**) and hence more net income for the higher tax brackets. The false assumption is that leaving the One Percent with more income will be an incentive for them to undertake more capital investment and job creation.

The sophistry continues by promising that inasmuch as corporations and rich people employ labor, cutting their taxes will enable them to employ more workers. (See **Trickle-Down Economics**.) This implies that the wealthy will create jobs by investing their gains in new production – not outsourcing, downsizing, looting pension funds and driving the economy into debt (see **Financialization**). Such lobbyists never mention corporate raiders, downsizing or outsourcing jobs.

What is "supplied" is simply more income, asset-price gains and hence political power to the vested interests, leaving them with yet more to lend back to the increasingly indebted 99 Percent. The effect is to shrink output and employment, and deterring rather than inducing new capital investment.

Sustainability: An economy's ability to be resilient and supply its members' basic needs while preserving environmental balance (avoiding pollution, depletion and climate change), financial balance (avoiding debt overhead, fraud and bad loans or toxic mortgages) and demographic balance (avoiding austerity that drives skilled labor to emigrate and older labor to die early from suicide and reduced health care). As such, sustainability is the antithesis to debt deflation, neoliberalism and supply-side economics.

Systems Analysis: A technique for viewing the impact of any given change on all parts of the economic, political and social system, based on positive feedback such as increasing returns, or damping negative feedback (diminishing returns). What neoclassical economics dismisses as externalities often turn out to be most important for the overall social system, *e.g.*, debt deflation. As such, macro-analysis is the antithetical to the *ceteris paribus* reasoning (Latin for "all other things remaining equal") that underlies mainstream economics. (See **X and Y Axes**.)

ENDNOTES

---

[1] See for instance Karl Marx's speech to the Chartists, as well as Terence McCarthy's introduction to Marx's *History of Economic Theories* (New York 1952, his title for *Theories of Surplus Value*), p. xvi: "Marx, in many of his basic precepts, was the last great member of the Manchester School of Thought," the free marketers of his day who spearheaded repeal of Britain's Corn Laws in 1846.

[2] *Ibid.*, p. xi; McCarthy adds that Marx castigated bureaucrats and civil servants "as parasites and unproductive laborers … [and] shared the lathing for waste, inefficiency and parasitism voiced by most of the progressive capitalists and economic theoreticians of the time he studied."

[3] Plato, *Republic*, 331c-d. The term for justice is *dīkaiosyne*, meaning "right behavior," from *dīke*, cognate to dexterous. I am indebted to Moritz Hinsch of Berlin for drawing my attention to this passage, in his paper on "Private Debts in Classical Greece,"

delivered to the international conference on "Debt: The First 3500 Years" in Tübingen, Germany, June 11, 2016.

[4] See the articles collected in L. Randall Wray, ed., *Credit and State Theories of Money: The Contributions of A. Mitchell Innes* (Edward Elgar, 2004).

[5] "How Interest Rates Were Set, 2500 BC - 1000 AD: *Máš*, *tokos* and *fænus* as metaphors for interest accruals," *Journal of the Economic and Social History of the Orient* **43** (Spring 2000), pp. 132-161.

is for
Trickle-Down Economics

Tableau Économique: The first formal national income account, developed by the **Physiocrat** François Quesnay on the analogy of how blood circulates through the human body. (See **Accounting**, **Economist** and **Say's Law**.) Its aim remained the focus of classical political economy: to quantify the economic surplus (*produit net*, net product) and to show who ended up with it (the landowning nobility and palace).

Today's main recipient of the rise in national income is still the FIRE sector and the One Percent that owns most of its wealth. Largely out of embarrassment at singling out how little of the economy's net gain is shared with the 99 Percent, mainstream economists talk as if there is *no* surplus. **NIPA** statistics have no suggestion of exploitation or unearned income, no meaningful categories for economic rent, and no measure for "capital" gains.

Taxation: Collection of a specified portion of income from citizens and businesses by government. But the tax burden is not evenly distributed. Society's victors view taxes as what they can extract from the losers as tribute and subsidy. The FIRE sector lobbies to untax real estate, natural resources and financial rent seeking, shifting the fiscal burden onto labor and consumers via regressive sales taxes, excise taxes and value-added taxes (VAT), and by disguising the Social Security tax as a user fee. (See **Tax Shift**.)

Taxes and money are closely linked. Levying taxes is what gives national value to money, by governments accepting it in payment of taxes and fees. (See **State Theory of Money**.)

At first it may seem that lower taxes would leave more income available for personal consumption and business investment. At a given moment of time this would be true – all other things remaining equal (*ceteris paribus*). But bankers realize that whatever revenue the tax collector relinquishes is available to be pledged for debt service. From their vantage point, land and its rent, monopolies and their rent, and even corporate cash flow are all targeted for paying interest. Lower real estate taxes leave more rent to be capitalized into bank loans, raising housing prices as banks lend more. Conversely, taxing this land rent would leave *less* for banks to collect as mortgage interest. So banks and real estate investors have led a populist ideology to limit government property taxation. This requires government spending to be cut back, while banks block government from creating its own money to finance its budget deficits (see **Modern Monetary Theory**).

California's notorious Proposition 13 froze real estate taxes on commercial properties as well as owner-occupied homes. The effect of leaving the rising land rent in private hands – to be paid to mortgage bankers for larger and larger loans – was to vastly increase California real estate prices. Bank profits soared, while the government had to roll back public services and impose more taxes on consumers. So labor's net disposable personal income (after paying the FIRE sector) ended up suffering by much *more* than the personal savings on home property taxes.

Tax Shift: A reversal of progressive taxation to favor finance and property (the FIRE sector). Taxes historically were levied mainly on land, because it is the largest and most visible form of wealth. From ancient times through medieval Europe, people living on the land were the source of corvée labor and service in the military. This was the archaic basis for assigning land tenure rights: land and its rent were for paying taxes, at first "in kind" and later in money.

But since about 1980 (following Margaret Thatcher's victory in Britain and Ronald Reagan's in the United States), taxes have been shifted off real estate onto labor. Wage withholding for Social Security and health insurance is a quasi-tax, rhetorically camouflaged as prepayment of user fees for public services paid for out of the general budget. And large corporations are allowed to establish "dummy affiliates" in offshore banking centers, pretending to make all their profits in countries that have no income tax. (The process was pioneered by the oil industry setting up flags of convenience in Liberia and Panama.)

The effect of these tax shifts is to intensify economic polarization, by adding fiscal deflation ("fiscal drag") to debt deflation for the 99 Percent, while spurring asset-price inflation benefiting the One Percent.

Teleology: An *a priori* approach (from Greek *telos*, "end") depicting any existing status quo as being a natural result of past trends and how past conflicts were resolved on a presumably constant upward trajectory. Such history is written as if there are no realistic alternative modes of economic or social organization (Mrs. Thatcher's TINA), only selected antecedents that lead to the present. (See **End of History** and **Stages of Development**.)

Thatcher, Margaret (1925-2013): As British Conservative Prime Minister (1979-1990), she claimed that "there is no such thing as society." This anti-social view sees no need to protect consumers or the environment from exploitation, or to protect economies from predatory financial behavior. Her trademark phrase was **TINA: There Is No Alternative**. (See **Neoliberal**, **Reaganomics** and **Social Market**.) Her **Labor Capitalism** was borrowed largely from Chile's Augusto Pinochet, who fled to her country for protection and indeed plaudits after his bloody military junta ended.

To persuade voters that they could make easy speculative gains and become capitalists-in-miniature, Mrs. Thatcher privatized public enterprises at low prices to provide quick price jumps. Starting with British Telephone, dumped at an initial public offering (IPO) discount for the company's retail customers, her selloff of public infrastructure provided windfalls, above all for speculators and large financial organizations. This created an illusion that producing financial gains helped "the economy" instead of polarizing it while making it high-cost. Meanwhile, high underwriting fees (an enormous 2% giveaway to investment bankers) shifted economic power to London's banking sector.

Privatizing public housing was a bonanza for mortgage bankers. Mrs. Thatcher's policy may be summarized as: "Sorry you've lost your job. I hope you made a killing on buying your Council House and are watching its price soar." But real estate's soaring prices left British workers unable to live in central London, forcing them to spend many hours each day on expensive travel to and from work (on privatized transportation). Thatcher lost power when she imposed a poll tax on the middle class instead of recapturing the soaring land prices by a windfall land tax, taxing people not property.

Thatcherism continued and even intensified after Thatcher. Tony Blair's New Labour Party celebrated financialization, and followed up Thatcher's rent and tax increases by privatizing the railroads and subways with **Public/Private Partnerships.** New Labour deregulated Britain's economy under Gordon Brown's "light touch," leading to the collapse in 2008 of the Royal Bank of Scotland (RBS), Icesave bank and other fraud-infested insider lootings.

"The Market": Advocates of the status quo have always vied with reformers to define and perpetuate the kind of market that serves their own interests. The modern faith that economies work fairly and equitably – even by natural law – is based on a definition of "the market" that deems *rentier* classes to be a natural part of economies. Critics urge political reform of the context within which markets operate. At issue is whether economic policy should focus on:

(1) Unbridled markets administered by the most powerful vested interests (the One Percent), or

(2) Society's need for economic growth by appropriate regulation, fair taxation and public spending and investment in infrastructure.

The choice will determine who will be the market's major beneficiaries – and victims. Opponents of public regulation construct academic models that depict the Progressive Era and New Deal reforms that created the American middle class as being "distortions" of "pure competition" and even "deadweight." Market failures since 2008 are blamed on "exogenous" factors that lie outside the scope of these narrow "market-oriented" models.

This **conservative** approach ignores the fact that economic inequality is widening and financial crashes are occurring because of the way in which markets have become malstructured (see **Structural Problem**). Rejecting government's historic role in shaping markets to prevent economic polarization from tearing communities apart, neoliberal theory goes so far as to idealize "the market" as having no public context at all.

This narrow view demonizes the past two centuries of classical and Progressive Era reforms to regulate credit, impose usury laws and treat money, health care and other basic infrastructure as public utilities so as to reduce the cost of living and doing business. If the Austrians and Thatcherites had their way, civilization never could have taken off, and China could not have risen to global economic power with its mixed public/private economy.

Classical economists analyzed how tax and regulatory policies shape markets. The major problem they addressed was landlords "reaping [land rents] where they have not sown" (as Adam Smith put it), collecting such rents "in their sleep" (as John Stuart Mill put it). Their solution was to free markets from economic rent by taxing it away or making basic infrastructure and other means of production public. (See **Fourth Factor of Production**.) A fictitious mythology of economic history brands the essence of Adam Smith, John Stuart Mill and their advocates as "socialist" as an epithet, as if there can be no such thing as a good proactive government policy with checks and balances that promote fair and sustainable economic growth.

By John Maynard Keynes's time, financial reform was taking its place alongside land taxation as a policy to free economies from the *rentier* financial class. (See **Euthanasia of the *Rentier***.) But today's neoliberal "markets" reverse financial regulation, public banking and debt write-downs by promoting the **"sanctity of debt."** This turnabout is rationalized by the unrealistic assumption that economies self-adjust in a fair and stable way without government action from "outside" or "above" the market. In a travesty of Adam Smith's "invisible hand," they denounce any such attempts as pernicious interference.

Freeing markets *from* predatory rent seeking requires (1) progressive taxation of the *rentier* class and its unearned income, and (2) either anti-monopoly legislation or public control of basic infrastructure to enable government to provide public services at cost or on a subsidized basis. These policies threaten the feudal epoch's legacy of vested interests, which strive to retain their time-honored free lunch (tax favoritism, untaxed capital gains and other tax loopholes, control of bank credit and as many natural infrastructure monopolies as they can take; see **Kleptocracy**). They seek to minimize regulation or "public option" competition from governments.

Rentier lobbyists aim is to mobilize anti-government resentment of insider dealing and oligarchy to discredit all government, especially socialist governments. The trick is to get the 99 Percent act against their own self-interest by not protecting themselves from these carry-overs of feudal privilege. (See **Stockholm Syndrome**.) To deter reforms, pro-*rentier* client academics define "the market" narrowly as a "free market" might exist without government regulations or a public option. (See **Learned Ignorance**.) This approach shifts blame for austerity onto "the market" **as if** it is a force of nature rather than being based on policies favoring the FIRE sector.

The Nobel Economics Prize for what is euphemized as "economic science" typically is given for the tautology that public regulations and subsidies impose transaction costs that "interfere" with free markets. But as David Graeber points out, contrary to the neoliberal assumption that markets came *before* governments (as if governments evolved simply to *enforce* payment of debts and contracts), the Bronze Age archaeological record shows that governments created and sponsored the earliest markets. The prototypical contracts were with (or mediated by) the palace or temples, sworn to by oaths to a god of commerce and/or justice. And in modern times, the first stock markets dealt mainly in royal debt. The 19th-century industrial takeoffs of Britain, the United States and Germany (and Japan after World War II) saw their governments take the lead in shaping markets with subsidies, tariffs (see **Protectionism**), taxes and direct investment.[1]

Markets always have been regulated and subsidized (see **Mixed Economy**). Antiquity's temples oversaw the purity and weight of monetary silver as part of their supervision of honest weights and measures. Mesopotamian rulers often started their reign by proclaiming price ratios for silver, grain, copper and other basic commodities in order to standardize fees for public services and other fiscal payments. (See **Money** and **Accounting**.) And nearly every Bronze Age ruler started his reign by annulling debts to create a Clean Slate. This long tradition prompted Karl Polanyi (1886-1964) to organize a group of academics to trace the extent to which markets are "embedded" in social rules that shape exchange, trade and credit by public regulation of prices, interest rates and, in modern times, anti-monopoly rules, consumer protection, usury and bankruptcy laws, and debt cancellations.[2]

By demonizing the past century's moves toward shaping markets more equitably, discussion of the reforms that built up a prosperous middle class has been airbrushed out of history and consigned to an Orwellian "memory hole." Voters are told that a market designed and controlled by the One Percent is a natural outgrowth of free markets, despite the fact that the middle class and industry are shrinking as a result of increasing debt overhead that concentrates property and financial wealth in the hands of the One Percent.

To endorse financial austerity and oppose public money creation to finance budget deficits or enactment of more humanitarian bankruptcy laws favoring debtors (the 99 Percent), anti-government ideologues seek to keep governments out of the monetary and financial regulatory sphere. Their sophistry depicts money as having been developed solely by individuals engaging in barter with each other. This mythology treats money simply as a commodity, not the legal and fiscal creation that it historically has been. (See **"As if"** and **Karl Menger**.) Budget deficits financed by public money creation to spend on public infrastructure investment and social welfare programs are defined as market "distortions," on the ground that they lead to different prices and incomes than would result without such intervention. Anti-usury laws, debt writedowns (see **Bankruptcy** and **Debt Forgiveness**) and more humanitarian treatment of debtors are deemed to interfere with the "freedom" of creditors ("capitalists" in their lexicon) to impose financial and fiscal austerity (often backed by U.S.-sponsored military juntas as in Augusto Pinochet's Chile).

The bankers' main fear is that government policies may favor labor, consumers and debtors over the power of inherited wealth, employers and creditors. The kind of "free market" envisioned by today's **Chicago Boys**, **Austrians** and **neoliberals** benefits the One Percent at the expense of society at large. This array of pro-financial policies requires a censorship of alternatives. To oppose claims that public regulation and oversight are necessary, neoliberals assert that **equilibrium** will occur automatically, without markets requiring government mediation to operate in a fair and equitable way.

Post-Soviet Russia gave U.S.-led neoliberals a free hand to create their travesty of a "free market." The result was a kleptocracy controlled by insiders and monopolists who impoverished labor and created a demographic collapse. Russia was turned from one of the world's most literate and high-technology populations into a raw-materials exporter, and its engineers and other professional classes were driven to emigrate abroad – along with about $25 billion of capital flight each year.

One recent writer summarizes the result: "In the early 1990s, a highly placed World Bank research economist ... argu[ed] that these countries were 'victims' of unreasonable egalitarianism, and all increases in inequality, linked as they must be to higher returns to more productive members of society, should be welcome."[3]

By contrast, look at China's socialist market economy to see how it avoided austerity and rose rapidly to great-power status by following active government policies akin to those of the United States and Germany during *their* industrial takeoffs.

Thorstein Veblen Theorem: Land prices tend to be higher than merely capitalizing existing property rents at the going rate of mortgage interest. In a bubble economy, prices reflect anticipated capital gains (to produce total returns; I review the math in the "Hudson Bubble Model" later in this book). Describing real estate as "the great American game," Veblen viewed it as "an enterprise in 'futures,' designed to get something for nothing from the unwary, of whom it is believed by experienced persons that 'there is one born every minute.'" Farmers and other rural families from the surrounding lands look "forward to the time when the community's advancing needs will enable them to realize on the inflated values of their real estate," that is, to find a sucker "to take them at their word and become their debtors in the amount which they say their real estate is worth." The entire operation, from individual properties to the town as a whole, is "an enterprise in salesmanship," with collusion being the rule.[4]

This excess of property prices over the capitalized value of their current rental income reflects the degree of "bubbling" – organized "puffing," that is, promoting hopes among potential buyers and investors that a property's site value will rise as a result of speculation, further economic development, easier bank credit and/or lower property taxes.

TINA (There Is No Alternative): The neoliberal principle that if one can censor awareness of policy alternatives to austerity, people will believe that poverty, inequality and economic polarization are natural, not manmade. To limit public awareness of alternatives, today's mainstream academic curriculum no longer includes the history of economic thought (or economic history for that matter). "Whoever controls the image and information of the past determines what and how future generations will think," wrote Orwell; "whoever controls the information and images of the present determines how those same people will view the past." When history is expunged from the common curriculum, there are no lessons of actual history. This enables an unrealistic mythology to be substituted, such as economic individualism and Austrian School fantasies.

Too Big To Fail/Jail: The 2008 crisis revealed that pervasive fraud by the largest U.S. banks was so systemic that the Obama Administration's Justice Department refrained from prosecuting the leading **banksters**. The excuse was that recovering the fraudulent exactions of banks would bring them down, and the economy with it. A more immediate political reason was that Wall Street had gained the power to direct President Obama to recruit Eric Holder and Lanny Breuer from the ranks of Wall Street law firms and put them in charge of the Justice Department (see **Regulatory Capture**). They pretended that jailing bankers would harm innocent spouses, children and bank employees.

No such concern was shown to victims of the banks' junk mortgage fraud, who were foreclosed on and evicted from their homes. The government not only rescued the biggest banks, it allowed them to grow even more dominant, using some of their gains to lobby Congress and pay millions of dollars to the political campaigns of leading Senators and Congressmen on key financial and other oversight committees to dilute reforms intended to prevent a recurrence of the collapse.

It is all reminiscent of what Voltaire wrote regarding the law: "It is forbidden to kill; therefore all murderers are punished unless they kill in large numbers and to the sound of trumpets. In such cases it is the rule."[5] (See **Criminal** and **Crime**.) Applying this principle to high finance, one may say that it is forbidden to defraud and falsify records, and banksters are punished unless they steal in large numbers and to the sound of applause by popular business media and the politicians they finance with their loot.

Total Return: The sum of current income (profit, interest and/or dividends) *plus* capital gains. In real estate, by far the major proportion of total returns consists of asset-price gains. Most corporate income – especially real estate rent and profits for financialized companies raided with junk bonds – is paid out as interest or used for stock buybacks to increase share prices. This leaves stockholders with capital gains instead of more highly taxed dividend income.

Totalitarianism: A propaganda term applied only to governments, not to creditor power. This term is used to terrorize people into believing that regulating prices, progressive tax policy and other social shaping of markets is a loss of democratic freedom, leading to control by government bureaucracy, and hence should be left to a financial oligarchy "free" of public regulation. The road to such control is paved by libertarians claiming that there is no such thing as society, but only "the market," which should be stripped of all public regulation. The aim of such **"Market Bolshevism"** is to remove all checks and balances from democratic government.

Hayek's *Road to Serfdom* is a prime example of defending the sell-off and privatization of the public domain to vest an oligarchy with control over all aspects of political and social life. No wonder his supporters, from Margaret Thatcher to the

Chicago Boys, admired Chile's Augusto Pinochet's assassination and terror campaign against academics, socialists, labor leaders and land reformers.

Traditionally assumed to be nationalist, today's trend toward totalitarian control is led by cosmopolitan financial institutions, as when the IMF, European Central Bank (ECB) and European Union overruled Greek voters to force privatization, cut back pensions and earmark all forms of economic surplus to pay creditors.

Tragedy of the Commons: A term coined in a lobbying effort claiming that the public domain should be privatized to prevent its overuse and depletion. The pretense is that users will overgraze and mismanage the **commons** in the absence of rules governing access – as if privatization will do a better job of conserving natural resources.

The term was coined by Garrett Hardin, who later acknowledged that the "tragedy" was limited to *unmanaged* commons, which rarely occurs in practice.[6] Neoliberals have ignored his back-tracking. It is their privatization that leads to short-term asset stripping – precisely what they accuse socialism of doing!

Transaction Cost: The overhead involved in commodity sales or financial transactions, such as the typical credit-card 3% fee to merchants and up to 29% interest (and even more in penalties) charged to buyers, or the money-management fees charged by stockbrokers and mutual funds for asset purchases. On the broadest level, financial management of society's savings includes such externalities as asset-price inflation and debt deflation resulting from diverting savings and credit away from industry toward financial speculation on real-estate and stock-market bubbles.

Rent seeking and its associated property privileges can be viewed as a transaction cost of permitting monopolies and private ownership of land and natural resources, as well as deregulated credit creation. However, neoliberal theorists such as Nobel Prize winner Douglass North only blame governments for increasing such costs, not deregulation increasing overhead in the form of fraud, cheating and looting.

Transfer Payment: A payment without a *quid pro quo*, such as immigrants' remittances to their families in their country of origin. Economic rent, interest and other payments to the financial and property sectors also fall into this category of **zero-sum activities**.

Transfer Price: Double-taxation treaties permit global conglomerates to choose *where* to pay their taxes. Multinational companies transfer oil, minerals or other products at fictitiously low tax-avoidance prices from the producer countries (where oil drilling or mining occur) to shipping affiliates domiciled in tax-free **offshore banking centers**.

The typical ploy starts by registering trading affiliates operating or hiring ships to fly "flags of convenience" in countries where income-tax rates are lowest, *e.g.*, in Panama or Liberia, or in Ireland, Liechtenstein or Monaco for industrial companies. Oil, minerals or other products are sold at low production prices to ships or "dummy" affiliates in low-tax jurisdictions, which make un-taxed gains by selling at a markup so high to refineries, marketing and distribution affiliates in North America and Europe that no taxable profit remains to declare.[7] Such transfer pricing ("tax shopping" in the world's fiscal race to the bottom) distorts trade and balance-of-payments statistics to reflect the fictions drafted by corporate tax accountants.

Traumatized Worker Syndrome: Federal Reserve Chairman Alan Greenspan's explanation to the U.S. Senate in July 1997 of why wages had not risen despite rising productivity (output per man-hour): "a heightened sense of job insecurity and, as a consequence, subdued wage gains."[8] Workers are afraid to go on strike or even to complain about working conditions, for fear of losing their paychecks or defaulting on their mortgage. (See **Exploitation**.) Falling behind on their monthly credit card bills would enable banks to sharply raise their interest rates and fees to reflect the debtor's lower credit rating.

Treasury: The proper role of a nation's Treasury should be to issue money or bonds to finance government spending, and levy taxes in ways to best promote employment and minimize payments to the financial sector. (See **State Theory of Money**.) By contrast, today's neoliberalized central banks seek to finance and bail out commercial banks and bondholders. (See **Regulatory Capture**.)

In the United States, the Federal Reserve was created in 1913 to shift monetary policy *away* from the Treasury to Wall Street and other business centers.[9] In 1951 the Treasury wanted low borrowing costs for the government, while the Federal Reserve urged higher interest rates, and won under the ensuing Accord. In 2008 the Fed blocked the Treasury's FDIC from taking over insolvent Citigroup, Bank of America and Wall Street firms whose net worth was wiped out by junk mortgage lending and other fraudulent practices such as NINJA loans.

Monetary policy throughout the world is passing from treasuries to central banks. The European Central Bank (ECB) prevents national public treasuries from financing budget deficits, thereby enforcing austerity. In Ireland the ECB insisted that the Treasury (and hence, Irish taxpayers) absorb the losses from massive bank fraud to pay uninsured depositors in full. Its neoliberal insistence on privatization and labor "reforms" has blocked recovery from Euro-austerity in Greece, Spain and other countries. Reviving employment requires rolling back the ability of central banks to serve financial oligarchies, returning treasuries to democratic control.

Trickle Down Economics: The pretense that reversing progressive taxation and giving more income to the wealthiest One Percent will maximize economic growth and prosperity for the 99 Percent. The actual effect is to help the rich get richer. (See **Demagogy, Laffer Curve** and **Supply-Side Economics.**) The *rentier* class has manipulated the tax code so that, as Leona Helmsley put it: "Only the little people pay taxes."

A supporting factoid is that the One Percent spends its income buying products produced by labor. That was Thomas Malthus's argument for why British landlords should receive agricultural tariff protection (the Corn Laws). His argument endeared him to John Maynard Keynes, but in practice the wealthy bought largely foreign luxuries and financial securities or more property. Today's One Percent lend out their income and wealth to further indebt the economy to themselves.

Another false assumption is that financiers and property owners (the FIRE sector) will save and invest their revenue to expand the means of production and employ more labor. (See **Parallel Universe.**) In practice, the wealthy wield creditor power to force governments to privatize the public domain and buy companies already in place. When the fictions of "trickle-down economics" lead to financial crises, the wealthy demand that governments rescue banks, give bailouts to uninsured depositors and bondholders, and shift taxes to further favor the FIRE sector at the expense of labor. (See **Moral Hazard.**) The result of trickle-down policy is thus economic polarization, not prosperity.

One of the earliest and most blatant expressions of trickle-down demagogy is found in the pleading by Isocrates in his *Areopagiticus* (VII, 31-34, written in 355 BC). Like most Sophist rhetoric teachers, he charged fees so high that only the wealthy could afford to study with him, so it hardly is surprising that his written speeches supported the oligarchy. "The less well-to-do among the citizens were so far from envying those of greater means that they ... considered that the prosperity of the rich was a guarantee of their own well-being." This may be the earliest written example of the Stockholm Syndrome.

Isocrates praised harsh judges for being "strictly faithful to the laws." This meant creditor-oriented laws. He noted that "judges were not in the habit of indulging their sense of equity," that is, what would be fair in the traditional morality of mutual aid. His over-the-top rationale for why Athenian judges "were more severe on defaulters than they were on the injured themselves" (meaning the creditors "injured" by not being paid in full) was that "they believed that those who break down confidence in contracts" (as if being unable to pay was a deliberate attack on pro-creditor laws) "do a greater injury to the poor than to the rich; for if the rich were to stop lending, they [the rich] would be deprived of only a slight revenue, whereas if the poor should lack the help of their supporters they would be reduced to desperate straits." It is as if usury doesn't deprive the poor of their land

and liberty, which **Socrates** did not hesitate to explain as the "sting" of usury that stripped debtors of their land and hence degraded their status as citizens.

Truthiness: A term coined by comedian and talk show host Stephen Colbert for a made-up fact or story accepted by many as true simply because it reflects their world view. An example: stories of "welfare queens" exploiting tax-payers, as if the free lunch is taken by the bottom of the economic pyramid instead of by the top. (See **Factoid** and **Mathiness**.) "Fake news" is now a worldwide phenomenon. And "postfaktisch" (post-fact) has been named Germany's Word Of The Year (2016), reflecting what people want to believe or what is consistent with their belief system, especially in cases where reality elicits **cognitive dissonance**.

Two Economies: Domestic private sectors are composed of two distinct systems. These are often conflated to mean "The Economy," but their dynamics are quite different.

(1) The **"real" economy** of current production and consumption, wages and industrial profits account for only part of the economy. (See **Circular Flow** and **Say's Law**.)

(2) The **FIRE sector** (Finance, Insurance and Real Estate) consists of land, monopoly rights and financial claims that yield *rentier* returns in the form of interest, financial fees, economic rent (unearned income) and monopoly gains, plus asset-price gains ("capital" gains).[10] Within the FIRE sector, the relationship between banks and real estate is dominant.

Since the 1980s, banks have created credit to lend mainly into the FIRE sector, not to businesses in the "real" economy of tangible investment and employment. This long credit buildup has inflated prices for real estate, stocks and bonds, leading borrowers to anticipate that capital gains will continue indefinitely (see **Asset-Price Inflation**).

Most of the FIRE sector's financialized "wealth" – the asset side of its balance sheet – is held by the *rentier* class. The magnitude is much larger than the GDP. Its debt counterpart on the liabilities side of the balance sheet consists mainly of mortgage debt, a financial overhead for homeowners and commercial real estate. Since World War II, the "real" economy has spent more and more income on real estate, insurance and payments to banks, pension funds and other financial transactions.

Bubbles are created when speculation on credit enters the phase in which debts rise as rapidly as asset valuations. When these financial bubbles burst, negative equity results as asset prices fall back, plunging below the face value of mortgages, bonds and bank loans attached to real estate and other assets. The post-2008 collapse is the result of the "real" economy having to pay down the debts it had run up, deflating consumer spending along with housing prices. This **debt deflation** is the final stage of the

"**Great Moderation**." Nearly all subsequent asset-price gains and income growth has accrued to the FIRE sector and the One Percent.

Interacting with these two private sector economies, governments either withdraw revenue by levying taxes and user fees, or (more frequently) spend more money into the "real economy" and the FIRE sector than it withdraws. It injects money into the economy by investing in public infrastructure and undertaking current spending (largely military and Social Security). But since 2008 the Obama Administration has subsidized mainly the FIRE sector, primarily with bank bailouts and the Federal Reserve's Quantitative Easing. (See **State Socialism** and **Socialism for the Rich**.)

Budget surpluses (taxing more than the government spends) drain income from the economy's flow of spending between producers and consumers. It is the government's way of "saving" by paying down public debt. Budget deficits

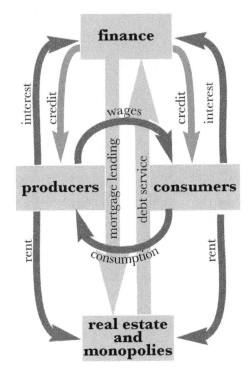

THE TWO ECONOMIES

#1. "Real" Economy (producers and consumers)

#2. FIRE Sector (**finance**, **real estate** and **monopolies.**

are financed either by borrowing from bondholders (obliging the government to pay interest to them), or by fresh money creation, usually by the central bank buying bonds from the FIRE sector. (The "Hudson Bubble Model" article in this book shows the government sector's role in the economy's flow of funds and the international sector.)

ENDNOTES

[1] David Graeber, *Debt: The First 5,000 Years* (Brooklyn, New York, 2011), pp. 50, 55, 344 and 358.

[2] For a discussion of how markets were shaped by administered pricing, see my afore-mentioned *Creating Economic Order: Record-Keeping, Standardization and the Development of Accounting in the Ancient Near East* (ed. with Cornelia Wunsch, Bethesda, 2004). Polanyi's approach is summarized in Karl Polanyi, Conrad M. Arensberg and Harry W. Pearson, *Trade and Markets in the Early Empires* (1957). See also Johannes Renger (1979), "Interaction of Temple, Palace, and 'Private Enterprise' in the Old Babylonian Economy," in Eduard Lipinski (ed.), *State and Temple Economy in the Ancient Near East* (Leuven, 1979): I, pp. 249-56, and his "Patterns of Non-Institutional Trade and Non-Commercial Exchange in Ancient Mesopotamia at the Beginning of the Second Millennium BC," in Alphonse Archi, ed., *Circulation of Goods in Non-Palatial Context in the Ancient Near East* (Rome, 1984), pp. 31-115. I contrast Polanyi's distinction between the reciprocity of gift exchange, redistributive markets via administered pricing and price-making markets with Marx's focus on modes of production in my review of surveys of Polanyi's work in *Archiv für Orientforschung* **51** (2005/2006), pp. 405-11.

[3] Branko Milanovic, "Why We All Care About Inequality (But Are Loath to Admit It)," 2 Challenge, vol. 50, no. 6, November–December 2007. https://www.gc.cuny.edu/CUNY_GC/media/CUNY-Graduate-Center/PDF/Centers/LIS/Milanovic/papers/2004/challenge_proofs.pdf

[4] Thorstein Veblen, *Absentee Ownership and Business Enterprise in Recent Times* (1923), pp. 142ff.

[5] "Il est défendu de tuer; tout meurtrier est puni, à moins qu'il n'ait tué en grande compagnie, et au son des trompettes; c'est la règle." *Dictionnaire philosophique* (Geneva, 1764), under *Droit*.

[6] Robert Andelson (ed.), *Commons without Tragedy* (1991).

[7] I describe the details in *Finance Capitalism and its Discontents* (ISLET 2012), chapter 9: "An insider spills the beans on offshore banking centers," pp. 135-156.

[8] Testimony of Chairman Alan Greenspan before the Committee on Banking, Housing, and Urban Affairs, U.S. Senate July 22, 1997: "The Federal Reserve's semiannual monetary policy," http://www.federalreserve.gov/boarddocs/hh/1997/july/testimony.htm

[9] I give the background in "How the U.S. Treasury avoided Chronic Deflation by Relinquishing Monetary Control to Wall Street," *Economic & Political Weekly* (India), May 7, 2016.

[10] See Dirk Bezemer and Michael Hudson, "Finance Is Not the Economy: Reviving the Conceptual Distinction," *Journal of Economic Ideas*, September 2016. See also my book, *The Bubble And Beyond: Fictitious Capital, Debt Deflation and Global Crisis*. 2014: Chapter 11, "Saving, Asset-Price Inflation and Debt Deflation," pp. 297-318.

is for
Unearned Income

Underdevelopment: A term coined by the economic historian and sociologist Andre Gunder Frank (1925-2005) to describe the policies by which Europe's colonies and subsequent Third World countries have been turned into indebted raw-materials exporters instead of balanced economies capable of feeding themselves and remaining free of foreign debt and its associated loss of sovereignty. (See **World System**.) The term implies that they will follow the same pattern as "developed" economies. But they are misshapen, often supported by violent creditor oligarchies. This maldevelopment is euphemized by **stages of growth** theory suggesting that malstructured economies need simply "wait their turn" to develop in a healthy way. Locked into debt dependency on the leading financial nations, they are forced to adopt neoliberal anti-labor policies and relinquish their public domains to rent-seeking monopolists. This is the opposite of U.S.- and European-style protectionist drive to ensure economic self-sufficiency in food and basic industry. (See **IMF**, **Conditionalities** and **Washington Consensus**.)

Unearned Income: See **Economic Rent**, **Free Lunch**, **Monopoly** and **Windfall**, as well as **Asset-Price Inflation** and **Capital Gain**.

Unexpected: The the media's preferred adjective when announcing bad economic news. Given the fact that to neoliberals the solution to any problem is to shrink government, cut taxes and subsidize the banks and real estate, it is appropriate to express great "surprise" when the 99 Percent are not helped, and when the dynamics of compound interest lead to debt deflation. When it is not politically possible to avoid reporting that a real estate or financial bubble has burst or that an austerity program has made the economy even worse than the government or IMF projected, reporters find it obligatory to show that their heart is in the right place by assuring their audience that nobody could have foreseen the economic disaster. It is politically incorrect to give credence to warnings that threaten mainstream trickle-down optimism.

Usury: Biblical sanctions against charging usury were aimed at agrarian usury. The royal Mesopotamian Clean Slates freed debtors from tax arrears and other fees owed to public collectors or other creditors, but did not apply to commercial lending. In medieval Europe, however, the word usury (from Latin *usus fructus*, "use of the fruits") referred to interest charged for *any* purpose – not only loans to individuals (usually to pay taxes or buy consumer goods) but also to the financing of profitable trade ventures. Thirteenth-century Churchmen replaced "usury" with the less unpleasant word "interest," having less negative connotations and suggesting a partnership between creditors and debtors for mutual gain. Since the Middle Ages the term "usury" has been limited to interest charges in excess of the legal maximum rate.

On a society-wide level, usury polarizes economies. It is worse than merely a zero-sum activity, because as Francis Bacon observed in his essay "On Usury": "Usury bringeth the treasure of a realm into few hands, for the usurer, being at certainties, and the other at uncertainties, in the end of the game most of the money will be in the box, and a State ever flourisheth where **wealth** is more equally spread." (See also: **Agio, Murabaha Loan** and **Sharia Law**.)

Utility Theory: The idea that the more of any commodity one has, the more one is satiated, so that each additional unit (say, of bananas) gives less utility. All commodities – food, housing and most recently medical care and education – are treated as freely chosen by "consumers," not simply out of need to live and pay debts or rent. Consumer "demand" is supposed to drive producers to "satisfy" them. This "consumer is king" approach depicts the economy as being steered by its victims instead of recognizing worker-consumers as exploited parties.

Assuming that individuals suffer the "disutility" of working in order to buy consumer goods, this psychological speculation implies that individuals with less money or consumer goods will be motivated to work harder and catch up with those with more wealth – who presumably find less "utility" in earning and consuming more. This idea of satiation as one gets richer (and presumably consumes more) is the opposite phenomenon of **wealth addiction**.

Marginal utility theory is part of the late 19th century's anti-classical reaction. Taking policy structures and the distribution of wealth for granted, it shifts the focal point of economics away from unearned *rentier* income (which involves no labor or "disutility" at all) and monopoly pricing, and hence away from institutional reforms to limit how wealth is obtained.

Utopia: A theocratic blueprint for society, such as Plato's *Republic* or Thomas More's *Utopia*. Most such utopias have been authoritarian and hierarchic, run by strong leaders enforcing a highly regimented uniformity. Real-world attempts to create such communities have tended to isolate themselves as sectarian cults.

Utopian Economics: A description of how to structure a society that would work harmoniously and equitably. Mainstream textbooks depict our own economy as nearly a utopia in which everyone earns in proportion to their contribution to production. (See **John Bates Clark** and **"As If" Argument**.) Free market economists have idealized an individualistic society removing public regulation, thanks to the workings of the invisible hand of personal self-interest. The result is held to be the best of all possible worlds (see **End of History**), but in practice turns out to be today's dystopian financialized oligarchy. War, fraud and crime make no appearance, and there seems to be no dependency or coercion, because all consumer goods and debts are assumed to be a matter of free choice. It is as if we have reached a utopian ideal, so it seems unnecessary to provide a guide to what government regulations or policies are needed to create a better world in practice.

is for
the Vested Interests

Value: For classical economists, value connoted the technologically and socially necessary costs of production. Ultimately these costs were resolved into the labor embodied in the cost of capital equipment, buildings and raw materials used up in the process of production. The **labor theory of value** was an analytic tool to isolate **economic rent**, **interest** and other property claims as **transfer payments**, that is, elements of market price in excess of value.

Today's post-classical era conflates value with price, not acknowledging the degree to which prices exceed the necessary costs of production. Consumer utility is viewed as defining prices regardless of their costs of production, subject to the assumption that free competition will bring these prices in line with costs, so that "utility" will reflect competitive costs. But this assumption becomes unrealistic as economies become **financialized** and **monopolized**.

Value Added Tax (VAT): The most anti-progressive form of taxation, the VAT avoids taxing non-production *rentier* income, falling on commodity sales at each stage of production. Neoliberal advocates of VAT typically urge a **tax shift** of fiscal policy away from income taxation, favoring a low flat tax equal for all income brackets instead of progressive income taxation or taxes falling specifically at *rentier* wealth. The VAT ultimately is passed on to consumers, increasing commodity prices while leaving rent, interest and assets such as stocks, bonds and real estate untouched. By contrast, a tax on property or *rentier* income would *lower* asset prices, by limiting the flow of "free lunch" revenue that can be capitalized into bank loans.

Value-Free Economics: The effect of "value-free" thinking is to prevent people from making value judgments questioning the status quo. The aim above all is to avoid characterizing rent and interest accruing to property owners and creditors as being unearned. The FIRE sector is counted as producing an economic product, not as overhead.

Veblen, Thorstein (1857-1929): American institutionalist who traced how financial managers for the **vested interests** load industry down with watered costs. Veblen's *Absentee Ownership* (1924) described urban development as a game of real-estate promotion (see **Thorstein Veblen Theorem**). His *Theory of The Leisure Class* (1899) coined the term "conspicuous consumption," showing how personal tastes were socially engineered in wasteful ways by advertising. He also discussed how academic economics brainwashes students with "trained incapacity" to understand the economy's actual structure and problems (see **Learned Ignorance**). His *Higher Learning in America* (1918) described how mainstream economic theorists sought to exclude from discussion the factors most important in shaping economic life.

Post-classical economists accused Veblen of being more a sociologist than an economist. The economics discipline narrowed its scope to exclude the *rentier* dynamics on which Veblen focused, calling them "externalities," not an inherent part of economies. Veblen responded by coining the term "strategic sabotage."

Vested Interests: A term coined by **Thorstein Veblen** to describe *rentiers* using their property and financial claims to buy control of government.

Virtual Reality: A parallel universe created by interlocking sets of assumptions and hypotheses based on the deductive method, usually to distract attention from how real economies function. (See **Junk Economics** and **Neoclassical Economics**.)

Virtual Wealth: A term coined by the physicist Frederick Soddy (Nobel Prize for Chemistry in 1924) to distinguish financial and property claims *on* the means of production and income from the tangible assets themselves (real wealth). Virtual wealth (bonds, bank loans and stocks) belongs on the liabilities side of the balance sheet. Its growth at compound interest may come to exceed the value of the asset side of the balance sheet, leaving a negative equity balance instead of net worth.[1]

ENDNOTE

[1] Frederick Soddy, *Wealth, Virtual Wealth and Debt: The solution of the economic paradox*. George Allen & Unwin, 1926.

is for
Wealth Addiction

Wall Street: Replacing government as the economic planning center on behalf of the FIRE sector, Wall Street is the major source and sponsor of financial overhead. Its business plan is to load corporations, households, real estate, natural resources and government with enough debt so that all profit, all wages above basic subsistence needs, and all rents will be paid to banks and bondholders as interest. (See **Finance Capitalism**, **FIRE Sector**, *Rentier*, the **One Percent** and **Zero-Sum Activity**.)

Financial short-termism is a distinguishing feature of junk economics. Corporate income is used for stock buybacks and higher dividend payouts instead of for new capital investment. Political contributions support politicians who vote to harden pro-creditor bankruptcy laws and sponsor regulatory capture to block prosecution of financial fraud. The resulting debt deflation slows economic growth, as debt service absorbs a rising proportion of personal and corporate income.

Wall Street's business plan thus is inherently self-destructive. A financial crisis can be averted only by an exponential creation of new credit to fuel more asset-price inflation, enabling debts to be paid by borrowing the interest against collateral whose price is being pushed up by easier bank loans. (See **Ponzi Scheme** and **Hyman Minsky**.) To defend subsidizing the rising debt overhead and bailouts of banks and bondholders, Wall Street has become the major political campaign contributor, and also the major sponsor of junk economics that blames the victims (debtors, labor, immigrants and foreigners) instead of the debt creation and tax favoritism that increase the *rentier* wealth of the One Percent.

War: The major cause of national debts, balance-of-payments deficits and price inflation, often followed by postwar deflation. Politically, war serves as an excuse to centralize control of government in the Executive Branch, which usually means in the hands of the few. **Pentagon capitalism** refers to the "cost-plus" pricing policy of America's military-industrial complex, by which industrial engineers seek to maximize production costs instead of minimize them. The higher the cost of production, the more the cost-plus contracts yield in profit add-ons.

Washington Consensus: The neoliberal **"conditionalities"** imposed on debtor countries by the **IMF** and **World Bank**, forcing governments to **privatize** their public domain to U.S. and other international finance capital. The policy achieved its greatest success in Russia after 1991, supporting the selloff of mineral and oil resources to kleptocrats, dismantling industry and imposing **monetarist austerity**, capping the U.S. Cold War victory by leading to depopulation and capital flight estimated at $25 billion annually since 1990. A similar policy stripped assets in Greece after 2015. (See **Underdevelopment**.)

Watered Costs: A 19th-century term for issuing new stocks or bonds to managers and insiders, "watering down" the securities held by the public. More generally, the term refers to economically unnecessary and often **fictitious costs** above labor and capital outlays. The term can be extended to include interest, stock options and bonds issued to financial and political insiders, as well as the management and underwriting fees charged by money managers and investment bankers.

Watered Stock: Stocks and bonds issued by companies that receive nothing in return for their increase in liabilities. (The original term referred to cattlemen driving their herds to market and filling them up on water before they were weighed for sale to the meat packers.) Railroad barons issued watered stock to themselves and their Congressional backers in exchange for land grants and public subsidy, not to raise money for investment. The practice anticipated the stock options that today's managers give themselves.

Wealth: The linguistic root of "wealth" bears a connotation of welfare and the common weal. But increasingly it has taken the form of financial and other *rentier* claims at the expense of social well-being. (See **Virtual Wealth**.)

Wealth Addiction: A Roman proverb observes: "Money is like sea water: The more you drink, the thirstier you get." The more money a rich man has, the more driven he is to accumulate more. Greek dramatists portrayed the limitless **greed** for money as a disease of the psyche. In Aristophanes' last play, *Ploutos* (388 BC), Karion remarks that a person may become over-satiated with food – bread, sweets, cakes, figs and barley – but no one ever has enough wealth. His friend Chremelos agrees:

> Give a man a sum of thirteen talents,
> and all the more he hungers for sixteen.
> Give him sixteen, and he must needs have forty,
> or life's not worth living, so he says.   (lines 189-93)

Compulsive wealth addiction tends to go hand in hand with **affluenza**.

Wealth Creation: Originally referring to society's means of production, the financial press has turned the term into a euphemism for inflating prices for stocks, bonds and other financial claims *on* the economy's tangible wealth and income. Popularized by Federal Reserve Chairman Alan Greenspan to describe rising prices for buying homes or stocks and bonds to yield a fixed retirement income, the term depicts **asset-price inflation** as increasing net worth. Frederick Soddy coined the term **virtual wealth** to depict such financial claims (on the liabilities side of the balance sheet) as the antithesis of tangible capital formation.

Who/Whom: Attributed to a 1921 speech by Vladimir Lenin to the Second All-Russian Congress of Political Education Departments: "The whole question is, who will overtake whom? (*kto:kogo*)." Initially referring to Soviet vs. capitalist world dominance, the term soon came to mean class struggle. In today's world in which most debts are owed by the 99 Percent to the One Percent, the main who/whom relationship is between creditors and debtors.

Widows and Orphans: When lawgivers from Babylonia through the Bible spoke of protecting widows and orphans, they meant the weak and needy: war widows and children of men killed in fighting on behalf of their community, or old and infirm individuals taken out of their family context on the land. But today's economics journalists speak of protecting widows and orphans who are heirs or divorcees of the wealthy, living off their inheritance, trust funds, pre-nuptial contracts and/or divorce settlements. They are to be protected from inflation eating away at financial securities in which funds for their support are invested.

The crocodile tears traditionally shed by financial elites for widows and orphans – at least those living on interest from the bonds in their trust funds – are now being shed for retirees as the pretended beneficiaries of policies favoring high finance. During the Bubble years, inflating asset prices (and not taxing "capital" gains) was defended on the logic that this would enable pension funds to enable retirees to live in a prosperous way.

Regarding poor widows and orphans as being in need of public support instead of being trust-fund *rentiers*, Herman Kahn's liberal wife Jane told me that when she asked Milton Friedman whether it was indeed desirable to provide support for them, he replied: "Mrs. Kahn, why do you want to subsidize the production of orphans?"

This view confuses correlation with causation, on the assumption that paying more for anything will increase its supply. The political message is that governments should not engage in social welfare spending, because this will cause dependency instead of helping recipients to be self-sustaining individuals.

Windfall: The preferred (originally British) term for **capital gain**, an increase in an asset's price without the owner having to exert effort. Ricardo described windfalls accruing to landlords in the form of **economic rent** as population growth forced the cultivation of poorer soils, raising costs and hence crop prices. But the major windfalls today take the form of asset-price inflation in the real estate and stock markets. John Stuart Mill called such windfalls an "unearned increment." (See **Free Lunch** and **Unearned Income**.)

World Bank: The International Bank for Reconstruction and Development (IBRD), created by the Allied Powers in 1944 along with the International Monetary Fund (IMF) to finance the postwar reconstruction of Europe as a market for U.S. exports, and loans to Third World countries to finance their trade dependency. Instead of emulating the successful protectionist U.S. policies supporting agriculture with import quotas, rural extension and credit services, the World Bank promoted plantation export monocultures. It does not make loans in local currency, and hence is precluded from promoting domestic food production by local agricultural extension services and related price supports of the sort that have made U.S. agriculture so productive since the 1930s. Countries following World Bank advice became heavily indebted, falling into the grip of the IMF, which withholds currency support if countries do not sell off their public domain to global investors. (See **Asset Stripping**, **Privatization** and **Washington Consensus**.)

World System: A view of the global economy in terms of an empire-building core that shapes and exploits the periphery (typically former European colonies) into debt and food dependency.

are for
the X and Y Axes

X and Y Axes: Economics is taught largely by isolating just two variables at a time. Y is the vertical axis (*e.g.,* supply and demand, income, and debt), and X the horizontal axis (usually time) to chart the relationship between prices, interest rates or income. Lower wages are supposed to increase employment, "all other things remaining unchanged." That is the problem: only two functions are analyzed, in isolation from the economic system and its complex dynamics.

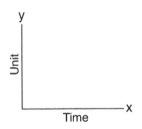

Charts using only the X and Y axes encourage two-dimensional flat-earth thinking, as if prices and incomes can be isolated on the individualistic level without involving feedback responses throughout the economy. (See **Systems Analysis**.) The problem is the tacit assumption that all other things really do remain equal. Economists use the Latin term *caeteris paribus* to legitimize tunnel vision in the same way that mathematical symbolism does. But the economic system rarely remains unaffected when major variables are changed.

It would take more than two dimensions to show that when IMF austerity programs lower wages and shrink markets, employment does *not* increase, but is obliged to emigrate (or die earlier). Lower interest rates, for instance, are supposed to spur direct investment (as if banks actually lend for new investment, which they don't). The actual effect of the Federal Reserve's Quantitative Easing since 2008 was that banks provided relatively low-interest credit that made corporate raiding and financial engineering (debt leveraging and arbitrage trading) more profitable, at the expense of new long-term capital formation. (See **Liquidity Trap**.) Industrial employment did not pick up, but the Fed's two-dimensional depiction cannot explain why.

Whenever one finds such tunnel vision and chronically repeated economic error, there is a special interest benefiting from such short-sightedness – usually the financial sector, which lives in the short run. In the case of Quantitative Easing, the beneficiaries are the banks receiving free reserves (on which the Fed has paid interest since 2008). Banks pretend that their gain will be that of the economy. That is our era's most characteristic wrongheaded pretense, and the leading premise of today's junk economics.

is for
Zero-Sum Activity

Zero-Sum Activity: Rent-seeking behavior in which one party's gain is another's loss. Such predatory transactions merely *transfer* income rather than producing real output or value. (See **Sterile**.) Such **transfer payments** usually take the form of **economic rent** or **usury**, and lead to economic polarization favoring the *rentier* class (see **FIRE Sector**) at the expense of tangible capital formation and living standards.

Viewed in terms of their economy-wide effects, zero-sum activities almost always turn out to be negative-sum activities on the macroeconomic level. (See **Usury**.) That is why defenders of *rentiers* promote an economic methodology that does not consider how economic polarization and debt deflation corrode economies. Junk economics deems such income and wealth distribution to be "exogenous" to its doctrinaire models.

The 22 Most Pervasive Economic Myths of Our Time

Socrates argued that the root of evil is ignorance, because no one knowingly sets out to do evil. But lawyers, politicians and lobbyists vie with each other to weave webs of economic rationalization and loopholes for the *rentier* One Percent by promoting economic ignorance and sophistry. The more successful their Doublethink, the more their clients need to pay, because misleaders charge more to persuade an audience of falsehood than well-meaning individuals charge to spread truth. In a world where financial success has become the new moral measure celebrating evil, the root of evil turns out to be money.

Plato describes the Sophist school as teaching an "appearance-making art, an uninformed and insincere art of contrary-speech-producing." The sophist is "a paid hunter after wealth and youth ... a merchant in the goods of the soul," and hence "in the class of magicians and mimics." Sophists became the first lawyers, advocates pleading cases for their clients by using the techniques of acquisition, not production.

Hardly surprising, the political tenor of this school was to oppose democracy. In contrast to other branches of philosophy, its teachers charged tuition fees, which could be afforded mainly by aristocrats. Today, the main political role of sophistry – Plato's "merchants of knowledge" – is to use superficially plausible logic to distract discussion away from real substance, above all by refining a demagogy of trickle-down economics. The aim is to compose a seemingly plausible cover story to convince the population – especially the lower classes – to identify their welfare with that of the oligarchy in an economy-wide Stockholm Syndrome. ("Only the One Percent can save/employ us and lend us enough to scrape by.")

National Income statistics (NIPA) are distorted by burying economic rent, omitting capital gains, and excluding fraud and crime

Sophistry applies not only to the use of language, but extends to seemingly objective statistics. Any set of accounting categories reflects an economic theory, and mainstream theory has been "cooked" to serve the FIRE Sector's *rentier* interests. Its cheerleaders promote false characterizations so persuasive that most people mistake them for economic science. That is especially the case when statistics give the illusion of objective reality, as long as one does not question the concepts underlying their categories.

MYTH #1:
The National Income and Product Accounts (NIPA) show how fortunes are built up.

The NIPA exclude "capital" (asset-price) gains. Along with *rentier* income syphoned off from the rest of the economy, these are the major means of acquiring fortunes in today's world. That is why many countries call financial wealth "invisible." What is unmeasured will be unseen, unresented and untaxed. (See the **Two Economies**.)

REALITY: Post-classical economics shies away from distinguishing land and real estate ownership, banking and monopolies from the industrial economy. Jumbling them together misses the fact that economic rent is extractive, and that although real estate does not make a taxable profit, rising property prices are the aim of most real estate investment. The goal of real estate investment is to ride the wave of debt-fueled asset-price inflation.

The myth is that fortunes are built up by saving out of "earnings," not by financially inflating asset prices. Yet the NIPA promote the fiction that the real estate sector does not make a profit. That sector reports no earnings for years on end. So where is "saving" to come from?

The answer is capital gains. But these are statistically invisible. NIPA statistics exclude the "capital" (asset-price) gains that are the dominant element of total returns.

NIPA statistics also do not indicate land rent and other forms of economic rent as such, and national balance sheet calculations by the Federal Reserve do not provide realistic estimates for land, or make any attempt to evaluate rent-extracting assets as distinct from manmade capital investment. Hence, there is no index of the rising cost of housing stemming from landlords or their mortgage lenders enjoying a free lunch "in their sleep."

Theories of the "falling rate of profit" that fail to segregate the FIRE sector from the industrial economy are swamped by the fact that real estate is the largest sector, and by far the largest debtor as well as reporting the most depreciation – a largely fictitious concept as used by real estate tax accountants. Buildings rarely lose value; their sales price tends to rise. But they can be depreciated again and again for tax purposes. The accounting fiction is that they start losing value with each change of ownership, but then miraculously recover this value – usually with a "capital gain" – with each change of ownership. I call this phenomenon *over-depreciation*.

Fortunately, the NIPA statistics measure overall ebitda: earnings before interest, taxes, depreciation and amortization. By far the largest component is interest, typically absorbing over two-thirds of real estate ebitda. Interest is paid out of overall rental income, but is tax deductible, on the pretense that it is a necessary cost of doing current business. Homeowners as well as commercial investors who borrow against their property can deduct interest charges (for transferring assets) from their reported taxable income.

Next to interest, depreciation is the largest element of real estate cash flow. These tax writeoffs for the depreciation tax loophole, as well as rising interest payments, rarely leave any income to be declared. The statistical pretense underlying the apparent falling rate of profit enables tax accountants for absentee real estate owners to claim "book losses" to offset income earned on their other operations, rendering them free of income taxation. This increases their actual returns. However, homeowners are not allowed to claim depreciation; only landlords and commercial owners can do this. As hotelier Leona Helmsley famously said: "Only the little people pay taxes." Tax favoritism for absentee property owners is one of the most anti-progressive elements in modern tax codes.

Finally omitted is the source of so many great fortunes: fraud and other crime. The NIPA include payments for the cost of burglar alarms, police and similar protection, but not the economic transfer payment to burglars, robbers and embezzlers.

MYTH #2:
All income is earned, reflecting the recipient's contribution to production.

The financial sector claims to be a necessary part of the production and consumption economy. Wall Street's enormously high earnings are said to reflect its contribution to productivity. Official statistics follow a circular reasoning that defines productivity as earnings per individual, ignoring the classical distinction between earned and unearned income (price and value), and hence between income and output. (See **John Bates Clark** and **Economic Rent.**)

REALITY: The private sector should be divided in two parts. (See **Two Economies.**) The production-and-consumption economy is wrapped in a web of financial and property claims that extract revenue without playing a directly productive role. The NIPA conflate rent extraction with "earnings" instead of depicting today's economy as bifurcated between a productive sector and rent-extracting overhead. The FIRE sector extracts interest and rents *from* the production-and-consumption economy. This distinction was essential to the classical economists. NIPA statistics treat the FIRE sector as if it actually creates "product," not as appropriating wealth.

A more realistic accounting format would isolate predatory zero-sum activities to quantify economic rent so that unearned income can be made into a the tax base.

But today's academic mainstream has consigned this concept to oblivion. This has enabled financial and other *rentier* interests to replace democratically elected governments and monopolize the fruits of economic growth for themselves, leaving the "real" economy floundering in austerity.

MYTH #3:
There is no such thing as unearned income.

Anyone's earnings are counted as payment for a corresponding contribution to Gross Domestic Product (GDP). Charges paid to the FIRE Sector are counted as part of GDP, not as transfer payments *extracted from* what the economy produces and earns.

REALITY: The only time "rent" appears in the NIPA statistics is for a category that is not really paid: "imputed rent" by homeowners, as if they were to pay the current rental value of their homes to themselves. The real-life rental income by absentee or other commercial owners is called "earnings." No other use of the word "rent" appears.

It is convoluted (but not impossible) to assign real estate income to land as distinct from capital investment in buildings, because the Federal Reserve's Flow-of-Funds statistics on the balance sheet of the U.S. economy (at the very end of its problematic Table Z) treat land as a residual, which minimizes its valuation. Buildings and other capital improvements are assumed to rise in value in keeping with the construction price index – even as absentee property owners pretend for tax purposes that buildings are *losing* their value as a result of "depreciation." This logic obliged the Federal Reserve to assign an absurdly *negative* $4 billion valuation to corporately owned land in 1994.

To isolate land rent it is necessary to calculate a more realistic balance between land and buildings, and apply the resulting ratio to the NIPA's statistic on real estate ebitda: earnings before interest, taxes, depreciation and amortization. A similar attempt should be made for the oil and mining sectors, privatized infrastructure monopolies such as the broadcasting and communications spectrum, pharmaceuticals and other rent-extracting sectors.

MYTH #4:
Economic rent is earned, and is simply another form of industrial profit.

REALITY: Economic rent is essentially a private tax (an unearned increment). This is most clear in the case of monopolists seeking to privatize public infrastructure for the purpose of rent extraction. Key infrastructure targeted to be monopolized includes land, water, mineral rights, air rights, communications and the broadcasting spectrum (see the Commons). These assets are provided by nature without cost. Appropriation of these assets is the result of a private law (literally a privilege) turning them into private property with the right to charge rent.

In the sphere of manmade technology, pharmaceutical patent owners, transportation routes, information technology and copyright owners extract similar tollbooth-like rents. Their "property right" takes the form of a legal chokepoint to deny access to basic needs and key technology. The aim of such patents and "rights" is to enable their owners to act as the landlords of the domain of scientific knowledge.

Economic rent also occurs in the financial sphere. Governments that pay interest to bondholders instead of creating their own money in effect are paying tribute for relinquishing government's money-creation function. Likewise, paying mortgage interest to bankers for credit to buy a home has the same effect as paying a tax, as far as the homebuyer is concerned. That is why banks want to monopolize the privilege of credit creation, and block public banking initiatives. It is why the FIRE sector seeks to become the economy's de facto government and privatizer of the otherwise public domain.

The essentially public nature of legal rent-extracting privileges is what makes them like a tax. *Rentiers* aim to extract charges for access to government-assigned property. But unlike public infrastructure investment, which aims to minimize costs for basic public services (like health care and money creation), privatizing public infrastructure, patent rights, scientific knowledge and natural resources for rent extraction aims to maximize the economy's cost structure in order to squeeze out more for the *rentier* sector. These charges do not reflect any cost of labor or actual enterprise (except for the cost of lawyers, lobbyists and kindred political influence) and thus are not in the character of industrial profits.

All countries should have access to scientific discoveries on the ground that technology is a universal and common asset of civilization. For this reason, most monopoly privileges and some patent rights for basic innovation granted by individual nations should not receive legal protection under international law (*e.g.*, basic pharmaceuticals, science and technology). A good example would be discoveries resulting from basic research by the National Institutes of Health (NIH).

MYTH #5:
The public sector is deadweight, and government activity is unnecessary overhead. The inference is that public spending should be minimized.

REALITY: Public infrastructure investment is a factor of production. Its role is to lower the economy's cost of living and doing business, by providing transportation, communications, health care and other services at cost, on a subsidized basis or freely. Public investment in such natural monopolies keeps them out of the hands of privatizers, rent extractors and financializers.

MYTH #6:
Any activity that makes money is part of "the market." The resulting status quo is morally justified as being simply "how the world works."

REALITY: Limiting the scope of analysis to current output and demand for goods and services (GDP) leaves out of account the property, financial and other *rentier* framework shaping the distribution of income and wealth. Where money is to be made, predatory activity tends to be legitimized and its gains financialized, mainly by the One Percent. All reforms, past and present, are called "distortions" of the market.

MYTH #7:
Capital gains are not income, and hence should not be subject to income tax or contributions to fund Social Security.

REALITY: Money managers define *total returns* as current income *plus* asset-price gains. Such gains are the major objective of FIRE sector investors. Yet nowhere in the NIPA or in the Federal Reserve's balance sheet statistics is there a measure of asset-price gains for land, stocks and other financial securities. As far as official statistics are concerned, the guiding principle seems to be that what is not seen will not be taxed or regulated. (See **Myth #1**.)

The 1913 U.S. income tax applied the same rates to capital gains as to income, on the ground that the effect was the same: an increase of wealth and "savings." Unlike wages and profits, asset-price gains result not so much from the owner's own efforts as from:

(1) Public infrastructure investment increasing the site-value of real estate (see **Thorstein Veblen Theorem**)

(2) National prosperity expanding market demand for housing and stocks

(3) Easy credit policies by the central bank (quantitative easing) to lower interest rates and increase bond prices.

These ways of enrichment receive tax favoritism over wage income and industrial profits earned on tangible capital formation. This is what has made the One Percent primarily a *rentier* class, enriched by public subsidy while taxes are cut on debt-leveraged financial and property gains.

* * *

Myths of Finance Capitalism that rationalize its predatory hold on the economy

MYTH #8:
Most debts can be paid without polarizing the economy and concentrating wealth in the hands of creditors.

COROLLARY: Business downturns ("recessions") are self-curing as wages and prices fall, providing profitable opportunities for new investment and employment to spur recovery. Hence, the economy appears to have no long-term structural problem of debt mounting up from one business upswing to the next in a financial super-cycle.

REALITY: The rate at which debts mount up at compound interest – plus new bank credit – tends to outrun the economy's ability to pay. The result is debt deflation, a widening wave of foreclosures, debt peonage and IMF privatization "condition-alities" that transfer the public domain to rent extractors.

Since World War II the debt overhead has increased from each business recovery to the next, growing exponentially beyond the ability to be paid. That is what led to the 2008 financial crash, and what is stifling subsequent economies in debt deflation. Rising debt service (interest and amortization) diverts spending away from goods and services, shrinking the economy and thus reducing investment and new hiring. The inevitable financial crash forces the economy to choose between writing down debts to the scale that *can* be paid (or in practice, an economy-wide Clean Slate), or letting creditors foreclose, transferring property ownership from defaulting debtors to the economy's top financial layer, while plunging the economy into chronic depression. In the ensuing fiscal crisis the financial sector uses its economic and political power to force governments to relinquish public assets (privatization).

MYTH #9:
Privatization is more efficient than public ownership and management.

REALITY: Public investment in infrastructure has been the major category of capital formation since time immemorial. Instead of seeking to make a profit on this investment, governments aim to subsidize prices charged for basic infrastructure services so as to make the economy more competitive. They are supposed to help the private sector function more profitably, not make a profit.

The most critical monopolies are those that governments have long kept in the public domain: roads and other basic transportation, the post office and communications, research and development, public health and education. Privatization builds in interest and other *rentier* ownership charges, executive salaries and bonuses, while offering opportunities for extortionate rent grabbing.

Using these sectors as opportunities to extract economic rent and pay it out as interest and financial fees is the dream of financial kleptocracies. The aim is to obtain capital gains, with tax preferences that reverse Progressive Era reforms.

The supply and pricing of transportation, communications, water and public health is largely responsible for international cost differences. Yet nowhere in "free market" trade theory is this role of public investment factored into comparative-cost ratios or absolute-cost analysis. The National Income and Product Accounts do not credit capital formation (public infrastructure) by the government as an asset against spending in calculating budget deficits or surpluses.

* * *

Myths of Labor Capitalism, Pension Fund Capitalism and Social Security

MYTH #10:
Employee stock ownership programs (ESOPs) and pension funds, along with personal saving via mutual funds, are elevating workers to the status of capitalists-in-miniature.

REALITY: Stock ownership remains concentrated in the hands of the top 10% of the population. Most capital gains accrue to this 10%, and to upper management for its stock options.

Pension funds in General Augusto Pinochet's Chile, Margaret Thatcher's Britain and the United States have not used their stock ownership to improve working conditions or wage levels. Pension and mutual funds tend to support management rather than using their stock ownership to promote policies in the interest of labor. The main effect has been to inflate equity prices by channeling labor's deferred wages (pension "savings") into the stock market.

When markets are rising, employers may declare pension plans to be overfunded and transfer their savings to the company's own account. This leaves the plans underfunded when markets turn down. Companies also use Employee Stock Ownership Plans (ESOPs) to pay for mergers and acquisitions, which dilute the plans and often wipe out most of their savings. The ultimate corporate ploy is to declare (or threaten to declare) bankruptcy to wipe out or substantially reduce pension-fund and healthcare promises. Bondholders are given priority over pensioners and employees, who are shunted onto the government's underfunded Pension Benefit Guarantee Corporation (PBGC).

MYTH #11:
Social Security should be pre-funded by its beneficiaries. Progressive income taxes should be abolished in favor of a flat tax – just one tax rate for everyone.

REALITY: The essence of progressive taxation is to levy higher taxes on the upper income and wealth brackets, whose revenue consists largely of economic rent, interest and other financial gains. When the U.S. income tax was legalized in 1913, it was recognized that the wealthiest layer of the population – the only layer obliged to file an income-tax report – were *rentiers*, deriving their income from property rents and speculative gains (largely from manipulating financial markets).

Like public health and other basic protections and infrastructure investment, Social Security should be funded out of the general budget. This means financing it out of government money creation or progressive income and wealth taxation. Either the present cut-off point for the Social Security tax ($115,000 and slowly rising) should be removed, or the program should be funded on a pay-as-you-go basis. In any case, pre-saving for Social Security should not be used to cut taxes on the higher income and wealth brackets.

MYTH #12:
Voters get what they vote for. It is their fault if public policy does not serve their needs.

REALITY: The Supreme Court's 2010 decision in *Citizen's United v. Federal Election Commission* permits the One Percent to buy elections. Campaigns for politicians running for office should be thought of as comprising two columns. Column A includes a list of what voters want. Column B lists what the major campaign contributors want. The demagogue's trick is to assign a Column A "voters' wish list" label to each Column B actual policy aim: to serve Wall Street and corporate backers.

Barack Obama provides a classic example. He promised voters "hope and change" in 2008. Instead, his policies *prevented* change – and made economic distress even worse by introducing each pro-Wall Street policy with an Orwellian vocabulary pretending to "revive employment" by trickle-down policies that left the debts in place to impose debt deflation, while bank bailouts and "Quantitative Easing" increased income and asset-price gains for the One Percent. The word "reform" is attached to laws that actually roll back Progressive Era reforms, betraying the hopes of the 99 Percent.

* * *

Financial mythology rationalizes saving the bankers instead of the economy

MYTH #13:
The September 2008 financial crisis was one of temporary illiquidity, not insolvency resulting from reckless and fraudulent lending.

REALITY: A bank is illiquid when a crisis freezes credit. The problem in such cases is economy-wide shock, not the bank's systemically bad loans. The freeze temporarily prevents banks from meeting withdrawals by selling their mortgages and other loans, so central banks provide credit to ride out the storm. However, they are supposed to charge a high enough interest rate to deter banks from borrowing to speculate. This is called the Bagehot Rule, named for the 19th-century British economic journalist Walter Bagehot.

That rule was not followed in 2008. Headed by Citigroup and Bank of America, some of the largest banks were insolvent as a result of reckless over-lending without regard for borrowers' ability to pay, or for what their mortgaged homes could sell for on the open market. The Federal Deposit Insurance Corp. (FDIC) was supposed to take over these banks instead of rescuing them. To avoid this fate, the large **Too Big To Fail/Jail** banks mainly responsible for junk-mortgage lending insisted that the market for these mortgages was only drying up temporarily, so banks were not insolvent – or responsible for the collapse of their balance sheets. Federal Reserve and Treasury officials pretended that junk mortgages *could* be paid, despite some ten million U.S. homeowners facing foreclosure, unable to sell their homes at prices that would reimburse the banks.

Instead of punishing executives of the biggest banks for the frauds that led the Department of Justice to collect civil fines of more than $65 billion from 2012 through mid-2015, the Federal Reserve trivialized the 2008 crisis as a liquidity problem. Treating junk-mortgage loans as basically sound, the Fed pretended that the economy could return to solvency by bailing out the banks. The cover story was that low interest rates would enable banks to begin lending again, with enough new debt leverage to bid up real estate prices so that mortgage lenders could avoid taking a loss. Continued bubbling was promised to make the mortgage crisis only temporary.

The Federal Reserve's bank bailout of 2008-2016 is a classic example of financial demagogy. The Fed pursued an easy-money policy for banks and their bondholders, hoping to manipulate markets by injecting $4.3 trillion for banks to buy reserves at interest rates of just a fraction of one percent (to 2016 and still running). The aim was to enable banks to work their way out of insolvency by making loans at a markup – that is, by making the economy even more debt-heavy. In practice, the banks speculated in currencies, stocks and bonds, and lent for corporate takeovers.

Quantitative Easing did *not* lead to new tangible capital investment and hiring ("real" economic activity). Only the financial markets were inflated. The Fed helped increase bank lending to inflate asset prices, not to revive employment and wage levels. Scant attempt was made to write down the economy's debt burden.

Nearly free central bank credit helped the economy "borrow its way out of debt," by lending to families to bid housing prices back up. The pretense was that reversing the decline in the valuation of real estate backing the mortgage loans – and re-inflating prices for stocks and bonds – would revive the economy, making it easier to carry the debt burden. The Federal Housing Authority, Fannie Mae and Freddie Mac revived the home mortgage market by guaranteeing new mortgage loans that absorbed up to an unprecedented 43% of borrowers' income. This imposed debt deflation on such households, while banks became the economy's most profitable sector. Their stocks soared.

MYTH #14:
Increasing the money supply inflates the general price level. This makes debts easier to pay out of rising wages and incomes.

REALITY: The Federal Reserve's money-dropping "helicopter" only flies over Wall Street, just as the Bank of England's helicopter only flies over London's financial City. The Greek central bank's helicopter only flies over Frankfurt and Paris, because it is run by the eurozone's bank-appointed planners.

The aim of central bank policy is to benefit its constituency – commercial banks and the financial sector – by Quantitative Easing that inflates the market for mortgages (and hence, real estate prices), stocks and bonds, held overwhelmingly by the top One Percent. This increases asset prices, not wages or consumer prices. Obliging the 99 Percent to pay for these higher-priced assets squeezes most household budgets and *deflates* consumer spending in the production and consumption economy.

Credit card rates and student loan rates did not decline during the Quantitative Easing years, and mortgage rates did not fall anywhere near as much as bank borrowing costs did. So bank profits soared, while the real estate collateral backing their mortgage loans was slowly re-inflated. The aim was **Asset-Price Inflation**.

MYTH #15:
Cutting real estate taxes makes housing less costly for homeowners.

REALITY: Cutting property taxes *raises* the cost of housing, because whatever rental income the tax collector relinquishes leaves more available to be pledged to banks as interest. So if taxes are reduced by $1,000 a year, this amount of rental value is "free" to be capitalized into a bank loan. At a 5% mortgage a $1,000 annual tax cut will raise the mortgagee's cost of a home by $20,000. Sellers will gain – but buyers in the next generation will suffer.

This explains why the financial sector backs the real estate sector in advocating lower property taxes. *Banks end up with the tax cuts.* This is followed by a shift of the tax burden onto consumers, via sales taxes, and onto local income taxes (from which absentee real estate investors are largely exempt.

It seems counter-intuitive that higher real estate taxes tend to *lower* the cost of housing. But FIRE-sector sophistry claims that property tax cuts help homebuyers, creating a cover story to distract attention from who actually ends up with the economic rent.

MYTH #16:
Higher real estate taxes make housing more costly, while cutting these taxes helps make housing more affordable.

REALITY: The site value of land (mainly the rent of location) is set by market conditions – the general level of prosperity, the desirability of living in prestigious neighborhoods with good schools and parks, access to transportation, and also the homeowner's income and hence ability to pay, and capped by the banks' willingness to lend enough to outbid rival buyers.

The question is, how much of this rent should be paid as taxes and how much remains available to be capitalized into bank loans. Whatever the property tax collector relinquishes is available to be paid to the bankers. If property taxes are increased, less rental value can be pledged to banks. They will not lend more to increase property prices – and the government will be able to use this land rent as the natural tax base.

* * *

Myths that the economy will achieve "balance" by shrinking government

MYTH #17:
Government budget deficits are bad, balanced budgets are good, and budget surpluses even better!

REALITY: When governments run deficits (except for bailing out banks and paying bondholders), they spend money *into* the economy. But if they run a balanced budget (or even worse, a budget surplus), this sucks revenue *out* of the economy. That is what happened when Andrew Jackson ran deflationary budget surpluses in the 1830s after he closed down the Bank of the United States. It happened again after the Civil War, when the United States sought to roll prices back to pre-1860 levels, causing prolonged depression.

Calls for balanced budgets stem from the banking sector's drive to replace national treasuries as the source of money and credit. When President Bill Clinton ran a budget surplus at the end of his administration in the late 1990s, this obliged the American economy to rely on commercial banks to supply the credit needed to grow. Unlike government spending that can be self-financed, banks charge interest and fees for their credit creation – and create credit mainly to bid up asset prices, not to spur employment and tangible capital formation.

MYTH #18:
Cutbacks in public spending will bring the government's budget into balance, restoring stability.

REALITY: Unlike private-sector debts, government debts cannot be written down. IMF loans to governments to bail out private bondholders (mainly banks and the One Percent) leave a residue of inexorable IMF claims on governments. IMF conditionalities – cutbacks in public spending, pensions and rising taxes on labor – shrink the debtor economy, deepening its budget deficit. This leads the IMF and finance ministers to call for even harsher austerity – as if their "medicine" is not actually bleeding and weakening the indebted victim.

The ensuing downward spiral is the actual aim of austerity, because worsening a government's financial crisis forces privatization sell-offs. This is especially clear in the financial conquest of Greece since 2010.

MYTH #19:
Providing social services freely or below cost "distorts" the self-regulating market. All goods and services should be paid for by their users at however much "the market" will bear. As Margaret Thatcher said, "there is no such thing as society," only the interests of asset owners and their bankers.

REALITY: Denying that society exists diverts attention from how financial managers have taken over the economy, government and planning. Imposing the libertarian fantasies of Margaret Thatcher and Ronald Reagan is largely responsible for pricing Britain and America out of global markets and deindustrializing their economies.

MYTH #20:
Deregulating the financial sector will free it from paperwork and enable it to pass the cost savings on to its customers.

REALITY: Like landlords, financial institutions charge as much as the market will bear. Cutting their paperwork and related compliance costs blocks the government from preventing fraud, enabling a rising swath of predatory financial rent to be extracted.

MYTH #21:
Markets return to balance if instability disrupts activity. Business cycles are cured by the economy's automatic stabilizers, so there is no need for government regulation or intervention from "outside" the market.

REALITY: Markets tend to polarize between creditors and debtors, and between property owners and users of basic infrastructure privatized from the public domain. The volume of debt accumulates at compound interest, faster than the "real" economy's trends of output, income and hence the ability to pay debts. Families, businesses and even governments are obliged to sell off their assets to pay creditors, until property and its income are so concentrated that the economy collapses or is conquered from without, or experiences a revolution from within. (See **Myth #7**.)

The great challenge is to free governments from control by the *rentier* interests. This requires reality-based economic principles to guide tax and regulatory policy. Turning the economy into an oligarchy is the price to be paid for failing to counter the sophistry of financial predators promising that their gains are those of the economy at large, not merely transfer payments *from* the economy to themselves.

MYTH #22:
The criterion of economic science is to demonstrate that economies tend to return to stability and an increasingly fair and equitable distribution of income and wealth. Models of polarization or atrophy have no simplistic mathematical resolution, and hence fall outside the definition of economic science proper.

REALITY: The financial and property sector seeks to control the educational curriculum and popular media to discourage reform that would slow its monopolization of wealth and political power. That is to be accomplished by changing the meaning of economic vocabulary and eliminating the study of economic history. The antidote to this junk economics must explain why economies tend to become more unstable and *more* polarized as a result of their own internal ("endogenous") dynamics – above all, credit and debt dynamics, and the untaxing of unearned economic rent.

* * *

Recovering from misleading economic mythology

Today's economics discipline is near collapse, awaiting a new paradigm. Academic journals remain committed to the mythology of financialization and its underbelly of rent seeking and privatization: the trickle-down idea that tax favoritism for debt financing, the FIRE sector and high income brackets will accelerate capital investment and raise living standards. There is a refusal to acknowledge that most savings are lent out to increase the economy's debt burden, subjecting it to debt deflation after the initial flush of asset-price inflation. That is why today's distribution of wealth and income is polarizing between creditors (the One Percent) and debtors (the 99 Percent).

Response to the devastation caused by living in this neoliberal illusion is likely to follow the Kubler-Ross 5 stages of grief model for dealing with loss:

1. Shock and denial. The eurozone and other finance-dominated governments refuse to admit that failure to write down debts is blocking economic growth. Politicians either don't care – passive-aggressive denial – or act as demagogues on behalf of their financial sponsors and campaign contributors. Seeing populations squeezed by debt service, neoliberal advisors insist that cutbacks in wages and consumption will prepare the way for a sounder takeoff. Latvia's debt deflation and tax shift off property and finance onto labor is depicted as a success story – as if reducing unemployment by driving labor to emigrate is a desirable. Greece is told to follow Latvia's "success," as if demographic collapse is part of the solution.

2. Anger and rage: Critics of neoliberalism are excluded from mainstream academic journals as neoliberals suppress any idea that alternative policies exist. General Pinochet's 1973 coup in Chile under the banner of "free markets" sponsored Operation Condor, assassinating labor leaders and academics across Latin America. In Greece, finance minister Yanis Varoufakis was accused of treason simply for trying to discover his own country's tax records and statistics. In the United States, financial lobbyists expressed their rage at serious reformers by blocking Elizabeth Warren from becoming head of the inaugural Consumer Financial Protection Bureau she helped design.

When Greece sought to hold a referendum on the terms of surrender demanded by Eurozone finance ministers in June 2015, the European Central Bank froze credit to Greek banks, forcing their closure. Eurogroup President Jeroen Dijsselbloem warned that pursuing an alternative policy would be countered by economic sanctions such as had been levied against Cuba, Iran and North Korea. "Ultimately, it is up to Greece whether it will become North or South Korea: absolute poverty or one of the richest countries in the world" under a ruling financial oligarchy.[1]

3. Bargaining: When IMF head Christine Lagarde insisted in summer 2015 on no writedowns of the debt that Greece owed the IMF and European Central Bank, she offered the palliative of reducing its short-run carrying charges by stretching out the loan payments over at a longer period and at a lower interest rate. Likewise in other countries, banks lent governments, homeowners and companies enough to pay the carrying charges falling due. Such bargains are essentially to "extend and pretend," that is, to pretend that in the end all debts can be paid.

Banks prefer to avoid writing down their creditor claims, and to receive an ongoing stream of interest payments and penalties (especially when these are publically guaranteed). Today's new bargain is: "You don't have to pay the debt. We'll just keep lending you more and more and charge you interest and late fees on the rising debt balance." Indeed, bank managers nickname credit-card users "deadbeats" if they pay off their balance each month instead of running up interest charges.

This bargain aims to block out reality. In the United States the Obama Administration enacted a modest budget-deficit stimulus, while promising to write down homeowners' debts. (It broke its promise.) Subsequent politicians suggested closing some of the most outrageous tax loopholes and passing laws to slow financial fraud – as long as these would not actually be enforced by the Justice Department and key financial regulatory agencies. Such bargains turn out to be chimerical and deceptive.

4. Sadness: Like cult members who come to realize that their hopes have been based on fantasy, the mythical "as if" beauty of mainstream economic dogma turns out to be a nightmare. The fictional 19th-century Golden Age of free market individualism was really the Gilded Age of robber barons whose insider dealings, privatization of railroads, western land grants and other financial maneuverings enriched an elite that celebrated itself in ego-driven luxury, castle-like estates and a vulgarization of fine art as *rentier* trophies.

Another dream that has been lost is that European integration can succeed in the context of today's eurozone giving finance ministries power to impose austerity and debt deflation. The financial devastation imposed on Greece confronts Portugal, Spain, Italy and Ireland with the daunting realization that democracy cannot survive within the eurozone's financial constraints dooming economies to debt peonage. To give democratic government control of central banks and tax policy to avoid austerity would require withdrawing from the eurozone's Lisbon and Maastricht treaties. Finding this prospect of losing the dream of the European Project too discouraging, voters acquiesce to the financial takeover. As oligarchies replace democracy, voting rates fall – the modern political symptom of social sadness and surrender. The resulting depression is both economic and psychological.

5. Acceptance. Arthur Schopenhauer observed: "All truth passes through three stages. First, it is ridiculed; second, it is violently opposed; and third, it is accepted as self-evident." But the fight for reality-based economics is not easily won. Will the vested interests accept change without a fight? And in such a fight, will populations surrender to debt peonage and chronic depression?

At issue is whether debt-strapped economies will let themselves be driven into a new Dark Age of debt serfdom. Will populations be able to survive by freeing their economies from debt by enacting Clean Slates and restoring progressive tax policy?

Roman creditors never lightened their demands until mass poverty led to Christian repudiation of usury. Pleas for Christian charity on a personal level replaced Jesus's call for an economy-wide Jubilee Year when he unrolled the scroll of Isaiah and announced that he had come to pronounce a Clean Slate (Luke 4). But subsequent Christian religion became one of resignation in the face of economies reduced to bare subsistence levels.

The lesson of history is that creditor elites will not acknowledge how destructive their mythology is. Manoeuvering to survive the economic collapse that they bring on, they turn their financial claims into direct land ownership and grabitization. They turn economies into gated communities like medieval manors, with hereditary ownership of the surrounding land and basic infrastructure, much as under feudal warlords. To accept this financial dark age is the equivalent of passivity in the face of economic and demographic death.

ENDNOTES

[1] Anastassios Adamopoulos, "Eurogroup President: Greece Can Choose to be Either North or South Korea," *Greek Reporter*, September 12, 2015.

Economics
as Fraud

Science of assumptions: An oxymoron in which the criterion for deeming a discipline scientific is simply whether its assumptions are logically consistent, not necessarily realistic. The result tends to be circular reasoning based on tautological definitions. (See **Junk Economics** and **Neoclassical Economics**.)

"In theory there is no difference between theory and practice. In practice there is."
— "Yogi-ism," attributed to Yogi Berra, among many others.

Lawyers have a saying: "When the facts are on your side, pound on the facts. When the law is on your side, pound on the law. If you have neither, pound on the table." Pounding is not enough, of course. The trick is to create an alternative hypothesis to distract attention from the facts *and* the law. In economics the law is the body of theory, its basic definitions and conceptual categories. The relevant facts are statistics tracing the course of wealth and income, who owns this wealth, how they obtain it, and who ends up owing how much to whom.

Distracting attention from these realities is a form of deception. That is what experts are hired to do. In court cases each side produces its own advocates, replete with academic credentials. In the sphere of economic policy, politicians and the popular media trot out prize-winning experts to give the appearance of respectability to arguments as to why taxes should be cut for the rich, why governments should not regulate, and why they should sell off the public domain to rent-extracting buyers.

When the facts do not back austerity, deregulation and a reversal of progressive taxation, textbook writers say that reality is not a criterion of economic validity. Much as in literary criticism, the discipline's main criterion for theoretical excellence is the internal consistency of assumptions, not reality. That is what makes the theory of international trade "pure," as if reality is an impurity marring the beauty of abstract logic. The effect – indeed, the aim – is to distract attention to an "as if" world.

Economics versus the Natural Sciences: The Methodology of "As If"

Today's leading economic textbooks turn economics into a mock-science by teaching students that the discipline's basic assumptions need not be based on reality. Typical is *Microeconomics* by William Vickrey, long-time chairman of Columbia University's economics department, president of the American Economic Association (1992–93) and winner of the 1997 Nobel Economics Prize. Professor Vickrey informs his students that "pure theory" need be nothing more than a string of tautologies:

> Economic theory proper, indeed, is nothing more than a system of logical relations between certain sets of assumptions and the conclusions derived from them. The propositions of economic theory are derived by logical reasoning from these assumptions in exactly the same way as the theorems of geometry are derived from the axioms upon which the system is built.
>
> The validity of a theory proper does not depend on the correspondence or lack of it between the assumptions of the theory or its conclusions and observations in the real world. A theory as an internally consistent system is valid if the conclusions follow logically from its premises, and the fact that neither the premises nor the conclusions correspond to reality may show that the theory is not very useful, but does not invalidate it. In any pure theory, all propositions are essentially tautological, in the sense that the results are implicit in the assumptions made.[1]

The phlogiston theory of combustion was logical and internally consistent. So was Ptolemaic astronomy, whose practitioners drew complex models of a solar system revolving around the earth rather than the sun. Astrology, former queen of the medieval sciences, also is highly technical and mathematized, and like economics it deals with forecasting. But these theories were built on false assumptions.

Why strive to be logically consistent if one's working hypotheses and axioms are misleading in the first place? The answer is that there is method in this seeming madness. As in science fiction, the trick is to convince readers to suspend their disbelief in the assumptions being proposed. The public is asked to look at the economy in terms of a universe in which money is either spent on producing current goods and services or saved, but not created as loans and debts to buy or gamble on real estate, stocks and bonds. There are no financial bubbles, junk-mortgage fraud or insider dealing, and hence no need for Quantitative Easing. Students are asked to believe that debts do not tend to grow beyond the means to pay, and that any disturbance in economic balance will be met by automatic stabilizing responses rather than requiring action from outside the market economy.

To believe that the growth in debt overhead is not a serious problem, we are to leave Planet Earth and think in terms of a parallel universe in which all debts can be paid without deranging foreign exchange rates or transferring vast swaths of assets to creditors. It is necessary to put our faith in simplistic models in which shifting the money supply will steer interest rates to a level that will keep the economy's growth in debt claims in line with the ability to pay while broadening home ownership.

Lacking empirical breadth and measurement, economics narrows into an otherworldly mock-science of assumptions without historical grounding. Today's mainstream economists use a self-congratulatory language that characterizes "pure" theory as drawing "heroic" generalities, that is, banal simplicities presented in a mathematical mode called "elegant" rather than air-headed.

At first glance the sophistical tendency would appear to find an antecedent in John Stuart Mill's 1844 essay "On the Definition of Political Economy; and on the Method of Investigation Proper to it":

> In the definition which we have attempted to frame of the science of Political Economy, we have characterized it as essentially an abstract science, and its method as the method a priori. … Political Economy, therefore, reasons from assumed premises – from premises which might be totally without foundation in fact, and which are not pretended to be universally in accordance with it. The conclusions of Political Economy, consequently, like those of geometry, are only true, as the common phrase is, in the abstract; that is, they are only true under certain suppositions, in which none but general causes – causes common to the whole class of cases under consideration – are taken into account.[2]

Recognizing that societies are multilayered, Mill's aim was to *transform* the policy environment. His logic treated land, labor and capital – along with money and the balance of payments – independently, but *then* tied their interactions together into an overall system. This was not logic for its own sake. He sought to tax the landed aristocracy so as to bring land (or at least its rent) into the public domain.

Post-classical economists have pursued logical consistency as an objective in itself, without necessary reference to how the real world would work with different policy alternatives. Economists project existing trends in a policy environment assumed to be unchanging ("all other things remaining equal," *ceteris paribus*), with merely marginal analysis instead of treating the economy as an interrelated system in which increasing financial strains tend to build up.

Looking at the mathematics, not the real world

Paul Samuelson typifies the problems inherent in the unrealistically abstract "as if" approach in the conclusion of his famous article on "The Gains from Trade": "In pointing out the consequences of a set of abstract assumptions, one need not be committed unduly as to the relation between reality and these assumptions."[3] He defended his Factor-Price Equalization Theorem (which states that under free trade, wages and profits will tend to equalize throughout the global economy) by claiming that:

> Our problem is ... a purely logical one. Is 'If H, then inevitably C' a correct statement? The issue is not whether C (factor-price equalization) will actually hold; nor even whether H (the hypothesis) is a valid empirical generalization. It is whether C can fail to be true when H is assumed to be true. Being a logical question, it admits of only one answer, either the theorem is true or false.[4]

This attitude did not deter Samuelson-type theorists from drawing policy conclusions affecting the real world in which people live. Mainstream orthodoxy treats the international economy as a thermodynamic system to be analyzed by entropy theory, despite the real-life world in which labor migrates and capital flows from low-income "cold" economies to high-income "hot" ones. This resource drain, especially of skilled labor, is a major loss for Latvia, Ireland and most recently Greece subjected to IMF and Washington Consensus austerity dogma.

Waving the banner of "free markets," special interests are always at work to reframe popular perceptions of reality to depict policies leading to widening inequality, austerity and emigration as the road to prosperity, not debt dependency and financial neocolonialism. Outgoing presidents of the American Economic Association often seek to atone by giving a speech showing that they know it is all just a game, and chastise their colleagues for not being more realistic. But they rarely make an effort to set things right.

It is now over a century since John Shield Nicholson remarked that: "The traditional method of English political economy was more recently attacked, or rather warped," by pushing the hypothetical or deductive side ... to an extreme by the adoption of mathematical devices.... less able mathematicians have had less restraint and less insight; they have mistaken form for substance, and the expansion of a series of hypotheses for the linking together of a series of facts. This appears to me to be especially true of the mathematical theory of utility. I venture to think that a large part of it will have to be abandoned. It savors too much of the domestic hearth and the desert island."[5]

The anti-classical reaction of the 1870s – what Veblen called the neoclassical revolution of William Stanley Jevons, Carl Menger, and later of Alfred Marshall and his followers, culminating in today's Chicago School – follows from the particular way in which mathematics has been applied. Its marginalist and monetarist abuses have become so nearsighted as to lose sight of the economy's structural instabilities. Contrasting mainstream trade theorems with the real-world tendency of international incomes and wages to polarize rather than equalize, Gerald Meier observes: "It need not ... come with any surprise that factor returns have been so different ... when in short, the restrictive conditions of the theorem have been so clearly violated in reality."[6]

But is it not sophistical to speak of reality violating a theory? Theory violates reality, not the other way around. And wrong-headedness is not accidental when it is maintained decade after decade. In such cases there always is a special interest involved to distract attention from economic reality. In the case of free-trade theory, global investors and exporters from lead nations oppose governments that protect their own domestic industry and agriculture. U.S. farm exporters, for example oppose foreign attempts to become self-sufficient in their own basic food needs by pursuing the domestic agricultural subsidies that the United States used to increase its farm productivity. Free traders accordingly denounce governments that have the temerity to withstand U.S. diplomatic sanctions against governments pursuing an independent foreign and domestic economic policy.

That was how Britain, the United States, France and Germany industrialized and rose to become world economic powers. The World Bank and IMF were created to bring financial leverage against governments defending their national interest, and to steer them to become dependent on U.S. agricultural exports as well as dollar credit, adding food dependency to debt dependency.

The resulting "as if" theorizing depicts a trickle-down economy in which financial *rentiers* are the driving force. As Goldman Sachs chief executive Lloyd Blankfein put matters: "The people of Goldman Sachs are among the most productive in the world."[7]

The question is, productive of what"? For Mr. Blankfein, it is simply productive of revenue, regardless of how it is earned – even when his firm and its Wall Street neighbors have had to pay billions and billions of dollars in civil fraud penalties. When the National Income and Product Accounts count the financial sector's extractive and often fraudulent earnings as part of Gross Domestic Product measuring real growth, we have entered an upside down Alice and Wonderland world.

Fictitious economic theories and vocabulary invariably serve special interests

If one must be logical, why not start with realistic rather than hypothetical assumptions? The obvious answer is that realistic assumptions do not lead to the policy conclusions pre-selected by pro-*rentier* ideologues depicting society's attempts to tax and regulate the banks and other natural monopolies as "the road to serfdom" rather than as the escape route from debt peonage and landlord rent extraction.

We are entitled to ask whose interests are served when economists claim that their assumptions need have no connection with reality, yet then proceed to make policy recommendations. Why do so many economics departments teach the assumptions of the Heckscher-Ohlin-Samuelson trade theory instead of starting from more realistic assumptions that would explain why the real world is economically polarizing? The answer is that they do not want to come to policy conclusions that oppose the vested interests that back today's economic mainstream.

A policy motive invariably is the starting point, as Gunnar Myrdal observed in his essay "How Scientific are the Social Sciences?": "Facts do not organize themselves into systematic knowledge, except from a point of view. This point of view amounts to a theory." He emphasizes that "contrary to widely held opinions, not only the practical conclusions form a scientific analysis, but this analysis itself depends necessarily on value premises."[8]

Modern economics lacks an epistemological dimension to evaluate these premises – the capacity for self-reflection to perceive the extent to which the discipline's theorizing is shaped by narrow self-interest to promote a bankers'-eye view of the world. The Chicago School's monetarism is the perspective of *rentiers*, financial speculators and traders, not nations seeking to develop their industry and agriculture.

The strength of Marxism, and sociology in the tradition of Simon Patten and Thorstein Veblen, lies is their recognition that economic theorizing is a product of self-interest and policy pleading. Perceiving class biases, Marx and Veblen viewed economic theory as apologetics for advocates of one policy or the other. Today's monetarist worldview is a rhetorical system serving the global financial interests that have come to dominate the "real" economy with an iron hand of ideological censorship to back the financial weaponry of debt leverage forcing privatization and dismantling of public sectors.

The more libertarian the theory, the more authoritarian the economic pedagogy tends to be, precisely because its reasoning rests on specious foundations. In General Pinochet's Chilean dictatorship after its 1973 coup, Chicago economists showed their intellectual intolerance of a free market in economic ideas by closing the economics and social science departments of all universities save for the Catholic University in which they ruled unchallenged. Consensus was established not through reason, but by removing from the scene all who disagreed with their extremist policies.

A rising volume of products of low-wage economies is traded for products made by better-paid labor, as long as low-wage economies do not produce a full range of output. Productivity differences have long been cited, but another factor also is at work: chronic depreciation of the currencies of low-wage countries as a result of debt service ("capital transfers") for loans taken out in an increasingly desperate attempt to carry their foreign debts. Accruing interest beyond the means to pay, these unpayable debts throw economies into the clutches of the IMF, whose austerity programs are defended by economists hired to persuade governments to surrender to models that fail to recognize how austerity destabilizes public budgets and the balance of payments. And when economic theory fails to persuade governments to submit voluntarily to smash-and-grab privatization programs, the objective is achieved at gunpoint, as in Chile under General Pinochet or Ukraine under President Petro Poroshenko and Prime Minister Arseniy Yatsenyuk.

Mainstream economics as mathematized tunnel vision

If today's economics has become less relevant to the social problems that formed the subject matter of classical political economy a century ago, its scope has narrowed in large part because of the technocratic role played by mathematics formulating problems in terms of only a few selected functions, excluding wealth (especially the pricing of land) and how it is acquired by rent seeking, asset price inflation and/or insider privatizations. Despite the emphasis that Ricardo gave to rent theory, the land nationalization debate stimulated by John Stuart Mill, Herbert Spencer and Henry George, and the role that Thorstein Veblen assigned to urban land speculation in *Absentee Ownership*, land-price gains have been ignored by today's price theory and its definition of economic returns.

In a similar vein the structure of society's long-term transformation is excluded from analysis on the ground that its dynamics cannot be sufficiently mathematized. Reiss has located an appropriate quotation from William Roscher:

> ... some scientists (attempted to) fit laws of economics in algebraic formulae ... But, of course, the advantage of the mathematical mode of

expression vanishes the more, the more complex the facts to which they are applied become.... In every description of the life of a nation the algebraic formulae would become so complicated that they render a continuation of work impossible.[9]

The resulting logical constructs of modern mathematical economics were not created without some degree of protest. Already a generation ago F. J. Dyson complained: "Mathematical intuition is more often conservative than revolutionary, more often hampering than liberating." Citing Ernst Mach's observation that "The power of mathematics rests on its evasion of all unnecessary thought and on its wonderful saving of mental operations," he worried that too much real-world complexity might be discarded.[10]

Wilhelm Launhardt's railway economics was considered too technical to be classified as political economy proper. His analysis did not deal with how lower transport costs affected the value of farmland, residential and commercial property along the trackway, making fortunes for real estate speculators. As any urban planner knows, this "external" effect on land prices is much larger than the direct costs of building railroads.

Early mathematical economists concerned themselves with narrower topics such as price formation from the vantage point business cost accounting. Hermann Gossen's mathematical formulation of utility theory was not widely noticed because he focused on problems hitherto considered too mundane to be deemed an essential part of political economy's core. Political economy had not yet narrowed into technical business planning or individualistic consumer preference. The technical problems with which the early mathematical economists dealt, such as psychological utility and price formation based on supply and demand, were far from being deemed the highest concern in an epoch when political economy remained an extension of moral philosophy and public policy making. Such early applications of mathematical notation and graphs were viewed as being more in the character of engineering or technical analysis than full-fledged political economy.

The marginalists made a breakaway by viewing the consumer rather than the producer/employer as the focal point of the economic system. The Austrians in particular discussed the economy from the vantage point of individual psychology, attributing wealth disparities to the "impatience" of consumers who failed to save and get rich. As with today's mathematical economics, the effect was to distract attention from what formerly was most important.

It has taken a hundred years to drive out the most vital concerns of classical political economy: the shape of social evolution, the strains it tends to develop and the range of democratic or oligarchic policy responses. As long as these concerns remained paramount, there was little reason to celebrate the early users of mathematical functions as having made a great breakthrough. Their "discovery" would have to await the time in which economics narrowed its scope and dropped its concerns with political reform.

As mainstream economics has come to take the institutional and political environment for granted, the effect has been to establish a *status quo* economics stripped of the classical focus on wealth, how it is acquired, and how its distribution (indeed, its polarization) affects social development. Comparative advantage models and regression analysis presuppose that social and cost structures remain constant. Economies are assumed to respond to disturbances automatically by settling at a new equilibrium without government intervention or radical policy change. Theories that show widening disparities in income and wealth are denied in principle.

What made political economy the queen of the social sciences in the 19th century was its focus on the transformation of nations by public policies most appropriate for their social evolution – their legal and institutional structure, technological breakthroughs and financial reform. Predecessors of Adam Smith noted that emigration, lack of industrial technology and a wealthy class living in luxury makes nations trade-dependent. Nothing like that was acknowledged by Ricardian free-trade theory, any more than it is by today's neoliberal austerity programs. The narrow *ceteris paribus* methodology ("all other things remaining equal") of marginalism assumes no change in economic policy. Such a politically trivialized approach does not have much appeal to reformers.

The main surviving classical alternative to the emerging marginalist *status quo* economics was Marxism. In addition to retaining the breadth of scope of classical political economy and the idea of stages of development, Marx used dialectics, irony and the idea of inner contradictions as a logical method to interpret economic history. Although he used arithmetic examples to illustrate the rates of profit and surplus value for enterprises employing differing proportions of labor and capital, this was not a mathematical model of the economy. No Marxist has tried to reduce the *Communist Manifesto* or dialectical materialism to mathematical formulae.

The semantics of marginalist equilibrium theory

Marginalist models imply that economic problems may be solved by small shifts in a narrow set of variables. Insolvency appears as an anomaly, not as inevitable as debt accruals grow exponentially, forcing the underlying economy to taper off and shrink. An impression is given that any economy can pay its debts without limit, by diverting more income from debtors to creditors. (That is why creditors love this approach that blames the victims of debt, not predatory finance.)

Looking over the countries in which such theorizing has been applied, one cannot help seeing that the first concern is to assert that the economy does *not* require public intervention. Mainstream models do not explain the quick bankruptcy of post-Soviet neoliberal "reform" (asset stripping) under Yeltsin and his oligarchy in Russia, or the rapid looting and bankruptcy of Chile's privatized pension funds under General Pinochet, or the subsequent bankruptcies and national resource selloffs caused by the financial deregulation and austerity programs imposed by the IMF on third world debtor countries, Ireland and Greece. Neoliberal "free market" theory thus has become part of the problem, not part of the solution.

The distortions of today's major statistical categories

Early statistics dealt with public finances, debt and the economy's tax-paying capacity. The focus was on the ruler's ability to finance deficits (mainly in times of war) through public debt and taxation. From this primary concern rulers developed an interest in the "Political Arithmetic" (a term coined by Sir William Petty of Ireland in 1672) of making their economies richer so that they could collect more revenue.

Opposing the proliferation of excise taxes that increased the price of labor and made economies less competitive, classical political economy developed largely out of the anti-royalist ideology of the French Physiocrats and Adam Smith. Instead, they urged taxing landlords and other rent recipients. Statistical categories and accounting formats were developed to quantify the emerging body of theory.

Any set of categories and their empirical statistics is a conceptual structure of how the world works. It is not possible to show where economies are generating wealth without dividing their activities into the classical categories of productive vs. unproductive, *i.e.*, real wealth-creating activity vs. overhead and mere transfer payments. This dichotomy was the focal point of a classical debate that lasted more than a century.

It differs from the GNP accounting format developed by Simon Kuznets, which has become the norm today. The National Income and Product Accounts depict any and all activities as being productive, rather than some (such as crime prevention, medical treatment, environmental cleanup costs and warfare) being in the character of overhead. The production and sale of cigarettes is counted as national product, along with the medical treatment of smokers. Crime prevention is counted, but not criminal takings.

These statistics do not reflect the major way in which the largest sectors – real estate, mining and fuels, banking and finance – take their economic returns. They seem to operate without reporting a profit, but their capital gains are not traced. Despite the fact that real estate and stock-market price gains have become the way in which most homeowners, investors and the One Percent have built up their wealth, this distinguishing financial phenomenon of the present era – asset-price inflation – does not appear in the NIPA or anywhere else. "Capital" gains are excluded as being "external" to the post-classical model of how the economy works. There is nothing akin to Mill's concept of landlords or other *rentiers* making land-price gains "in their sleep."

What is not seen has less chance of being taxed. That is why real estate and financial lobbyists have opposed collection of realistic statistics on land-price gains. Federal Reserve flow-of-funds statistics attribute so much of the price rise to the inflation of construction costs that in 1994 the value of all corporately owned land in the United States appeared to be a negative $4 billion! On the basis of the Census Bureau reports, I estimate that the actual land value of U.S. real estate was then over $9 trillion.

Instead of viewing the economy as multi-layered, the NIPA group "households" together, from wage earners to *rentiers*, from the One Percent to the 99 Percent. Increased income for anyone is supposed make everyone else better off, because "the market" or GDP expands, and all other variables are plugged into it – as if it does not seem to matter for *whom* this wealth accrues, or whether they get it by rent extraction, financial gains, wages or profits on new direct investment. There is no recognition that economies may collapse from enriching financial or other *rentier* elites at the majority's expense.

How junk economics treats savings and debt

Economies are supposed to be able to pay their debts by saving more. The implicit assumption is that saving (and new bank credit) is invested productively, not just lent out to create new debts. Productive investment of saving is assumed to enable any society's growth in debt to proceed *ad infinitum*, because creditors are assumed to invest their earnings in expanding output, not to shift the ownership of assets and wealth.

Any increase in saving is held to be good, without regard for whether it may be lent out for purely financial transactions instead of being invested to expand production and consumption. In practice, most saving and new bank lending finds its counterpart in financial claims on wealth – bonds, mortgages and bank loans – to transfer ownership of real estate, stocks and bonds. The effect is to bid up their price on credit, that is, by debt leveraging. Little saving and credit takes the form of tangible capital formation.

Since 2008, most household savings (among the 99 Percent, that is) have been used to pay down debts that were rung up earlier. The NIPA treat a negation (paying down) of a negation (debt) as a positive (saving). This is true mathematically, of course. But would it not help to show what *kinds* of savings are being made?

The effect is to enlarge the volume of financial claims attached to existing productive assets. This debt overhead extracts interest charges, which are recycled into yet more new loans. Instead of financing new means of production to help economies "grow their way out of debt," this dynamic submerges economies more deeply in debt.

According to today's national income concepts, the domestic U.S. saving rate was reported to be a negative 2% of national income at the end of 1998. (Foreign central bank purchases of Treasury securities accounted for an inflow of 2%, bringing the overall balance up to zero). It continued negative for about a decade. Yet *gross* savings (mainly savings by the One Percent that were loaned out to the 99 Percent) were building up at an unprecedented rate. The low reported net savings rate simply reflected the high degree to which new savings have found their counterpart in debt – that is, being lent out, in the form of loans to real estate and stock market players seeking capital gains, not invested to create new tangible capital.

These seemingly objective official statistics distract attention from *why* so large a proportion of the economy's savings is being diverted away from new direct investment and into real estate and stock market speculation – namely, the search for asset-price gains. The aim of national statistics has been inverted from its original function of informing the tax collector how much can be taxed, to concealing such gains from public view.

Problems, dilemmas and quandaries

A dilemma is a situation in which whatever path or "horn" one chooses, it involves pain and sacrifice. Obstacles present themselves on every side, and if the economy avoids being impaled on one horn, it will fall on the other. Economies fall into a quandary when the conditions for a real solution are lacking. Since 2008, economies have sought to escape from such dilemmas and quandaries as if they are solvable problems – solvable without changing economic rules to write down debts, without prosecuting systemic financial fraud, and without shifting taxes back off labor and industry and onto finance and real estate.

A mathematically optimum position is one in which one cannot move without making matters worse. When debtors defaulted, banks stopped lending. Real estate prices fell, and so did prices for bonds and stocks. Banks were unable to cover their deposit liabilities as the market value of the collateral backing their loan portfolios fell.

Governments tried to solve this quandary by leaving the debts in place, shrinking the "real" economy but bailing out the banks. They then sought to pay for this by raising taxes and cutting back social spending. When this shrank the economy all the more in Europe and other countries, public enterprises were sold to foreign investors, whose remission of profits and dividends created a balance-of-payments drain that lowered the currency's exchange rate. This made dollar-denominated and other foreign currency debt even more costly, exacerbating debt deflation.

So economies went from bad to worse. That is what happens when one defines economic problems so narrowly that without radical change, nations face a downward spiral – or rather, an upward flow of property and income to the *rentier* One Percent. The economy's problem is the One Percent's windfall. The Great Moderation deeply indebted American homeowners, students and consumers to the One Percent. This debt has blocked recovery and painted the economy into a corner.

Some kinds of economic equilibrium are not happy. Falling on one's face is a state of equilibrium. Death is the ultimate state of equilibrium. So is economic austerity, emigration and the transfer of property from debtors to creditors. But marginalist and monetarist equilibrium economics employ a mathematics that does not recognize serious dilemmas developing, or economies falling into quandaries whose financial and economic constraints prevent technological potential from being realized.

Washington Consensus policies have led many economies into a quandary – unless we look at matters from the vantage point of global bankers and the foreign investors and privatizers that they fund, permitting them to act like vultures transferring the public domain into their hands while leaving economies more debt-strapped. This half-century-long policy of austerity has led to privatization and deeper indebtedness. But in today's epoch in which finance has become the new mode of warfare, to accuse such neoliberal policies of being a "failure," when they keep on producing the same effect without change, misses the point that such economic devastation must really be their *aim*.

That is why the economic situation becomes worse when governments borrow from the IMF and are forced to enact austerity programs. IMF riots break out, governments fall and dictatorships that are oriented to serve global financial interests are installed, permitting capital flight that strips the economy of its resources all the faster. Money-capital flees abroad and skilled labor emigrates as the economy shrinks, with no technological cause indicated in the policy models being applied.

To *rentiers*, the problem is how to strip economies of income and assets. Their success leaves the 99 Percent in a quandary, where they must remain until they recognize that their quandary stems from the failure to understand and change the system.

To *rentiers*, the problem is to deter the economics discipline from providing any escape from this victimization. Marginal analysis avoids dealing with such quandaries and the policy alternatives necessary to escape. A narrow set of phenomena (labor and materials costs, the interest rate, income and the pattern of demand) is selected to produce models that fail to explain how and why the world economy is being pushed further and further out of balance.

Not all trends proceed at the same rate. At some point, certain major trends must intersect, and something must give. This is the definition of a crisis – literally a crossing or intersection of trends where the political structure must accommodate itself to promote one trend or the other.

Mainstream economics shies away from using mathematical analysis in this way. Students are taught that economics is about making choices between scarce resources. When resources really become scarce, economists call it a crisis. Only marginal problems are recognized – problems that are not structural but can be solved by marginal adjustments in incomes, prices and wage levels, the money supply and interest rates. The idea is that a slightly higher price will spur more output, while unemployment can be solved by reducing wage levels or increasing public spending – "scarcity" plays only a minor role

Looking for small adjustments within the existing economic policy structure, marginal analysis doesn't go very far. Its financial short-termism misses the degree to which economies are locked into debtor dependency. Nearly all approaches view savings as financing new capital investment, which is assumed to take the form of tangible capital formation, not just a stock market or real estate bubble.

The solvable problem in such cases is to recognize that what has come to pass for mainstream economics is junk economics in the service of a *rentiers'*-eye view of what they can get out of the economy. This reverses the classical focus on what resources are available to governments to promote economic growth and higher living standards.

Mainstream economics in today's Age of Deception and Fraud

Over the past generation, courses in mathematical economics have displaced the traditional courses in the history of economic thought and economic history. This knowledge might have familiarized students with alternatives to today's neoliberal orthodoxy, especially where the dynamics of debt are concerned. The ongoing and indeed deepening failure to explain our epoch's debt crisis suggests that the aim of this dumbed-down ahistorical economics has not really been to explain the world, but rather to censor perceptions that imply that the financial system under current policies is unstable and must be regulated and changed.

Such findings are not congenial to monetarist economists in their capacity as political lobbyists for the banking sector. By treating the growing debt overhead as self-stabilizing, monetarist orthodoxy has removed public regulation from the democratic political process, centralizing planning and public spending policies in the hands of finance ministries and central banks. That is what an "independent central bank" means – beyond the control of elected political representatives.

Nineteenth- and eighteenth-century writers explained the mathematical tendency for financial claims – bonds, bank loans and other financial securities – to grow by purely mathematical principles of self-expansion, faster and independently from underlying trends in wealth and income, and hence from the ability of debtors to pay the interest (much less to actually pay off the loans). Savers/creditors load tangible capital assets and real estate down with debts that in many cases are not repayable except by transferring ownership to creditors. This transfer changes the economy's political shape.

Neglect of the self-expanding debt overhead is a prerequisite for economic models to generate laissez faire conclusions. To acknowledge the tendency of financial dynamics to create structural quandary would imply what it did back in Sumerian and Babylonian times, when economic balance had to be restored by royal fiat, from "outside" the economic system.

In recent decades debt claims have grown more rapidly than tangible investment in factories and farms, buildings and homes, transport and power facilities, communications and other infrastructure. Corporations and also governments have been obliged to pay their debts by cutting back new research, development and new physical reinvestment. Such cutbacks in long-term investment often are the product of corporate raids financed by high-interest junk bonds. At the government level, this is the essence of IMF austerity plans, which "stabilize" the currency by international borrowing on terms that further shrink and destabilize the economy.

Cutting back tangible investment leaves corporations and governments less able to carry their debt burden. They are forced to live even more in the short run. Interest rates rise as loans become riskier. And as interest rates rise, more money is shifted away from direct investment into lending at interest, until the system is torn apart from within. That is why Adam Smith remarked that "interest rates usually are highest in countries going fastest to ruin."[11] Capital flees abroad, the currency falls and unemployment rises. In the end the global economy must be obliged to do what Adam Smith said every debtor government historically was obliged to do: let its debts go.

Now that global debts are becoming dollarized, it is less possible for national economies simply to inflate their way out of debt so as to make what Smith called a "pretended payment." The only options are default or outright repudiation.

Reality economics: Debts that can't be paid, won't be

No government has ever repaid its debts, Smith concluded. That is why savings do not accumulate exponentially without limit. Most early medieval loans were wiped out by wars. The 13th-century accumulation of wealth of the Knights Templar was seized by Philip the Fair, who dissipated it in warfare. The wealth of the great Italian banking families was lost in loans to Britain's kings, who likewise dissipated the proceeds in waging their perpetual wars with France. Fortunes have been lost through confiscation, and bad judgment with risky foreign investment or government-organized stock market bubbles, South Sea-style.

Financial fortunes cannot continue to accumulate *ad infinitum* because the mathematics of compound interest is economically unsustainable. Creditors plow back their interest receipts into increasingly risky new loans, creating a financial overhead that ends up impoverishing and polarizing economies. Just how far the modern pro-creditor models diverge from early economic thought is reflected in the closing words of David Hume's *Enquiry Concerning Human Understanding*:

> When we run over libraries, persuaded of these principles, what havoc must we make? If we take in our hand any volume; of divinity or school metaphysics, for instance; let us ask, Does it contain any abstract reasoning concerning quantity or number? No. Does it contain any experimental reasoning concerning matter of fact and existence? No. Commit it then to the flames: for it can contain nothing but sophistry and illusion.[12]

Mathematizing the economy's financial dimension

Debt may be viewed as financial pollution, entailing major cleanup costs to cope with the inability of consumers, businesses and governments to pay their stipulated debt service, except by transferring an intolerably high proportion of their assets to creditors. These transfers are done through bankruptcy proceedings, liquidation of corporate or personal assets under distress conditions, and (in the case of government debts) privatization selloffs. Monetarists – the people who claim to have mastered financial science – urge economies to surrender to financial austerity by sanctifying debts rather than saving the economy, its labor force and living standards.

This is happening because financial securities are not simply a mirror image of "real" economic activity. They are claims for payment, the "other" side of the balance sheet. When it comes to deciding what must give, the economy or its financial overhead, the latter turns out to be more powerful – and hence, more "real" – than the economy's tangible flows of output and income. Entire economies are being crucified on the altar of debt and subjected to austerity and its foregone economic development.

The wealthiest economies tend to be the most highly indebted precisely because they have the most savings and because their banks have the ability to create new credit, often with just a few computer keystrokes. More wealth is being generated by debt pyramiding and asset-price inflation than by building new factories to employ more people. The classical distinction between productive and unproductive credit has been replaced by an ostensibly value-free theory claiming that money earned in one way is as economically worthwhile as money earned in any other way, without regard for the effect on employment or national prosperity. These effects are held to be extraneous to purely financial concerns.

As an ideology of global planning, "free market" economics threatens to bring about a poorer and more unfree world. Its models have a blind spot when it comes to how financial planning subjects the world to austerity to pay debts to a creditor class absorbing a soaring proportion of the world's wealth.

Guideposts leading the public along today's road to financial serfdom are put in place much like the strategy of selling cigarettes. Popular fears of coughing, lung cancer, strokes and other adverse effects are countered by advertising claims that cigarettes freshen the breath and are associated with vigorous outdoor life as epitomized by the Marlboro Man – and a sign of individualism and daring against authority and regulation. Scientists are hired to provide a veil of professionalized confusion to dispute statistical evidence that smoking causes ill health.

In a similar way economists have been mobilized to serve, wittingly or unwittingly, as public relations lobbies for global financial interests. Chicago graduates and their clones, trained in strategy at Goldman Sachs or similar financial breeding grounds, monopolize the staffs of finance ministries, treasury departments, central banks and the leading global financial institutions. Their task is to depict austerity as laying a sound foundation for future growth rather than promoting self-feeding collapse. When poverty intensifies, governments are urged to bail out the economy's savers (the One Percent) at the taxpayer's (the 99 Percent) expense, and to cut wages and pensions while shifting the tax burden onto labor and consumers.

When the promised prosperity fails to materialize, the austerity lobby argues that monetarist policies have not been followed intensively enough to "work their magic." But like most magic, the purported "magic of the marketplace" is as much a trick as the "magic of compound interest." The aim is to distract voters and policy makers from understanding why debt dependency increases as jobs are downsized, lives are shortened, emigration accelerates and the quality of life declines.

The requisite starting point for the study of economics

There is an alternative, of course. That is to make the starting point of economics *the inexorable tendency of debt to grow beyond the ability to be paid.* What is needed is a policy to save the economy, not its creditors. This requires reversing the oligarchic takeover that has enthroned a body of junk economics designed to make it appear that an economy's debts can all be paid – by lowering wages, taxing consumers more, making workers (and ultimately, businesses and government) poorer, and selling off the public domain (mainly to foreigners from the creditor nations).

Rationalizing this financial grab is what passes for economic prestige today. Its economy-wide effects can be seen recently in Greece at the hands of the IMF and European Central Bank. James Galbraith points out that unlike army officers who lose battles or naval captains whose ships run aground, mainstream economists "are not held accountable in the same way that others are … Economists are not ranked by the results of their recommendations. They are ranked by what one might call the a priori analytical correctness of their point of view … according to the judgment of others in their profession."[13]

Galbraith contrasts economists to doctors, whose professional motto is "do no harm." Economists do harm. Ever since the German reparations debate after World War I, their most widely applauded practitioners have defended the policy of bleeding economies to pay creditors. They cannot avoid harming the economy as long as their priority is to save bankers and bondholders from absorbing a loss – by shifting it onto governments and the overall economy. Their aim is not to save the economy, but to endorse the downward spiral of debt deflation and widening fiscal deficits that force debt-ridden countries to sell off their land and mineral rights, their public buildings, electric utilities, phone and communications systems, roads and highways at distress prices – and then to applaud such privatizations as progress away from "the road to serfdom."

This syndrome has become a constant over so many decades that by now it must be seen as conscious and deliberate, not just an oversight that can be fixed. There is no way to sustain the rise in debt without killing the economy. But the criterion for success by economists reflects the prestige of the vested interests that employ them, headed by the IMF and World Bank, central bankers and the policy think tanks and business schools they sponsor.

Professional success in these arenas requires endorsing and defending a set of wrongheaded assumptions that serve to distract attention from reality, denying that the FIRE sector's gains are inherently opposed to those of the "real" economy. The resulting body of junk economics recognizes no limits on the ability to pay.

At first glance this seems to be insanity – defining insanity as doing the same thing again and again, hoping that the results will be different. But what if mainstream junk economists are not insane? What if they simply seek prestigious academic status and high-paying appointments at the major international institutions where professional success is achieved by endorsing politics favored by their patrons? In today's world, the wealthiest and most politically powerful patrons are the *rentiers*, and the economic mainstream acts as their priesthood legitimizing their predatory gains.

ENDNOTES

[1] William Vickrey, *Microeconomics* (New York 1964), p. 5.

[2] John Stuart Mill, "On the Definition of Political Economy; and on the Method of Investigation Proper to it" in *Essays on Some Unsettled Questions in Political Economy* (London 1844): V, p. 46.

[3] Paul Samuelson, "The Gains from Trade," *Canadian Journal of Economics and Political Science* **5** (1939): 205: reprinted in *Papers*, 1966 **II**, p. 782 [781–971].

[4] Paul Samuelson, "International Factor-Price Equilibrium Once Again," *Economic Journal* **59** (1949), p. 182 [181–197]; reprinted in *Papers* (1966) **II**: 869–885.

[5] John Shield Nicholson, *Principles of Political Economy* (London 1893), p. 122.

[6] Gerald Meier, *The International Economics of Development; Theory and Policy* (New York 1968), p. 227.

[7] Quoted by Greg Farrell, "Goldman chief defends employees' pay," *Financial Times*, November 11, 2009.

[8] Gunnar Myrdal, "How Scientific are the Social Sciences?" see *An International Economy: Problems and Prospects* (New York 1956), p. 336.

[9] William Roscher, *Grundlagen*, 67 f. quoted by J. Reiss, "Mathematics in Economics: Schmoller, Meyer and Jevons," *Journal of Economic Studies* **27** (2000): 477–91.

[10] Freeman J. Dyson, "Mathematics in the Physical Sciences," *Scientific American* **211**/3 (Sept. 1964): 132f.

[11] Adam Smith, *Wealth of Nations*, Ch. 11 (III, p.3).

[12] David Hume, *Enquiry Concerning Human Understanding* (1748), p. 132 (section xii, part iii).

[13] James K. Galbraith, *Welcome to the Poisoned Chalice* (Yale University Press, 2016), p. 100.

Economic Methodology is Ideology, and Implies Policy

Economics ultimately is political economy. To claim that it is "disinterested" and scientific is to cover up its political motives. The entire history of political economy has centered on the conflict between reformers seeking to free society from *rentiers* – landlords, creditors and monopolists – and the reaction by these wealthy vested interests to maintain their grip on the status quo that favors them.

Each side in this centuries-long conflict has its own methodology. Reformers say that distribution matters, and that a *rentier* oligarchy extracting economic rent or interest without adding to production will lead to general impoverishment and collapse. Beneficiaries of special privileges argue that the distribution of wealth does not matter, only its overall magnitude.

Reformers and conservatives both start with a policy conclusion, and then reason backward to choose a logic or "model" leading to their pre-selected conclusion. Support for (or opposition to) progressive taxation vs. a flat tax, public regulation vs. deregulation, or protectionism vs. free trade rest on underlying definitions and concepts that may strike outsiders to be merely technical issues, but are really a conflict over the scope and basic assumptions of economics.

A tipoff as to the politics of any economic theory is whether it distinguishes between earned and unearned income. That distinction is all but expunged from today's mainstream orthodoxy. It determines how economists measure output and, in particular, the economic surplus. This was central to the doctrines of Adam Smith, John Stuart Mill and other classical reformers seeking to free society from the burdensome legacies of feudalism: the landed aristocracy defending its hereditary rents, and the financial class prying away the public domain to create monopolies and indulge in price gouging. To create a streamlined competitive economy, they sought to tax away or nationalize the rent of land and natural resources, and to keep natural monopolies and basic infrastructure in the public domain – including banking so as to minimize the cost of financial services. This campaign led them to contrast market prices from intrinsic cost-value so as to isolate "unproductive" overhead charges, defined as economic rent in excess of intrinsic value.

By the late 19th century, defenders of landlords, financial fortunes and monopolists mounted a reaction. They claimed that what classical economists called "economic rent" actually was earned. This new post-classical school accused public regulation of being an inefficient "intrusion" into "free" markets.

The etymological root of *regulation* reflects the essence of government: *reg*, as in *regal*, *regime* and *royal*. So what is at issue is whether society is to relinquish government to predatory rent extractors, or govern itself by progressive tax policy, public infrastructure investment and ownership of natural monopolies, and regulations to protect labor, consumers and the public interest.

Political scope of economic theorizing about markets

Reformers explain how markets are embedded in institutions and tax policies, monetary policy and public regulations that determine who will end up with rent, interest and capital gains, and how this will affect economic growth and the distribution of income.

Opponents of reform define "the market" more narrowly. They look at individuals instead of overall society; at the short term, not the long term; and only at marginal changes within existing social and political structures so as to avoid discussing alternative policies and regulation of markets. All transactions are deemed voluntary, simply because they occur. Limiting their vantage point to that of individuals interacting with each other enables social reactionaries to exclude the effects of change on the economy at large. Insisting that There Is No Alternative (TINA, to use Margaret Thatcher's phrase), conservatives take the existing social institutions for granted, not as objects of reform.

To shift attention away from how markets favor the vested interests and the *rentier* class, they exclude political power relationships as being external ("exogenous") to their economic models. From the Austrian School and marginal utility theorists to today's anti-government libertarians, such self-proclaimed individualists deny that there is any such thing as society. Their economic models exclude broad society-wide effects as "externalities," especially financial crises, which they deem "exogenous" to their calculations.

All varieties of economic theorizing fall into one of these two broad divisions between reformers and conservatives. The progressive line extends from the mercantilists through Adam Smith, John Stuart Mill and later, Karl Marx, evolving into the institutionalists and sociologists in the Progressive Era. The common political aim of these reformers was to free society from the legacy of feudalism and its inherited *rentier* privileges. Their successors in the United States were the socialists, New Deal Democrats, Keynesians and post-Keynesians. These reformers try to show the impact of economic policies on society. Marx and the German Historical School looked at history to draw examples and analyze where various policies would lead.

Opponents of reform assume that the status quo will go on forever, with economies keeping their existing shape as they grow. They prefer to base their discussion on how hypothetical individuals might act on a desert island – or how we ourselves might act if we were transported in a time machine back to the Neolithic to "invent" a market economy, replete with all our own property laws and credit rules.

The role of government: Productive or intrusive?

Governments are either democratic or oligarchic. When oligarchies make their wealth hereditary, they become aristocracies. Europe's 19th-century industrial bourgeoisie saw democratic parliamentary reform as the means to break the political control of the landed aristocracies. And many high-born aristocrats came over to their side, hoping to vest government power in classes whose economic interests favored progressive taxation and public investment. "Socialism" became the late 19th century's word for policies to end the power of aristocracies to impoverish industrial economies by living off land rent, monopoly rent and interest. Across the political spectrum it simply meant reform.

Seeing their power threatened, the vested *rentier* interests sought to block such reforms. They depicted governments not under their control as intrusive and burdensome, playing no productive role but only as acting bureaucratically to interfere with the supposed efficiency of the status quo. These anti-government interests depict privatization as more efficient, and insist that public infrastructure should be counted as part of the budget deficit. Statisticians accordingly report government spending as deadweight, not as an investment in a distinct factor of production to hold down the cost of living and doing business.

Polarization vs. equilibrium theory and its "automatic stabilizers"

By depicting downturns and other economic imbalances as self-curing, mainstream business cycle theory aims to make government intervention seem unnecessary. Markets are depicted as self-regulating, so that any problems will be cured without any need for public regulation.

This is a highly political message. If "automatic stabilizers" really restore economies to a state of equilibrium when "disturbed," there is no structural problem (much less reform) requiring governments to intervene from "outside" the market.

The same logic is found in international trade theory. Equilibrium theorizing leaves no reason for protectionist trade policy or public subsidies. Free trade theory treats every nation as "trading" what it is best at producing most cheaply at any given moment of time, under existing productivity and income conditions. This approach avoids looking at long-term potential changes in productivity or the role of debt accumulation and tax policy on international price competition.

Systems analysts recognize that imbalances tend to make economies more polarized and unstable. Positive feedback loops lead trade imbalances to widen, so that gaining (or losing) industrial productivity advantages is self-reinforcing. Creditor economies get richer while poor countries sink deeper into debt dependency and suffer a downward spiral if their governments do not act to rebalance their economies by "interfering" with polarizing market forces.

Intrinsic cost-value vs. value-free *rentier* price theory

Factories and farms that produce commodities are different from rent-extractors who set up monopolies as legal tollbooths to charge for access to land, water and other natural resources, or for credit, roads and other infrastructure, or drug company patents and information technology. The costs of tangible capital investment in industry and agriculture ultimately can be resolved into the expense of labor to make products, the machinery that produces them, and the raw materials or other inputs needed for their production. But land rent, natural resource rent, monopoly rent, interest and financial fees have no intrinsic cost, except that of paying lawyers and lobbying politicians for favors and privileges. The resulting technologically unnecessary charges add to prices without reflecting real value based on the cost of producing the "service" being provided.

That is why socialist economies can adopt technology and operate with lower costs of living and doing business. They are free from having to bear a *rentier* overhead. This is the kind of free market that classical economists wanted. It is industrial capitalism at its most efficient. It can only exist in a mixed economy, which is now vilified as socialist – which was not a bad word in the 19th century. The question was, into what kind of socialism was capitalism evolving? Into a mixed economy of state socialism, Christian socialism, a utopian religious plan such as the Fourier communities, or labor socialism?

Whatever the answer, certain common denominators spanned the reform spectrum, based on classical moral philosophy that viewed economic rent as socially coercive and unfair as well as unnecessary for applying the new industrial technologies.

Landlords, monopolists and other vested interests defended their privilege to charge what "the market" will bear by denying that there is any such thing as unearned income. High prices that included heavy economic rents were viewed as reflecting consumer "utility" – otherwise, users of monopolies and renters simply would not pay the prices being charged (assuming that they have a "choice" not to eat or live in a dwelling).

The proverbial "idle rich" and other recipients of economic rent applaud economists who depict them as productive and even necessary for society to function. *Rentier* income and wealth is supposed to "reward" its beneficiaries in proportion to what they are assumed to contribute to the economy's output. This is the economic theory of John Bates Clark and his followers. It assumes that everyone earns whatever income and wealth they manage to obtain, regardless of how they do this.

The resulting orthodoxy depicts finance, insurance and real estate as part of GDP, not as a subtrahend or transfer payment *from* the economy to rent takers. This practice rejects any distinction between intrinsic value and market price, or between productive labor and credit as compared to unproductive "zero-sum transactions."

To cap matters, any transaction is said to be a voluntary exercise in choice by definition – even borrowing to avoid starvation, or sleeping under a bridge. Accepting at face value whatever "the market" obliges consumers and investors to pay for a house, education or food in a famine sidesteps the classical focus on the extent to which an economy can minimize prices for its services, housing and other goods or assets. They key for classical economists was to change the tax laws and regulate monopoly prices to bring them into line with "real" costs of production, and indeed to provide goods and services at public subsidy. Today's economic mainstream has rejected the analytic framework and even the ideology necessary to do this. "Value-free" theory lacks any criterion for regulation. For deregulators, that is its political virtue.

Debt is an overhead cost polarizing economies vs. "Debt doesn't matter"

Financial and monetary reformers look at how the buildup of debt increases the economy's cost structure, leading in due course to debt deflation and austerity. Defenders of creditor interests view debts simply as bargains between individual creditors and borrowers, implicitly voluntary and hence presumably mutually beneficial. They conclude that any government "interference" with this private "choice" must reduce its overall benefits. This individualistic approach misses the tendency of overall debt levels to rise steadily with each business recovery – and with this debt, the flow of interest to banks and bondholders. This buildup blocks market growth by diverting income from consumption and investment to pay creditors, making each recovery weaker.

On the international plane, Ricardo asserted that neither debt service nor military spending abroad would lead to chronic balance-of-payments deficits, because automatic income shifts in nations receiving any money inflow would recycle it to the payments-deficit economy (by importing or lending more). This was analogous to Say's Law on an international level. It failed to see that debt service drains the circular flow of international payments, just as occurs in domestic debt-ridden economies. Ricardo's pro-banker "debt doesn't matter" view was refuted by John Stuart Mill in 1844, who showed the effects of debt service on exchange rates and hence on the terms of trade. But like a zombie that won't die, Ricardo's pro-bank theory has been revived by Milton Friedman's Chicago School.

Marginalist and "monetarist" theory ignores how debt dynamics empower creditor elites to turn democracies into oligarchies by sucking income and property into financial hands, enabling bondholders to use debt leverage to force indebted governments to privatize the public domain – land, natural resources and basic infrastructure. The resulting austerity does not enable debtors to pay their creditors. Just the opposite: It drives governments, households and businesses deeper into debt and instability.

IMF doctrine does not view economic collapse, lower living standards and deepening government dependency on the IMF and vulture funds. Just the opposite: It is the condition that bankers and bondholders lobby to bring about! To paraphrase what former Cleveland Mayor Tom Johnson said about the city's electric utilities: Either the people will own the banks, or banks will own the government and the people. That is where debt dynamics lead. The resulting concentration of income is incompatible with democracy, and hence overrides attempts to reform the financial system and tax *rentier* income.

Few people a century ago anticipated that sophisticated mathematical defenses of deregulated privatized wealth concentration would be awarded with global economics prizes and applauded as economic philosophers carrying the torch of Western civilization. The past century's about-face in economic ideology would have been viewed as rolling back the Enlightenment.

The problem confronting financial elites is how to make this takeover seem desirable and even natural. Their solution has been to distract attention from the predatory maldistribution of income and wealth. When inequality finally must be acknowledged (as in the recent work of Thomas Piketty, Immanuel Saez *et al.*), it is attributed to the high productivity of smart innovators (today's euphemism for "greedy") with their "creative destruction," not to debt and finance, real estate, monopolies or similar rent seeking. The best Piketty can do is to urge taxation of inherited wealth, not a change in the system itself.

Chicago School monetarists depict money and debt as merely a "veil" for the economy's transactions, inflating all prices and assets in equal proportion, not as changing the distribution of wealth and income to enrich creditors by impoverishing debtors. The poster boy for junk economics along these lines is Robert Lucas, the Chicago School's 1995 Nobel Economics Prize winner for his theory of "rational expectations" that "proves" mathematically that markets reflect realistic analysis and accurate expectations. He insists that money and finance – and hence, credit and debt – are "neutral," having no effect on distribution, cost structures or relative prices of goods, services and assets.[1] These prices are supposed to expand or contract like a balloon with a pre-printed design that is not distorted as it is inflated or deflated.

This "debt doesn't matter" assumption led Lucas to insist that money and debt could not lead to a financial crisis. His celebratory 2003 presidential address to the American Economic Association in 2003 showed that he had no clue that the 2008 crisis would occur in five years, or even that an endogenous monetary and debt cause of instability was possible. He claimed that the era of depressions and recessions was over, except for "exogenous" shocks that no economist could be expected to foresee. The "central problem of depression-prevention has been solved, for all practical purposes, and has in fact been solved for many decades,"[2] thanks to supply-side economics and the underlying rationality of market forecasts ("expectations").

One can't make this stuff up. Lucas's smug, self-satisfied right-wing refusal to acknowledge the downside of a debt-leveraged economy is typical of his profession. That is why he has achieved such acclaim, after all. Economists who follow his methodology are unable to foresee how the growth of debt leads to debt deflation, austerity, economic collapse and a free-for-all property grab. That tunnel vision is what endears them to the financial donor class. Leaving debt out of account lulls indebted populations into quiescence.

But creditors know that in the end the debts cannot be paid. Bondholders are busy preparing their grabitization strategy for when foreclosure time arrives. Such strategists utilize Lucas and other Chicago Boys as the proverbial useful idiot savants educating students in "learned ignorance" (an inability to see the economy's major strains). These individuals are appointed as censors to referee mainstream economic journals and keep them non-threatening to today's rapidly deteriorating status quo.

The importance of how income and wealth are distributed

Wages have drifted downward in the United States since 2008 (and indeed, for some decades before that). But to hear politicians and the One Percent talk, one would think that economies are growing, even when all their growth in income and asset valuation has accrued only to the richest 5% while the rest of the economy shrinks. No wonder the wealthiest layer of the population assures the 99 Percent that "distribution doesn't matter."

Branko Milanovic sums up their insistence "that concerns with distributional matters are irrelevant – or worse, pernicious. Distributional matters are often viewed as a distraction, a nod to populism, and a waste of time that is ultimately destructive: A fight about the slices of the pie reduces the size of the pie and makes everybody worse off. ... how much better to focus on hard work and investment and to make the pie grow."[3] He cites Martin Feldstein's address to the 1998 Federal Reserve conference on inequality, asserting that no one should be worried about inequality (least of all the workers) as long as overall income is increasing: "I want to stress that there is nothing wrong with an increase in well-being of the wealthy or with an increase in inequality that results [solely] from a rise in high incomes."[4]

The afore-mentioned Robert Lucas joins in this censorial dismissal: "of the tendencies that are harmful to sound economics," he writes, "the most seductive, and in my opinion, the most poisonous, is to focus on questions of distribution."[5] He claims that gains in welfare will come from better fiscal policies, by which he means "providing people with better incentives to work and to save, not from better fine-tuning of spending flows." It is all about "'supply-side' fiscal reforms," cutting taxes to provide more "incentives," for the wealthy – while squeezing debtors to work harder and harder to carry their debt load. Diverting spending to pay debt service can be ignored, because giving more after-tax income to the wealthy instead of to workers and consumers will enable economies to work their way out of debt.

By their logic – that distribution does not matter – there is no need for governments to pursue redistributive policies such as the mortgage writedowns that Congress promised when it bailed out U.S. banks in 2008 under the Troubled Asset Relief Program (TARP). Also, there would be no reason for progressive income or wealth taxation, no public option for health care or other basic infrastructure, no anti-monopoly rules to prevent price gouging. But once one acknowledges that debt is the major dynamic polarizing economies between the One Percent and the 99 Percent, a political rationale follows logically for reforming the financial sector and the monopolies it promotes.

For centuries it was recognized that distribution and economic polarization are indeed important, because the wider the disparity, the more the waste and top-heavy overhead. As Jonathan Swift wrote in *The Run upon the Bankers* (1734):

Money, the life-blood of the nation,
    Corrupts and stagnates in the veins,
Unless a proper circulation
    Its motion and its heat maintains.

The "distribution problem" brings us back to the question of whether we should measure economic welfare by looking at aggregate GDP or analyze how the economy's production-and-consumption sector is wrapped in the FIRE sector's debt and property claims.

The scope of economic analysis: Social vs. individualistic

Markets are embedded in a political and social context of property rights and laws, power relationships and regulations. Marx and Karl Polanyi criticized defenders of the status quo favoring landlords, bankers and monopolists for shifting attention away from the fact that deregulated "free" markets tend to be predatory and prone to crime and exploitation of labor, debtors and consumers.

At issue is whether "the market" is the whole economy, or only part of it. To put matters another way, is overall GDP all we need to measure how the economy is doing? What if GDP rises while most of the economy is falling into poverty?

Some revisionist historians, for example, have decided that the post-Roman Dark Age was not so dark after all. True, Rome's harsh pro-creditor laws did lead to the vast latifundia that Pliny accused of ruining Italy. But recent reconstructions of the epoch's GDP suggest that the affluence of wealthy families at the top of the social pyramid may have made up for the declining fortunes of the 99 Percent. Most of the subsistence economy may have been stripped of money, but the luxury trade remained monetized.

An analogous polarized state of affairs is emerging today (2017). If we look at overall GDP since 2008 there seems to have been a modest recovery. But it turns out that all growth in income has accrued to the top 5 percent of the population. The bottom 95 percent have seen their incomes and net worth decline. So "the economy" has gone in two different directions. Finance has gained since it was saved in 2008. Stock and bond prices have shot up, benefiting mainly the wealthy ownership class. The bailout was for them, because the Federal Reserve's monetary helicopter only drops money over Wall Street. The production and consumption economy wasn't saved. Its debts were left in place, and its 95 Percent are limping along, squeezed by debt deflation.

Does it matter? Yes, if economic progress is measured mainly by rising living standards for the population at large. Checking the oligarchy's power grab is appropriate is one perceives today's financial sector as playing the extractive *rentier* role that landlords played in the 18th and 19th centuries.

To restore the broad scope of the classical political economy, it is necessary to reject the reactionary methodology that looks only at small marginal changes in supply and demand, income and prices within the economy's existing institutional structures. That approach rejects the distribution of property and income as inconsequential. The starting point should be to recognize that the economy is malstructured. But Junk Economics excludes consideration of structural problems, so it cannot play a role in the solution. Its tunnel vision labels credit and debt accumulation, tax policy and debt financing of real estate and corporate finance "exogenous."

That is the problem with today's mainstream economics. It excludes structural analysis and the causes of internally generated polarization and instability. Failure to place these phenomena at the center of economic analysis lets debt deflation, privatization and regressive tax shifts continue, plunging the economy into permanent depression.

Reality Economics vs. a parallel universe "science of assumptions"

The *rentier* class seeks to distract popular pressure away from reform by saying to its client economists, "If the eye offends thee (or more to the point, offends the vested interests), pluck it out." Paul Samuelson and other "as if" economists claim that their discipline need not be realistic, merely logically consistent. The effect is to distract attention away from the real-world phenomena of unfair, parasitic and predatory behavior. This distraction is achieved by redefining economics as a purely abstract mode of reasoning.

To prevent deceptive logic, an economic map must be grounded in statistics reflecting realistic categories. The next chapter, "Economics as Fraud," describes how *rentier* elites have submerged the discipline in the junk economics of Chicago school monetarism, Austrian marginalism, free trade assumptions at odds with reality, and trickle-down logic that distracts attention from the need for structural reform. The stage is set to sterilize realistic analysis by requiring students to spend most of their time discussing a fictitious map of the economy – replete with a failure to distinguish between earned and unearned wealth and overhead or to recognize fictitious capital based on debts that cannot realistically be paid without impoverishing and polarizing society.

Graduate students who take courses in economics in hope of making the world better face a professional and intellectual gauntlet as they seek teaching positions or other professional employment. Their status is based on publication in the main refereed journals, whose neoliberal or monetarist editorial boards insist on the methodology of junk economics that this book has described.

Trapping would-be reformers into an anti-reform methodology

The futility of trying to defend progressive reforms by using a methodology intended from the start to thwart the logic of reform has undermined many would-be reformers. Henry George fell into this trap. A popular journalist in the 1870s through the 1890s, he advocated taxing the land's full economic rent. It had provided the basis for public revenue from antiquity down through the Norman Conquest and other land grabs by medieval warlords. When the barons (heirs of the conquerors) privatized the land, this created a parasitic landlord class. That is what led the Physiocrats, Adam Smith, John Stuart Mill and other reformers to develop their value, price and rent theory and its associated analysis of national income flows.

Unfortunately, George's anti-academic prejudice (defensive over his lack of a formal education) led him to try to re-invent the analysis of rent without classical value and price theory. Jumping on the post-classical fad of consumer utility to explain prices, he lacked a meaningful definition of rent to quantify its magnitude as the excess of market price over intrinsic cost-value.

As for explaining land prices, George did not relate them to bank lending. His blind spot regarding finance and debt blocked him from anticipating that land prices would be set by how much banks were willing to lend. He failed to see that most rent would end up as interest, and that this would lead bankers to throw their political support behind landowners to reduce property taxes. His discussion of "interest" conflated it with profits made from physical productivity gains – a confused fable about men on a desert island. Eugen von Böhm-Bawerk dismissed it as a "naïve productivity" theory.

George became increasingly libertarian as he got bitten by the political bug, and spent more effort fighting socialists and labor reformers than landlords. Advocating taxing land rent as an alternative to nationalizing the land, he opposed strong government. This left no authority powerful enough to overcome resistance to a land tax by the *rentier* alliance of real estate and the financial sector.

George's followers petered out into a sectarian geriatric cult. Their political ineffectiveness reflected George's failure to view the economy as a complex multi-layered system. Failing to place real estate in its financial context blocked them from seeing that the land's rent ends up being paid to mortgage bankers. The fact that today's banks find their largest market to be mortgage lending has led to a symbiosis of high finance with the landed interest.

Herbert Spencer and others in the late 19th century suggested that governments should buy out the landlords so as to gain control the land and collect its rent without confiscation. This would have turned the landed aristocracy directly into a creditor class. That is what in fact has occurred informally. Landlords gradually sold out, keeping their hereditary fortunes mainly in the form of bonds and stocks.

George opposed outright state buyouts, saying that this would be like paying slave owners to buy the liberty of their slaves. He insisted on the moral principle that land rent was wrong because it was not earned. But he only said this journalistically, and criticized only landlords, not the financialization of land rent and other forms of economic rent.

Against such reformers, defenders of the status quo insist that an analysis of distribution and flow of rents and debt service throughout the economy is not a relevant dimension to study. A focus on the One Percent would lead people to question how the vested interests obtained their wealth and how they "earn" so much *rentier* income. Statistics show that most revenue is obtained via the FIRE sector and via patents for the right to charge monopoly prices for technologies under financial control.

A common symptom of ignoring structural analysis along these lines is for reforms to assume that the financial system needs to be left in place as it is. That was the problem with George's proposals to tax land rent, and also the recent proposals of Thomas Piketty to counter polarization and redistribute wealth simply by taxing inheritance – without addressing the need to regulate or tax away rent seeking or reform the financial system. Effective monetary reform to stop the flow of unproductive credit issued against land rent and other economic rent requires a parallel fiscal reform to tax away these rents at their source. Otherwise the rent will be available to be financialized.

All these reforms require democratic politics to limit the power of financialized wealth to control the election process and promote "regulatory capture" of treasuries and central banks. That is why economics must be political economy, recognizing the tendency of democracies to turn into oligarchies unless predatory wealth is checked.

Rentier interests deter such progress by sponsoring a tunnel vision that leaves today's students facing a profession not amenable to recognizing debt and economic polarization as the major problems of our time. Many students seek economics degrees in the hope of making society better. But the textbooks used to indoctrinate today's students do not emphasize thinking about the economy as a multi-layered political as well as economic system. Students are confronted with a methodology that sidesteps the most important financial and political dynamics that threaten to derail our epoch onto the road to debt peonage. To make professional headway, graduates are confronted with pressure (and rewards) to bypass financial and institutional analysis of these problems.

A limited scope and methodology based on a fictitious "as if" parallel universe is bound to lead to serious economic destruction. If universities were subject to defective product recalls for the debt-financed degrees they sell, they would require former graduates to undergo rehabilitation courses in reality economics. That would be the intellectual equivalent of safer seatbelts to prevent policy accidents.

It is not necessary to re-invent the analytic wheel

The essence of classical political economy is to explain how an unproductive *rentier* debt overhead polarizes economies and brings economic growth to a stop. What passes for mainstream New Economic Thought today excludes consideration of this problem, along with the distinction between earned and unearned income, and the logic of public infrastructure investment to lower the cost of living while creating a higher standard of living and competitive edge against rival nations that fail to create a successful mixed economy.

Today this aim is vilified as "socialist," as if the drive to free economies from unnecessary charges was not the essence of classical political economy. All but forgotten is the classical belief that the destiny of industrial capitalism was to reform economies by eliminating the *rentier* legacies of feudalism. That was to be done by taxing and regulating unearned wealth so as to free society from economic rent, predatory finance and other unnecessary burdens.

"Ricardian" socialism and other 19th-century versions of socialism lay the analytic groundwork for Marx to point out that not only were the aristocratic *rentier* privileges of land rent, natural resource rent, monopoly rent and interest exploitative, but so were the miserable employment conditions and subsistence wages preferred by industrial capitalists. Just as the first wave of socialism hoped to make land, mineral rights and basic infrastructure public, Marx believed that future socialism would take manufacturing and other production into the public domain as appropriate. Providing the services from socialized assets at subsidized prices or freely instead of through private-sector markets would enable future "leisure" economies to supply all basic needs.

Today's economic and political mainstream rejects even moderately mixed economies as inherently socialist. Tarring socialism with the misbegotten Soviet version of Marxism has been used to reject not only Marx but all the classical economists before him in favor of a "free market" run by the *rentier* One Percent. An umbrella of guilt by association has been used to reject the entire classical analytic toolkit.

It is not really the Soviet model that mainstream economists fear. It is Marx's grounding in classical political economy's own value, price and rent theory providing the logic to strip away the rents, interest and monopolies inherited from the feudal epoch. Marx's analysis of industrial capitalist reform emerged out of Adam Smith, Ricardo, Mill and their contemporaries. To portray them as patron saints of freeing *rentier* income *from* taxation and regulation, it has been necessary to expurgate their actual logic from the history of economic thought. The theory of cost-value and economic rent as unearned income has been dismissed, as if all such analysis is a "socialist" step along the slippery slope to serfdom, not away from it.

What is at stake?

One future is for *rentiers* to privatize and deregulate economies. This travesty of a classical free market ends up driving populations, industry and governments into deepening debt, leading to global neofeudalism and debt peonage. The increasingly financial sector's implicit business plan is to achieve the same predatory conquest of the land, natural resources and public infrastructure that required military conquest a millennium ago. This is now happening all over the world.

The alternative future is to create governments strong enough to save economies from this conquest. The classical ideal was a mixed economy with checks and balances to steer private gain seeking in keeping with the long-term public interest. Freeing society from the rentier legacy of feudalism seemed well on the way to being achieved by the late 19th century. Leading economists backing democratic reform movements mobilized public opinion by describing parasitic economic tendencies (and showing where taxes were least burdensome) in ways that nearly everyone could understand. Today's expurgation of the history of economic thought and its classical vocabulary threatens to reverse that understanding. The *rentiers* have sponsored a rewriting of history that is a travesty of the moral principles and toolkit provided by the Enlightenment's classical political economists. Their tunnel vision and idealization of short-term cut-and-run financial markets threatens economic and ecological collapse on an unprecedented scale.

ENDNOTES

[1] Robert Lucas, "Expectations and the Neutrality of Money," *Journal of Economic Theory* **4** (1972): 103–24.

[2] Robert E. Lucas Jr., "Macroeconomic Priorities," *American Economic Review* **93** (March 2003), pp. 1-14, also available at
http://pages.stern.nyu.edu/~dbackus/Taxes/Lucas%20priorities%20AER%2003.pdf

[3] Branko Milanovic, "Why We All Care About Inequality (But Are Loath to Admit It)," *Challenge*, vol. 50, no. 6, November–December 2007.
https://www.gc.cuny.edu/CUNY_GC/media/CUNY-Graduate-Center/PDF/Centers/LIS/Milanovic/papers/2004/challenge_proofs.pdf

[4] Martin Feldstein, "Reducing Poverty Not Inequality." *Public Interest* #137 (1999), pp. 35–36.

[5] Robert Lucas, "The industrial revolution: Past and Future." In Federal Reserve Bank of Minneapolis *Annual Report*, 2003. Available at http://minneapolisfed.org/pubs/region/04–05/essay.cfm.

Does Economics Deserve
A Nobel Prize?

(And, by the way, does
Paul Samuelson deserve one?)

This article was first published in *Commonweal*, Vol. 93 (Dec. 18, 1970) pp. 296-98, on the occasion of Mr. Samuelson's being awarded the second annual Nobel Economics Prize (the Swedish National Bank's Prize in Economic Sciences in Memory of Alfred Nobel) that year. My initial optimism that a revolution would overthrow his theories obviously did not bear fruit. I was teaching international trade theory at the Graduate Faculty of the New School for Social Research at the time. Subsequently, I criticized Mr. Samuelson's methodology in "The Use and Abuse of Mathematical Economics," *Journal of Economic Studies* 27 (2000):292-315. Most unrealistic of all is Mr. Samuelson's factor-price equalization theorem, whose misleading assumptions I survey in *Trade, Development and Foreign Debt: A History of Theories of Polarization v. Convergence in the World Economy.*

It is bad enough that the field of psychology has for so long been a non-social science, viewing the motive forces of personality as deriving from internal psychic experiences rather than from man's interaction with his social setting. Similarly in the field of economics: since its "utilitarian" revolution about a century ago, this discipline has also abandoned its analysis of the objective world and its political, economic productive relations in favor of more introverted, utilitarian and welfare-oriented norms. Moral speculations concerning mathematical psychics have come to displace the once-social science of political economy.

To a large extent the discipline's revolt against British classical political economy was a reaction against Marxism, which represented the logical culmination of classical Ricardian economics and its paramount emphasis on the conditions of production. Following the counterrevolution, the motive force of economic behavior came to be viewed as stemming from man's *wants* rather than from his productive capacities, organization of production, and the social relations that followed therefrom. By the postwar period the anti-classical revolution (curiously termed neo-classical by its participants) had carried the day. Its major textbook of indoctrination was Paul Samuelson's *Economics*.

Today, virtually all established economists are products of this anti-classical revolution, which I myself am tempted to call a revolution against economic analysis *per se*. The established practitioners of economics are uniformly negligent of the social preconditions and consequences of man's economic activity. In this lies their shortcoming, as well as that of the newly-instituted Economics Prize granted by the Swedish Academy: at least for the next decade it must perforce remain a prize for non-economics, or at best superfluous economics. Should it therefore be given at all?

This is only the second year in which the Economics prize has been awarded, and the first time it has been granted to a single individual – Paul Samuelson – described in the words of a jubilant *New York Times* editorial as "the world's greatest pure economic theorist." And yet the body of doctrine that Samuelson espouses is one of the major reasons why economics students enrolled in the nation's colleges have been declining in number. For they are, I am glad to say, appalled at the irrelevant nature of the discipline as it is now taught, impatient with its inability to describe the problems which plague the world in which they live, and increasingly resentful of its explaining away the most apparent problems which first attracted them to the subject.

The trouble with the Nobel Award is not so much its choice of man (although I shall have more to say later as to the implications of the choice of Samuelson), but its designation of economics as a scientific field worthy of receiving a Nobel prize at all. In the prize committee's words, Mr. Samuelson received the award for the "scientific work through which he has developed static and dynamic economic theory and actively contributed to raising the level of analysis in economic science. . . ."

What is the nature of this science? Can it be "scientific" to promulgate theories that do not describe economic reality as it unfolds in its historical context, and which lead to economic imbalance when applied? Is economics really an *applied* science at all? Of course it is implemented in practice, but with a noteworthy lack of success in recent years on the part of all the major economic schools, from the post-Keynesians to the monetarists.

In Mr. Samuelson's case, for example, the trade policy that follows from his theoretical doctrines is laissez faire. That this doctrine has been adopted by most of the western world is obvious. That it has benefited the developed nations is also apparent. However, its usefulness to less developed countries is doubtful, for underlying it is a permanent justification of the status quo: let things alone and everything will (tend to) come to "equilibrium." Unfortunately, this concept of equilibrium is probably the most perverse idea plaguing economics today, and it is just this concept that Mr. Samuelson has done so much to popularize. For it is all too often overlooked that when someone falls fiat on his face he is "in equilibrium" just as much as when he is standing upright. Poverty as well as wealth represents an equilibrium position. Everything that exists represents, however fleetingly, some equilibrium – that is, some balance or product – of forces.

Nowhere is the sterility of this equilibrium preconception more apparent than in Mr. Samuelson's famous factor-price equalization theorem, which states that the natural tendency of the international economy is for his wages and profits among nations to converge over time. As an empirical historical generality this obviously is invalid. International wage levels and living standards are diverging, not converging, so that the rich creditor nations are becoming richer while poor debtor countries are becoming poorer – at an accelerating pace, to boot. Capital transfers (international investment and "aid") have, if anything, aggravated the problem, largely because they have tended to buttress the structural defects that impede progress in the poorer countries: obsolete systems of land tenure, inadequate educational and labor-training institutions, pre-capitalist aristocratic social structures, and so forth. Unfortunately, it is just such political-economic factors that have been overlooked by Mr. Samuelson's theorizing (as they have been overlooked by the mainstream of academic economists since political economy gave way to "economics" a century ago).

In this respect Mr. Samuelson's theories can be described as beautiful watch parts which, when assembled, make a watch that doesn't tell time accurately. The individual parts are perfect, but their interaction is somehow not. The parts of this watch are the constituents of neoclassical theory that add up to an inapplicable whole. They are a kit of conceptual tools ideally designed to correct a world that doesn't exist.

The problem is one of scope. Mr. Samuelson's three volumes of economic papers represent a myriad of applications of internally consistent (or what economists call "elegant") theories, but to what avail? The theories are static, the world dynamic.

Ultimately, the problem resolves to a basic difference between economics and the natural sciences. In the latter, the preconception of an ultimate symmetry in nature has led to many revolutionary breakthroughs, from the Copernican revolution in astronomy to the theory of the atom and its sub-particles, and including the laws of thermodynamics, the periodic table of the elements, and unified field theory. Economic activity is not characterized by a similar underlying symmetry. It is more unbalanced. Independent variables or exogenous shocks do not set in motion just-offsetting counter-movements, as they would have to in order to bring about a meaningful new equilibrium. If they did, there would be no economic growth at all in the world economy, no difference between U.S. per capita productive powers and living standards and those of Paraguay. Mr. Samuelson, however, is representative of the academic mainstream today in imagining that economic forces tend to equalize productive powers and personal incomes throughout the world *except* when impeded by the disequilibrating "impurities" of government policy. Empirical observation has long indicated that the historical evolution of "free" market forces has increasingly favored the richer nations (those fortunate enough to have benefited from an economic head start) and correspondingly retarded the development of the laggard countries. It is precisely the existence of political and institutional "impurities" such as foreign aid programs, deliberate government employment policies, and related political actions that have tended to counteract the "natural" course of economic history, by trying to maintain some international equitability of economic development and to help compensate for the economic dispersion caused by the disequilibrating "natural" economy.

A Revolution

This decade will see a revolution that will overthrow these untenable theories. Such revolutions in economic thought are not infrequent. Indeed, virtually all of the leading economic postulates and "tools of the trade" have been developed in the context of political-economic debates accompanying turning points in economic history. Thus, for every theory put forth there has been a counter-theory.

To a major extent these debates have concerned international trade and payments. David Hume with the quantity theory of money, for instance, along with Adam Smith and his "invisible hand" of self-interest, opposed the mercantilist monetary and international financial theories that had been used to defend England's commercial restrictions in the eighteenth century. During England's Corn Law debates some years later, Malthus opposed Ricardo on value and rent theory and its implications for the theory of comparative advantage in international trade. Later, the American protectionists of the 19th century opposed the Ricardians, urging that engineering coefficients and productivity theory become the nexus of economic thought rather than the theory of exchange, value and distribution. Still later, the Austrian School and Alfred Marshall emerged to oppose classical political economy (particularly Marx) from yet another vantage point, making consumption and utility the nexus of their theorizing.

In the 1920s, Keynes opposed Bertil Ohlin and Jacques Rueff (among others) as to the existence of structural limits to the ability of the traditional price and income adjustment mechanisms to maintain "equilibrium," or even economic and social stability. The setting of this debate was the German reparations problem. Today, a parallel debate is raging between the Structuralist School – which flourishes mainly in Latin America and opposes austerity programs as a viable plan for economic improvement of their countries – and the monetarist and post-Keynesian schools defending the IMF's austerity programs of balance-of-payments adjustment. Finally, in yet another debate, Milton Friedman and his monetarist school are opposing what is left of the Keynesians (including Paul Samuelson) over whether monetary aggregates or interest rates and fiscal policy are the decisive factors in economic activity.

In none of these debates do (or did) members of one school accept the theories or even the *underlying assumptions and postulates* of the other. In this respect the history of economic thought has not resembled that of physics, medicine, or other natural sciences, in which a discovery is fairly rapidly and universally acknowledged to be a contribution of new objective knowledge, and in which political repercussions and its associated national self-interest are almost entirely absent. In economics alone the irony is posed that two contradictory theories may both qualify for prize worthy preeminence, and that the prize may please one group of nations and displease another on theoretical grounds.

Thus, if the Nobel prize could be awarded posthumously, both Ricardo and Malthus, Marx and Marshall would no doubt qualify – just as both Paul Samuelson and Milton Friedman were leading contenders for this year's prize. Who, on the other hand, can imagine the recipient of the physics or chemistry prize holding a view not almost universally shared by his colleagues? (Within the profession, of course, there may exist different schools of thought. But they do not usually dispute the recognized positive contribution of their profession's Nobel prizewinner.) Who could review the history of these prizes and pick out a great number of recipients whose contributions proved to be false trails or stumbling blocks to theoretical progress rather than (in their day) breakthroughs?

The Swedish Royal Academy has therefore involved itself in a number of inconsistencies in choosing Mr. Samuelson to receive the 1970 Economics Prize. For one thing, last year's prize was awarded to two mathematical economists (Jan Tinbergen of Holland and Ragnar Frisch of Norway) for their translation of other men's economic theories into mathematical language, and in their statistical testing of existing economic theory. This year's prize, by contrast, was awarded to a man whose theoretical contribution is essentially untestable by the very nature of its "pure" assumptions, which are far too static ever to have the world stop its dynamic evolution so that they may be "tested." (This prompted one of my colleagues to suggest that the next Economics Prize be awarded to anyone capable of empirically testing any of Mr. Samuelson's theorems.)

And precisely because economic "science" seems to be more akin to "political science" than to natural science, the Economics Prize seems closer to the Peace Prize than to the prize in chemistry. Deliberately or not, it represents the Royal Swedish Academy's endorsement or recognition of the political *influence* of some economist in helping to defend some (presumably) laudable government policy.

Could the prize therefore be given just as readily to a U.S. president, central banker or some other non-academician as to a "pure" theorist (if such exists)? Could it just as well be granted to David Rockefeller for taking the lead in lowering the prime rate, or President Nixon for his acknowledged role in guiding the world's largest economy, or to Arthur Burns as chairman of the Federal Reserve Board? If the issue is ultimately one of government policy, the answer would seem to be affirmative.

Or is popularity perhaps to become the major criterion for winning the prize? This year's award must have been granted at least partially in recognition of Mr. Samuelson's *Economics* textbook, which has sold over two million copies since 1947 and thereby influenced the minds of a whole generation of – let us say it, for it is certainly not all Mr. Samuelson's fault – old fogeys. The book's orientation itself has impelled students away from further study of the subject rather than attracting them to it. And yet if popularity and success in the marketplace of economic fads (among those who have chosen to remain in the discipline rather than seeking richer intellectual pastures elsewhere) is to become a consideration, then the prize committee has done an injustice to Jacqueline Susann in not awarding her this year's literary prize.

To summarize, reality and relevance rather than "purity" and elegance are the burning issues in economics today, political implications rather than antiquarian geometrics. The fault therefore lies not with Mr. Samuelson but with his discipline. Until it is agreed what economics *is*, or *should be*, it is as fruitless to award a prize for "good economics" as to award an engineer who designed a marvelous machine that either could not be built or whose purpose was unexplained. The prize must thus fall to those still lost in the ivory corridors of the past, reinforcing general equilibrium economics just as it is being pressed out of favor by those striving to restore the discipline to its long-lost pedestal of political economy.

Hudson Bubble Model*

From Asset-Price Inflation to Debt-Strapped Austerity

Today's form of finance capitalism is an evolution (or detour) of industrial capitalism into an economy dominated by large banks and money-management institutions controlled by the One Percent. Its idea of "wealth creation" (indeed, its business plan) is to inflate asset prices for real estate, stocks and bonds on credit. This creates financial bubbles that leave borrowers and governments debt-strapped, leading in due course to debt deflation.

The term "financialization" refers to the degree to which this debt leverage rises as a proportion of asset valuations and, in the process, extracts a rising proportion of national income. This increases the power of banks and the One Percent over labor and industry in seven ways:

(1) **Inflating asset prices** obliges buyers to take on more debt, increasing the cost of home ownership and buying a retirement income, while creating more "capital" gains for the One Percent.

(2) **Increasing debt** is owed mainly to the One Percent, largely by the 99 Percent, including for education as the cost of schooling (like housing prices) reflects how much banks are willing to lend to buyers.

(3) **Paying interest and carrying charges** for mortgage debt, education debt, credit-card debt and bank debt leaves less personal after-tax income available to spend on goods and services, thereby slowing new investment and employment.

---

* For a more in-depth discussion see my book *The Bubble And Beyond: Fictitious Capital, Debt Deflation and Global Crisis* (2013), Ch. 8: "The Real Estate Bubble at the Core of Today's Debt-Leveraged Economy," and Ch. 11: "Saving, Asset-Price Inflation and Debt Deflation."

(4) **Debt-leveraging** of corporate balance sheets leads to insolvency, which managers use as a threat to downsize pension obligations.

(5) **Financialization leads to a fiscal crisis** as the tax deductibility of interest (and similar subsidies for real estate) reduces federal and local tax revenue. This forces a **tax shift** onto labor and consumers via higher sales and excise taxes, higher income taxes, and cutbacks on social programs and infrastructure spending. The fiscal squeeze leads to an underfunding or elimination of pensions. (See **Financialization**.)

(6) **Paying public debts and financing budget deficits by selling off the public domain** turns user fees for hitherto public services into rent-extraction opportunities. Privatization of public education is financialized on credit with student loan debt, while health care and Social Security are turned into profit opportunities instead of being financed out of the general budget.

(7) **Non-prosecution of financial crime** as the banking sector invests its gains in buying control of the political process and election campaigns to back client politicians. The resulting regulatory capture of public agencies is accompanied by rewriting of bankruptcy laws (decriminalizing usury) to favor creditors instead of enabling debtors to make a fresh start.

The result of these tendencies is that the center of social and economic planning shifts from governments to Wall Street and other financial centers – under the banner of "free markets."

The symbiotic Finance, Insurance and Real Estate (FIRE) Sector

Instead of spurring capital investment and output or raising living standards and employment, these financialization trends polarize the economy and ultimately shrink it. Almost 80% of bank credit is to buy real estate, and much of the remainder is to buy stocks (including corporate takeover loans). The result is a symbiotic Finance, Insurance and Real Estate (FIRE) sector, which accounts for most of the economy's *rentier* income, "capital" gains and debt overhead.

Since 1980 the Federal Reserve has driven down U.S. interest rates from 20% to nearly zero since 2008. Leading up to the 2008 crash, easier credit terms (lower interest rates, lower down payments, slower amortization and higher debt/equity ratios) inflated stock market prices and a real estate bubble, while the bond market enjoyed the greatest boom in history. "Creating wealth" in the form of higher asset prices in this purely financial way was achieved by creating debt on the liabilities side of the balance sheet.

Raising household debt by creating bank credit mainly to bid up prices for housing and other real estate leaves less wage income available to buy what labor produces. The debt deflation resulting from asset-price inflation has caused wealth and debt to increase much faster than wages. Since 1980 a rising proportion of wages has been diverted to

---

Hudson Bubble Model:

Two Types of Inflation Contrasted

The following ratios trace the financial *rentier* mode of exploiting labor and the economy by inflating asset prices (P_A) faster than real wages (W/P_C).

$$\frac{\Delta P_A}{\Delta W / \Delta P_C} = \text{1. The inflation rate for asset prices (on credit) compared to that of real wages}$$

A rising ratio benefits the One Percent

$$\Delta W / \Delta P_C = \text{2. Money wages deflated by the Consumer Price Index (CPI), commonly referred to as "real wages"}$$

A declining ratio hurts the 99 Percent

KEY

Δ: Change from one time period to the next

P: Price

P_A: Asset prices (an index number composed of a weighted average of price indices for real estate, stocks and bonds)

P_C: Consumer goods prices (the Consumer Price Index [CPI]), the usual measure of "inflation"

ΔP_A: The rate of "capital gains" in the form of rising asset prices, *e.g.*, Asset-Price Inflation

ΔP_C: The rate of consumer price inflation (or deflation)

W: Money wages for labor

---

pay interest and other financial charges, insurance and rent to the FIRE sector.

Mainstream economists assure the public that the rise in debt is benign, because "we owe it to ourselves." Whatever the indebted 99 Percent ("we") pay in interest and fees to creditors ("ourselves") is supposed to be spent or lent back into the economy by "job creators" (the One Percent's euphemism for itself).

The reality is that the One Percent do not use their gains to buy goods and services or hire labor. They lend out more money to increase the economy's debt ratios, and buy more assets. See **Hudson Bubble Model** chart above for the two formulas that trace the financial *rentier* mode of exploiting labor and the economy by inflating asset prices (P_A) faster than real wages (W/P_C).

How financialization and the tax shift off the One Percent strip the 99 Percent of its disposable personal income

Financializing home ownership, education, pensions and industry leaves less of the family paycheck available for consumer spending after paying debt service and suffering from taxes being shifted off the FIRE sector. The government withholds a rising percentage of wages to pay FICA contributions for Social Security and Medicare (now over 15% of paychecks) and federal and local income taxes (up to about 20%). Instead of progressively taxing the One Percent, taxes on wage earners are increased, along with sales taxes to close the budget gaps caused by tax favoritism for the higher wealth and income brackets. What is left to wage earners after paying these taxes is called disposable personal income or DPI. (See the discussion in the A-to-Z section of this book.)

National income statistics (see NIPA) define DPI as what wage earners take home after deduction of taxes and FICA withholding. But what remains is not fully disposable:

• **Housing charges.** For starters, families must pay their monthly housing "nut" to the bank for their mortgage, or to the landlord for rent. U.S. federal housing programs guarantee bank mortgages that absorb up to 43% of the homebuyer's personal income, and rents in many areas have reached this level.

• **Other debts.** Payments on student loan debt, credit card debt, auto debt and other debts (not to speak of payday loans) typically absorb over 10% of consumer income.

• **Forced saving.** After the 2008 financial crash many wage-earning households were obliged to "save" by paying down their debt as banks scaled back their lending and credit card exposure. Such quasi-saving is squeezed out, not available for discretionary spending. The result is what Richard Koo has called a balance sheet recession.

• **Insurance and pensions.** Also taken off the top are payments for compulsory health insurance, and in come cases non-government pension plans and health care charges. Taken together, these charges leave only between a quarter and a third of wage income disposable for spending on goods and services. (See **Wage-Earner DPI** chart on opposite page.)

• **A tax shift off the One Percent onto the 99 Percent.** Household income does not get the same tax breaks afforded to businesses. Businesses deduct payroll and all other operating costs and depreciation, as well as taxes and interest from their taxable income. Wage earners have analogous basic expenses but receive no such

---

Wage-Earner DPI*

... and what actually is available for discretionary spending

Gross Wages

| *less* | up to 35% Taxes
(15% FICA wage withholding for Social Security and Medicare and up to 20% Federal and local income tax and sales taxes) |

---

equals	**Disposable Personal Income (DPI)***
less	up to 43% for housing: either mortgage payments (government-guaranteed up to 43%), or rent (typically a similar percentage)
less	10% (or more) for credit card debt, student debt, personal loans, auto loans and retail credit.
less	Compulsory and/or voluntary saving via pension funds and other retirement savings plans

---

leaves	Only about 25% to 30% of wages actually available for discretionary consumer spending

* DPI = Disposable Personal Income as defined by the U.S. National Income and Product Accounts (NIPA)

---

tax favoritism. If income-tax policy treated labor like capital, only this net after-expense income would be taxed, not the entire wage. Yet many Americans are in favor of cutting taxes without realizing that this usually means cuts overwhelmingly for the One Percent.

• **Inequality of "total returns" between families and businesses.** Just as businesses measure "total returns" to include the rise (or decline) in the market price of homes and financial securities, consumers and wage earners should have a parallel measure. This would show the decline in their net worth (and hence, spending power) after prices for homes fell after 2008. That decline toward negative equity offsets the gains that many homebuyers imagined they were obtaining when they rode the Bubble Economy's rising wave of debt-inflated housing prices.

How financialization deflates the "real" economy

When a bubble economy and "Quantitative Easing" (central bank support for bank credit creation to drive down interest rates) raise asset prices, this results in lower returns on stocks and bonds. That requires more saving to be set aside to generate a given retirement income from financial securities. Trying to financialize pensions by obliging workers, employers and public agencies to save more for their retirement and health care in advance thus leaves less to spend on goods and services.

This holds down economic growth, and hence employment and real wages. If corporate, state and local budgets cannot meet this pension schedule, they run up shortfalls on defined-benefit pension plans. Government also has been forced into deficit by the corporate shift to pay earnings to bondholders and banks as tax-exempt interest instead of after-tax dividends to shareholders.

FIRE-sector lobbyists urge governments to make up the resulting budget shortfalls debts by selling off the public domain. This reverses the classical aim of minimizing the economy's cost of living and doing business by supplying public infrastructure services at cost, on a subsidized basis or freely. When transportation, communications, water and other basic infrastructure assets are privatized, the new owners build in interest, dividends and management salaries, stock options and bonuses to the prices they charge for these basic needs.

Leaving corporations with less post-financialized income to invest

While corporate lobbyists promise that lower taxes will lead to more investment and hiring, this is merely a myth to lull voters into a trickle-down fantasy (an economic Stockholm Syndrome). When companies adopt financial engineering rather than industrial engineering, rolling back corporate taxes (or taking profits in offshore tax-avoidance centers) simply leaves more revenue available for share buybacks, dividend payouts and management bonuses.

The counterpart to tracing how FIRE-sector charges and taxes eat into household income is the diversion of corporate cash flow – ebitda – to pay the FIRE sector (see **Business Cash Flow (ebitda) to Pay the FIRE Sector** chart on opposite page).

To help ensure that the aim of corporate managers will be to engineer asset-price gains (called "creating shareholder value"), they are rewarded with stock options and bonuses based on how much they push up the price of their shares. This prompts companies to use their profits for stock buybacks and higher dividend payouts instead of re-investing to expand their business. An enormous 92% of corporate cash flow in 2014 was paid out as dividends or used for share buybacks. Higher asset

---

Business Cash Flow (ebitda) to Pay the FIRE Sector

Ebitda
(Earnings Before Interest, Depreciation and Amortization)

less	taxes
less	interest charges
less	depreciation and amortization
less	addition to pension fund reserves (and loss reserves)

equals	business profits
less	dividend payouts
less	stock buy-backs
less	management fees and bonuses linked to raising stock prices

equals	net retained earnings available for new investment

---

prices also are achieved by cutting costs – eliminating staff and product lines, and downsizing pension plans and employer contributions to healthcare.

The FIRE Sector's extraction of *rentier* revenue

Most people think of the economy in terms of wages being spent on consumer goods, while profits are invested to build more factories and machinery to keep the economy growing (see **Two Economies**, Economy #1). Less familiar is how this economy of production and consumption is encased in the FIRE sector's superstructure of financial and property claims (see **Two Economies**, Economy #2). Classical economists spent over a century explaining how this superstructure was extraneous to production, siphoning off rents to pay landlords who make little contribution to production except by charging access fees to land and natural resources, and to financial "coupon clippers" (see ***Rentier* Financial Class**) holding bonds and stocks. Seeking to free economies from rent and interest payments, the classical economists defined such economic rent as the excess of market price over real and necessary cost-value, and hence as extractive rather than "earned" (see **Unearned Income**).

Today's accounting formats do not disclose any measure of land rent or other forms of economic rent. The U.S. National Income and Product Accounts (NIPA) depict rent, interest and fees as actual costs of production contributing to real output, not as a rake-off. Rent is conflated with profits by calling it "earnings."

Neither national income accounts nor central bank statistics distinguish productive credit to fund new means of production from lending that merely transfers ownership of property already in place. Corporate takeover loans, for instance, do not create new means of production, but build in interest charges paid to the junk-bond holders that back financial raiders. It thus seems bizarre to depict these charges as payments for providing a "service" that increases Gross Domestic Product (GDP). That is not the aim of financial raiders. Such extractive credit bloats the financial overhead with unnecessary costs.

What has been lost from today's discussion is the classical free-market emphasis that economies are made lower-cost not only by new technology's productivity gains, but by freeing society from rent and interest charges (overhead). Today's technology potential is universal, but the power of banking, *rentier* income and interest seeks policies that will monopolize the economy's technology gains for a narrow elite (the One Percent). As originally promised, technology by itself should have raised wages, living standards and shortened the workweek. What is called for is an explanation of why this has not occurred.

Financialization differs from the industrial exploitation of labor

Industrial capitalism's internal contradiction is that seeking profits by exploiting labor leaves it unable to buy what it produces. To avoid a market crash, the shortfall in purchasing power must come from outside the "closed" economy, by:

(1) **Selling products in foreign markets**, spurring a drive for colonialism in the 19th century, and reliance on China today
(2) **Selling to the government**, as in today's military-industrial economy
(3) **Selling on credit**, to an increasingly indebted economy

What kept Western economies expanding in the decades leading up to the 2008 crash was mainly the third option: bank lending to infuse purchasing power. However, this merely financial mode of "wealth creation" has its own internal contradiction. Leaving this expansion of credit in the hands of bankers and bondholders comes at a price: interest charges. The debt overhead grows by the mathematics of compound interest, to the point where it exceeds the ability of households, business and governments to pay.

Furthermore, banks create money mainly to lend against assets in place (real estate, corporate takeovers and privatization of public infrastructure monopolies), not to fund new tangible capital investment and hiring. The result of such lending is to bid up asset prices. Today's investors aim at "total returns," defined as current income *plus* asset-price gains. For real estate and the stock and bond markets since 1980, asset-price gains have far exceeded current income. This increasing role of asset-price inflation has transformed finance capitalism away from promoting industry and employment to a strategy of financial engineering. Yet these gains do not appear in any national accounts to show why the Bubble Economy has widened inequality so sharply – and so rapidly.

When credit is extractive, rising debt levels impoverish real estate, public infrastructure and industry. That is what is causing today's austerity. The more debt service and other *rentier* income is extracted, the higher the probability of default, ending in a crash that leaves a residue of debt deflation. Foreclosures ensue, transferring assets to creditors – unless the loans are resolved by debt writedowns, bankruptcy and Clean Slates.

Austerity caused by financialization thus exploits labor not only as wage earners and consumers, but also as debtors and even as forced savers (via pension fund capitalism and Social Security contributions used to cut taxes on the FIRE sector and the One Percent). The current rent and financial dynamic that has led to austerity was first described in Volumes II and III of Karl Marx's *Capital* (see **Rent Theory**). Interest-bearing credit, he explained, has its own mathematical dynamic of compound interest, external to the industrial economy of production and consumption.

Most classical economic reformers of the mid to late 19th century optimistically expected capitalism to prepare the ground for socialism and a better living standard by freeing economies from the *faux frais* (unnecessary expenses) of production in the form of interest, land rent and other forms of monopoly rent (see **Monopoly**). The task of industrial capitalism seemed logically to be to make banking productive instead of usurious and predatory, mainly by democratic parliamentary reform. Industrial capitalism's drive for efficiency and cost-cutting was expected to lead to "socialism" in one form or another as democratic governments would tax away land rent and unearned financial returns, and nationalize basic infrastructure and natural monopolies to finally free society from the legacy of feudalism.

However, bankers, landlords and other vested interests did not remain passive in the face of this Progressive Era drive. Seeking to morally justify their "free lunch," they fought back to sponsor a pro-*rentier* ideology that depicts rent and interest (and capital gains) as being productively earned, as if their recipients contribute to economic growth rather than burdening society with an extractive overhead.

That ideological rollback has now become mainstream. Today's national income statistics avoid reporting the unearned income that was a central focus for classical political economy. This state of denial has shielded *rentier* wealth and power from criticism. The Bubble Economy leading up to 2008 was applauded as a boom, as if its business model was making economies rich and enabling them to pay pensions out of purely financial engineering instead of paying current income to retirees.

The Bubble Economy's sponsors called it the Great Moderation, oblivious to the mounting debt. What was moderate was simply the lack of protest among mainstream economists, media and politicians. Federal Reserve chairman Alan Greenspan assured voters that the economy was getting richer by debt leveraging to bid up the prices that people had to pay for homes. Those who said that the financial emperor had no clothes were ignored, as if they simply failed to understand how the rising tide of debt was lifting all yachts, not submerging the economy around them.

This financial game plan goes far beyond the scope of what mainstream textbooks describe. It seeks government subsidy and tax favoritism (see **Socialism for the Rich**), while preventing governments from issuing their own money (leaving this function to commercial banks) and privatizing basic infrastructure for creditors and the buyers they finance. Seeing credit and debt creation as the main lever to obtain property income, financial lobbyists realize that housing and corporate ownership can be left nominally in non-financial hands as long as the middle class and business owners pay all of their disposable income to the banks and the bondholders who finance them.

The reason why the economy has polarized between the One Percent and the 99 Percent is thus largely financial. Nearly all growth in income and wealth has been sucked up to the top of the economic pyramid. Most economists treat this narrowly monopolized growth as if the economy at large is growing, but the financial business plan involves diverting income away from tangible capital formation, shrinking the economy.

The result is that instead of helping nations undersell competitors by minimizing the cost of living and doing business, financialization adds to costs in two ways:

(1) **Interest and financial charges are built into the break-even costs of living and doing business**. On a deeper level, financial bubbles inflate asset prices on credit (debt leveraging), while shifting political power to the *rentier* class whose aim – the unearned increment – is the opposite of what 19th-century democratic reformers intended.

(2) **The tax burden is shifted onto labor and industry** by the regressive VAT tax ("value added" taxes on each stage of production, passed on to consumers), sales taxes and a flat (low) income tax. The alternative would be to tax land and make banking and natural monopolies into public utilities. Social Security and health care are treated as user fees that are pre-paid by wage earners instead of financed by pay-

as-you-go progressive taxation (so much for the "entitlement" fiction). To cap matters, privatizing the creation of money and credit blocks governments from self-financing their budget deficits. Insistence that governments should not run such deficits (and urging them actually to pay down the public debt) forces economies to rely on banks for the credit needed to grow.

As the world has suffered since 2008, this favoritism toward the FIRE sector leads to a fiscal and financial crisis. Neoliberal economic theory – epitomized by the eurozone's financial demands on Greece – urges that pensions and public services be scaled back, and that the resulting austerity and fiscal shortfalls be resolved by privatizing natural resources and public infrastructure that can be turned into rent-extracting monopolies.

Instead of public investment to lower the economy's cost structure, privatized transportation and communications, water and other key utilities already in place provide opportunities for banks to lend even more. Financializing education with student loan programs, for instance, requires prospective graduates to go deeply into debt to banks to pay for training to obtain work. Meanwhile, the content of economics education is turned into junk economics depicting this post-industrial finance capitalism as being the natural "end of history," as if there is no practical alternative going forward (see **TINA**). Austerity for labor/consumers, downsizing of industry and privatization of the public infrastructure – including public health, pensions, Social Security, and the banking and credit system – is depicted as inevitable, not as a hijacking of economic potential.

The feeling of inevitability relies on a censorship of the history of economic thought, and of economic history. That intellectual degradation provides the protective shell for financial exploitation of labor and industry, effectively eliminating the lessons of history.

Any long-term analysis of how economies evolve must recognize this misshaping of academic understanding and its corollary statistical representations of reality. Economic theory can play either a productive or regressive role. What is important to recognize is that each economic class promotes its own worldview. The resulting conflation of subjective self-interest with objective reality makes the economics discipline unscientific and prone to sophism. Today's mainstream worldview is that of financial *rentiers*, not industry or labor. Given today's official financial policy of monopolizing all economic growth for *rentiers* atop the economic pyramid, any realistic model of the economy must recognize that society does not always progress forward. It can retrogress. That is what the world has been seeing for the past generation and, at present, that looks like our foreseeable future.

Author Interview:
KILLING THE HOST

The following interview with Michael Hudson by Eric Draitser
was aired on CounterPunch Radio, Episode 19, September 21, 2015.[1]
This transcript has been edited for clarity.

ERIC DRAITSER (ED): Today I have the privilege of introducing Michael Hudson to the program. Doctor Hudson is the author of the new book *Killing the Host: How Financial Parasites and Debt Bondage Destroy the Global Economy*, available in print on Amazon and an e-version on CounterPunch.

Michael Hudson, welcome to CounterPunch Radio. As I mentioned already, the title of your book, *Killing the Host*, is an apt metaphor. You explain that parasitic finance capital survives by feeding off what you call the real economy. Could you draw out that analogy a bit? How does finance behave like a parasite toward the rest of the economy?

MICHAEL HUDSON (MH): Economists for the last 50 years have used the term "host economy" for a country that lets in foreign investment. The word "host" implies a parasite. The term parasitism has long been applied to finance by Martin Luther and others in the sense of simply taking something from the host.

But in nature, biological parasitism works in a more complex and sophisticated way. The key is how a parasite takes over a host. It has enzymes that numb the host's nervous system and brain. So when it stings or gets its claws into the host, there's a soporific anesthetic to block it from realizing that it's being taken over. The parasite then sends enzymes into the host's brain to control its behavior.

A parasite cannot take anything from the host *unless* it takes over the brain. The brain in modern economies is the government, the educational system, and the way that society makes economic policy for how to behave.

In nature the parasite makes the host think that the free rider, the parasite, is its baby, part of its body. Its aim is to convince the host to protect the parasite over itself. That's how the financial sector has taken over the economy. Its lobbyists and client academics persuade governments and voters that they need to protect banks, and even need to bail them out when they become overly predatory and face collapse. Politicians are persuaded to save banks instead of saving the economy. It is as if the economy can't function without banks being left in private hands to do whatever they want, free of serious regulation and even from prosecution when they commit fraud. This worldview saves creditors – the One Percent – not the indebted 99 Percent.

It was not always this way. A century ago, two centuries ago, three centuries ago and all the way back to the Bronze Age, almost every society saw finance – that is, debt – as the great destabilizing force. Debt grows exponentially, ultimately enabling creditors to foreclose on the assets of debtors. Creditors end up reducing societies to debt bondage. That is how the Roman Empire ended in serfdom.

About a hundred years ago in America, John Bates Clark and other pro-financial ideologues argued that finance is *not* external to the economy. They said that it's not extraneous, it's *part* of the economy, just like landlords claim to be part of the economy's production process, not an overlay to it. This implies that when the financial sector takes more revenue out of the economy as interest, fees or monopoly charges, it's not merely siphoning it off this revenue from producers; it's because Wall Street and the One Percent are an inherent and vital part of the economy, adding to GDP. So our economic policy protects finance as if it helps us grow instead of siphoning off our growth.

A year or two ago, Lloyd Blankfein of Goldman Sachs said that the reason his firm's managers are paid more than anybody else is because they're so productive. The question is, productive of *what*? The National Income and Product Accounts (NIPA) say that everybody is productive in proportion to the amount of money they make or take. It doesn't matter whether it's extractive income or productive income. It doesn't matter whether it's made by manufacturing products or simply by taking money from people via the kinds of fraud for which Goldman Sachs, Citigroup, Bank of America and others paid tens of millions of dollars in fines for committing. Any way of earning income is considered to be as productive as any other way.

This is a parasite-friendly mentality, because it denies that there's any such thing as unearned income. It denies that there's a free lunch. Hence, there seems to be no such thing as economic parasitism. Milton Friedman got famous for promoting this idea that there's no such thing as a free lunch, but Wall Street knows quite well that from its perspective, the economy is all about how to get a free lunch – and how to get the risks picked up by the government. No wonder they back economists who deny that there's any exploitation, or any such thing as unearned income!

ED: To get to the root of the issue, what's interesting to me about this analogy is that we hear the term neoliberalism all the time. It is an ideology that's used to promote the environment in which this parasitic sort of finance capital can operate. Could you talk a bit about the relationship between finance capital and neoliberalism as its ideology?

MH: Today's vocabulary is what Orwell would call Doublethink. If you're going to erase the memory of what Adam Smith, John Stuart Mill and other classical economists described as free markets – markets free of *rentier* income – you claim to be *neo*liberal, misrepresenting these reformers as endorsing today's anti-classical "freedom" *from* taxation for *rentiers*. This inversion of classical liberalism requires a rewriting of the history of economic thought to suppress the 19th-century distinction between earned and unearned income – that is, between real wealth and mere overhead.

The parasite's strategy is to replace the meaning of everyday words with their opposite. It's Doublethink. This rewriting of the history of economic thought involves inverting the common vocabulary that people use. The focus of Smith, Mill, Quesnay and the whole of 19th-century classical economics was to distinguish between productive and unproductive labor – that is, between people who earn wages and profits, and *rentiers* who, as Mill said, "get rich in their sleep." That is how he described landowners receiving groundrent and rising land prices over time. It also describes the financial sector receiving interest and "capital" gains.

The first thing the neoliberal Chicago School did when they took over Chile was to close down every economics department in the country except the one they controlled at the Catholic University. They started an assassination program of left wing professors, labor leaders and politicians, and imposed neoliberalism at gunpoint. Their breakthrough idea was you cannot have deregulated "free markets" stripping away social protections and benefits *unless* you have totalitarian control. You have to censor any idea that there's ever been an alternative, by rewriting economic history to deny the progressive tax and regulatory reforms that Smith, Mill, and other classical economists urged. You have to reject the classical economists' guiding objective: to free industrial capitalism *from* the surviving feudal privileges of landlords and predatory finance.

Democratic vs. oligarchic government and their respective economic doctrines

ED: I don't want to go off on a tangent, but you mentioned the example of Chile's 1973 coup and the assassination of Allende to impose the Pinochet dictatorship. That was a Kissinger/Nixon operation as we know, but in the process, Chile was transformed into a sort of experimental laboratory to impose the Chicago School's economic model of what we now call neoliberalism. Later in our conversation I want to talk about some recent laboratories we have seen in Eastern Europe, and now in Southern Europe as well. The important point about neoliberalism is its anti-democratic relationship with totalitarian government.

MH: Neoliberals say they're against government, but what they're really against is democratic government. The kind of government they support is pre-referendum Greece or post-coup Ukraine. As Germany's Wolfgang Schäuble said, "democracy doesn't count." Neoliberals want the kind of government that will create gains for the banks, not necessarily for the economy at large. Such governments basically are oligarchic. Once high finance takes over governments as a means of exploiting the 99 Percent, it's all for active government policy – for itself.

Aristotle talked about this more than 2,000 years ago. He said that democracy is the stage immediately proceeding oligarchy. All economies go through three stages repeating a cycle: from democracy into oligarchy, and then the oligarchs make themselves hereditary. Today, Jeb Bush wants to abolish the estate tax to help the emerging power elite make itself into a hereditary aristocracy. Then, some of the aristocratic families will fight among themselves, and take the public into their camp and promote democracy, so you have the cycle going all over again. That's the kind of cycle we're having now, just as in ancient Athens. It's a transition from democracy to oligarchy on its way to becoming an aristocracy of the power elite.

ED: I want to return to the book in a second, but I have to interject that one particular economist hasn't been mentioned yet: Karl Marx. His labor theory of value was that value ultimately is derived from labor. Parasitic finance capital is the opposite of that. It may increase prices without value.

MH: Correct, but I should point out that there's often a misinterpretation of the political context in which the labor theory of value was formulated and refined. The reason why Marx and the other classical economists – William Petty, Smith, Mill and the others – talked about the labor theory of value was to isolate that part of price that *wasn't* value. They defined *economic rent* as something that was *not* value. It was extraneous to production, a free lunch – an element of price that has *no* basis in labor, *no* basis in real cost. It is purely a monopoly price or return to privilege. This was mainly a survival of the feudal epoch, above all via the landed aristocrats who were the heirs of the land's military conquers, and also the banking families and *their* heirs.

The aim of the labor theory of value was to divide the economy between price gouging and labor. The objective of the classical economists was to bring prices in line with value to prevent a free ride, to prevent monopolies, to prevent an absentee landlord class so as to free society from the legacy of feudalism and the military conquests that carved up Europe's land a thousand years ago and that still underlies our property relations.

The concept and theory of economic rent (unearned income)

ED: That's a great point, and it leads me into the next issue I want to touch on. You've mentioned the concept of economic rent a number of times. We all know rent in terms of what we have to pay every month to the landlord, but we might not think about what it means conceptually. It's one of the fabrics with which you've woven this book together: one of the running themes, rent extraction and its role in what we've termed this parasitic relationship. So, explain for laymen what rent extraction means, and how the concept evolved.

MH: To put the concept of economic rent in perspective, I should point out when I got my PhD over a half a century ago, every university offering a graduate economics degree taught the history of economic thought. That topic is now erased from the curriculum. People get mathematics instead, so they're unexposed to the concept of economic rent as unearned income. It's a concept that has been turned on its head by "free market" ideologues who use "rent seeking" mainly to characterize government bureaucrats taxing the private sector to enhance their authority, not free lunchers seeking to untax their unearned income. Neoclassical economists define rent as "imperfect competition" (as if their myth of "perfect competition" really exists) stemming from "insufficient knowledge of the market," patent privileges and so forth.

Rent theory was developed in Britain, and also in France. English practice is more complex than America. The military conquers imposed a groundrent fee on the land, as distinct from buildings and improvements. So if you buy a house from a seller in England, somebody else may own the land underneath it. You have to pay a separate rent for the land. The landlord doesn't do anything at all to collect land rent, that's why they call them *rentiers* or coupon clippers. In New York City, for example, Columbia University long owned the land underneath Rockefeller Center. (Finally they sold it to the Japanese, who lost their shirt.) This practice is a carry-over from the Norman Conquest and its absentee landlord class.

The word "rent" originally was French, for a government bond (*rente*). Owners received a regular income every quarter or every year. A German pensioner is a *Rentner*. A lot of bonds used to have coupons, and you would clip off the coupon and collect your interest. It's passively earned income, that is, income not actually earned by your own labor or enterprise. Rent and interest are claims that society has to pay, whether to government bondholders or to land owners.

This concept of income without labor – simply from privileges that have been made hereditary – was extended to the ideas of monopolies like the East India Company and other trade monopolies. They could produce or buy goods for, let's say, a dollar a unit, and sell them for whatever the market will bear – say, $4.00. The markup is "empty pricing." It's pure price gouging by a natural monopoly, like today's drug companies.

To prevent such price gouging and keep economies competitive with low costs of living and doing business, European countries kept the most important natural monopolies in the public domain: the post office, the BBC and other state broadcasting companies, roads and basic transportation, as well as early national airlines. This prevents monopoly rent, by providing basic infrastructure services at cost, or even at subsidized prices or freely in the case of roads. The guiding idea is for public infrastructure to lower the cost of living and doing business. So you should think of this government investment as a factor of production, along with labor and capital.

By privatizing this infrastructure, Margaret Thatcher turned Britain into a tollbooth economy. Privatization leads to economic rent being charged, a rise in prices that is paid out in the form of interest, stock options, soaring executive salaries and underwriting fees. The economy ends up being turned into a collection of tollbooths instead of factories. So, you can think of rent as the "right" or special legal privilege to erect a tollbooth and tell consumers, "You can't get television over your cable channel unless you pay us, and what we charge you is whatever the market will bear."

This price doesn't have any relation to what it costs to produce what the privatizers sell. Such extortionate pricing is now sponsored globally by U.S. diplomacy, the World Bank, and what's called the Washington Consensus forcing governments to privatize the public domain and create such rent-extracting opportunities for foreign investors. This has become the new financial imperialism.

When Mexico was told to be more "efficient" and privatize its telephone monopoly, the government sold it to Carlos Slim, who became one of the richest people in the world by making Mexico's phones among the highest priced. The government provided an opportunity for price gouging, and called this the "free market." It was free from government investment and price regulation. Similar high-priced privatized phone systems plague the post-Soviet economies that have become neoliberalized.

Classical economists viewed this as a kind of theft. The French novelist Balzac wrote about this more clearly than most economists when he said that every family fortune originates in a great theft. He added that this not only was undiscovered, but has come to be taken for granted so naturally that it just doesn't seem to matter any more.

If you look at the Forbes 100 or 500 lists of each nation's richest people, most made their fortunes through insider dealing to obtain land, mineral rights or monopolies. If you look at American history, early real estate fortunes were made by insiders bribing the notoriously corrupt British Colonial governors. The railroad barrens bribed Congressmen and other public officials to let them privatize the railroads and rip off the country. Frank Norris's *The Octopus* is a great novel about this, and many Hollywood movies describe the kind of real estate and banking rip-offs that made the American West what it is. Most of the nation's power elite basically begun as robber barons, as they did in England, France and other countries.

The difference, of course, is that in past centuries this was viewed as corrupt and a crime. Today, neoliberal economists actually recommend it as the way to raise "productivity" and make countries wealthier, as if it were not the road to neofeudal serfdom.

The Austrian School vs. government regulation and pro-labor policies

ED: I don't want to go too far off on a tangent because we have a lot to cover from your book. But I heard an interesting story when I was doing my own research through the years about the evolution of economic thought, and specifically about the so-called Austrian School of Economics – people like von Mises and von Hayek. In the early 20th century they were essentially, as far as I could tell, creating an ideological framework in which they could make theoretical arguments to justify exorbitant rent and make it seem like a product of natural law – something akin to a phenomenon of nature.

MH: The key to the Austrian School is its hatred of labor and socialism. It feared and opposed democratic government spreading social reform to the Habsburg Empire, and sought to reverse it. The Austrian idea of a free market was one free from democratic government regulating and taxing *rentiers*. To the wealthy they said: "It's either *your* freedom or that of labor." It was a short step to fighting in the streets, using the police, army and targeted murder as a "persuader" for the particular kind of "free markets" they wanted – a privatized Thatcherite deregulated kind.

Kari Polanyi-Levitt has recently written about how her father, Karl Polanyi, was confronted with these right wing Viennese and their fake history of how economics and civilization originated. His *Great Transformation* and subsequent "substantivist" analysis of exchange showed the shortcomings of "market exchange" and demonstrated an array of alternatives, from redistributive exchange to administered pricing since the beginning of civilization. This led him to expand economics into the realm of anthropology, as David Graeber has shown in *Debt: The First 5000 Years*.

One of the first Austrians was Carl Menger in the 1870s. His individualistic theory about the origins of money saw no role for the temples, palaces or other public institutions that actually created money. Just as Margaret Thatcher said, "There's no such thing as society," the Austrians developed a picture of the economy without any positive role for government. It was as if money were created by farmers, craftsmen and merchants bartering their output.

This is a travesty of history. All ancient money was issued by temples or public mints so as to guarantee standards of purity and weight. You can read Biblical and Babylonian denunciations of merchants using false weights and measures to see why money had to be public. The major trading areas were *agora* spaces in front of temples, which kept the official weights and measures. And much exchange was between the community's families and the public institutions – on credit.

My archaeological and assyriological group, the International Scholars Conference on the Ancient Near East (ISCANEE) started twenty years ago at Harvard has published a series of five colloquia showing that money was not brought into being for trade, but for paying debts. Most early debts were owed to the temples and palaces for public services or taxes. But to the Austrians, the idea is that anything the government does is deadweight overhead.

Above all, they oppose governments creating their own money, *e.g.* as the United States did with its greenbacks in the Civil War. They want to privatize money creation in the hands of commercial banks, to receive interest on the private banking privilege of credit creation to transfer wealth ownership – and also to control the allocation of resources, mainly for non-public purposes and speculation.

Today's neoliberals follow this Austrian tradition of viewing government as a burden instead of freeing infrastructure from rent extraction. As we said in the previous discussion, the greatest fortunes of our epoch have come from privatizing the public domain. Obviously the government isn't just deadweight. But it is becoming so as it falls prey to the financial interests, and to the smashers and grabbers they have chosen to back.

ED: You're right, I agree 100%. You encounter this ideology even in the political and sociological realm with Joseph Schumpeter, or in the quasi-economic realm with von Hayek in *The Road to Serfdom*.

MH: Its policy conclusion actually advocates neo-serfdom. Real serfdom was when families had to pay all their income to the landlords as rent. Centuries of classical economists backed democratic reform of parliaments to roll back the landlords' power. But Hayek claimed that this rollback was the road *to* serfdom, not *away* from it. He said democratic regulation and taxation of *rentiers* is serfdom. In reality it's the antidote.

Finance as the new mode of warfare

ED: That's the inversion you were talking about earlier. We're going to go into a break in a minute but I want to touch on one other point that is important in your book: debt. I had the journalist John Pilger on this program a few months ago. He and I touched on how debt is used as a weapon. You can see this in the form of debt enslavement in postcolonial Africa. You see the same thing in Latin America where I know you have a lot of experience in the last couple of decades. So let's talk a little bit about debt as a weapon, because I think this is an important concept for understanding what's happening now in Greece, and is really the framework through which we have to understand the looming 21st-century austerity.

MH: If you treat debt as a weapon, the basic idea is that finance is the new mode of warfare. That's one of my chapters in *Killing the Host*. In the past, in order to take over a country's land and its public domain, its basic infrastructure and mineral resources, you had to mount a military invasion. But that's very expensive. And politically, almost no modern democracy can afford a military invasion anymore.

The objective of the financial sector – Wall Street, the City of London or Frankfurt in Germany – is to obtain land, natural resources and to privatize key infrastructure away from the public domain. You can look at what's happening in Greece. What its creditors, the IMF and European Central Bank (ECB) want are the Greek islands and the gas rights in the Aegean Sea. They want buildings and property there is, including the museums ad prime tourist sites, as well as ports and transport hubs.

In the private sector, if you can get a company or individual into debt, you can strip away the assets they have when they can't pay. A Hayek-style government would block society from protecting itself against such asset stripping. Defending the "property rights" of creditors, such "free market" ideology subordinates the rights of indebted businesses, individuals and public agencies. It treats debt writedowns as the road to serfdom, not the road *away* from debt dependency.

In antiquity, creditors (often palace collectors or infrastructure managers) obtained labor services by making loans to families in need, and obliging their servant girls, children or even wives to work off the loan in the form of labor service. When new Bronze Age rulers started their reign, it was customary to declare an amnesty to annul personal debts and return such bondservants to their families, as well as to return whatever lands were forfeited. So in the Bronze Age, debt serfdom and debt bondage was only temporary. The biblical Jubilee Year was a literal translation of Babylonian practice going back two thousand years.

In colonial America, sharpies (especially from Britain) lent farmers money that they knew couldn't be paid, and then would foreclose just before the crops came in. Right now you have corporate raiders forcing companies into debt, and then smashing and grabbing, starting with their pension funds and Employee Stock Ownership Plans (ESOPs).

Globally, you now have the IMF, European Central Bank and Washington Consensus taking over whole countries, like Ukraine. The financial tactic still hasn't changed much. It is to lend them the money that clearly cannot be repaid, and then force them either to become economic pariah states like Iran or Argentina, or accept the neoliberals' solution: sell off public enterprises, land and natural resources to pay creditors. In Greece's case, 50 billion euros of its property, everything that it has in the public domain, is supposed to be sold off to foreigners (including Greek oligarchs operating out of their offshore accounts in tax-avoidance enclaves). Debt leverage is thus the way to grab what it took armies to take over in times past.

ED: Exactly. I want to get your comment on Africa after the French and the British nominally gave up control of their colonies. Debt became an important lever to maintain hegemony within their spheres of influence. Of course, asset stripping and seizing control, smashing and grabbing was part of that. But it also was debt service – the vicious cycle of taking out new loans to service the original debts. This is also an example of debt servitude or debt bondage.

MH: That's correct, but mainstream economics denies this. The idea that debt cannot create serious problems began with Ricardo, whose brothers were major bankers while he himself was England's leading bank lobbyist. Right after Greece won its independence from Turkey, the Ricardo brothers made the country a rack-renting loan, issued far below par (that is, below the face value that Greece committed itself to pay). Greece tried to pay over the next century, but the terms of the loan stripped away its export earnings and kept it on the edge of bankruptcy well into the 20th century.

Ricardo testified before Parliament that there could be *no* debt-servicing problem. An automatic stabilization mechanism (via shifts in demand, not exchange rates) he said, enables every country to pay. This is the theory that underlies Milton Friedman and the Chicago School of monetarism: the misleading idea that debt cannot be a problem. It is taught in international trade and financial textbooks as mainstream wisdom, but it's false pleading. It draws a fictitious "What If" picture of the world.

When criticized, the authors of these textbooks, from Paul Samuelson to Bill Vickrey, say that it doesn't matter whether economic theory is realistic or not. The judgment of whether economics is scientific is simply whether it is internally consistent.

So you have the authors of these economic fictions given Nobel Prizes for promoting an upside down view of how the global economy works. And their common denominator is that government regulation is bad (increasing "transactions costs" with all that paperwork), privatization is efficient and hence good, markets produce fair prices that reflect the necessary costs of production but no free lunches, and debt is not a problem that threatens to slow economic growth and impoverish or polarize economies. This is all the reverse of what most people believed a century ago and what actually happens.

ED: One other thing they no longer teach is what used to be called political economy. The influence of the Chicago School, neoliberalism and monetarism has removed classical political economy from the academic canon. As you said, it's now all about mathematics and formulas that treat economics like a natural science instead of as a historically grounded social science.

MH: The formulas that they teach don't have government in them. If you have a theory saying that everything is simply an exchange, a trade, and that there isn't any useful role for government, then your theory has nothing to do with the real world – except to oppose public authority and thus leave it open to the financial class to manage the economy in its own narrow interests. The result will be bad policies favoring predatory behavior.

The classical economists – Adam Smith, John Stuart Mill, Marx, Thorstein Veblen – all sought to reform the world. They wanted to free society from the legacy of feudalism, to get rid of land rent and take money and credit creation into the public domain. Whether they were right wingers or left wingers, Christian socialists, Ricardian socialists or Marxian socialists, all the theorists of 19th-century industrial capitalism called themselves socialists, because they saw capitalism as evolving into socialism in one way or another.

But after World War I a reaction against this approach set in, especially as Germany and other countries were threatened with revolution in the wake of Russian Communism, against the vested post-feudal interests. The post-classical aim is to strip away of the idea that governments have a productive role to play. If government is not going to regulate and plan the economy, then who is? The answer is, the financial sector – Wall Street. And if the government is not going to tax the economy and be responsible for providing basic infrastructure services, then who is? Again, the answer is Wall Street – banks, bondholders and money managers. So the essence of neoliberalism that you were mentioning before turns out to be a doctrine of central planning, but it states that this planning should be done by Wall Street, by and for the financial sector.

The objective of central planning by Wall Street is not to raise living standards, and certainly not to increase employment. It's to smash and grab. That is the society we're now rushing toward.

A number of chapters of my book (I think five), describe how the Obama administration has implemented this smash and grab, doing the opposite of what he promised voters. Obama has implemented the Rubinomics [Robert Rubin] doctrine of Wall Street to force America into what looks like a chronic debt depression, so as to minimize wages and maximize the power of banks, high finance and the One Percent behind them.

The case of Latvia: Is it a success story, or a neoliberal disaster?

ED: I want to go back to some of the issues we alluded to in the first part of our discussion. A few years ago I twice interviewed your colleague Jeffrey Sommers, with whom you've worked and co-published a number of papers. We talked about many of the same issues that you and I are touching on. Specifically Sommers – and I know you as well – worked in Latvia, a country in the former Soviet space in Eastern Europe on the Baltic Sea. Your *Killing the Host* has a whole chapter on it, as well as references throughout the book. So let's talk about how Latvia serves as a template for understanding the austerity model. It is touted by technocrats of the financial elite as a major success story – how austerity can work. I find it absurd on many levels. So tell us what happened in Latvia, what the real costs were, and why neoliberals claim it as a success story.

MH: Latvia is the disaster story of the last two decades. That's why I cited it as an object lesson. You're right, it was Jeff Sommers who first brought me over to Latvia. I then became Director of Economic Research and Professor of Economics at the Riga Graduate School of Law.

Latvia was given its independence when the Soviet Union broke up in 1991. A number of former Latvians had studied at Georgetown University, and brought neoliberalism over there – the most extreme grabitization and de-industrialization of any country I know. Latvia, Russia and other post-Soviet countries were under the impression that U.S. advisors would help them become modernized like the U.S. economy, with high living standards. But instead of advice as to how to emulate American experience – with protective agricultural and industrial tariffs, government subsidies for economic modernization and education, progressive taxation and New Deal type checks and balances – what they got was the opposite: how to let foreign investors and bankers back domestic kleptocrats to carve up the economy, dismantle its industry, and drive its young workers abroad to find employment. Latvia became a bizarre neoliberal experiment, featuring the world's fastest real estate bubble.

You may remember one of the 2008 Republican presidential contenders, Steve Forbes, who proposed a flat tax to replace progressive taxation. The idea never could have won in the United States, but Latvia was another story. They set the flat tax at an amazingly low 12 percent of income – and no significant property tax on real estate or capital gains. It was a financial and real estate dream, and created a classic bubble.

Jeff and I visited the head of the tax authority, who told us that she had written her PhD dissertation on Latvia's last land value assessment – which was in 1917. They hadn't updated assessments since then. The Soviet economy didn't have private land ownership, and didn't even have a concept of rent-of-location for planning purposes.

Latvia emerged from the Soviet Union without any debt, and also with a lot of real estate and a highly educated population. Latvia had been a computer center and also the money-laundering center of the Soviet leadership already in the late 1980s (largely as a byproduct of Russian oil exports through Ventspils). But its political insiders turned over most of the government enterprises to themselves, and Riga remains the money-laundering portal for today's Russia.

Privatizing housing and other property led to soaring real estate prices. But this wasn't financed by domestic banks. The Soviet Union didn't have private banks, because the government simply created the credit to fund the economy as needed. The main banks in a position to lend to Latvia were Swedish and other Scandinavian banks. They pounced on the lending opportunities opened up by a nation whose real estate had almost no tax on it. The result was the biggest real estate bubble in the world, along with Russia's. Latvians found that to buy housing of their own, they had to go deeply into debt. Assets were only given to insiders, not to the people.

A few years ago there was a reform movement in Latvia to stop the economic bleeding. The country was going broke because its population had to pay so much for housing and business sites, and was under foreign-exchange pressure because debt service on its mortgage loans was being paid to the Swedish and foreign banks. Jeff and I brought over American property appraisers and some economists from various countries. We visited the bank regulatory agency, whose head regulator explained to us that her agency's clients are the banks, not the native population. The regulators thought of themselves as working for the banks, even though these were foreign-owned. She acknowledged that the banks were lending much more money than property actually was worth. But her regulatory agency had a solution: It was to obligate not only the buyer to pay the mortgage, but also the parents, uncles or aunts. Get the whole family involved, so that if the first signer couldn't pay, the co-signers could be billed.

That is how Latvia stabilized its banking system. It did so by destabilizing the economy. This is why Latvia has lost 20 percent of its population over the past decade or so – for much the same reasons that Greece has lost 20 percent of *its* population, with Ireland in a similar condition. The Latvians have a joke: "Will the last person who leaves in 2020 please turn off the lights at the airport."

The population is shrinking because the economy is being run by looters, domestic and foreign. I was shown an island in the middle of the Daugava river that runs to the middle of Riga, and was sold for half a million dollars. Our appraisers said that it's potentially worth half a billion dollars. The giveaway could be recaptured by a realistic land tax, but there are no plans to do this to recover these gains for the country. That would enable Latvia to lower its labor taxes, which are the heaviest in the world. Nearly half of each paycheck goes for income tax and "social security" spending, so that finance and real estate don't have to be taxed. This tax shift off finance and property onto labor is what neoliberals applaud for the Baltic Tigers as their dream tax policy.

A few years ago I was invited to the only meeting of INET (George Soros's group) that I've attended, and one of the first talks was on how Latvia was a model that all countries could follow to balance their budgets. Latvia's government has balanced its budget by selling off whatever remains in the public domain while cutting public spending, reducing employment and lowering wage levels while indebting its population and forcing it to emigrate.

These giveaways at insider prices have created a kleptocracy obviously loyal to neoliberal economics. I go into the details in my chapter on Latvia in *Killing the Host*. It's hard to talk about it without losing my temper, so I'm trying to be reasonable but Latvia is a country that was destroyed and smashed. That is the U.S. neoliberal alternative to post-Stalinism. It isn't an economy taking the path that America did. It is a travesty.

Why then does the population continue to vote for these neoliberals? The answer is, the neoliberals say, the alternative is Stalinism. To Latvians, that keeps alive the memories of the old pro-Russian policy, deportations and exile. The Russian-speaking parties are the main backers of a social democratic platform. But neoliberals have merged with Latvian nationalists. They are framing elections over the ethnically divisive issue of stirring up resentment against the Russian-speaking population, including the fact that many are Jewish.

I find it amazing to see someone who is Jewish, like George Soros, allying with anti-Semitic and even neo-Nazi movements in Latvia, Estonia, and most recently, of course, Ukraine. He has funded a foundation in Latvia similar to ones he started in other post-Soviet countries apparently to position himself to get a part of the loot. It's an irony that you could not have anticipated deductively. If you had written this plot in a futuristic novel twenty years ago, no one would have believed that politics could turn more on national and linguistic identity politics than economic self-interest.

The issue is whether you are Latvian or Russian-Jewish, not whether you want to untax yourself and recapture what the kleptocrats have taken? Voting is along ethnic lines, not over whether Latvians really want to be forced to emigrate to find work instead of making Latvia what it could have been: an successful economy free of debt. Everybody could have gotten their homes free instead of giving real estate to the kleptocrats. The government could have taxed the land's rental value rather than letting real estate valuation be pledged to pay banks – and foreign banks at that. Latvia could have been a low-cost economy with high living standards, but neoliberals turned it into a smash and grab exercise. They now call it an ideal for other nations to follow, most notoriously for the U.S.-Soros strategy in Ukraine.

ED: That's an excellent point. It's a more extreme case for a number of reasons in Ukraine, but the same tendency. They talk about "Putin and his gaggle of Jews" – the idea that Putin and the Jews will come in and steal everything – while neoliberals scheme to appropriate Ukraine's land and other resources themselves.

In this intersection between economics and politics, Latvia, Lithuania, Estonia – the Baltic States of the former Soviet Union – have become the front lines of NATO expansion. They were some of the first, most pivotal countries brought into the NATO orbit to counter the "threat of Russian aggression" from the enclave at Kaliningrad, or Russia in general. That is the threat they use to justify the NATO umbrella, and simultaneously to justify continuing these economic policies. So Russia serves as a convenient villain on a political, military and economic level.

MH: It's amazing how the popular press doesn't report what's going on. Yevgeny Primakov, who died a few months ago, said during the last crisis a few years ago that Russia has no need to invade Latvia, because it already owns the oil export terminals in Ventspils and other key points. Russia has learned to play the Western game of taking countries over financially and acquiring ownership. It doesn't need to invade to control Latvia any more than America needs to invade to control Saudi Arabia or the Near East. If it controls exports or access to markets, what motive would it have to spend money and lives to invade? As things stand, Russia uses Latvia it as a money-laundering center.

The same logic applies to Ukraine. The U.S. promotes the idea that Russia is expansionary in a world where no one can afford to be militarily expansionary any more. After Russia's disaster in Afghanistan, no country that's subject to democratic checks can invade another country, whether it's America after the Vietnam War or Russia or Europe today. All they can do is drop bombs. This can't capture a country. For that you need a major troop commitment.

In the trips that I've taken to Russia and China, I've seen that they're in a purely defensive mode. They're wondering why America is forcing all this ethnic and religious hostility. Why is it destroying the Near East, creating a refugee problem and then telling Europe to clean up the mess it's created? And why is Europe willing to keep doing this? Why does it back NATO's fight in the Near East? When America tells Europe, "Let's you and Russia fight over Ukraine," that puts Europe in the first line of fire. Why would it have an interest in taking this risk, instead of trying to build a mutual economic relationship with Russia, as seemed to be developing in the 19th century?

ED: That's the ultimate strategy the United States has used – driving a wedge between Russia and Europe. This is the argument that Putin and the Russians have made for a long time. You can see tangible examples of that sort of a relationship if you look at the Nord Stream pipeline connecting Russian energy to German industry. That is a tangible example of the economic relationship, which is only just beginning between Russia and Europe. That's what I think the United States wants to put the brakes on, in order to be able to maintain hegemony. The number one way it does that is through NATO.

MH: It has not only put the brakes on, it has created a new iron curtain. Two years ago Greece was supposed to privatize 5 billion euros of its public domain. Half of this, 2.5 billion, was to be the sale of its gas pipeline. But the largest bidder was Gazprom, and Greece was told, "No, you can't accept the highest bidder if its Russian." Same thing in Ukraine. It has just been smashed economically after the coup, but the U.S. says, "No Ukrainian or Russian can buy into the Ukrainian assets to be sold off. Only George Soros and his fellow Americans can buy into this." This shows that the neoliberalism of free markets, of "let's everybody pay the highest price," is only patter talk. If the winner in the rigged market is not the United States, it sends in ISIS or Al Qaeda and the assassination teams, or backs the neo-Nazis as in Ukraine.

So, we're in a New Cold War. Its first victims, apart from the post-Soviet Baltics and Southern Europe, will be the rest of Europe. This is just beginning to tear European politics apart, with Germany's Die Linke and similar parties making a resurgence on the left and on the right.

The Troika and IMF doctrine of austerity and privatization

ED: I want to turn back to your book and some other key issues that you bring up. We hear in the news all the time about the Troika – the IMF, the European Central Bank (ECB) and the European Commission. I guess we could call them the political arm of finance capital in Europe. They impose and manage austerity in the interest of the finance capital ruling class. These are technocrats, not academically trained economists (maybe with a few exceptions), but I want you to talk a bit about how the Troika functions and why it's so important in what we could call this crisis stage of neoliberal finance capitalism.

MH: Basically, the Troika is run by Frankfurt bankers as foreclosure and collection agents. Former Greek finance minister Yanis Varoufakis and his advisor James Galbraith recently have written that when Syriza [their left-wing radical party] was elected in January, they tried to reason with the IMF. But it said that it could only do what the European Central Bank said, and that it would approve whatever the ECB decided to do. The European Central Bank said that its role wasn't to negotiate democracy. Its negotiators were not economists. They were lawyers. "All we can say is, here's what you have to pay, here's how to do it. We're not here to talk about whether this is going to bankrupt Greece. We're just interested in how you're going to pay the banks what they're owed. Your electric companies and other industry will have to go to German companies, the other infrastructure to other investors – but not to Russians."

What's happening in Greece today is much like what happened when England and France divided up the Near East after World War I. There's a kind of a gentlemen's agreement as to how the creditor economies will divide up Greece, carving it up much like neighboring Yugoslavia to the north.

In 2001 the IMF made a big loan to Argentina (I have a chapter on that), which went bad after a year. So the IMF passed a rule, called the "No More Argentinas" rule, stating that the Fund was not going to participate in loans to government that obviously could not pay.

A decade later came the Greek crisis of 2011. The staff found that Greece could not possibly pay a loan large enough to bail out the French, German and other creditors. So there had to be a debt write-down of the principal. The staff said that, and the IMF's board members agreed. But its Managing Director, Strauss-Kahn wanted to run for the presidency of France, and most of the Greek bonds were held by French banks. French President Sarkozy said, "You can't win political office in France if you stiff the French banks." And German Chancellor Merkel said that Greece had to pay the German banks. Then, to top matters, President Obama came over to the G-20 meetings and they said that the American banks had made such big default insurance contracts and casino gambles betting that Greece *would* pay, that if it defaulted – that is, if the Europeans and IMF did not bail out Greece – then the American banks might go under. The implicit threat was that the U.S. would make sure that Europe's financial system would be torn to pieces as collateral damage.

ED: Michael, I just want to clarify: These were credit default swaps and collateralized debt obligations?

MH: Yes. U.S. officials said that Wall Street had made so many gambles that if the French and German banks were not paid, they would turn to their Wall Street insurers. The Wall Street casino would go under, bringing Europe's banking system down with it. This prompted the European Central Bank to say that it didn't want the IMF to be a part of the Troika *unless* it agreed to support the ECB bailout – regardless of whether Greece could repay or not. If not, creditors would be backed to smash and grab. This led some of the IMF European staff to resign, most notably Susan Schadler, who later acted as a whistle blower to write up what happened.

The IMF capitulated to the EB's hard line toward Greece earlier this year. The incorrigible Christine Lagarde said that the IMF doesn't do debt reduction, but would give them a little longer to pay. Not a euro will be written down, but the debt will be stretched out and perhaps the interest rate will be lowered – as long as Greece permits foreigners to grab its infrastructure, land and natural resources.

The IMF staff once again leaked a report to the *Financial Times* (and I think also the *Wall Street Journal*) that said that Greece couldn't pay. There's no way it can later turn around and sell off the IMF loan to private bondholders, so any bailout will be against the IMF's own rules. Lagarde tried to save face by saying that Germany has to agree to stretch out payments on the debt – as if that marginal concession somehow will enable Greece to pay. Its assets pass into foreign hands, which will remit their profits back home and subject Greece to even steeper deflation, making the bailout debt even more impossible to pay off.

Then, a few weeks ago, you had the Ukraine debt crisis. The IMF is not allowed to make loans to countries that cannot pay. But now, the whole purpose is to make loans enabling creditors to turn around and demand that debtor countries pay by selling off their public domain – and force more of their population to emigrate.

ED: Also, technically the IMF is not supposed to be making loans to countries that are at war, and they're ignoring that rule as well.

MH: That's the second big violation of IMF rules. At least in the earlier Greek bailout, Strauss Kahn got around the "No More Argentinas" rule by having a new

IMF policy say that if a country is "systemically important," the IMF can lend it the money even if it *can't* pay, even though it's *not* credit-worthy, if its default would cause a problem in the global financial system – meaning in practice, a loss by Wall Street or other bankers. But Ukraine is not systemically important. It's part of the Russian system, not the western system. Most of its trade is with Russia.

As you just pointed out, when Lagarde made the IMF's last Ukrainian loan, she said that she hoped its economy would stabilize instead of waging more war in its eastern export region. The next day President Poroshenko said that now that it had got the loan, it could go to war against the Donbass, the Russian-speaking region. Some $1.5 billion of the IMF loan was given to banks run by Kolomoisky, a kleptocrat who fields his own army. His banks sent the IMF's gift abroad to his own foreign banks, using his domestic Ukrainian money to pay his own army allied with Ukrainian nationalists flying the old Nazi SS insignia and fighting against the Russian speakers. So in effect, the IMF is serving as an arm of the U.S. military and State Department, just as the World Bank has long done.

ED: I want to interject two points here for listeners who haven't followed it so closely. Number one is the private army that you're talking about – the Right Sector, which is essentially a mercenary force of Nazis in the employ of Kolomoisky. They're also part of what's now called the Ukrainian National Guard, a paramilitary organization being paid by Kolomoisky. Number two – and this relates back to something you were saying earlier, Michael – the recent IMF loan went to pay for a lot of the military equipment that Kiev has now used to obliterate the economic and industrial infrastructure of Donbass, which was Ukraine's industrial heartland. So from the western perspective it's killing two birds with one stone. If they can't strip the assets and grab them, at least they can destroy them, because the number one customer was Russia.

MH: Russia had made much of its military hardware in Ukraine, including the liftoff engines for its satellites. The West doesn't want that to continue. It wants its own investors to take over Ukraine's land, its gas rights in the Black Sea, electric and other public utilities, because these are major tollbooths to extract economic rent. Basically, US/NATO strategists want to make sure, by destroying Ukraine's eastern export industry, that Ukraine will be chronically bankrupt and will have to settle its balance-of-payments deficit by selling off its private domain to American, German and other foreign buyers.

ED: That's Monsanto, and that's Hunter Biden on the Burisma board (the gas company). It's like you said earlier, you wouldn't even believe it if someone had made it up. What they're doing in Ukraine is quite transparent.

Financialization of pension plans and retirement savings

ED: I want to switch gears a bit in the short time we have remaining, because I have two more things I want to talk about. Referring back to this parasitic relationship on the real economy, one aspect that's rarely mentioned is the way in which many regular working people get swindled. One example that comes to my mind is the mutual funds and other money managers who control what pension funds and lots of retirees invest in. Much of their savings is tied up in heavily leveraged junk bonds and in places like Greece, and also recently in Puerto Rico, which is going through a similar scenario right now. So in many ways, U.S. taxpayers and pensioners are funding the looting and exploitation of these countries and they're then financially invested in continuing the destruction of these countries. It's as if these pensioners are being used as human shields for Wall Street to justify exploitative policy on the ground that otherwise pension savers will suffer if the One Percent has to take a loss.

MH: This is a main theme of my book – financialization putting on a populist face. Half a century ago a new term was coined: pension fund capitalism, sometimes called pension fund socialism. Then we got back to Orwellian doublethink when Pinochet came to power behind the alliance of the Chicago School with Kissinger at the State Department. They organized what they called labor capitalism – with labor as the victim, not the beneficiary. The first thing they organized was a compulsory set-aside of wages, ostensibly in the form of pension funds controlled by employers, who could do whatever they wanted with the money. Ultimately they invested these corporate pension funds in their own stocks or turned them over to their own captive banks, around which their *grupo* conglomerates were organized. They then drove the businesses with employee pension funds under. Left as empty corporate shells, their pension fund liabilities were wiped out, after having moved the assets into their banks.

Something similar happened in America a few years ago with the *Chicago Tribune*. Real estate developer Sam Zell borrowed money to buy the *Tribune*, using the Employee Stock Ownership Plan (ESOP) essentially to pay off the bondholders. He then drove/looted the Tribune into bankruptcy and wiped out the stockholders. Employees brought a fraudulent conveyance suit.

Already fifty years ago, critics noted that about half of the ESOPs are wiped out, because they're invested by the employers, often in their own stock. Managers give themselves stock options, while ESOP purchases helped bid up their price. Something similar occurs with pension funds on an economy-wide basis. Wage set-asides are paid into pension funds, which buy and thus bid up prices for the stocks that managers award themselves. That's pension fund capitalism.

The underlying problem with this kind of financialization of pensions and retirement savings is that modern American industry is being run more for financial purposes than for industrial purposes. The major industrial companies have been financialized. For many years General Motors made most of its profits from its financial arm, General Motors Acceptance Corporation. Likewise General Electric. When I was going to school 50 years ago, Macy's reported most of its profits not from selling products but by getting customers to use its credit cards. In effect, it used its store to get people to use its credit cards.

The purpose of running a company in today's financialized world is to increase the price of the stock, not to expand the business. Last year, 92% of the earnings of the Fortune 100 companies were used for stock buy-backs — corporations buying back their stock to support its price – or for dividend payouts, also to increase the stock's price (and thus management bonuses and stock options).

There's a lot of money coming into the market from pension funds. Social Security contributions would fuel a bonanza if they were steered into the stock market. George W. Bush's attempt to privatize Social Security was Wall Street's dream: to turn the +15% that FICA withholds from workers paychecks every month over to money management firms and the big banks. Along with speculators, they would get an enormous flow of commissions in addition to asset-price gains – until the American population began to age or, more likely, begin to be unemployed. At that point the funds would begin to sell their stocks to pay retirees. Withdrawing money from the stock market would crash prices as speculators sold out. The savings that workers had put into the scheme would plunge in price.

The basic idea is that when Wall Street plays finance, the casino wins. When employees and pension funds play the financial game, they lose.

Obama's demagogic role as Wall Street shill for the Rubinomics gang

ED: Right, and just as an example for listeners – to make what Michael was just talking about it even more real – if we think back to 2009 and the collapse of General Motors, it was not General Motors automotive manufacturing that was collapsing. It was GMAC, their finance arm, which was leveraged on credit default swaps, collateralized debt obligations and similar financial derivatives – what they call exotic instruments. So when Obama comes in and claimed that he "saved General Motors," it wasn't really that. He came in for the Wall Street arm of General Motors.

MH: That's correct. He was the Wall Street candidate, promoted by Robert Rubin, who was Clinton's Treasury Secretary. Basically, American economic policies have been run by Goldman Sachs and Citigroup.

ED: This was demonstrated in the first days of Obama taking office. Who did he meet with to talk about the financial crisis? He invited the CEOs of Goldman Sachs and JP Morgan, Bank of America, Citi and all of the rest of them. They're the ones who come to the White House. It's been written about in books, in the *New Yorker* and elsewhere. Obama basically said, "Don't worry guys, I got this."

MH: Ron Suskind wrote this up. He reported that Obama said, "I'm the only guy standing between you and the pitchforks. Listen to me: I can basically fool them." (I give the actual quote in my book.) The interesting thing is that the traces of this meeting were quickly erased from the White House website, but Suskind has it in his book. Obama emerges as one of the great demagogues of the century.

ED: So much of it is based on obvious policies and his actions. He came to power at a critical moment when action was needed. Not only did he not take the right action, he did exactly what Wall Street wanted. In many ways we can look back to 2008 when he was championing the TARP, the bailout and all the rest. That's something that Democrats like to avoid in their conversations.

MH: That's exactly the point. It was Orwellian rhetoric. He ran as the candidate of Hope and Change, but his real role was to smash hope and prevent change. By keeping the debts in place instead of writing them down as he had promised, he oversaw the wrecking of the American economy. Banks, uninsured depositors and bondholders were saved, at the economy's expense – in terms that brought on depression by leaving the bad debts in place.

Obama had done something similar in Chicago when he worked as a community organizer for the big real estate interests to tear up the poorer Black neighborhoods. His role was to gentrify them and jack up property prices to move in higher-income Blacks. This made billions for the Pritzker family. So Penny Pritzker introduced him to Robert Rubin. Obama evidently promised to let Rubin appoint his cabinet, headed by the vicious anti-labor Rahm Emanuel (now Chicago's mayor) as his Chief of Staff to drive any Democrat to the left of Herbert Hoover out of the party. Obama pushed the Democrats to the right, as the Republicans gave him plenty of room to move rightward and still be the "lesser evil."

So now you have people like Donald Trump saying that he's for what Dennis Kucinich was for: a single payer healthcare program. Obama fought against this, and backed the lobbyists of the pharmaceutical and health insurance sectors. His genius is being able to make most voters believe that he's on their side when he's actually defending the Wall Street special interests that were his major campaign contributors.

ED: That's true. You can see that in literally every arena in which Obama has taken action. From championing so-called Obamacare, which is really a boon for the insurance industry, to the charter schools to privatize public education and also become a major boon for Wall Street, for Pearson and all these major education corporations. In terms of real estate, gentrification, all the rest – literally from every angle from which you look at Obama, he is a servant of finance capital, not the people. And that's what the Democratic Party has become, delivering its constituency to Wall Street.

An alternative for the 99 Percent

MH: The problem is how to get the 99 Percent to realize this. How do we get people to talk about economics instead of ethnic identity and sexual identity and culture alone? How do we get the left to do what they were talking about a century ago – economic reform and how to take the side of labor, consumers and debtors? How do we tell the Blacks that the way to gain power is to get a well paying job? Deng said: "Black cat, white cat, it doesn't matter as long as it catches mice." How do we say "Black president, white president, it doesn't matter, as long as they support Wall Street instead of giving us well-paying jobs and helping our communities economically?"

ED: I think that's important, and I want to close with this issue: solutions. One of the things I appreciate in reading your book is that it is broken up into sections. The final section, I think, is really important: "There *Is* An Alternative." That is of course a reference to Margaret Thatcher's TINA (There Is No Alternative). That ideology and mindset took over the left, or at least the nominally left-wing parties. So you're saying that there *is* an alternative, and you propose a number of important reforms that you argue would restore industrial prosperity. I won't ask you to name all of them, but maybe touch on a bit of what you included in the list, and why it's important to build your alternative.

MH: I start with two age-old aims. One is to free society from unproductive debt. People shouldn't have to spend their lives working off personal debt, whether it's simply for living or to obtain a home and get an education as is becoming normal in today's world. Second, you want to fund industry by equity, not by debt. That is what the Saint-Simonians urged in France, and what German banking became famous for before World War I. There was a debate in Britain over whether it and the Allies might lose World War I because their banks were running the economy instead of subordinating finance to fund industry.

Finance should be used to help the economy grow, not be parasitic. Instead, our tax laws make debt service tax deductible. That is why the American stock market has become a vehicle for corporate raiding, replacing equity with debt over the past thirty years. If a company pays $2 billion a year in dividends, a corporate raider can buy it on credit and, if there's a 50% tax rate, he can pay $4 billion to bondholders instead of $2 billion to stockholders. But that makes break-even costs much higher.

The other point I'm making concerns economic rent. The guiding idea of a classical economic and tax system should be to minimize the cost of living and doing business. But if you look at what the average American wage earner has to pay, under the most recent federal housing authority laws the government guarantees mortgage loans that absorb up to 43% of family income. Meanwhile, 15% of wages are set aside for Social Security under FICA, in addition to about 20% that ends up being paid for income tax, sales taxes and various other taxes that fall on consumers. Perhaps another 10% goes for credit card debt service, student loans and other bank debt.

That leaves only about 25% of what American families earn to be spent on goods and services – unless they borrow to maintain their living standards. This means that if you give wage earners all their food, all their transportation and all their clothing for free, they still could not compete with foreign economies, because so much of the budget has to go for finance, insurance and real estate (FIRE). That's why our employment is not going to recover. That's why our living standards are not going to recover.

Even if wages do go up for some workers, the price for trying to join the middle class by getting higher education and buying a home requires them to spend the rest of their lives paying for education loans, mortgage loans (or rent), bank debt and credit card debt, and now also for our expensive and rent-extracting medical insurance and medications. The result is that workers won't end up keeping their higher wages and spending more disposable income on consumption. They'll pay their wage gains to the banks. That has been what's happening for over thirty years now.

ED: You don't have to tell me. I'm living that reality. Interestingly, in that final section of your book you talk about alternatives, like a public banking option that many people are discussing. You talk about paying Social Security out of the general budget, and focus on taxing economic rent to keep down housing prices while cutting personal taxes. Some critics would suggest that these sorts of reforms are not going to be able to salvage the capitalist model that is so ensconced in the United States. So I want to give you a chance to sort of address that argument or maybe rebut it.

MH: I won't rebut that criticism, because it's right. Marx thought that it was the task of industrial capitalism to free economies from the legacies of feudalism. He saw that the bourgeois parties wanted to get rid of the "excrescences" of the industrial marketplace. They wanted to get rid of the parasites, the landowners and usurious creditors. But then Marx pointed out that even if you get rid of the parasites, even if you socialize the land and finance that he dealt with in Volumes II and III of *Capital*, you're still going to have the Volume I problem. You're still going to have labor/capital exploitation.

My point is that most academic Marxists and the left in general have focused so much on the fight of workers and labor unions against employers that they tend to overlook that the huge FIRE sector tsunami – Finance, Insurance and Real Estate – is swamping the economy. Finance is wrecking industry and government, along with labor. The reforms that Marx expected the bourgeois parties to enact against *rentiers* haven't occurred. He was overly optimistic about the role of industrial capitalism and industrialized banking in preparing the ground for socialism.

Until you complete the task of freeing society from feudalism – corrosive banking and economic rent as unearned income – you can't solve the industrial and labor problems that Marx dealt with in Volume I. And of course, even when you *do* solve the *rentier* problems, labor exploitation and markets will still exist.

ED: Yes, absolutely. Well we're out of time. I want to thank you for coming onto the program. Listeners, you heard it. There's so much information to digest here. The book is really brilliant, I think essential reading, required reading – *Killing the Host: How Financial Parasites and Debt Bondage Destroy the Global Economy*, available through CounterPunch, as well as on Amazon. Michael Hudson, professor of economics at University of Missouri Kansas City, his work is all over the place. Find it regularly on CounterPunch, as well as on his website, michael-hudson.com. Michael thanks so much for coming on CounterPunch Radio.

MH: It's great to be here. It's been a good discussion.

ENDNOTE

---

[1] http://store.counterpunch.org/category/counterpunch-radio-podcasts/

*Michael Hudson at the Egyptian Temple of Dendur
exhibit, Metropolitan Museum,
New York City.*

Michael Hudson is a Distinguished Research Professor of Economics at the University of Missouri, Kansas City (UMKC), and Professor of Economics at Peking University in China. He gives speeches, lectures and presentations all over the world for official and unofficial groups reflecting diverse academic, economic and political constituencies.

Before moving into research and consulting, Prof. Hudson spent several years applying flow-of-funds and balance-of-payments statistics to forecast interest rates, capital and real estate markets for Chase Manhattan Bank and The Hudson Institute (no relation). His academic focus has been on financial history and, since 1980, on writing a history of debt, land tenure and related economic institutions from the Sumerian period, antiquity, and feudal Europe to the present.

Since 1996 as president of the Institute for the Study of Long Term Economic Trends (ISLET), he has written reports and given presentations on balance of payments, financial bubbles, land policy and financial reforms for U.S. and international clients and governments.

He organized the International Scholars Conference on Ancient Near Eastern Economies (ISCANEE) in 1993, and to-date has co-edited the preceedings of six academic conferences on the evolution of property, credit, labor and accounting since the Bronze Age.

A selected list of his books, articles, and papers appears at the end of this book. His website and blog can be found at *michael-hudson.com*. He has been interviewed on *Democracy Now*, *Marketplace*, and *Naked Capitalism*. Many of his interviews and public appearances can be seen on YouTube.

• • •

Paul Craig Roberts' Bio of Michael Hudson

(excerpted from an introduction to Michael Hudson's book, *Killing the Host*, originally posted on his website and at *NakedCapitalism.com* on February 6, 2016)

Michael Hudson did not intend to be an economist. At the University of Chicago, which had a leading economics faculty, Hudson studied music and cultural history. He went to New York City to work in publishing. He thought he could set out on his own when he was assigned rights to the writings and archives of George Lukács and Leon Trotsky, but publishing houses were not interested in the work of two Jewish Marxists who had a significant impact on the 20th century.

Friendships connected Hudson to a former economist for General Electric who taught him the flow of funds through the economic system and explained how crises develop when debt outgrows the economy. Hooked, Hudson enrolled in the economics graduate program at N.Y.U. and took a job in the financial sector calculating how savings were recycled into new mortgage loans.

Hudson learned more economics from his work experience than from his Ph.D. courses. On Wall Street he learned how bank lending inflates land prices and, thereby, interest payments to the financial sector. The more banks lend, the higher real estate prices rise, thus encouraging more bank lending. As mortgage debt service rises, more of household income and more of the rental value of real estate are paid to the financial sector. When the imbalance becomes too large, the bubble bursts. Despite its importance, the analysis of land rent and property valuation was not part of his Ph.D. studies in economics.

Hudson's next job was with Chase Manhattan, where he used the export earnings of South American countries to calculate how much debt service the countries could afford to pay to U.S. banks. Hudson learned that just as mortgage lenders regard the rental income from property as a flow of money that can be diverted to interest payments, international banks regard the export earnings of foreign countries as revenues that can be used to pay interest on foreign loans. Hudson learned that the goal of creditors is to capture the entire economic surplus of a country into payments of debt service.

Soon the American creditors and the IMF were lending indebted countries money with which to pay interest. This caused the countries' foreign debts to rise at compound interest. Hudson predicted that the indebted countries would not be able to pay their debts, an unwelcome prediction that was confirmed when Mexico announced it could not pay. This crisis was resolved with "Brady bonds" named after the U.S. Treasury Secretary, but when the 2008 U.S. mortgage crisis hit, just as Hudson predicted, nothing was done for the American homeowners. If you are not a mega-bank, your problems are not a focus of U.S. economic policy.

Chase Manhattan next had Hudson develop an accounting format to analyze the U.S. oil industry balance of payments. Here Hudson learned another lesson about the difference between official statistics and reality. Using "transfer pricing," oil companies managed to avoid paying taxes by creating the illusion of zero profits. Oil company affiliates in tax avoidance locations buy oil at low prices from producers. From these flags of convenience locations, which have no tax on profits, the oil was then sold to Western refineries at prices marked up to eliminate profits. The profits were recorded by the oil companies' affiliates in non-tax jurisdictions. (Tax authorities have cracked down to some extent on the use of transfer pricing to escape taxation.)

Hudson's next task was to estimate the amount of money from crime going into Switzerland's secret banking system. In this investigation, his last for Chase, Hudson discovered that under U.S. State Department direction Chase and other large banks had established banks in the Caribbean for the purpose of attracting money into dollar holdings from drug dealers in order to support the dollar (by raising the demand for dollars by criminals) in order to balance or offset Washington's foreign military outflows of dollars. If dollars flowed out of the U.S., but demand did not rise to absorb the larger supply of dollars, the dollar's exchange rate would fall, thus threatening the basis of U.S. power. By providing offshore banks in which criminals could deposit illicit dollars, the U.S. government supported the dollar's exchange value.

Hudson discovered that the U.S. balance of payments deficit, a source of pressure on the value of the U.S. dollar, was entirely military in character. The U.S. Treasury and State Department supported the Caribbean safe haven for illegal profits in order to offset the negative impact on the U.S. balance of payments of U.S. military operations abroad. In other words, if criminality can be used in support of the U.S. dollar, the U.S. government is all for criminality.

When it came to the economics of the situation, economic theory had not a clue. Neither trade flows nor direct investments were important in determining exchange rates. What was important was "errors and omissions," which Hudson discovered was a euphemism for the hot, liquid money of drug dealers and government officials embezzling the export earnings of their countries.

The problem for Americans is that both political parties regard the needs of the American people as a liability and as an obstacle to the profits of the military/security complex, Wall Street and the mega-banks, and Washington's world hegemony. The government in Washington represents powerful interest groups, not American citizens. This is why the 21st century consists of an attack on the constitutional protections of citizens so that citizens can be moved out of the way of the needs of the Empire and its beneficiaries.

Hudson learned that economic theory is really a device for ripping off the untermenschen. International trade theory concludes that countries can service huge debts simply by lowering domestic wages in order to pay creditors. This is the policy currently being applied to Greece today, and it has been the basis of the IMF's structural adjustment or austerity programs imposed on debtor countries, essentially a form of looting that turns over national resources to foreign lenders.

Hudson learned that monetary theory concerns itself only with wages and consumer prices, not with the inflation of asset prices such as real estate and stocks. He saw that economic theory serves as a cover for the polarization of the world economy between rich and poor. The promises of globalism are a myth. Even left-wing and Marxist economists think of exploitation in terms of wages and are unaware that the main instrument of exploitation is the financial system's extraction of value into interest payments.

Economic theory's neglect of debt as an instrument of exploitation caused Hudson to look into the history of how earlier civilizations handled the buildup of debt. His research was so ground-breaking that Harvard University appointed him Research Fellow in Babylonian economic history in the Peabody Museum.

Meanwhile he continued to be sought after by financial firms. He was hired to calculate the number of years that Argentina, Brazil, and Mexico would be able to pay the extremely high interest rates on their bonds. On the basis of Hudson's work, the Scudder Fund achieved the second highest rate of return in the world in 1990.

Hudson's investigations into the problems of our time took him through the history of economic thought. He discovered that 18th and 19th century economists understood the disabling power of debt far better than today's neoliberal economists who essentially neglect it in order to better cater to the interest of the financial sector.

Hudson shows that Western economies have been financialized in a predatory way that sacrifices the public interest to the interests of the financial sector. That is why the economy no longer works for ordinary people. Finance is no longer productive. It has become a parasite on the economy. Hudson tells this story in his recent book, *Killing the Host* (2015).

Paul Craig Roberts is former under-secretary of the U.S. Treasury (Reagan Administration) and author of *The Failure of Laissez Faire Capitalism and Economic Dissolution of the West*. His blog is at *paulcraigroberts.org*.

Selected Publications by Michael Hudson

Books

(available on *Amazon.com*)

The Lost Tradition of Biblical Debt Cancellations (forthcoming full-length book 2017)

Absentee Ownership and its Discontents: Critical Essays on the Legacy of Thorstein Veblen (2016), edited with Ahmet Öncü

Killing the Host: How Financial Parasites and Debt Destroy the Global Economy (2015)

Finance As Warfare (2015)

The Bubble and Beyond: Fictitious Capital, Debt Deflation and Global Crisis (2012)

Finance Capitalism and Its Discontents: Interviews and Speeches 2003-2012 (2012)

America's Protectionist Takeoff 1815-1914: The Neglected American School of Political Economy (New Edition 2010)

Trade, Development and Foreign Debt: How Trade and Development Concentrate Economic Power in the Hands of Dominant Nations (New Edition 2009)

Global Fracture: The New International Economic Order (New Edition 2005)

Super Imperialism: The Origin and Fundamentals of U.S. World Domination (New Edition 2003)

A Philosophy for a Fair Society (1994), edited with G.J. Miller and Kris Feder

Canada in the New Monetary Order: Borrow? Devalue? Restructure? (1978) – Reprint

The Myth of Aid: The Hidden Agenda of the Development Reports (with Dennis Goulet) (1971) – Reprint.

Ancient Near Eastern Economies Colloquia

Labor in the Ancient World (2015), edited with Piotr Steinkeller

Creating Economic Order: Record-Keeping, Standardization and the Development of Accounting in the Ancient Near East (2004), edited with Cornelia Wunsch

Debt and Economic Renewal in the Ancient Near East (2002), edited with Marc Van De Mieroop

Urbanization and Land Ownership in the Ancient Near East (1999), edited with Baruch Levine

Privatization in the Ancient Near East and Classical World (1996), edited with Baruch Levine

Articles and Papers

"The New Road to Serfdom: An illustrated guide to the coming real estate collapse." *Harper's* Magazine (May 2006).

"The $4.7 Trillion Pyramid: Why Social Security won't be enough to save Wall Street." *Harper's* Magazine (April 2005).

"Real Estate and the Capital Gains Debate" (with Kris Feder), The Jerome Levy Economics Institute of Bard College, Working Paper No. 187 (March 1997).

"A Payments–Flow Analysis of U.S. International Transactions: 1960-1968." NYU Graduate School of Business Administration, *The Bulletin*, Nos. 61-63 (March 1970).

The Lost Tradition of Biblical Debt Cancellations (1993). Free booklet/PDF @ *http://michael-hudson.com*

A-to-Z Guide – Mini Index

(Entry pages also contain selected cross-references in **boldface**.)

TOPIC INDEX

A-to-Z Guide entries are in boldface.
A-to-Z Guide Entries also contain selected cross-references in text in **boldface**.

R

CPSIA information can be obtained
at www.ICGtesting.com
Printed in the USA
BVOW09s0918250817

492853BV00004B/30/P

9 783981 484250